Alan Moore and the Gothic tradition

Manchester University Press

Alan Moore and the Gothic tradition

Matthew J. A. Green

Manchester University Press

Copyright © Matthew J.A. Green 2013

The right of Matthew J.A. Green to be identified as the author of this work has been asserted by him in accordance with the Copyright, Designs and Patents Act 1988.

Published by Manchester University Press
Altrincham Street, Manchester M1 7JA, UK
www.manchesteruniversitypress.co.uk

British Library Cataloguing-in-Publication Data is available

Library of Congress Cataloging-in-Publication Data is available

ISBN 978 1 7849 9363 4 *paperback*

First published by Manchester University Press in hardback 2013

This edition first published 2016

The publisher has no responsibility for the persistence or accuracy of URLs for any external or third-party internet websites referred to in this book, and does not guarantee that any content on such websites is, or will remain, accurate or appropriate.

Printed by Lightning Source

Contents

List of illustrations	*page* vii
A note on references and quotations	ix
Notes on contributors	xiii
Preface	xvii
Acknowledgements	xxi

PART I: MONSTROUS POLITICS

1. Alan Moore and the Gothic tradition — 3
   Matthew J.A. Green
2. 'Soap opera of the paranormal': surreal Englishness and postimperial Gothic in *The Bojeffries Saga* — 21
   Tony Venezia
3. A Gothic politics: Alan Moore's *Swamp Thing* and radical ecology — 42
   Maggie Gray

PART II: GOTHIC TROPES

4. 'Is that you, our Jack?': an anatomy of Alan Moore's doubling strategies — 65
   Jochen Ecke
5. 'Nothing ever ends': facing the apocalypse in *Watchmen* — 84
   Christian W. Schneider
6. Gothic liminality in *V for Vendetta* — 103
   Markus Oppolzer

PART III: INHERITANCE AND ADAPTATION

7   'The Sleep of Reason': *Swamp Thing* and the intertextual
    reader   121
    Michael Bradshaw
8   Madness and the city: the collapse of reason and sanity in Alan
    Moore's *From Hell*   140
    Monica Germanà
9   'I fashioned a prison that you could not leave': the Gothic
    imperative in *The Castle of Otranto* and 'For the Man Who Has
    Everything'   159
    Brad Ricca
10 Radical coterie and the idea of sole survival in *St Leon*,
    Frankenstein and *Watchmen*   179
    Claire Sheridan
11 Reincarnating Mina Murray: subverting the Gothic heroine?   195
    Laura Hilton

PART IV: ART, MAGIC, SEX, OTHER

12 'These are not our promised resurrections': unearthing the
    uncanny in Alan Moore's *A Small Killing*, *From Hell* and
    A Disease of Language   215
    Christopher Murray
13 Medium, spirits and embodiment in *Voice of the Fire*   235
    Julia Round
14 A darker magic: heterocosms and bricolage in Moore's recent
    reworkings of Lovecraft   253
    Matthew J.A. Green

Bibliography   276
Index   300

List of illustrations

2.1 Alan Moore and Steve Parkhouse, 'The Rentman Cometh', *The Complete Bojeffries Saga* (Northampton, MA: Tundra, 1992), 17.iv–vii. © Alan Moore and Steve Parkhouse   24

2.2 Alan Moore and Steve Parkhouse, 'The Rentman Cometh', *The Complete Bojeffries Saga* (Northampton, MA: Tundra, 1992), 18. © Alan Moore and Steve Parkhouse   25

2.3 Alan Moore and Steve Parkhouse, 'One of Our Rentmen is Missing', *The Complete Bojeffries Saga* (Northampton, MA: Tundra, 1992), 24.iii–vi. © Alan Moore and Steve Parkhouse   31

2.4 Alan Moore and Steve Parkhouse, 'One of Our Rentmen is Missing', *The Complete Bojeffries Saga* (Northampton, MA: Tundra, 1992), 26.iv © Alan Moore and Steve Parkhouse   32

3.1 Alan Moore and John Totleben, 'The Garden of Earthly Delights', *Swamp Thing*, 53 (Oct. 1986), 11. ©DC Comics   52

3.2 Alan Moore and John Totleben, 'The Garden of Earthly Delights', *Swamp Thing*, 53 (Oct. 1986), 24–5. ©DC Comics   53

3.3 Alan Moore, Stephen Bissette and John Totleben, 'The Nukeface Papers Part 1', *The Saga of the Swamp Thing*, 35 (Apr. 1985), 19. ©DC Comics   57

3.4 Alan Moore, Stephen Bissette and John Totleben, 'The Nukeface Papers Part 2', *The Saga of the Swamp Thing*, 36 (May 1985), 23. ©DC Comics   58

4.1 Alan Moore, Stephen Bissette and John Totleben, 'The Anatomy Lesson', *Swamp Thing*, 21 (Feb. 1984), 22. ©DC Comics   75

4.2	Alan Moore and Eddie Campbell, *From Hell* (London: Knockabout Comics, 2006), II.4. © Alan Moore and Eddie Campbell	78
7.1	Alan Moore, Stephen Bissette and John Totleben, 'The Sleep of Reason', *The Saga of the Swamp Thing*, 25 (June 1984), 23.iv–vii. ©DC Comics	135
8.1	Alan Moore and Eddie Campbell, *From Hell* (London: Knockabout Comics, 2006), IX.36.i–vi. © 2006 Alan Moore and Eddie Campbell	155
11.1	Alan Moore and Kevin O'Neill, *The League of Extraordinary Gentlemen Volume I* (La Jolla, CA: America's Best Comics, 2000), cover image (cropped). © Alan Moore and Kevin O'Neill	201
12.1	Alan Moore and Oscar Zarate, *A Small Killing* (Urbana, IL: Avatar, 2003), p. 84. © 2003 Alan Moore and Oscar Zarate	219
12.2	Alan Moore and Eddie Campbell, *From Hell* (London: Knockabout Comics, 2006), VII.24. © 2006 Alan Moore and Eddie Campbell	223
12.3	Alan Moore and Eddie Campbell, 'Snakes and Ladders', *A Disease of Language* (London: Knockabout Comics, 2010), 9. ©Alan Moore and Eddie Campbell, 2010	229
14.1	Alan Moore and Jacen Burrows, *Neonomicon*, I (2010), auxiliary cover. © 2010 Alan Moore and Avatar Press	268
14.2	Alan Moore and Jacen Burrows, *Neonomicon*, III.4–5 © 2011 Alan Moore and Avatar Press	270
14.3	Alan Moore and Jacen Burrows, *Neonomicon*, I.25 © 2011 Alan Moore and Avatar Press	271

Every effort has been made to contact copyright holders.

A note on references and quotations

Reference format

References to all works in the comics medium employ the following format: volume or book (V or B followed by the appropriate Arabic numeral; e.g. V1, B5), chapter (upper-case Roman numeral), page number (Arabic numeral) and panel number (lower-case Roman numeral), as in the following examples:

- reference to *V for* Vendetta, Book 1, Chapter 4, page 4, panel 7: B1.IV.4.vii.
- reference to *From Hell*, Chapter 4, page 35, panel 4: IV.35.iv.

Panel numbering runs from left to right across the page and then down; where panels do not follow a standard grid, the most likely direction of reading the page has been followed. Where any of the above divisions is not present, the relevant digit has been omitted (as in the example of *From Hell* above, which has chapter divisions but not book or volume divisions).

Chapter and issue numbers

Chapter numbering has replaced original issue numbers where these are the same, as in the case of *Watchmen*, or where the original publication included the same chapter divisions as the collected edition (e.g. *V for Vendetta* and *From Hell*). Where chapter numbers differ from issue numbers, as in the case of *Swamp Thing*, references cite the original magazine publication with corresponding references to the trade paperback collection provided in the bibliography. Chapters in *V for Vendetta* do not consistently begin on the page where the chapter number and title are given; readers of the collected editions are advised, however, that chapter breaks are indicated by a small Guy Fawkes mask in the bottom outside corner of each chapter's final page.

Pagination

Pagination is by issue/chapter, excluding any pages that included advertisements in the original magazine publications. Where no pagination is provided, numbering begins on the page in which the narrative or prologue begins, excluding cover reproductions. Where the trade paperback collection includes continuous pagination across multiple issues/chapters (as with collected editions of *Swamp Thing* and *V for Vendetta*), non-continuous pagination is retained in view of the considerable variation in practice across different editions. Interpolated material that is included at the end of a volume/issue/chapter (e.g. 'Under the Hood' in *Watchmen*) is also paginated separately and, where given, follows the pagination as presented in the cited text.

Editions

For the majority of these works, no standard edition exists and reference is, in general, given to the trade paperback or hardback collection most readily available when this book went to press.

Quotations

Ellipses: given the preponderance of ellipses in Moore's comics, it has been necessary to differentiate their presence in the original texts from editorial omissions made when quoting from these. Across all quotations, ellipses that appear enclosed in square brackets – [. . .] – indicate editorial omissions, while those that appear without brackets – . . . – are present in the original.

Line breaks in block quotations indicate a full or partial break in a speech balloon, either in the same panel or split across panels. In short quotations, line breaks are indicated by a forward slash: / .

Lettering: in general, the typescript for quotations has been standardised and there has been no attempt to replicate changes in letter-weighting. Practice varies across scholarly publications in the discipline. It was felt that because the gradations possible in comics are not possible in conventional typesetting and because discerning such weightings involves considerable subjectivity whilst yielding little change in the overall sense of the quoted material, this would be the most practical approach to take; however, where emphasis is clearly fundamental to the sense of the passage – as in the case of underlining, a change in font, or changes in capitalisation – these are indicated in the quotations.

For Thomas who gets first dibs on the
Swamp Thing collection

Notes on contributors

Michael Bradshaw is the author of *Resurrection Songs: the Poetry of Thomas Lovell Beddoes* (2001), the co-editor of *The Ashgate Research Companion to Thomas Lovell Beddoes* (2007), the editor of *Death's Jest-Book: the 1829 text* (2003) and the co-editor of *Beddoes's Selected Poetry* (1999). He has published critical articles on a range of Romantic authors and themes, including George Darley, Thomas Hood, John Keats, Mary and Percy Shelley, Walter Savage Landor, *The London Magazine* and Romantic fragment poems. Currently writing on Hood's comic poetry, and on Romanticism and disability, he is Professor of English at Edge Hill University, Liverpool.

Jochen Ecke teaches English literature at the Johannes Gutenberg University, Mainz, Germany. He has written his Master's thesis on concepts of time and space in Alan Moore's works and is currently preparing his doctoral thesis on British comics of the 1980s. In addition to co-editing *Comics as a Nexus of Cultures* (2010), he has published a number of essays on Alan Moore and Warren Ellis. He has also done extensive work in the German comics industry, serving as German editor and occasional translator on works by Ed Brubaker, Greg Rucka and Alan Moore.

Laura Hilton holds a Ph.D. in English Literature from the University of Birmingham, where she also completed her BA and MA degrees. Her doctoral research analyses representations of the Gothic double in the contemporary graphic novel and focuses on the work of Neil Gaiman, Frank Miller and Alan Moore. She is co-founder and co-editor of the first two issues of the *Birmingham Journal of Literature and Language (BJLL)* and has recently published articles in *Gothic Science Fiction: 1980–2010* and *Investigating Heroes: Truth, Justice and Quality TV*. She also has an article forthcoming in *Comment Rêver la Science-fiction à Present?* Laura has presented papers at several national and international conferences and her wider research interests include nineteenth-, twentieth- and twenty-first-century literature, comic book and graphic novel studies, and Gothic studies.

Monica Germanà is a writer and Senior Lecturer in English Literature and Creative Writing at the University of Westminster, London. Her research interests and publications concentrate on contemporary British literature, with a specific emphasis on the Gothic, gender and popular culture. Her first monograph, *Scottish Women's Gothic and Fantastic Writing*, was published by Edinburgh University Press in 2010. She is currently working on a monograph exploring the politics of body and dress in Ian Fleming's narrative and subsequent cinematic adaptations, provisionally entitled 'Bond Girls: Body, Style, and Gender'.

Maggie Gray was awarded her Ph.D. in the History of Art at University College London in 2010, with a thesis entitled *'Love Your Rage, Not Your Cage' Comics as Cultural Resistance: Alan Moore 1971–1989*. Her work has been published in *Studies in Comics*, the *Journal of Graphic Novels and Comics* and *Kunst und Politik*. She has taught comics, aesthetics and the history and theory of art and design at Middlesex University, UCL and Central St Martin's College of Art and Design, and works part-time at Mega-City Comics, London.

Matthew J.A. Green is Associate Professor of English Literature at the University of Nottingham. In addition to articles published on William Blake, Alan Moore and Lord Byron, he is author of *Visionary Materialism in the Early Works of William Blake* (2005) and co-editor of *Byron and the Politics of Freedom and Terror* (2011). He is currently completing a monograph on William Blake and Alan Moore.

Markus Oppolzer holds a Ph.D. from the University of Salzburg, Austria, where he is Assistant Professor (PostDoc) in the Department of English and American Studies. In his thesis he applied Victor Turner's theory of liminality to a study of early British Gothic fiction. Since then, his research interests have shifted to the comparative study of narrative strategies in various media, focusing mainly on comics.

Christopher Murray is Head of the English Department at the University of Dundee, Scotland, and lecturer in English, Film and Comics. He runs the UK's first Comics Studies M.Litt. programme, is editor of the peer-reviewed journal *Studies in Comics* (Intellect Books) and Anthology, a series publishing the work of comics students. He is the author of a monograph on superhero comics and propaganda, *Champions of the Oppressed* (Hampton Press, 2011), as well as articles on British comics, and the work of Grant Morrison and Alan Moore. He organises two annual conferences on comics, and chairs the Scottish Centre for Comics Studies.

Brad Ricca received his Ph.D. in English from Case Western Reserve University, Cleveland, Ohio, USA, where he is currently a SAGES Fellow. His work has been published in *The Emily Dickinson Journal*, *Leviathan* and *Critical Approaches to Comics and Graphic Novels*, among others. His book *Super Boys: Jerry Siegel, Joe Shuster, and the Creation of Superman* is forthcoming in 2013 from St. Martin's Press.

Julia Round (MA, Ph.D.) is senior lecturer in the Media School at Bournemouth University, UK, and edits the academic journal *Studies in Comics* (Intellect Books). She has published and presented work internationally on cross-media adaptation, television and discourse analysis, the application of literary terminology to comics, the 'graphic novel' redefinition, and the presence of Gothic and fantastic motifs and themes in this medium. She is currently writing a monograph on comics and the literary Gothic (provisionally entitled *Ghosts in the Gutter*, McFarland 2013) and editing the collection *Real Lives Celebrity Stories* (Continuum, 2013). For further details please visit www.juliaround.com.

Christian W. Schneider studied English Literature and Political Science at Ruprecht-Karls-Universität Heidelberg, Germany, and at the University of Wales Aberystwyth. He then went on to pursue a doctoral degree at Heidelberg. His doctoral dissertation on the Gothic mode in graphic literature will hopefully be finished by the time this reaches print, including an extended version of his arguments about *Watchmen*. He has written about the Gothic in other comics; his further research interests include contemporary American fiction, the narrativity of digital media and the postmodern transformation of popular literary genres.

Claire Sheridan has completed a Ph.D. at Queen Mary, University of London. Her research looks at representations of solitary survival and sociability, especially in the writings of William Godwin and Mary Shelley. She has published work in the *European Romantic Review* and written papers on Godwin as 'last man', Mary Shelley's *The Last Man* and biographies of Percy Bysshe Shelley.

Tony Venezia is a Ph.D. candidate at Birkbeck, University of London, completing a thesis on Alan Moore and the historical imagination. He is a tutor at Birkbeck and visiting lecturer at London South Bank University. His research interests include genre fiction, critical theory and post-millennial literature and culture. He has published articles and reviews in *Radical Philosophy*, *New Formations* and *Studies in Comics* and will be guest editing a special issue of *Studies in Comics* on comics and cultural theory (2013). He established the annual Comica Transitions symposium at Birkbeck, and is co-convenor of the Contemporary Fiction Seminar.

Preface

The following collection explores a number of Alan Moore's works in various forms, including comics, performance, short prose and the novel. It presents a scholarly study of these texts that examines the ways that Moore's work draws upon, and intervenes in, what can loosely be described as 'the Gothic tradition'. Though the project was originally conceived through conversations with other scholars who, predominantly though not exclusively, specialise in the Gothic, it has expanded to those working in Comics Studies and other cognate disciplines. Accordingly, the chapters below adopt a range of methodologies and vocabularies, some more readily associated with a specific discipline or school than others, giving rise to a plurality of voices that express the variety of ways in which Moore's work is being received at the present moment.

Though there are a range of connections across various chapters, for ease of reading the collection has been grouped into four parts. Part I, 'Monstrous politics', overtly explores the political dimension of Moore's works. In the first chapter, I highlight the collection's overarching themes, drawing on material from each of the subsequent chapters and presenting additional readings to argue for a politically charged sense of Moore's position within the Gothic tradition. Chapters 2 and 3 flush out this argument, through Tony Venezia's investigation of the sociohistorical context of *The Bojeffries Saga* and Maggie Gray's examination of *Swamp Thing*'s environmentalism.

The investigation of Moore's deployment of three specific Gothic devices occupies the chapters in Part II, 'Gothic tropes'. This part opens with Jochen Ecke's discussion of the döppelganger in *Swamp Thing* and *From Hell*, relating this to a close reading of Sheridan Le Fanu's novella,

Carmilla, followed by Christian W. Schneider's treatment of the apocalyptic in *Watchmen*, which analyses the use of atmosphere and fragmentation as well as the intersection of form and intertextuality. Markus Oppolzer's discussion of *V for Vendetta* closes the section with a reassessment of the significance of liminality in this text and others from the Gothic tradition.

The penultimate part, 'Inheritance and adaptation', explores the relationship between Moore's work and broader textual traditions, placing particular emphasis on the political and cultural significance of intertextual relationships and adaptations. Michael Bradshaw situates Moore's work within a larger post-enlightenment tradition, arguing that the work uses intertextuality to enhance the aesthetic and political sensibilities of the readership, while Monica Germanà provides an historically sensitive reading of *From Hell* that connects Moore's concern with the urban environment to his engagement with a range of historical discourses. Brad Ricca and Claire Sheridan situate Moore's treatment of the superhero in relation to key novels from the Gothic genre, with Ricca providing a compelling reading of *Superman Annual*, 11 in relation to Horace Walpole's *The Castle of Otranto*, while Sheridan combines an informed reading of William Godwin and Mary Shelley in their historical context with a careful analysis of the nexus of group politics and survival in *Watchmen*. Laura Hilton's chapter completes this part by directly addressing the adaptation of Mina Harker in Moore and O'Neill's *The League of Extraordinary Gentlemen* and Stephen Norrington's cinematic adaptation of *The League*.

The final part of the collection – 'Art, magic, sex, other' – turns attention to Moore's recent work in different genres and media, while at the same time engaging with his theories of art and magic and considering the significance, in this respect, of his representations of violence and sexuality. Christopher Murray and Julia Round provide extensive discussions of the intersection of magic and the Gothic in Moore's comics, performance pieces and the novel *Voice of the Fire*, while my closing chapter explores the insight that Moore's adaptations of Lovecraft can yield for broader understandings of his forays into the occult.

By examining Moore's diverse and longstanding engagements with the Gothic tradition, the chapters in this collection contribute both to Gothic Studies and Comics Studies. The underlying premise of the collection is that Moore, and the artists with whom he works, engage in a process of dialogue with a diverse array of source material. Accordingly, the chapters outlined above address two interrelated topics: how an understanding of the Gothic can enhance our understanding of Moore's work and, conversely, the ways in which the ideas and reading practices engendered by Moore's work might impact on a reflexive analysis of one or more of the traditions out of which it emerges.

Matthew J.A. Green
University of Nottingham, 2012

Acknowledgements

This collection truly has been a collaborative endeavour, and I am indebted to the conversations and correspondence with each of the contributors over the course of its creation. Alan Moore has been exceptionally generous with his time and his interest – I am tremendously grateful to him for taking time away from his many projects to discuss ideas about this book and other work in progress, as well as for permission to quote extensively from his texts. Many thanks also to Eddie Campbell, Kevin O'Neill, Steve Parkhouse, Avatar Press, Bryan Talbot and Oscar Zarate for permission to reproduce the visual art for which they hold copyright. Tony Bennett, William Christensen and Chris Staros were each instrumental in fielding correspondence; for their co-operation and support I am also very thankful. Equally, I would like to thank Matthew Frost and Kim Walker, whose enthusiasm for the book has been unwavering, as well as the anonymous readers whose comments have considerably strengthened it. Huge thanks are also due to Stephen L. Holland, Jonathan Rigby and Dominique Kidd of Page 45, whose suggestions and encyclopaedic knowledge have been invaluable – as a man far more knowledgeable than me once said, Page 45 is the best graphic novel shop I've ever been to. I am also obliged to my many colleagues in the School of English at the University of Nottingham, who have provided support and guidance at various stages in the project, and to successive years of students whose passion and interest for the Gothic and the comics form are inspirational. Last but not least, I could not have completed this collection without my wife Louise, whose enduring belief and advice mean more than words can say, and my daughter Abigail, who has kept me from disappearing too far into the shadows.

Part I

Monstrous politics

1
Alan Moore and the Gothic tradition

Matthew J.A. Green

> It's about the vital message that the stiff lips of decapitated men still shape; the testament of black and spectral dogs written in piss across our bad dreams. It's about raising the dead to tell us what they know. It is a bridge, a crossing-point, a worn spot in the curtain between our world and the underworld, between the mortar and the myth, fact and fiction, a threadbare gauze no thicker than a page. It's about the powerful glossalia of witches and their magical revisions of the texts we live in. None of this is speakable.
> Alan Moore, *Voice of the Fire*[1]

> Stories shape the world. They exist independently of people, and in places quite devoid of man, there may yet be mythologies.
> The glaciers have their legends. The ocean bed entertains its own romances.
> Alan Moore, *Swamp Thing*[2]

Alan Moore's comics, performance and prose works abound with Gothic tropes and beings. Alongside archetypal vampires, zombies, werewolves and witches lurk creatures extracted from the personal bestiaries of writers such as Robert Louis Stevenson, H.G. Wells and H.P. Lovecraft. And while the ancient beasts and pagan gods of British myth who appear in the novel, *Voice of the Fire*, do not exactly rub shoulders with the swamp monster created by Len Wein and Berni Wrightson, Moore's syncretic imagination erects bridges and opens byways that facilitate traffic between territories as seemingly distinct as pulp fiction and fading folklore, quantum science and anarchist politics, underground comics and the literary canon. His position within the Gothic tradition stems from the ability of his writing to tap into what Fred Botting identifies as the 'darker undercurrent to the literary tradition'[3] coursing through the culture of modernity. In staging the world-shaping capabilities of writing, his work enhances our understanding of the uncanny and the abject while further illustrating David Punter's sense that the Gothic 'serves to demonstrate [...] the perverse in the very ground of being'.[4] Uniting works as diverse as *Voice of the Fire*, *From Hell* and *Swamp Thing* is an unwavering belief in the intercourse between the fictional and the real. And underpinning Moore's understanding of these exchanges and communications is his longstanding interest in the occult and language, which reached a new stage in 1993 when, on the occasion of his fortieth birthday, he proclaimed himself a magician, giving tangible expression to his reflections on the craft of writing: 'There is something very magical at the heart of writing, and language, and storytelling. The gods of magic in the ancient cultures, such as Hermes and Thoth, are also the gods of writing.'[5]

Viewing Moore's work in relation to the Gothic tradition focuses attention on significant similarities across his diverse body of work, highlighting the political import of a variety of spectral or marginal continuities. The relevance of this tradition to Moore's oeuvre beyond the relatively small number of works that explicitly invoke the Gothic is connected to a shared preoccupation with the intersection of the popular and the literary, as well as with the problems of textuality which unfold into wider cultural anxieties over the heterogeneity and instability inherent to the self and its world(s). These concerns are, in other words, tied to what Moore identifies as the magic at the heart of writing which imbues fiction with its creative and destructive capabilities. This occult dimension of writing, so often disavowed in the narrowly defined economics and instrumentalism of contemporary culture, is expressed overtly in the Gothic's obsession with the supernatural; that is, with beings or occurrences that disrupt hegemonic structurings of everyday experience.

While the efficacy of storytelling is illustrated – often coercively, in Moore's view – by religion, the potential of writing to alter human consciousness also provides a link between magic and politics, offering a way of 'giving something back'.[6] Punter's remark that 'Gothic is the paradigm of all fiction, all textuality' itself suggests that the rupturing effects of Gothic writing make it particularly well placed to intervene in the wider social discourses that produce our experiences of self and of the world.[7] While such discussions of Gothic textuality draw overtly on poststructuralist critical theory, they are also commensurate with *Voice of the Fire*'s self-presentation, in which fiction is constitutive of non-fiction and writing gives a textual form to this interplay between the speakable and the unspeakable. But they also recall *Swamp Thing*'s evocative proposition that the non-human also has its stories to tell, and that the telling of them can be a magical intervention that recodes the discursive worlds we inhabit.

Representations of the sublime and of the abject – together with the staging of the inability of semiotic and legal systems to accommodate that which exceeds, precedes or otherwise annihilates the codifying capacities of language – motion outward to a 'relation between writing and the animal' that incorporates 'the mess, the shit, the refusal of confinement, the pacing tiger and its face of fury'.[8] Moore's work, from *Miracleman* onwards,[9] repeatedly depicts encounters with figures that disrupt hegemonic and self-aggrandising claims about what it means to be human. This is not the place to explore parallels between the sorcerer, whose memories are evoked by Deleuze and Guattari's *A Thousand Plateaus*, and the voice of the magus that reverberates throughout Moore's corpus; however, it is worth noting that the link between writing and the animal discussed by the sorcerer and the use of writing to present a world beyond illusory myths of human mastery that we find in works like *Swamp Thing* both owe something to the Gothic's propensity for unsettling boundaries and destabilising hierarchies. Thus, in their account of becoming animal, Deleuze and Guattari quote Lovecraft, whose works provide the jumping-off point for Moore's most overtly Gothic work in recent years, *Neonomicon*: 'Lovecraft recounts the story of Randolph Carter, who feels his "self" reel and who experiences a fear worse than that of annihilation: "Carters of forms both human and non-human, vertebrate and invertebrate, conscious and mindless, animal and vegetable."'[10] Lovecraft's passage indicates another way in which the Gothic in general, and Moore's work in particular, moves beyond the becoming-animal to include all those modes of existence that Deleuze and Guattari associate with the plane of nature: 'what if one became animal or plant *through* literature, which certainly does not mean literally?'[11]

Political ecologies

The transformative capacity of literature as a device for reconnecting the human with the non-human is a central aspect of Moore's work on *Swamp Thing*, which communicates an environmental politics that registers across his texts. Compare, for example, the guest story for Eclipse Comics' *Mr. Monster*, in which the protagonist, himself part vampire, must save a city being savaged by a monster composed from garbage. Staging a literal, if lightly depicted, return of repressed waste, 'The Riddle of the Recalcitrant Refuse' draws explicitly on the Freudian conception of the death drive in its articulation of environmentalism: 'No greater monster faces man than that which he has inadvertently created himself: Garbage! /[...] [I]n his wanton squanderings, man displays an unconscious tendency towards destruction / Surely, this repressed Thanatic curse is the greatest menace of them all!'[12] Though not widely discussed, this story experiments with ideas that would be further developed 12 months later in *Swamp Thing*, 53 (Oct. 1986), 'The Garden of Earthly Delights'. Recalling this issue, Moore underscores the way it foregrounds humanity's disavowed dependence on nature:

> we had an entire tropical rainforest [...] smothering the city in vegetation. In the resulting chaos and carnage all of the animals escaped from the local zoo so that you have [...] escaped tigers padding through the cosmetics department of the local chain store. [...] [E]ven though mankind can cover nature, and smother the wilderness with a layer of concrete [...] underneath our feet [...] the wilderness is still there. And though man might boast of having conquered nature that's not the case, for if nature were to shrug or to merely raise its eyebrow then we should all be gone.[13]

As Maggie Gray demonstrates in Chapter 3 below, the series as a whole deploys Gothic devices to engender a new environmental sensibility by moving beyond the instrumental attitude towards nature fostered by Enlightenment thought. Moreover, as Gray argues, Moore's revision of Swamp Thing's character destabilises distinctions between self and environment, animal and plant, human and non-human.

This sense of ecological interconnectedness is, moreover, subject to a doubling effect whereby Moore's commitment to environmentalism intersects with his longstanding engagements in the areas of gender and sexuality. The irruption of the wilderness in Gotham City occurs in a story arc that stretches across issues 51–4 (Aug.–Nov. 1986) and represents Swamp Thing's attempt to force Batman and Gotham City to release his lover, Abigail Cable, who, as a result of their relationship, is facing extradition to Louisiana for 'crimes against nature'.[14] Batman here becomes an unthinking agent of law, describing the eruption of the wilderness as 'terrorism' and insisting that Abby will not be released 'until she's been through the judicial process' ('Garden', 13.ii). The issue develops into a conflict between an urban, sci-fi Gothic – displaying the terrifying aspect of law and technocracy embodied in Batman and his monstrous technologies – and a Green Gothic that, as Batman is compelled to acknowledge, is on the side of 'love and justice' ('Garden', 27.iii). The confrontation between the wilderness and the city thus expresses not only Moore's own environmental politics but also his opposition to discrimination on the basis of sexual orientation or practice evident in 'The Mirror of Love', included in Moore's self-published anthology, *Artists Against Rampant Government Homophobia*.[15] This political dimension positioned *Swamp Thing* at the vanguard of a renewed engagement between comics and society, which developed in part out of the growing visibility of creators associated with the underground press.[16] While the interventionist stances adopted by such projects efface the boundary between the text and its social context, as Michael Bradshaw discusses in Chapter 7, *Swamp Thing* specifically utilises a series of intertextual connections to foster a deep sense of a cultural context stretching back over centuries.

The political uncanny and the human abject

To the extent that Moore's writing accelerates the experience of the text overflowing its own boundaries, it is constituted by the uncanny, which, Nicholas Royle observes, 'overruns, disordering any field supposedly extraneous to it'.[17] Here too, the magical dimension of writing makes its presence felt – as Sigmund Freud suggests in his seminal essay, the 'uncanny effect' can result from facing 'the reality of something' previously 'considered imaginary', and 'this is at the root of much that is uncanny about magical practices'.[18] Moore's work goes beyond this by demonstrating that the 'real' world depends upon the imagination, and it consistently deploys uncanny structures and thematics from early revisions of *Miracleman*, which confront the imaginary superhero with real life in 1980s Britain, to *Promethea*, which narrativises the magical capacities of the imagination. It is, moreover, no accident that there is an uncanny resemblance between the later magical works and the revisionary treatments of the superhero, given that 'another name for uncanny overflow might be deconstruction'.[19]

Anxieties over the collapse of the logos in fin-de-siècle London are, as Monica Germanà demonstrates in Chapter 8, embodied in *From Hell*, which posits an irrational ground for the psychological, geographical and historical structures required to sustain patriarchy and western imperialism. Concentrating on recurrent anxieties expressed by the Gothic, Germanà extends consideration of Moore's intertextuality, noted by Bradshaw in the previous chapter, to include a diversity of source documents, further illustrating the overlap of art and life. The corrupting and obliterative capacity of language itself is evidenced directly in Moore's responses to Lovecraft, which begin to appear in the mid-1990s, just as *From Hell* was being completed. As discussed by Matthew Green in Chapter 14, the short story, *The Courtyard*, and its comics sequel, *Neonomicon*, make the reality-altering capacity of language a central plot device, whereas the uncanny overflow of art into life is testified in Moore's report that writing the *The Great Old Ones* made him physically ill, as a result of the 'big, ugly energies that I was trying to contain in these words'. This struggle to linguistically embody the spectral similarly permeates the narrative form and structure of *Voice of the Fire*. As Julia Round discusses in Chapter 13, this novel – which also occupied a good deal of Moore's attention in the 1990s – embodies the spirits of Northampton through several cryptomimetic elements. Here too, Moore's writing incorporates Gothic representations of the body – as a site of abjection and violence – to give a form to his own reimagining of local history, developing this reading of the past into a reflection on textual form. In Chapter 12, Christopher Murray observes the uncanny effect exerted by the interconnectedness of beings, times and places in *A Small Killing*, *From Hell*, *The Birth Caul* and *Snakes and Ladders*. But Murray's discussion also suggests another connection to the abject, noting that Moore introduces fear into the superhero genre by undermining the presumed inviolability of the superheroes.

Julia Kristeva describes the ways that 'refuse and corpses *show me* what I permanently thrust aside in order to live',[20] presenting an analysis of the abject which anticipates Judith Butler's discussions of the centrality of vulnerability in identity formation, and it speaks to Moore's remarks about the superhero's ubiquitousness in mainstream comics. While Moore suggests that in its 'current incarnation' the superhero might be 'a symbol of American reluctance' to get involved 'in any kind of conflict without massive tactical superiority',[21] Butler outlines a concept of the subject capable of supplanting 'one in which the US subject seeks to [...] define itself as [...] radically invulnerable to attack'.[22] Butler's analysis of this nationalistic disavowal involves her in an explicitly Gothic vocabulary of 'spectral versions' of the subject, of a 'remainder [...] that limns and haunts every normative instance', and of life as 'haunted by its ontologically uncertain double'.[23] Such lexis is no mere rhetorical flourish for, in addition to Kristeva's theorisation of abjection, Butler's argument is indebted to Derridean conceptualisations of spectrality, themselves bound up with uncanny experiences of the subject.[24]

As a cultural icon of moral, mental and corporeal inviolability, the superhero – and Superman in particular – tends to confirm the hegemonic idealisations of the self at both personal and national levels. Thus, despite the concerted suspension of belief required to accept the sublime dimensions of these heroes in tights, they retain a central position within the comics industry, as Moore observes: 'I would have thought that sex would have been a more mainstream preoccupation [...] but... apparently not!'[25] He suggests that 'the brutality of *From Hell* or the sexuality of *Lost Girls* might be taking people into areas which they're not comfortable with',[26] and it is clear that these works remind readers of what is disavowed at both individual and societal levels. An excellent example of the disruptive effect of the abject on the symbolic is the final sequence in *Lost Girls*, where the displacement of sexual pleasure with militaristic violence is metonymically encoded in images of a mutilated dead soldier (III.30.8.i–iv). Here the symbolic power of the phallus is reduced to the pathetically disturbing image of his severed penis. Though *Lost Girls* directly contrasts sexual freedom with physical violence, it nevertheless debunks the myth that carnal love can ever be free, drawing a sharp distinction between imaginative liberties and the entrenchment of actually existing sexuality within exploitative power structures, evidenced by child prostitution and molestation (III.25.3.iii–iv, I.9.3–5).

V for Vendetta represents the specifically political use of sexual violence in its opening scene, where the narrowly averted gang rape and murder of Evey operates as a metonym for the state's violation of its subject's bodies and minds.[27] As Markus Oppolzer argues in Chapter 6, the text repeatedly demonstrates the vulnerability of the self to imposition from the state and its opponents, as V himself becomes drawn into the role of oppressor seeking to remake Evey in his own image. Oppolzer explores the problematics of such identity (re)formation and deconstruction in relation to a longstanding tradition of Gothic liminality that includes works by William Godwin, Ann Radcliffe and Mary Shelley. In Chapter 10, Claire Sheridan makes a compelling case that *Watchmen* also partakes of this literary inheritance, noting that although Moore and Godwin are both committed to anarchist politics, each remains acutely aware that it is only by the social dimension of existence that humans can overcome the present imperfections of their species.

The interrogation of identity provoked by the double in much Gothic fiction provides a related means of tracing intertextual relationships in Moore's texts. Thus, Jochen Ecke situates the presentations of the doppelgänger in *From Hell* and *Swamp Thing* alongside a close reading of Sheridan Le Fanu's 'Carmilla', exploring how doubling generates a sense of the uncanny related to the destabilisation of identity. The double links directly to the abject, as material that haunts the 'I' as 'a massive and sudden emergence of uncanniness, which, familiar as it might have been in an opaque and forgotten life, now harries me as radically separate, loathsome'.[28] For the superhero, this second self is expressed in the convenient fiction of his/her humanity, usually crystallised into an alter ego whose domesticity and mundanity make it the hero's key point of vulnerability. This presentation of the domestic as a site of violent crisis links the first of Moore's Superman stories penned for the US market, 'For the Man who has Everything', to what many regard as the founding text of the Gothic genre, Horace Walpole's *The Castle of Otranto*. As Brad Ricca argues in Chapter 9, these texts exhibit striking similarities that point to a Gothic undercurrent in Moore's Superman work. Jack Teiwes has described 'Jungle Line' and 'For the Man' as expressing Superman's 'deeply repressed trauma over being the sole survivor of a planetary holocaust';[29] however, while both stories definitely portray the Man of Steel suffering hallucinations and flashbacks suggestive of post-traumatic stress, Ricca's chapter identifies the repressed content of Superman's unconscious as the desire for a normal life lived on a human scale. It is not simply that Superman feels guilty for surviving, but that this guilt is compounded by his longing for the lacklustre life of a common man on Krypton.

As Christian W. Schneider notes in Chapter 5, it is precisely the fact of the heroes' human weaknesses – subject to alienation and the ravages of time – that generates many of *Watchman*'s Gothic effects. Significantly, the sense that its heroes are living in a world beyond their control provides an overarching context that imbues the representation of their sexual and non-sexual desires – passions that in the mid-1980s were themselves transgressive for the prototypical hero – with a sense that their identities are orientated around an abyssal absence. Nevertheless the text does not seek to supplant the human with the superhuman, but rather to emphasise the heroism inherent in everyday, fallible human beings such that *Watchmen* actually works against the abjection of the human. This rehabilitation of the average person is similarly identified in 'Whatever Happened?', which appeared in the same month (September 1986) as *Watchmen*'s first issue. Superman, we are told by his imaginary alter ego, Jordan Elliot, 'weren't nothin' special. Us ordinary workin' slobs, son . . . we're the real heroes' (36.v).

If it is the human that becomes the abject in the realm of the superhuman, then a considerable portion of what makes Moore's work Gothic is directly related to his vivid depictions of (super)human bodies in their animalistic and sexual dimensions. It is significant that in both 'For the Man' and 'Whatever Happened?' an imaginary child of Superman triggers the anagnorisis in the hero and the reader, respectively, because fatherhood involves not just sexuality, which 'strays on the territories of *animal*', but sexual generation, which 'confronts us [. . .] with our earliest attempts to release the hold of the *maternal* entity'.[30] The reclamation of the abject feminine within Moore's conception of magic is demonstrated in *Promethea*, 22 (Aug. 2002), in 'The Wine of Her Fornications', which celebrates female sexuality on both material and symbolic levels,[31] but it is also a seminal dimension of his inaugural revision of the superhero archetype in *Miracleman*. Though not published under the aegis of the Comics Code, issue 9 (July 1986) carried an alert to parents warning of the 'graphic scenes of childbirth', which include realistic, full-colour close-ups of Miracleman's baby emerging from Liz Moran's vagina (11–15). This issue elicited visceral responses from readers, whose letters – excerpted in *Miracleman*, 10 (Dec. 1986) –

deploy a range of adjectival phrases ranging from 'right', 'true' and 'EXACTLY what I was hoping for', to 'unnecessarily graphic', 'messy' and 'disgusting'. T.M. Maple's letter, in particular, demonstrates the scene's communication of the abject's power to disrupt mental coherence: 'my mind was saying several things at the same time as I read the story'.[32] Moore's repeated transgressions of genre conventions and disregard for regulatory bodies like the Comics Code Authority exemplify Punter's sense that the Gothic's disregard for the standards of its denigrators is connected to its concern 'with the animal';[33] moreover, in reminding us that, in Butler's words, 'animality is a precondition of the human',[34] his work interrogates the archetypes and ideals underpinning conceptualisations of the self and community, exploring the interplay between the waking world and that of the dream. Maple's letter describes this effect from a different angle, stating that the *Miracleman* birth scene 'demonstrates quite vividly how the previously dreamlike Miracleman is becoming more and more rooted in "mundane" humanity'.[35]

Of all Moore's superhero stories, his stand-alone Batman story, *The Killing Joke*, is perhaps the most overtly Gothic. Contemporaneous with both *Watchmen* and 'Whatever Happened?', this tale remains one of Moore's most brutal stories, a fact which has led him subsequently to disavow it publicly: 'too nasty, it was too physically violent'.[36] The plot unfolds on two levels, providing a traumatic origin story for the Joker alongside an account of his attempt to drive Commissioner Gordon insane through personal humiliation and torture, including a paralysing attack on his daughter. As Round notes, the text 'links psychological themes of repression and memory to the internal/external divide, calling to mind gothic notions of inversion and reversal via psychoanalytic criticism'.[37] Moreover, in its presentation of the Joker and Batman as doubles, the text appears to express the perverse symbiosis of transgression and law, a subject so prevalent in Gothic fiction from Walpole to the present that it might well be described as one of the genre's foundational tropes. Nevertheless, despite its deployment of Gothic devices, despite its capacity to generate a sense of horror and despite its presentation of abject (sub)human grotesquerie, *The Killing Joke* does not show the same relationship to story – and to storytelling – as the works discussed elsewhere in the present collection. While Moore's other works from this period – particularly *Swamp Thing* – anticipate his subsequent understanding of the interconnection between writing and magic, these aspects are absent from *The Killing Joke*. Furthermore, though the text is undeniably Gothic, it presents a vision of triumphal individualism anathematic to Moore's other work of the time. 'I spoke to Commissioner Gordon before I came in here. He's fine', Batman tells the Joker. 'Despite all your sick, vicious little games, he's as sane as he ever was' (41.i). The evocative effacement of the line of light separating Batman and the Joker on the final page thus does not so much signify the symbiosis between (para)legal violence and criminal transgression, but rather shows that hero and villain are both acting in accordance with the logic of the law. That this logic is insane and unfounded does nothing to undermine its authority as the closing image of light giving way to watery darkness is contraposed in advance with the image of the Police Commissioner's agonistic triumph. As in Moore's other superhero works from the period, the heroism of humanity is represented, but the triumph here depicted is that of the autonomous individual at the heart of the liberal–capitalist hegemony who successfully rejects his own vulnerability and animality. Moreover, while Batman appears to partake in the Joker's madness, his innermost desires for revenge are not only restrained but elided with the law:

> *Joker:* I shot a defenseless girl. I terrorized an old man.
> Why don't you kick the hell out of me and get a standing ovation from the public gallery?
> *Batman:* Because I'm doing this one by the book . . .
> . . . And because I don't want to.[38]

Batman's position here echoes that which he is accorded in *Swamp Thing*, and despite appearances to the contrary, it is the Joker who becomes infected by Batman's mad commitment to the law. In what is presented as a fight to the death – at least on the Joker's side – he misses the opportunity to shoot Batman because he is holding a toy gun rather than a real one; while the disappointment on his face suggests that this is not intentional, it appears that at least on an unconscious level the villain has decided to play by the hero's rules (43.iii–vi). The graphic violence confronts us with a series of abject forms that are ultimately disavowed, and while this conservative impulse is not uncommon within the Gothic tradition, it is almost unheard of in Moore's work.

Monstrous stories: magic, textuality and adaptation

That the abject coincides with – even as it disrupts – a conservative impulse within the genre relates directly to Moore's own sense of the emergence of the Gothic as 'an attempt to tame death – to remove the real evidence of death in our lives and to substitute a parade of demons and devils and monsters'.[39] Moore's description of Gothic writing as a transformation of 'all the trappings of death' into a '"sugary fantasy" that people could delight in' suggests it actually participates in the process of disavowal by substituting fictional objects of horror for real-life confrontations with vulnerability;[40] however, Moore's recurrent emphasis on the centrality of stories to human (and non-human) experiences of being and his understanding of the imagination as the creative faculty that allows for the construction of the world(s) we inhabit render untenable any attempt to establish an impermeable border between real and fictional objects of horror.

This slippage between the real world and the realm of story is dramatised in Moore's contribution to *Vampirella/Dracula: The Centennial*, published to mark the hundredth anniversary of Bram Stoker's novel. Moore's story, 'The New European', defamiliarises the Dracula story by bringing it 'into the murky borderlines of fact and fiction',[41] setting its story within a set of realistically depicted environments containing elements immediately recognisable to its intended audience (a Balkan war zone, a jumbo jet, the *Friends* television show), while at the same time introducing supernatural characters. Within the story, the protagonist, Jack Halloran, experiences a similar blurring of fact and fiction as he realises that his own identity, and those of his family and friends, are haunted by their precursors from Stoker's novel: 'it was only when I said Lucy's name that I realized how similar all our names were to those in the original story' ('New European', 10.i). Notably, it is this recognition that his everyday experience is structured by a fictional story that Halloran identifies as the greater source of fear: 'Dracula was a vampire. That frightened me. Dracula was fictional: that frightened me more' ('New European', 10.iii). The diegesis thus stages the text's uncanny effects, while also complicating the distinction between the uncanny and the abject, for it is precisely the uncanny haunting of the real by the fictional that gives form to the abject acts and objects represented, from the reiteration of Harker's encounter with the three vampire women, in which Halloran awakens at the centre of a four-way orgy in a bombed-out mansion, to a re-presentation of the arrival of the *Demeter* in Whitby, in which the ship becomes a plane full of bleeding corpses, with the dead pilot and co-pilot lashed to the controls.[42] Not only is the uncanniness of the supernatural more extreme than we would normally encounter in everyday life,[43] but so too is the abject, which is taken to levels impossible within the real world. 'The New European' not only depicts the power of stories to underwrite the world, but also suggests that this is a power that can be both insidious and malefactory. The story literally becomes the monster as Dracula becomes one with his tale: 'Oh, I'm a story, Mr. Halloran. A rather old European story, endlessly retold' (12.iii).

That stories themselves can become monstrous relates directly to a perception of tradition – of tradition in general and the Gothic tradition in particular – as fraught with conflict. Jerrold Hogle's work has been of seminal importance in conceiving of the Gothic as 'a site of "abjection" in Julia Kristeva's sense, a "monstrous other" into which the members of an increasingly uncertain Western culture could "throw off" (one literal meaning of ab-ject) much that seemed anomalous in themselves and their changing society'.[44] As Raymond Williams argues, tradition is not simply 'the surviving past', but rather a 'selective' force that expresses 'the dominant and hegemonic pressures and limits'.[45] More recent examinations have identified hegemonic practices as 'suturing' the field of the social by attempting to 'fill in' an 'original lack'.[46] That history itself is subject to such hegemonic practices is suggested by Jacques Derrida, who remarks that, while 'historical knowledge occludes, confines, or saturates', there nevertheless remains 'at the heart of this history [...] an abyss that resists totalizing summary'.[47] Significantly, Derrida names this ineradicable openness 'the gift of death', linking freedom and identity to the very experience of mortality that, as Moore observes, is disavowed by the sanitising impulses of the Enlightenment: 'as a culture, we no longer wanted to have the smell of death around us'.[48] The Gothic tradition thus presents a series of reminders of that very absence, here named death, which it appears to conceal, filling in the terror of personal annihilation with various demonic apparitions. Moreover, the heterogeneity of the genre, its ability to assimilate and recycle material from multiple sources, not only makes explicit the indebtedness and violence included in the concept of bricolage that

Derrida links to every act of creation, but it also involves the Gothic in a process of adaptation equally manifest in comics. Thus, Andy W. Smith speaks of 'areas of generic hybridity' in which comics and the Gothic find a shared textual *and* contextual space'.[49] While *Swamp Thing*, *From Hell* and *The League of Extraordinary Gentlemen* provide the foci in Smith's study, Punter identifies adaptation as a key feature of *Watchmen*, describing the text as 'a tissue of referentiality, taking us back to Blake, Nietzsche and the Gothic and romantic traditions'.[50]

Moore's most sustained and self-reflexive adaptations of Gothic texts and figures are *The Bojeffries Saga* and *The League of Extraordinary Gentlemen*, though the latter casts its net far wider than the Gothic to include the entirety of western culture. Both works demonstrate the 'hyperconsciousness' that Jim Collins associates not simply with postmodernism, but with popular culture more generally,[51] invoking intertextual relations in a manner capable of producing trenchant cultural critiques and of dissolving the distinction between text and world. As Tony Venezia demonstrates in Chapter 2, *The Bojeffries Saga* develops premises familiar from programmes like *The Munsters* and *The Adams Family* into a work with a distinctly English sensibility and a capacity for astute sociopolitical commentary. Specifically, as Venezia shows, *Bojeffries* represents a counter-cultural intervention exposing the absurdities inherent in a social climate dominated by Thatcherite politics. That the adaptation of the same Gothic character can have drastically different consequences, ranging from provocatively progressive to trenchantly conservative, is illustrated in Laura Hilton's discussion of Mina Harker in Chapter 11, which compares the presentation of her character in Bram Stoker's *Dracula*, Moore's *League* and Stephen Norrington's adaptation of the latter. Drawing on adaptation theory, Hilton explores the ways in which the comics and film versions of *League* radically diverge in their interpretations of Stoker's character, seizing upon diametrically opposed tendencies evident in *Dracula*.

The contention of this chapter – and a view at least implicit in most of the others in this volume – is that it is possible to propose a workable definition of the Gothic tradition emergent from, but not limited to, the study of Moore's work. Drawing on existing Gothic scholarship cited throughout, we can define the Gothic text as manifesting an uncanny temporal disjunction that disrupts mundane experience to expose the innermost vulnerabilities of the self (the abject); it can then be argued further that the Gothic tradition makes explicit the often occulted internal dynamics of tradition in general. Punter notes that the Gothic 'derives its overall vitality [...] from its attempt to come to grips with and to probe matters of concern to the society',[52] and as incorporated in Moore's work it represents instances where writing reflects on its own practice and effects. Symptomised by a series of meta-textual interruptions, the Gothic tradition circulates in Moore's corpus as an awareness of the weight of the past on the present and of the irrational or pre-rational origins of the worlds we create and inhabit.

Notes

1 Alan Moore, *Voice of the Fire* (Atlanta, GA: Top Shelf, 2009), p. 302.
2 *Swamp Thing Annual*, 2 (1985), 1.i–ii.
3 Fred Botting, *Gothic* (London: Routledge, 1996), p. 15.
4 David Punter, 'Introduction: of Apparitions', in *Spectral Readings: Towards a Gothic Geography*, ed. Glennis Byron and David Punter (Basingstoke: Macmillan, 1999), pp. 1–8 (p. 3).
5 *Alan Moore Spells It Out*, interview with Bill Baker (Milford, CT: Airwave, 2005), p. 10.
6 Ibid., p. 30.
7 *Gothic Pathologies: The Text, the Body and the Law* (Basingstoke: Macmillan, 1998), p. 1.
8 Ibid., p. 9.
9 As a continuation of the Marvelman story, the *Marvelman* title (under which Moore's initial run appeared in *Warrior*) is preferential for several reasons; however, as the present discussion will refer to Moore's later work on the series as well as to its reception in the letters column of the Eclipse publication, the later title, *Miracleman*, will be used throughout.
10 Gilles Deleuze and Félix Guattari, *A Thousand Plateaus*, trans. Brian Massumi (London: Continuum, 2004), p. 264; although the authors cite a different edition and imply sole authorship, the quotation from Howard Phillips Lovecraft and E. Hoffmann Price's story, 'Through the Gates of the Silver Key', originally published in *Weird Tales* (July 1934), can be found in Lovecraft, *Necronomicon: The Best Weird Tales of H.P. Lovecraft*, ed. Stephen Jones (London: Gollancz, 2008), pp. 393–421 (p. 406).
11 Deleuze and Guattari, *Thousand Plateaus*, p. 5.
12 Alan Moore, Michael T. Gilbert, William F. Loebs and Ken Bruzemak, 'The Riddle of the Relcalcitrant Refuse', in *Mr. Monster*, 3 (Oct. 1985), 16.iii–iv; reprinted in *The Extraordinary Works of Alan Moore: Indispensable Edition*, ed.

George Khoury (Raleigh, NC: TwoMorrows, 2008), pp. 129–44.
13 'Monsters, Maniacs, and Moore', dir. Norman Hull, ed. Kevin Lester and prod. David Naden, *England Their England* (Central Independent Television, 1987): www.youtube.com/watch?v=Ucba9NtF3cE.
14 *Swamp Thing*, 51 (Aug. 1986), 4.v.
15 Alan Moore, Stephen Bissette and Rick Veitch, 'The Mirror of Love', in *AARGH!* (Northampton: Mad Love, 1988), pp. 2–9.
16 Cf. e.g. *Strip Aids* (London: Willyprods/Small Time Ink, 1987), a collection of comic strips begun, as the inside front cover states, to 'counteract the use of a cartoon to perpetuate ignorance, fear and prejudice'. Also see Alan Moore and Bill Sienkiewicz, 'Shadowplay – The Secret Team', in *Brought to Light: A Graphic Docudrama* (Forestville, CA: Eclipse Books, 1989), pp. 1–30.
17 Nicholas Royle, *The Uncanny* (Manchester: Manchester University Press, 2003), p. 2.
18 Sigmund Freud, 'The Uncanny', in *The Uncanny*, trans. David McLintock (London: Penguin, 2003), pp. 121–62 (pp. 150–1).
19 Royle, *Uncanny*, p. 25.
20 Julia Kristeva, *Powers of Horror: An Essay on Abjection*, trans. Leon S. Roudiez (Chichester and New York: Columbia University Press, 1982 [1980]), p. 3.
21 'Hipster Priest: Unearthing the Magical World of the Comic Book Genius', interview by John Doran, *Stool Pigeon* (7 July 2010): www.thestoolpigeon.co.uk/features/alan-moore-interview.html.
22 Judith Butler, *Frames of War* (London: Verso, 2009), p. 47.
23 Ibid., pp. 4, 7.
24 For an extended discussion of Derridean spectrality and the uncanny, see Royle, *Uncanny*, pp. 277–88.
25 'Hipster Priest'.
26 Ibid.
27 Alan Moore and David Lloyd, *V for Vendetta* (London: Titan, 2009), I.3.
28 Kristeva, *Powers of Horror*, p. 2.
29 'A Man of Steel (by any other name): Adaptation and Continuity in Alan Moore's "Superman"', *ImageText*, 4:55 (2011), 17: www.english.ufl.edu/imagetext/archives/v5_4/teiwes/.
30 Kristeva, *Powers of Horror*, pp. 12–13.
31 Reprinted in Alan Moore, J.H. Williams III and Mick Gray, *Promethea*, 5 Books (La Jolla, CA: America's Best Comics, 2000–05), 4.3. For further discussion see Matthew J.A. Green, '"She Brings Apocalypse": Sex, Imagination and Redemptive Transgression in William Blake and the Graphic Novels of Alan Moore', *Literature Compass*, 8:10 (2011), 739–56.
32 'Miraclemail', in Alan Moore, Rick Veitch and John Ridgway, *Miracleman*,

10 (Dec. 1986), 17–19 (p. 19).
33 Punter, *Gothic Pathologies*, p. 215.
34 Butler, *Frames of War*, p. 19.
35 'Miraclemail', *Miracleman*, 10, 19.
36 'Alan Moore Reflects on Marvelman: Part 2', interview by Kurt Amacker, *Mania* (10 Sept. 2009): www.mania.com/alan-moore-reflects-marvelman-part-2_article_117529.html.
37 Julia Round, 'Cryptomimetic Tropes in Yoshinori Natsume's Batman: Death Mask', *Foundation*, 37:106 (Summer 2009), 41–52 (pp. 43–4).
38 *Batman: The Killing Joke*, with Brian Bolland, deluxe edn (London: Titan, 2008), 43.viii–ix.
39 'Alan Moore: Dracula Reborn', interview by David Bogart, in *The Best of Vampirella: Lost Tales*, ed. David Bogard and Bon Alimagno (New York: Harris, 2008), n.p. (p. 1); ellipsis in original. Though this interview, and 'The New European', also included in this collection, are not paginated, for ease of reference I will provide page numbers assuming that both the interview and the story are paginated separately. For 'The New European', page 1 is the first page with story content.
40 *Ibid.*
41 *Ibid.*, p. 2.
42 This doubling of the uncanny corresponds neatly with Freud's account of the relationship between the imagination and the uncanny; cf. Freud, *Uncanny*, pp. 150, 156–7.
43 Cf. *ibid.*, p. 157: 'But the writer can intensify and multiply this effect far beyond what is feasible in normal experience; in his stories he can make things happen that one would never, or only rarely, experience in real life.'
44 Jerrold E. Hogle, '"Christabel" as Gothic: The Abjection of Instability', *Gothic Studies*, 7:1 (May 2005), 18–28 (p. 22).
45 Raymond Williams, *Marxism and Literature* (Oxford: Oxford University Press, 1977), p. 115.
46 Ernesto Laclau and Chantal Mouffe, *Hegemony and Socialist Strategy*, 2nd edn (London: Verso, 2001), p. 88n.
47 Jacques Derrida, *The Gift of Death*, trans. David Wills (London: University of Chicago Press, 1995), p. 5.
48 Moore, 'Dracula Reborn', p. 1.
49 Andy W. Smith, 'Gothic and the Graphic Novel', in *The Routledge Companion to Gothic*, ed. Catherine Spooner and Emma McEvoy (London: Routledge, 2007), pp. 251–9 (p. 251).
50 Punter, *The Literature of Terror: A History of Gothic Fictions from 1765 to the Present Day*, 2nd edn, 2 vols (London: Longman, 1996), II, p. 147.
51 Jim Collins, 'Batman: The Movie, Narrative: The Hyperconscious', in *The*

Many Lives of the Batman: Critical Approaches to a Superhero and his Media, ed. Roberta E. Pearson and William Uricchio (London: BFI Publishing, 1991), pp. 164–81 (p. 165).
52 *Literature of Terror*, II, p. 181.

2

'Soap opera of the paranormal': surreal Englishness and postimperial Gothic in *The Bojeffries Saga*

Tony Venezia

> It's a thing that I've done that I've come closest to actually describing the flavour of an ordinary working class childhood in Northampton. And the inherent surrealism in British life.
> Alan Moore[1]

Originally serialised in *Warrior* in the early 1980s, featuring a cast of vampires, werewolves, Lovecraftian Old Ones and council rent collectors, *The Bojeffries Saga* by Alan Moore and Steve Parkhouse transplants various Gothic archetypes into a recognisably English suburban environment and bears a superficial resemblance to American television comedies *The Addams Family* and *The Munsters*. Like these sitcoms, *Bojeffries* is premised on the inversion of conventional representations of the family and family values, all the more potent coming as it did during a period marked by the uncanny return of so-called 'Victorian values' that emphasised unproblematic familial and national identities. This was also a period in which a sense of postimperial Englishness was increasingly foregrounded in political and cultural discourses, signalled by such disparate contemporary examples as the British Nationality Act of 1981, the Falklands conflict of 1982, inner-city riots and the growth of a heritage culture that peddled nostalgic representations of empire. The strip can be read in many ways as participating and commenting on these discourses, but also has as much in common with a kind of pulp Surrealism, as derived from comedic sources, as with the Gothic. This is signalled by the inversions, incongruities and juxtapositions embedded in the narrative and visual representations that often work to produce a satiric effect. *The Bojeffries Saga* can be seen as an optic through which to read what Stuart Hall and Martin Jacques identified as the 'New Times'.[2]

Reading *Bojeffries* as cultural history provides a conceptual framework capable of suggesting connections between form and content, and the multiple, overlapping contexts that inform material production and textual meaning. However, I would also like to trace dialogical connections across media and genres to other modes of representation, such as children's comics, film and television. Cultural history is 'history at the level of the signifier',[3] a level which is arguably marked by contradiction and overdetermination. Any critical reading needs to take into account how a comic narrative like *Bojeffries* is, on the one hand, a rich and overdetermined system of signification and on the other, speaks directly to contemporary concerns.

It is perhaps surprising given the evident fondness that Moore feels for *Bojeffries*, and the steady growth in academic interest that his work has attracted, that more critical attention has not been paid to the strip. Part of the reason it has been overlooked is undoubtedly due to the problem in accessing copies. Like Moore's other contributions to *Warrior*, *Bojeffries* has been published across a variety of formats. The temptation is to speculate that Moore's work at *Warrior* was subject to a Gothic curse that has prevented much of it from being republished in accessible formats.[4] Subtitled 'a soap opera of the paranormal', the *Saga* introduced the eccentric Bojeffries family who live in a council house for which they have not paid any rent since the reign of Queen Victoria. The family members are the relatively normal if somewhat ineffective patriarch Jobremus Bojeffries, overgrown schoolboy son Reth, troll-like daughter Ginda, vampire Uncle Festus Zlüdotny, werewolf Uncle Raoul Zlüdotny, Lovecraftian Elder Grandpa Podlasp and the gargantuan Baby, who resides in the basement. *The Independent* described the *Saga* as '*The Munsters* written by Alan Bennett high on episodes of *Coronation Street*, all beautifully rendered in a style equal parts Robert Crumb and *The Bash Street Kids*' Leo Baxendale.'[5] I want to take a close look at the first *Bojeffries* stories that introduced the characters and setting before working through their different social and cultural contexts. I will conclude by briefly returning to the Bojeffries family and the story 'Raoul's Big Night Out'.

The two-part story 'The Rentman Cometh'/'One of Our Rentmen

is Missing' was initially published across issues 12 and 13 of *Warrior* in 1983.[6] The narrative follows an over-inquisitive local council employee, the improbably named Trevor Inchmale, as he investigates why the Bojeffries family appear to have defaulted on their rent. Through the course of his investigations the reader is introduced to the family, and in the process the uncanny, surreal qualities of the family and of their domestic space are revealed. The focalisation begins with the annoying Inchmale, as he walks through the streets of an anonymous town to the Bojeffries residence. However, this perspective shifts to that of the Bojeffries, thereby identifying the reader with the family shortly after.

Steven Connor has suggested that the 'addressivity of a text is what opens or orientates a text to its actual reception in particular acts of reading'.[7] In terms of a comics narratology, Harry Morgan points out a distinction between perspective and focalisation that takes into account the positioning of the spectator and the reading of a sequence through a character.[8] Focalisation here works to orientate the reader between two external points of view. This shift maps a decisive move in terms of addressivity from the outside (and petty-minded authority) to the inside (and the community of the Bojeffries clan). What is evident, of course, is that the Bojeffries do not conform to the model of the traditional nuclear family. For a start, the family is not entirely English: the foreign Gothic is relocated firmly within the domestic national sphere, literally at home.

As Inchmale spies on the family, he and the reader build up a picture of the household. The reader is first introduced to the marginally grotesque Jobremus and Ginda. As the perspective shifts once again to Inchmale, even as sympathy remains with the Bojeffries, this picture is added to as the council officer first speaks to a neighbour – 'Polish people I think. Or Irish. Lovely people' (see Figure 2.1) – and then conducts surreptitious surveillance on the family. Later, he notes an anachronistically dressed gentleman and a wolflike dog with a football scarf wrapped around its neck entering the house (see Figure 2.2). By this stage the reader is well in on the joke, as Inchmale's petty-minded bureaucratic thinking renders him clearly a figure of fun to be mocked – 'Keeping of pets without council permission' – while the focalisation switches back and forth between him and the Bojeffries.

The 'realist' setting evokes kitchen-sink dramas – comics are never realistic in the sense that film and photography can be by their collaps-

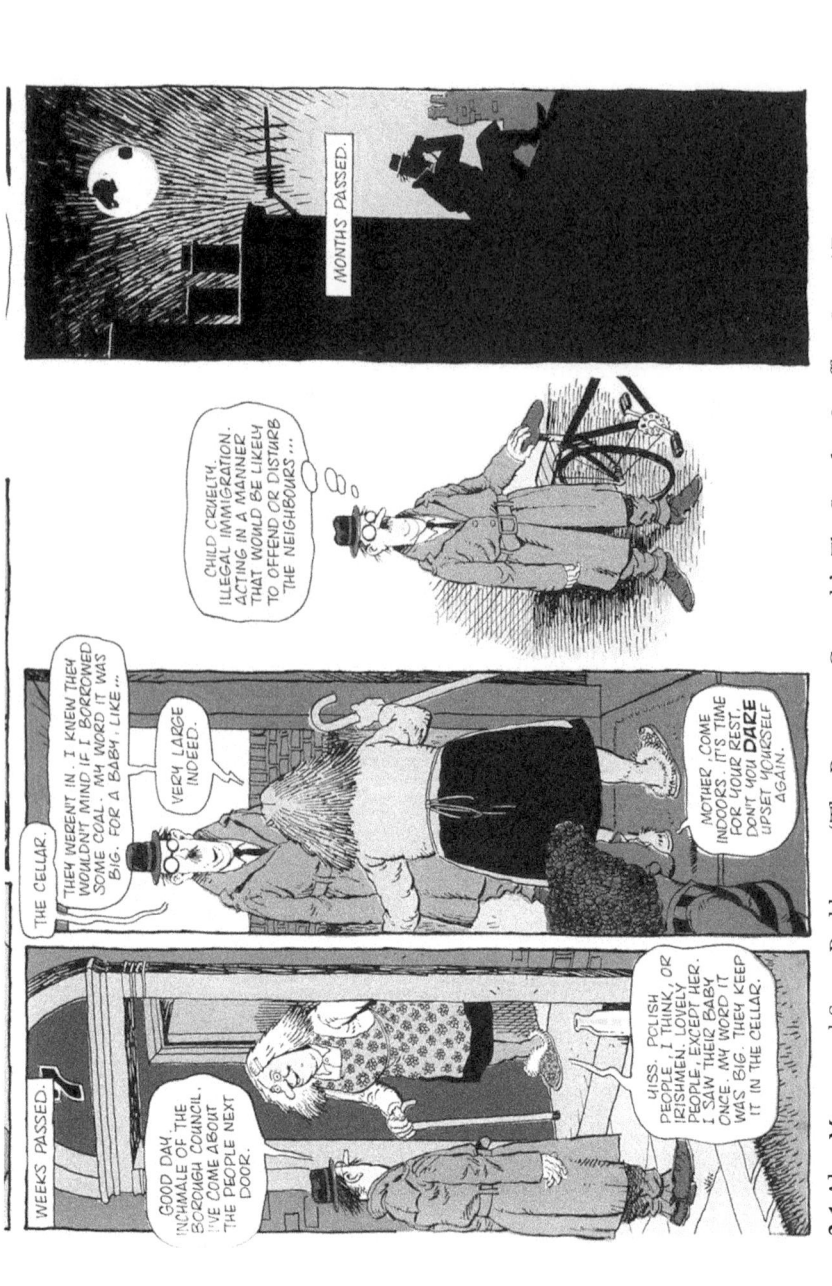

2.1 Alan Moore and Steve Parkhouse, 'The Rentman Cometh', *The Complete Boiettries Saga*, 17.iv–vii

2.2 Alan Moore and Steve Parkhouse, 'The Rentman Cometh', *The Complete Bojeffries Saga*, 18

ing of the distance between referent and sign in their reproduction of visual and aural surface textures – but comics are able to signify realism iconographically and indexically through the articulation of image and text. We can see this here in the use of visual and verbal shorthand, in the cobbled streets and terraced houses and in the use of localised dialect – 'Yus?' ('Rentman', 19.ii) – and vocational idiolect (Inchmale's bureaucratese). Although the town has been identified with Moore's own home town of Northampton, there is a lack of specificity in the presentation.[9] This contributes to the drab 'everywhere' status of the environment, and is important in establishing the humour, which derives from the embedding of the fantastic in a 'real' setting and inverting normative expectations to comment on that setting.

David Gilbert and Rebecca Preston have argued that the emergence of modern suburbia in the nineteenth century was accompanied by a set of usually disparaging figurative tropes 'that emphasised both the positive qualities of the suburbs and their hidden depths'.[10] Even the term 'suburbia' is characterised by a referential slipperiness, as it has been applied to a range of referents:

> In Britain this has included Victorian 'villadom', late nineteenth-century and Edwardian terraced suburbs [such as the Bojeffries house], inter-war semi-detached suburbs, New Towns and suburban public estates of the 1950s, and the owner-occupied estates of the building booms of the 1980s and 1990s.[11]

One connection that has seemingly lingered is the association of the suburban with a vague notion of Englishness.[12] This sense of an ordinary everyday Englishness first called into question and then reconfigured is crucial to any reading of *Bojeffries*. The family are a fantastic intrusion into the provincial/suburban townscape; they represent the uncanny appropriation of visual signifiers of the Gothic derived from popular culture. This is evident in the graphic presentation of Festus and Raoul as vampire and werewolf, evoking memories of the classic Universal Studios' horror-film cycle from the 1930s and 1940s that have become part of a general Gothic imaginary. Tzvetan Todorov's influential structuralist analysis of the fantastic theorises the term as a moment of uncertainty when the reader is confronted with the fictional supernatural, a hesitation between uncanny and marvellous explanations; the former opting for a rational explanation, the latter for the irrational.[13] What I want to suggest is that what we have here is the re-routing of the fantastic to the absurd, as signposted in the visual and narrative frameworks and the referential allusiveness. I will return to this story and the Bojeffries family, but first I want to elaborate connections between the Surreal and the Gothic.

Chris Baldick has proposed that Gothic fiction 'should combine a fearful sense of inheritance in time with a claustrophobic sense of enclosure in space, these two dimensions reinforcing one another to produce an impression of sickening descent into disintegration'.[14] This is most often manifested by archaic intrusions into the present, materialising as monstrous revenants or spectres. Gothic's literary historiography charts a movement from the margins to the centre, both spatially and temporally. The classic Gothic novels of the eighteenth century such as Horace Walpole's *The Castle of Otranto* (1764), Ann Radcliffe's *The Italian* (1797) and Matthew Lewis's *The Monk* (1796) all made extensive use of feudal settings on the Catholic fringe of Europe, but as the nineteenth century progressed, Gothic fiction shifted in time and space, moving into the contemporary metropolis.[15] Gothic tropes in the nineteenth century were also peculiarly suited to over-determined allegorical representations of imperial anxieties. The imperial Gothic is overtly concerned with the blurring of boundaries between the colonial margin and the imperial centre, whether in specific fears of individual regression or going native, or in the invasion of civilisation by dark demonic forces unhappily relegated to the colonial fringes.[16]

For Catherine Spooner the Gothic illustrates 'the radically provisional or divided nature of the self [and] the construction of peoples or individuals as monstrous or "other"'; as such, the Gothic is 'pervasive precisely because it is so apposite to the representation of contemporary concerns'.[17] Julia Kristeva's conceptualisation of abjection is particularly relevant. This involves the throwing off and under of anything that threatens autonomy and completeness, leading to an embodiment of contradictions and inconsistencies in the abject figure.[18] In this sense the Bojeffries family can be interpreted as abjected figures, expelled and grotesque, that act as the over-determined and constitutive other for a unified notion of Englishness: the Surreal Englishness the Bojeffries signify may be read as an example of a postimperial Gothic.

The striking and sometimes extreme effect of the Gothic can result in a tipping-over into comedy. Indeed, the relationship between the Gothic and the comedic can be quite close. Avril Horner and Sue

Zlosnik suggest that there is an affinity between the two: 'it is precisely because the Gothic is always liminal and poised on boundaries [that it is] already halfway to sending itself up'.[19] The 'fearful sense of inheritance in time with a claustrophobic sense of enclosure in space' is reproduced in *Bojeffries* within a regionalised, domestic setting, the incongruity resulting in a Surreal comedic effect: 'thus the tendency to the sinister grotesque is easily converted to the comic flamboyance of the grotesque as excess, particularly during periods of rapid change resulting in a sense of instability and flux'.[20]

There is, of course, more than a coincidental resemblance between the Surreal and the Gothic. As aesthetic modes, both envisage the irruption of the fantastic and the irrational and the erasure of boundaries. The Surrealists were fascinated by British Gothic novels and their preoccupation with the strange and the uncanny that often threatened to overwhelm coherence, reason and social order.[21] In fact, André Breton had composed a list of proto-Surrealists that included the English Gothic novelists Walpole, Radcliffe and Lewis, as well as Lewis Carroll and the slapstick cinema of Mack Sennett; as an avant-garde programme, however, Surrealism's impact in Britain was muted, to say the least.[22] According to David Pirie, elements of continental Surrealism found a more accommodating home in popular British Gothic films rather than as part of a systematic intellectual movement.[23] This argument is seconded by Andrew Spicer, who proposes that Surrealist ideas were cognate with an indigenous fantasy tradition that stretched back through the mid-Victorian 'nonsense genre' of Carroll and Edward Lear to the Gothic novels of the eighteenth century.[24] Spicer notes that Hammer horror films attracted the interest of French critics, 'who admired their Surreal qualities, in contradistinction to British critics who tended to regard them as vulgar and devoid of artistic or intellectual merit'.[25] This lineage manifested itself in other divergent strands; in the 'madcap' comedy that developed out of music hall and migrated to radio and television, and in elements of auteur cinema such as that of Michael Powell and Emeric Pressburger, Ken Russell and Derek Jarman.[26] To these could be added the tradition of British children's comics such as *The Beano* and *The Dandy* that featured marvellously absurdist tropes and incorporated a range of intertextual references.

Roger Sabin has pointed out that for most of the twentieth century, certainly well into the 1960s, comics in the UK were produced almost exclusively for children and were seen as 'an integral part of "British childhood", a romanticised and fiercely guarded state of innocence'.[27] Just how fiercely guarded is evident in the folk panic around US horror comics in the immediate post-war period. This was generated over what was perceived as the extreme violent content of American crime and horror comics, and fed into anxieties over juvenile delinquency, with the former often blamed for the latter. Although this panic had its foundation as far back as the 1940s, the argument was fuelled by and found its apotheosis in US-based psychiatrist Dr Fredric Wertham's book, *The Seduction of the Innocent*.[28] 'Should US "Comics" be banned?' asked an influential article in *Picture Post* in 1952, to which Parliament replied 'yes' just three years later, banning American horror comics from being imported, published or distributed in Britain until 1959, by which time the self-regulatory Comics Code was in effect, prohibiting sex, violence and anti-establishment messages.[29]

The Gothic in anglophone comics was thus restricted but nonetheless survived. Some comics, such as DC's *House of Mystery* and *House of Secrets*, structured around suggestion rather than gore, published within the confines of the Comics Code, while others bypassed the Code altogether by publishing in magazine formats.[30] In Britain, children's comics such as *Shiver and Shake* and *Monster Fun* featured characters like Ken Reid's *Frankie Stein*. *Warrior* also published Gothic stories, notably *Shandor, Demon Stalker*, as well as carrying advertisements for the *Halls of Hammer* magazine. This provided a material textual context that framed the early *Bojeffries* stories. Clearly the Gothic has had a close historical relationship with anglophone comics, and this in turn is indicative of how the Gothic has been remediated.

While *Bojeffries* works as a horror parody, a Gothic comic, it references and recalls other Gothic media, such as cinema, with the importation of generic visual archetypes, as we have seen, and especially television. The name parodies John Galsworthy's *The Forsyte Saga*, a series of Edwardian novels that followed the fortunes of an upper middle-class family that was famously televised in 1967. The resemblances to the 1960s American situation comedies *The Addams Family* and *The Munsters* have already been noted, and indeed are perhaps unavoidable. Both sitcoms presented recognisably Gothic characters and placed them in an everyday, suburban setting.[31]

The family-centric nature of these programmes resulted in a curious contradiction: the comedic *frisson* derives largely from the inversion of the ideal family usually presented in contemporary sitcoms, but these particular comedies ironically reinvest the family as 'a hallowed sacred institution, with very traditional parental gender roles established from the outset'.[32] This conservative reinvestment in Eisenhower-era values, albeit rendered quirky and eccentric, made these shows uncannily ideal for rediscovery in the 1980s. Channel 4 started broadcasting in 1982, shortly before the first publication of *Warrior*, and among the first shows it broadcast were repeats of *The Addams Family* and *The Munsters*. But while these shows, as entertaining as they are, ultimately appear to reinscribe the very conservative values that they mock, I want to propose that what is happening with *The Bojeffries Saga* is slightly different, given the altered national, cultural and historical contexts.

Returning to Trevor Inchmale and the Bojeffries household, the embattled council employee acts as an exaggerated representative of normality as he inspects the increasingly strange council house. The disorientating involutions of Gothic space are reproduced in the Bojeffries house as Inchmale discovers that the trapdoor to the attic opens out not into the expected loft space but instead into the back garden (see Figure 2.3). Such a Surreal topological passage disturbs the expected orientation of how a terraced house is supposed to be ordered. This spatial displacement further emphasises the shifting focalisation that characterises this story: point of view is mobile and unstable, moving transitionally from subject to subject and scene to scene, to borrow Scott McCloud's terms.[33] Inchmale is eventually confronted by Grandpa Podlasp (see Figure 2.4), a mutated mass of animal and vegetable who resides in the greenhouse and is a perfect example of what Kelly Hurley calls the 'abhuman', the 'not-quite-human subject, characterised by its morphic variability'.[34]

Grandpa's comic grotesque status is evident visually in his amorphous form that recalls the ambiguous bodily excess of Lovecraft's alien gods, and is further enhanced by his language, which manages to be reminiscent of both the portentous, insistent, indescribable horror of Lovecraft *and* the nonsense verse of Carroll and Lear. Inchmale has been confronted by consecutively greater degrees of alterity in the Bojeffries family, from the relatively normal Jobremus, Reth and Ginda, to the vampiric Festus and lycanthropic Raoul, and finally the enraged and abhuman Grandpa who, in a fit of pique, transforms Inchmale into a potted geranium.

3 Alan Moore and Steve Parkhouse, 'One of Our Rentmen is Missing', *The Complete Bojeffries Saga*, 24.iii–vi

2.4 Alan Moore and Steve Parkhouse, 'One of Our Rentmen is Missing', *The Complete Bojeffries Saga*, 26.iv

This metamorphosis marks a point at which the shifting patterns of focalisation merge and fuse. Inchmale, that emasculated representative of state interference, is transformed into a flower that acts as visual index of banal domesticity, and decides he is happier as an ornament in the Bojeffries household than as a rent collector. There is a complex cultural dialectic at work here, one associated with the contemporary Gothic: the monstrous is now fully identified with the domestic, while the normative becomes exclusionary. This is evident in *The Bojeffries Saga* in which, as we have seen, the reader is positioned to identify with the family against an intrusive, petty authority. In fact, rather ironically, this story evidences a distinct anti-statist strand that resonates with the aims of the New Right to roll back the frontiers of the state. This is to confirm the overdetermined status of the text, and to highlight the at times contradictory qualities invoked by the Gothic's encounter with the suburban. This narrative movement from outside in enacts a Surreal Englishness against which can be contrasted an exceptional Englishness, one ironically no less absurd (in fact perhaps more so) than the abjected figurations of the Bojeffries family. This sharply marks a text like *Bojeffries* against the nationalist discourses of Thatcherism and Powellism, the contexts for which I will elaborate now.

The period from the late 1970s/early 1980s marks an important cultural and historical shift in Britain. The election of Margaret Thatcher as Conservative Prime Minister in 1979 decisively buried the compact of the post-war consensus to which both main political parties had adhered, and saw the beginning of a new era characterised by the unsteady alliance of neo-liberal economics and social conservatism often referred to as 'Thatcherism.' Writing at the time, Stuart Hall famously anatomised Thatcherism as an 'authoritarian populism' that 'combines the resonant themes of organic Toryism – nation, family, duty, authority, standards, traditionalism – with the aggressive themes of a revived neo-liberalism – self-interest, competitive individualism, anti-statism'.[35]

Unsurprisingly, culture became a battleground against what was often perceived as a deeply reactionary government. In an interview, Moore notes that this period, in which he started writing comics, was an 'overcast time politically. Most of the liberal world looked on in horror at the inexorable rise of the Reagan–Thatcher fuck-buddy coalition.'[36] The election of the Iron Lady saw the installation of possibly the most right-wing political party in post-war British history, one that historian

Eric Hobsbawm characterised as 'profoundly and viscerally nationalist and distrustful of the outside world'.[37]

'Of all the media during eighteen years of Thatcherism,' write Paul Gravett and Peter Stanbury, 'comics were among the most politically outspoken.'[38] They point to Moore and David Lloyd's *V for Vendetta*, the revived and revisionist Grant Morrison-authored *Dan Dare* in *Revolver* and the general polemical thrust of the radical *2000AD* offshoot *Crisis*. Morrison also wrote *St. Swithin's Day*, which narrated the fantasy of assassinating the Iron Lady from the point of view of an alienated, angry teenage boy. Predictably, the reaction from both a predominately right-wing press and Conservative MPs was one of outrage. The rabidly Thatcherite *Sun* newspaper ran the headline: 'Death to Maggie Book Sparks Tory Uproar' (19 Mar. 1990), and Tory MP Teddy Taylor eagerly condemned the comic in much the same terms he had used to attack Tony Harrison's poem *V* when a televised reading had been broadcast by Channel 4 three years earlier ('Four-letter TV poem fury', *Daily Mail*, 12 Oct. 1987).

V for Vendetta, set in a dystopian near-future, was serialised alongside *Bojeffries* in *Warrior* and was an eerily effective allegorisation of what Roger Luckhurst, after Ian Baucom and Paul Gilroy, has called 'postimperial melancholy', a structure of feeling evident in much science fiction of the 1970s and 1980s in which narratives of an exclusive Englishness are centred on circumscribed locales.[39] This is narrativised in *V for Vendetta* in the imagining of an overtly Fascist Britain turning in on itself to eradicate the 'enemy within', whether homosexuals, political radicals or immigrants. But *V for Vendetta* arguably skirts the Gothic as much as science fiction, with its portrayal of an anti-hero who kidnaps, imprisons and tortures a young woman in a subterranean lair. This is surely a narrative that explicitly evokes Baldick's formulation of the Gothic as 'a fearful sense of inheritance in time with a claustrophobic sense of enclosure in space'. Postimperial melancholy is unmistakably attached to a postimperial Gothic, different aspects of which are articulated in *V for Vendetta* and *The Bojeffries Saga*. A key feature of the postimperial Gothic is the (dis)articulation between Britishness and Englishness.

Englishness is often elided with Britishness, a slippage evident at the level of language as English maintains a linguistic/symbolic hegemony over the Celtic fringe. As Krishnan Kumar points out, England remains a synechdochical expression 'not just for the island of Britain but for the whole [North Atlantic] archipelago'.[40] In an age of post-war decolonisation, a theoretically inclusive Britishness was increasingly displaced by an exclusive sense of Englishness that sought to ameliorate the long process of imperial decline. In this context, the British Nationality Act of 1981 marks an explicit attempt to define Englishness in a racially exclusionary manner, particularly when faced with migrations from the postcolonial margins. The Act was part of a transitional process that included the Immigration Acts of 1962, 1968 and 1971 that fundamentally reorganised the relationship between England and the Commonwealth and actively sought to exclude the postcolonial subject from the boundaries of an English national locale. Ian Baucom has given a historicised account of precisely this process in which he argues that an increasingly Anglocentric view of Britishness sought to simultaneously avow and disavow the history of empire and its determination of national identity.[41] But this new sense of nationalism was arguably riven by destabilising contradictions during the 1980s as the forces of the market, calls for devolution and European integration, alongside already established patterns of migration from former colonies, called into question any sense of a coherent and unified national identity.

Such concerns are filtered through the story 'Raoul's Night Out', which followed the poodle-eating werewolf over a day at work and a night out with his workmates from the Slesidge & Harbuck factory. The incorporation of Gothic tropes into a postimperial suburban English setting finds its near-perfect example in this story of Raoul attending a works function and metamorphosing into a werewolf in a restaurant. The tweedy foreman Stanley, who introduces Raoul to his wife Unity as 'one of us', gives Raoul a leaflet for the nationalistic League of St. Swithin, with instructions to pass it on once he has read it. Oblivious to its contents, at the dinner he passes it on to George, an Afro-Caribbean colleague, who is understandably shocked to find he has been given racist propaganda and remonstrates with his workmates, leading to the police being called. At this point Raoul, having mixed up the nights of that month's full moon, transforms. The police arrive shortly after Raoul has turned into a werewolf; ignoring him, they assault and arrest George, having made the automatic assumption that, as a black man, he is clearly guilty.

The story makes a number of references to contemporary (and not so contemporary) debates on Englishness. Most topically is the representation of police racism and brutality, which would have been immediately recognisable to the contemporary reader. The 1980s saw a series of inner-city riots generally ascribed to high unemployment and deprived environments but exacerbated by insensitive methods of community policing in neighbourhoods with high populations of ethnic minorities, especially Afro-Caribbean.[42] The League of St. Swithin is an allusion to the League of Empire Loyalists, a fringe group that campaigned against decolonisation in the 1950s and 1960s and were led by Arthur K. Chesterton, cousin of G.K. Chesterton, a former member of the British Union of Fascists.[43] Various splinter groups split off to form the British National Party (which, despite its name, remains a fundamentalist English organisation), with which the League eventually amalgamated.[44] Most telling and subtle is the appropriation of the phrase 'one of us', specifically associated with Margaret Thatcher in contradistinction to the enemy within. The phrase was elegantly interrogated by Hall:

> We can now see Thatcher's question – 'Are you one of us'? – as not only a search for converts to the Gospel of Market Forces, but as only the latest effort, still continuing, to resurrect that rapidly vanishing species, the late twentieth century 'true born Englishman' [...] and to rediscover, by a virulent form of regressive modernisation (an attempt to capture the future by a determined long detour through the past) those discursive forms of manly and entrepreneurial 'greatness' which could restore 'Englishness' as a beleaguered national identity: that cultural identity into which all the other diverse cultures of the British Isles and, at its peripheries, the colonised societies, were so often and so brutally collapsed.[45]

The story continues with the device of incorporating the Gothic into the everyday by presenting Raoul as someone who has an average job alongside a range of colleagues who themselves represent a social spectrum.

The general tone of *Bojeffries* was similar in some respects to that of contemporary alternative comedy, and especially the television sitcom, *The Young Ones*. Alternative comedy had grown as a reaction against what was seen as the inherent conservatism prevalent on the traditional club circuit for stand-up comics and expressed as a tendency towards racist and sexist jokes.[46] Very much a post-punk phenomenon, often political and/or absurd (or both, as in the comedy of Alexei Sayle, for instance), alternative comedy had started out initially in live performance before migrating over to television. *The Young Ones* was first broadcast in 1982, shortly before *Warrior* was first published, and in many ways both appealed to the same audience. Written by and featuring performers associated with alternative comedy, the show introduced a household of four undergraduate students and combined aspects of the traditional sitcom (such as the predominant focus on a single setting) with often violent slapstick and anarchic surrealism. The link between *Bojeffries* and *The Young Ones* is made explicit by comedian Lenny Henry in the introduction to the collected edition.[47]

Slesidge & Harbuck stands in as a generic factory in an anonymous industrial town whose employees put up with the monotony of the Fordist production line because they have little choice. In other words, they are working for exactly the kind of employer that was disappearing throughout the 1980s as the economy shifted from manufacturing to services, and with it, a particular idea of the working class as an homogenised identity. This is a production line whose workers, after all, include Raoul, who is of indeterminate but clearly non-English origin, as well as George and the punk Colin Council Estate alongside the arbiter of ethnic identity, Stanley. What this story illustrates very well, both in a literal and figurative capacity, is a working class structured by difference rather than similarity. In fact it is a class that, on this representation, seems ruptured by this difference, haunted by an idea of a unified identity associated with ethnicity and nation; attempts to police an exceptional Englishness in this context are rendered absurd.

The automatic assumption that George is the guilty party gives the narrative its satirical charge, underlined by a remark from the police sergeant to Stanley that identifies him as racist ('See you at the meetin' next Wednesday, Stan'). The intrusion of the Bojeffries family into the everyday is evidently not as Surreal as everyday life itself. The construction of a unified, exceptionalist English identity becomes untenable when confronted by a contingent and conjunctive Surreal Englishness.

The Bojeffries family, then, would seem to be English/un-English. The Anglicised Bojeffries stand in contrast to their apparent cousins from the East, the Zlüdotnys, and both stand in contrast to the abhuman Grandpa Podlasp. Having long established themselves, since Victoria no less, in the heartlands of suburbia, they represent over-determined signifiers of the abjected Gothic other that denies a coherent and unified English identity. According to Spicer, a common trope in post-war comedy from the Goons to Monty Python was to play off the fantastic against the real, to reveal how it is actually the everyday that is irrational, a trend that continued in later alternative comedy.[48] A similar conclusion is reached by Murray Smith in his reading of *The Young Ones*, which, he argues, is characterised by a double inversion: first in its representation of that which is typically marginalised in the sitcom and then in the re-presentation of what is 'outside' the initial representation (normal, middle-class family life) as being just as grotesque as that 'inside'.[49] What I have tried to show is that a similar reading can be made of *The Bojeffries Saga*, in which a Surreal Englishness is contrasted with an absurd English exceptionalism.

Moore has stated that he and Parkhouse intend to revisit and continue *Bojeffries*:

> The family's probably completely broken up and Ginda Bojeffries is probably one of the Blair babes, Labour new women M.Ps. The son of the family is probably a Booker prize winning author who spends most of his time at the Groucho club, having reached fame by writing what people take to be witty, magic realist stories about his working-class upbringing.[50]

Given that we are now in a post-Blair era, this would be a fascinating exercise. With council houses virtually all but sold off, devolution a political fact, postimperial adventures in the Middle East, an influx of migration from Europe rather than former colonies and a 'progressive' Conservative Party happy to associate with extremist elements in the European Parliament, the surreal Gothic of *The Bojeffries Saga* would be a welcome relief.

Notes

1 Alan Moore interviewed in George Khoury and Friends (eds), *The Extraordinary Works of Alan Moore* (Raleigh, NC: TwoMorrows, 2003), p. 60.
2 Stuart Hall and Martin Jacques, 'Introduction', in *New Times: The Changing Face of Politics in the 1990s*, ed. Stuart Hall and Martin Jacques (London: Lawrence & Wishart, 1989), pp. 11–22.
3 Catherine Belsey, 'Reading Cultural History', in *Reading the Past: Literature and History* (Basingstoke: Palgrave Macmillan, 2000), pp. 103–17 (p. 106).
4 *The Bojeffries Saga* started in *Warrior*, 12 (Aug. 1983) and 13 (Oct. 1983), and continued in issues 19 (June 1984) and 20 (July 1984). These were subsequently reprinted and colourised in *Flesh and Bones*, issues 1–4 (1986), with a new preface added in *Dalgoda*, issue 8 (Apr. 1986). New instalments

were published in *A1*, issues 1 (May 1989), 2 (Sept. 1989), 3 (Feb. 1990), 4 (Apr. 1990) and in *The A1 True Life Bikini Confidential* (Feb. 1991). All of this material was collected and colourised in *The Complete Bojeffries Saga* (1992), along with additional new material. For an overview of the series' development, including a publication history, see Lance Parkin, *The Pocket Essential Alan Moore* (Harpenden: Pocket Essentials, 2001), pp. 73–4 and Gary Spencer Millidge, *Alan Moore: Storyteller* (Lewes: ILEX, 2011), pp. 90–3, 313 (including unpaginated insert material). A new collected edition is scheduled for publication by Top Shelf but has not been released at the time of writing.

5   Mike Moran, 'Arts and Book Review', *Independent* (10 Nov. 2006), p. 4.
6   Republished in Alan Moore and Steve Parkhouse, *The Complete Bojeffries Saga* (Northampton, MA: Tundra Press, 1992), pp. 13–21, 22–7; all subsequent references are to this edition, hereafter cited in the main body of the text.
7   Steven Connor, *The English Novel in History: 1950–1995* (London: Routledge, 1996), p. 10.
8   Harry Morgan, 'Graphic Shorthand: from Caricature to Narratology in Twentieth-Century *Bande Dessinée* and Comics', *European Comic Art*, 2:1 (2009), 21–39.
9   The international hero fan website unequivocally identifies the town as Northampton. See www.internationalhero.co.uk/b/bojeffriesaga.htm.
10 David Gilbert and Rebecca Preston, '"Stop being so English": Suburban Modernity and National Identity in the Twentieth Century', in *Geographies of British Modernity*, ed. David Matless and Brian Short (Oxford: Blackwell, 2003), pp. 187–203 (p. 188).
11 *Ibid.*, p. 188.
12 *Ibid.*, p. 190.
13 Tzvetan Todorov, *The Fantastic: A Structural Approach to a Literary Genre*, trans. Richard Howard (Ithaca, NY: Cornell University Press, 1973), p. 25.
14 Chris Baldick, 'Introduction,' in *The Oxford Book of Gothic Tales*, ed. Chris Baldick (Oxford: Oxford University Press, 1992), pp. xi–xxiii (p. xix).
15 The seminal historical account of Gothic literary fiction remains David Punter's *The Literature of Terror: A History of Gothic Fictions from 1765 to the Present Day*, 2nd edn, 2 vols (London: Longman, 1980). More recently, Andrew Smith's *Gothic Literature* (Edinburgh: Edinburgh University Press, 2007) provides a convenient chronology in his introduction that traces the Gothic through literary forms to cinema and television (pp. ix–xxvi).
16 Patrick Brantlinger, *Rule of Darkness: British Literature and Imperialism, 1830–1914* (Ithaca, NY: Cornell University Press, 1988), pp. 230–1.
17 Catherine Spooner, *Contemporary Gothic* (London: Reaktion, 2006), p. 8.
18 Julia Kristeva, *Powers of Horror: An Essay on Abjection*, trans. Leon S. Roudiez

(Chichester and New York: Columbia University Press, 1982 [1980]), p. 4.
19 Avril Horner and Sue Zlosnik, *Gothic and the Comic Turn* (Basingstoke: Palgrave Macmillan, 2005), p. 17.
20 Ibid.
21 J.H. Matthews, *Surrealism and Film* (Ann Arbor: University of Michigan Press, 1971), pp. 21–8.
22 Gérard Durozoi, *History of the Surrealist Movement* (Chicago: University of Chicago Press, 2002), p. 305.
23 David Pirie, *A Heritage of Horror: The English Gothic Cinema 1946–1972* (London: Gordon Fraser, 1973), pp. 21–2.
24 Andrew Spicer, 'Occasional Eccentricity: The Strange Course of Surrealism in British Cinema', in *The Unsilvered Screen: Surrealism on Film*, ed. Graeme Harper and Rob Stone (London: Wallflower Press, 2007), pp. 102–14 (pp. 102–3).
25 *Ibid.*, p. 103.
26 Ibid.
27 This stands in contrast to the American experience: 'Because American culture was never so strictly demarcated between children and adults, a system of "dual address" evolved whereby both audiences would be targeted simultaneously'. Roger Sabin, *Adult Comics: An Introduction* (London: Routledge, 1993), p. 286, n.4.
28 Roger Sabin, *Comics, Comix and Graphic Novels: A History of Comic Art* (London: Phaidon, 1996), p. 68. This episode has been well covered. See the classic accounts from Amy Kiste Nyberg, *Seal of Approval: The History of the Comics Code* (Jackson: University Press of Mississippi, 1998) and Martin Barker, *A Haunt of Fears: The Strange History of The British Horror Comics Campaign* (London: Pluto Press, 1984) for the British context.
29 Sabin, *Adult Comics*, pp. 30–1.
30 Sabin, *Comics*, pp. 75–7.
31 Helen Wheatley, *Gothic Television* (Manchester: Manchester University Press, 2006), p. 130.
32 Ibid., p. 134.
33 Scott McCloud, *Understanding Comics: The Invisible Art* (New York: HarperCollins, 1994), pp. 70–4.
34 Kelly Hurley, *The Gothic Body: Sexuality, Materialism, and Denigration at the Fin de Siècle* (Cambridge: Cambridge University Press, 1996), p. 4.
35 Stuart Hall, 'The Great Moving Right Show', in *The Politics of Thatcherism*, ed. Stuart Hall and Martin Jacques (London: Lawrence & Wishart, 1983), pp. 19–39 (p. 29).
36 *The Mindscape of Alan Moore*, dir. DeZ Vylenz (London: Shadowsnake Productions, 2003).

37 Eric Hobsbawm, *The Age of Extremes: The Short Twentieth Century 1914–1989* (London: Abacus, 1994), p. 412.
38 Paul Gravett and Peter Stanbury, *Great British Comics: Celebrating a Century of Ripping Yarns and Wizard Wheezes* (London: Aurum, 2006), p. 127.
39 Roger Luckhurst, *Science Fiction* (Cambridge: Polity Press, 2005), pp. 172–80. Luckhurst has adapted the term from Paul Gilroy, who characterised it as a cultural pathology centred on England, decolonisation and decline.
40 Krishnan Kumar, *The Making of English National Identity* (Cambridge: Cambridge University Press, 2003), p. 7.
41 Ian Baucom, *Out of Place: Englishness, Empire, and the Locations of Identity* (Princeton, NJ: Princeton University Press, 1999).
42 See Colin Leys, *Politics in Britain: From Labourism to Thatcherism*, rev. edn (London: Verso, 1989), pp. 355–69.
43 Stan Taylor, *The National Front in English Politics* (London: Macmillan, 1982), p. 12.
44 Ibid., p. 18.
45 Stuart Hall, 'Culture, Community, Nation', *Cultural Studies*, 7:3 (1993), 349–63 (p. 356).
46 Brett Mills, *Television Sitcom* (London: BFI, 2005), pp. 46–7. Roger Wilmut and Peter Rosengard, *Didn't You Kill My Mother-in-Law? The Story of Alternative Comedy in Britain from The Comedy Store to Saturday Live* (London: Methuen, 1989), pp. xiii–xvii.
47 Lenny Henry, 'Under the Settee with Len', in Moore and Parkhouse, *The Complete Bojeffries Saga*, pp. 6–7. Henry had started out as a teenage stand-up performer in the 1970s, appearing on *The Black and White Minstrel Show* and *New Faces*. His career was subsequently rejuvenated by an association with alternative comedy, and in 1984 he appeared as a postman in 'Summer Holiday', the final episode of *The Young Ones*. Other established comics found themselves in tune with the comedy 'new times', notably the laconically Surreal Arnold Brown and the deadpan absurdist Norman Lovett.
48 Spicer, 'Occasional Eccentricity', pp. 107–9.
49 Murray Smith, 'Flatulent Conceptions: "The Young Ones," Inoculation, and "Emesis"', in *Television Studies: Textual Analysis*, ed. Gary Burns and Robert J. Thompson (London: Praeger, 1989), pp. 57–78 (p. 62).
50 Khoury et al., *Extraordinary Works*, p. 60.

3

A Gothic politics: Alan Moore's *Swamp Thing* and radical ecology

Maggie Gray

> You blight the soil . . . and poison the rivers. You raze the vegetation till you cannot even feed . . . your own kind . . . / A . . . And then you boast . . . of man's triumph . . . over nature.
> Alan Moore, *Swamp Thing*[1]

Radical environmental activism, particularly as manifest in the contemporary social movement against man-made climate change, can be conceived as a Gothic politics invoking the malevolent spectre of a cataclysmic eco-apocalypse, which can only be averted through drastic societal transformation and the development of a new ecological sensibility. The sublime threat posed by a significant rise in global temperatures, in terms of the almost incomprehensible total devastation of the planet and the unprecedented possible end to the sustainability of life upon it, raises problems of both perception and representation. Hollywood ecothrillers can tend to downplay and simplify the crisis through staging formulaic confrontations, resulting in 'quick, violent fixes' and the restoration of near-normality.[2] On the other hand, more adequately eschatological and terrifying narratives of climate change (including much scientific discourse) can, like other apocalyptic narratives, act as 'justification for human passivity in the face of history', condoning 'the abdication of personal responsibility' and deterring people from taking action.[3] This problem of political agency and motivation is compounded by the indeterminacy of environmental narratives, the difficulty in imagining the distant and uncertain consequences of present-day actions and their global impact. Much ecocriticism stresses the need for a reorientation of our 'habitually foreshortened environmental perception' and an alteration of the way in which we conceive the relationship between humanity and non-human nature, through the construction of new attitudes, values and visions.[4] This has led to a keen critical interest in cultural practices that engage with these problems and can imagine these new ways of thinking and being.

In their mid-1980s run on DC's *Swamp Thing*, Alan Moore, Steve Bissette, John Totleben and their many other collaborators turned a generic horror comic into a complex visual narrative that articulated a radical green politics, by not only depicting the threat of an imminent and manifold environmental apocalypse but also affirming just such an ecological consciousness. It rehearsed many of the debates within the environmental movement of the period between various ecosophical positions, such as deep and social ecology, and also offered heuristic formal strategies for overcoming the problem of agency and compelling an activist response from the reader, combining self-consciously ecological composition with Brechtian alienation effects. This was achieved through the transformation of the conditions of US mainstream comics production, and particularly through the mobilisation and interrogation of the tropes and techniques of the Gothic.

Shadowing the Enlightenment, frequently cast as the source of instrumental attitudes towards nature and the social institutions that perpetuate its destruction, the early Gothic novels drew on a countervailing ecological sensibility and a transformed concept of wild and sublime nature, which much ecocriticism has aligned more explicitly with Romanticism, as Michael Bradshaw discusses in greater detail in Chapter 7 of this collection. Significantly, the Gothic is a mode not only concerned with representing the unrepresentable, but which consistently and self-consciously interrogates the very 'limits, effects and power of representation'.[5] It therefore constitutes a rich resource of imagery, themes, stylistic conventions and self-reflexive formal strategies for Moore and his co-creators to draw on in delineating an environmentalist critique. Like comics themselves, Gothic literature is the source of much cultural anxiety and stigmatisation, often derided as a low popular form that appeals to a readership lacking in literary sophistication. The horror genre of comic books, in particular, received a large part of the opprobrium of the post-war anti-comics crusade, and it was to that genre that radical underground cartoonists such as Greg

Irons and Richard Corben turned when contributing to environmental activist comix like *Slow Death Funnies*. For the creators of *Swamp Thing*, therefore, the horror comic offered an effective space for green political subversion aimed at a wide audience, a fruitful site from which to challenge established ideological constructions of our relationship to the natural world.

'Swamp Thing' began as a one-shot story in *House of Secrets*, 92 (June–July 1971). Written by Len Wein and illustrated by Bernie Wrightson, it told the story of Alex Olson, an early twentieth-century scientist transformed into a muck-encrusted swamp monster. The issue was the best-selling DC title of that month and so it was decided to launch a new series based on the character, DC's first major attempt to publish a horror-themed comic with a recurring protagonist. Wein and Wrightson updated the story to a contemporary context by creating a new character, Alec Holland, with an essentially identical origin story. The bi-monthly series, which ran for only 24 issues from 1972 to 1976, revolved around Holland's futile attempts to regain his lost humanity, while battling various adversaries in episodes that employed classic Gothic riffs. As Wein put it, 'we did the *Island of Dr Moreau* in issue two, *Frankenstein* in issue three, *The Wolf Man* in issue four. In issue five it was witches.'[6] Like Mary Shelley's archetypal monster, who cameoed as Patchwork Man, Swamp Thing was a grotesque hybrid, existing in a liminal space between human and non-human, life and death, nature and culture.

DC relaunched the title as *The Saga of Swamp Thing* in 1982, to capitalise on the release of a Wes Craven film based on the character.[7] The artist for the new series, Tom Yeates, was a graduate of the Joe Kubert School of Cartoon and Graphic Art, the first technical school devoted to comics art. Due to schedule pressures he was assisted by fellow alumni John Totleben and Steve Bissette as 'ghost' artists.[8] They shared a commitment to the potential of comics as an artistic medium and had a particular interest in the horror genre, not only in terms of mainstream comics but also underground and avant-garde European titles. Bissette and Totleben subsequently took over as artists from issue 16 (August 1983). Shortly thereafter, Moore was invited to script the comic, which was suffering from poor sales, and he joined the title from issue 20 (January 1984).

Writing for *Swamp Thing* marked the first time Moore worked within the more quasi-Fordist division of labour in the US industry, with different pencillers and inkers, joined by a separate colourist. However, more concretely than Bissette and Totleben, his approach to comics was forged in the countercultural ethos of the 1970s comix scene, and together all three creators attempted to overcome the constraints of entrenched mainstream practices. Transcending conventional assembly-line production, their creative process was intensely collaborative, aiming at a complete synthesis of narrative and visual styles. Moore corresponded with the artists via international post and telephone, integrating their vision regarding characters and storylines, discussing the overarching thematics of the series and exchanging articles. They reciprocated by sending Moore examples of their artwork, and Bissette went against DC's practice of not providing inkers with access to the script by posting Totleben copies of Moore's lengthy notes. They were also gifted with the virtue of non-intrusive editors and a lack of executive interest in the project, meaning, at least early on, that they were free to experiment, 'pretty much unrestrained for a good period of time ... [as] ... DC's attitude was that it was just a nowhere book on the verge of cancellation – "so who cares what they do with it"'.[9]

However, the collaboration between Moore, Bissette and Totleben extended beyond a commitment to artistic autonomy and formal sophistication, to a shared political conviction of the potential for comics to intervene in key debates and struggles of the contemporary environmental movement. Although environmental activism in both the UK and USA had its roots in the late nineteenth century, it was the 1970s that witnessed the ascendancy of the environment as a discrete area of public policy, and environmentalism as a distinct social movement. However, that period had also marked the beginnings of a split over political strategy. Where mainstream organisations, including many of the older conservation groups, were becoming increasingly professionalised, focusing on lobbying, legislation and litigation, alternative groups perceived the incorporation of such 'envirocrats' into existing state institutions as compromising and undemocratic. They advocated grassroots community organising and direct action; it was these groups that grew in the 1980s in the face of the New Right backlash against existing environmental policies and commitments. Both the Reagan and Thatcher governments were antipathetic to state regulation and intervention in this area, seeing it as a threat to private enterprise, and both administrations were therefore increasingly unresponsive to the mainstream environmental lobby.[10]

Accompanying this argument regarding effective forms of political action was a critical debate about the political philosophies behind the green movement. In the 1970s, the Norwegian philosopher Arne Naess formulated the theory of deep ecology, a philosophy popularised in the USA in the 1980s by George Sessions and Bill Devall. Næss criticised the 'shallow environmentalism' of reformist groups for focusing on limited technocratic solutions that failed to challenge the instrumental rationality of advanced industrial society, which saw nature as inert environment, separate from humanity and existing solely for human exploitation.[11] Naess countered what he considered to be this anthropocentric view, with a deep ecological perspective based on biospherical egalitarianism, asserting the intrinsic value of every species and their equal right 'to live and blossom'.[12] He advocated a co-participative relationship with nature based on the satisfaction of only vital human needs, appearing to mandate a substantial decrease in the human population. The Malthusian implications of deep ecology were attacked, particularly by veteran anarchist thinker Murray Bookchin, who elaborated an opposing theory of social ecology. He criticised deep ecology for its failure to address the foundation of exploitative attitudes to nature in exploitative social relations, echoing Herbert Marcuse's connection of the technocratic domination of nature with the total administration of human nature and hierarchical class society.[13] Other green philosophies also emerged during this period, including bioregionalism, ecofeminism and the Gaia hypothesis, all of which challenged Enlightenment notions of progress as the triumph of man over nature and demanded a radical restructuring of society in political, economic and ideological terms.

Moore had personally become engaged in green politics as his partners were involved in the local Northampton Green Party group, for which he illustrated posters.[14] Although it was somewhat spurned by the established conservation lobby and drew many of its members from comparatively more radical groups such as Friends of the Earth and Greenpeace, the party's focus on electoral politics distinguished it from alternative direct-action groups.[15] Moore became increasingly dissatisfied with the kind of conventional power politics involved, even at a local level, and ultimately decided to focus on his creative work rather than 'fundraising for a local party I wasn't sure of the integrity of anymore'.[16] *Swamp Thing* thus became the key locus of his political intervention in the ecology movement, and Bissette and Totleben, who were similarly 'full of piss and vinegar in the 1980s', shared his vision that it was possible to effectively address such sociopolitical issues in comics and to contest the New Right anti-environmentalist hegemony.[17] The creators used the title to raise issues of air and water pollution, the greenhouse effect, nuclear weapons testing, pesticide use, littering, desertification, toxic waste, acid rain, deforestation, soil erosion, animal testing and vivisection. Combined, these threats – which appeared as both the central foci of plots and more incidental details, such as 'the odd bit of garbage in panels meant to be showing lush vegetative panoramas' – created a constant subtext of wide-ranging environmental destruction, even in issues where this topic was not addressed directly.[18]

However, it was through the total revision of the character of Swamp Thing itself that they asserted a radical ecology which implicitly criticised instrumentalist attitudes towards the natural world. Moore identified that the major limitation of the comic's existing plot was that its central premise was false. Alec Holland's quest to regain his lost humanity was ultimately dissatisfying because 'even the most brain damaged reader realised that the moment he became human again, the strip finishes'.[19] Both Moore and Bissette felt that this rendered the character one-dimensional, representing him, in Moore's words, as 'Hamlet covered in snot',[20] and reducing the title to a 'monster of the month treadmill' that lacked narrative development as it was compelled incessantly to return to the status quo.[21] In 'The Anatomy Lesson', the new creative team completely transformed the character into an entirely vegetable entity, redefined not as a hybrid creature but as an earth elemental, a figure indebted to the Green Man of folklore.[22] Swamp Thing was thus able to harness the power of the natural world, change shape and travel instantaneously from one point to another via the 'green'. This change in ontological status overcame the narrative limitations of the existing character (who had to hide in the boots of cars to get anywhere) and allowed the artists free rein to experiment visually, as its physical orientation could now change according to location, season and mood. Rather than looking like 'a guy in a green suit', he appeared covered in patches of fungus, pin mould and lichen, sprouting thorns when angry and flowers when placid.[23]

As well as this visual plasticity, the revision of the character also led to a revision of the relationship between actors and the environment in which the action of the story takes place, as the character essentially *was* the environment. Bissette and Totleben consistently played with this conflation, having Swamp Thing surprise other characters by suddenly emerging from background plant life, or drastically altering his size to become as big as mountains. Crucially, in its revised conception, the character no longer occupied an irresolvable space between culture and nature, or human subject and Othered non-human nature, but represented a re-subjectified and re-sacralised nature that defied such binary oppositions altogether. Unlike the dualism of conventional superhero characters, the new Swamp Thing no longer had a secret human identity, but became a pagan earth-god given equitable, if not superior, agency and voice to any human character. Through the connection to the green, its consciousness operated at a global ecological dimension, evinced by slow speech patterns that signified geological thought processes. As such he could relate the legends of the glaciers and the romances of the ocean bed, the interconnected narratives of the natural world.

This difference between this retconned Swamp Thing and the more conventional composite monster was explored in the confrontation between the protagonist and Jason Woodrue/Floronic Man. Having accessed the green and become suddenly attuned to the suffering of the natural world, Woodrue declares war on humanity, vowing to 'destroy the creatures ... that would destroy the ecosphere with their poisons and bulldozers'.[24] His justifiable rage at environmental devastation is given a powerful presentation, playing on the chainsaw motif of contemporary horror films to highlight the destruction wrought by the logging industry. However, Swamp Thing admonishes him for his residual dualistic modes of thought, poisoning the green with human forms of consciousness: 'This ... is not ... the way ... of the wilderness. / This ... is the way ... of man.'[25] Woodrue merely inverts the epistemological schism between human subjectivity and objectified nature, reducing humans to 'screaming meat'. Swamp Thing defeats him by revealing that were he to eradicate all animal life on earth there would be nothing left to convert oxygen into the carbon dioxide required by plant life. This reveals Swamp Thing's more relational understanding of biospherical interdependency, echoing ecosophical notions of harmony between humanity and nature. However, it also counters some of the misanthropic attitudes of deep ecology, and the tendency to merely invert the culture/nature binary and hierarchical conceptions of human versus non-human nature. As a whole, this story arc can be seen to stage many of the debates occurring within the contemporary green movement between anthropocentric and biocentric positions, through an exploration of the Gothic trope of monstrosity.

As a horror comic, *Swamp Thing* employed many other stock Gothic features, including graveyards, haunted houses, black magic, madness and hallucinations, metamorphic bodies, reanimated corpses, dramatic meteorological conditions such as dense fog and raging storms and shady cyberpunk corporations. The geographical context of Louisiana allowed the creators to draw particularly on the conventions of Southern Gothic, which explored the region's 'indeterminate status between now and then, the New and the Old World' as a mysterious mix of French, Cajun and West African cultures.[26] The swamp, too, was a wild landscape rich in Gothic qualities which they could exploit, particularly at night, when many characters lose their way in its bewildering and unstable topography. This use of Gothic tropes was playful, and, as with much of the Gothic canon itself, extremely self-conscious. Most importantly, however, the creators deployed Gothic techniques and styles in order to posit different relations between subjectivity and object-world that suggested a new environmental consciousness. In terms of narrative style this meant non-linear, fragmented or elliptical storylines that not only contributed the necessary suspense but reflected a more interconnected and complex time-frame perspective. This weblike narrative structure was elaborated across episodes, with characters returning from previous issues and crossing paths in an unpredictable and organic way, or small details gaining greater significance retrospectively, revealing a more ecological diegesis. Rather than using third-person narration in captions and objective point of view in panels, the creators relied overwhelmingly on first-person narration, often exploiting the complex semiotics of comics to oppose visual and verbal elements. Stories were frequently related through the cumulative, overlapping accounts of multiple narrators, some of whom were unreliable owing to mendacity or madness. This effect was amplified by the use of close-ups or subjective points of view in panels that placed the reader in the space of one of the characters, which often switched from panel to panel in a single page, juxtaposing different and sometimes conflicting standpoints. A common structure in Gothic fiction, this use of montage meant that the creators could examine the subjective emotional and psychological states of the characters, but it also meant that there was no singular and objective perspective from which to approach the events narrated, resulting in a less definitive split between interiority and exteriority, self and environment. This polyphony also mandated a more active and relational reading: in the absence of a guiding authorial voice, readers are required to adjudicate themselves between competing discursive positions.

Visually, *Swamp Thing* was radically distinct from the clear bold lines, geometric forms and simple strong colours of most mainstream comics, particularly in the dominant superhero genre. As Gothic revival architecture differed from neoclassical order in its excessive ornamentation, Bissette and Totleben gave precedence to the decorative both within panels and in page layouts. Their style was characterised by asymmetry and intricacy, with soft and textured line work building up to dense hatching (particularly in the rendering of facial expressions), and ornate compositions registering the influence of psychedelic comix, specifically the work of artists like Irons and Rick Griffin. The colour palette was diverse, using a wider range of secondary colours and tonal variations, drawing on Bissette's training in stage-lighting design and familiarity with the use of colours as emotional keys. Both Bissette and Totleben made detailed suggestions to colourist Tatjana Wood to ensure that the colouring matched the depth and subtlety of the line work, and Totleben even experimented with inking onto the separate acetate colour overlays, to overcome the separation between flat colour and black line that characterised the four-colour printing process.

More importantly, the creators gave unprecedented attention to location. Moore carefully researched the bayou habitat, its flora and fauna and the cultural and social environment of Louisiana, even getting character names from a Houma telephone directory.[27] Following fan mail which criticised the comic for geographical inaccuracies, Bissette travelled personally to Houma to do location research. As a result the environment was rendered with a level of detail and 'intensity that American comics traditionally eschew'.[28] The natural world was not purely the 'setting' for the story, a term which, Lawrence Buell points out, 'deprecates what it denotes, implying that the physical environment serve for artistic purposes merely . . . as backdrop, ancillary to the main event'.[29] Rather, the location of the swamp was presented in as much

Swamp Thing *and radical ecology* 51

detail and animation as the character of Swamp Thing itself, blurring this conventional demarcation of background environment and foreground characters. Indeed, in the story-arc in which Swamp Thing confronts Batman in order to save Abby from imprisonment, the conflict focused as much on the struggle between the natural and urban environment as on a conventional showdown between two superheroic protagonists. Although Batman is possibly the most Gothic of superheroes, it was his technocratic aspect that was emphasised in these issues, echoed by a depiction of Gotham, not as a city of dark alleyways or neo-Gothic architecture, but a modernist bastion of steel and glass laid out in a strict grid plan. As the clean lines of Gotham are invaded by the flowing organic forms of plants – Swamp Thing mobilising the total power of the green – many of the panels reflect an intertwining of character and location, figure and ground (see Figure 3.1). Swamp Thing appears simultaneously in both background and foreground (alternatively as a figure and flora), and it is unclear where the character stops and the environment begins, revealing their essential integration.

However, it is not only at the level of content or composition that this intimation of an alternative philosophical relationship with nature is expressed, but in the overall structure of the comic, which subverts conventional illusionism of neutral page layouts in the standard orthogonal grid pattern.[30] As the 'excessively ornate rhetorical gestures' of the Gothic undermine the standard devices of literary realism or pictorial mimesis,[31] Bissette and Totleben use elaborate and highly expressive page layouts as a 'graphic emotional component' of the story.[32] In the showdown with Batman, Swamp Thing becomes as large as a giant redwood tree, his size emphasised by the single panel taking up the entire page (see Figure 3.2). On the adjacent page the contours of his face become the panel borders and bleed to the page edges. Swamp Thing is thus not only background and foreground at the same time, but also the narrative frame, his anger dwarfing the city's population in terms of scale and emotional pitch. This frequently used device represents a dramatic transcendence of more traditional conceptions of the mechanics of comics as a transparent carrier for the narrative; the panel is no longer an objective 'window on the world'; the page is no longer a neutral narrative structure. This transformed relationship between the visual narrative and its material frame, in which the two become interdependent rather than exclusively demarcated spaces, further

3.1 Alan Moore and John Totleben, 'The Garden of Earthly Delights', *Swamp Thing*, 53 (Oct. 1986), 11

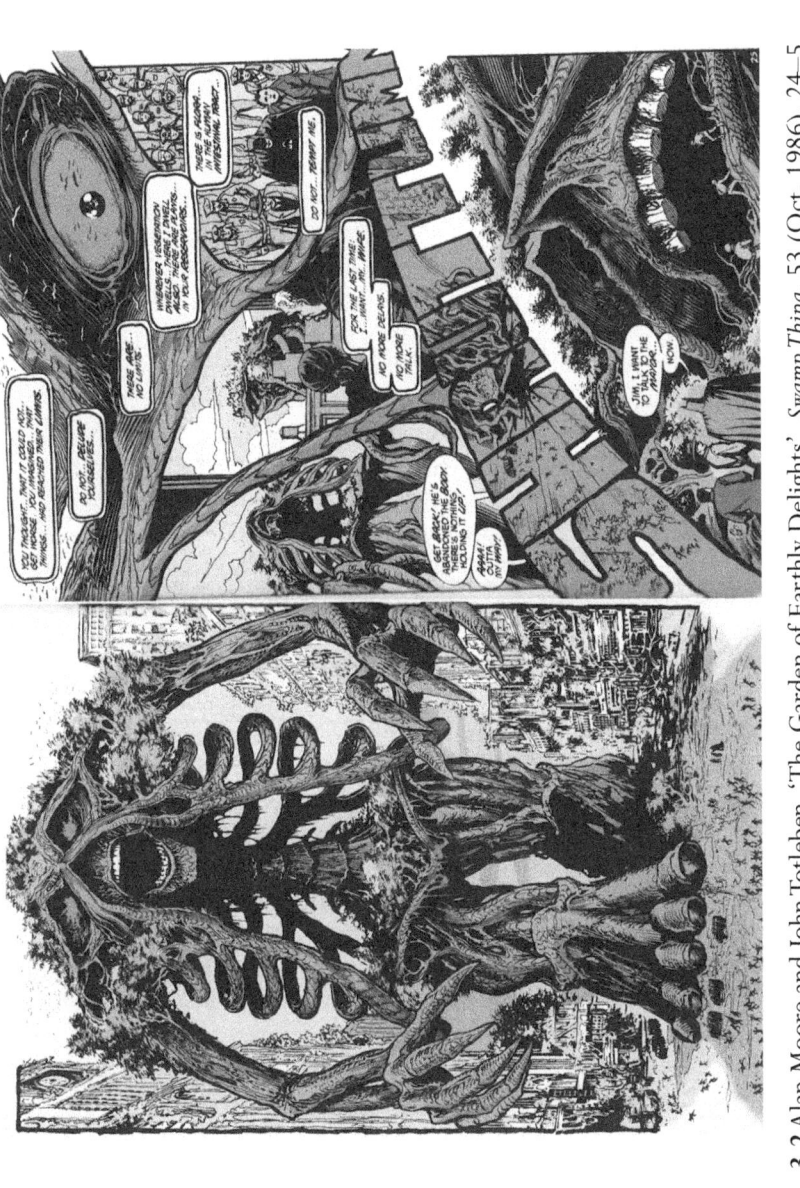

3.2 Alan Moore and John Totleben, 'The Garden of Earthly Delights', *Swamp Thing*, 53 (Oct. 1986), 24–5

emphasises the way that the comic resonated with the holism of green philosophies like deep ecology.

However, the comic's most extensive and self-reflexive engagement with the Gothic reveals a more explicit affinity with social ecology. As Bradshaw discusses at length, the narrative arc known as 'American Gothic' opposes Swamp Thing to many of the clichéd horrors of the Gothic tradition. However, in a very canny collapse of the uncanny, revealing an intertextual awareness of Gothic criticism itself, it is made inescapably and unambiguously clear that the horrific monsters are actually metaphors for 'the darkness [...] in the heart of America'.[33] The horrifying effect of these issues is not a result of the terror of the indescribable or the sublime, but lies rather in the chilling recognition of these monsters as the revenant victims of the crimes of America's history. Collectively they reveal how the classic construction of bourgeois identity, and its ideology of rationalist progress and unlimited economic growth, is founded on the ejection and repression of a history of exploitation and oppression. These issues explicitly situate the overarching theme of the misappropriation and destruction of the natural world in relation to inequalities of class, race and gender, articulating a social-ecological position that insists that 'the history of man's efforts to subjugate nature, is also the history of man's subjugation by man'.[34]

Crucially, as with American Gothic texts by figures like Nathaniel Hawthorne and Toni Morrison, this exposes the 'materialist roots of the Gothic', bearing witness to the real horrors of history rather than imaginary terrors.[35] However, this kind of self-consciously materialist Gothic, disclosing actual historical processes and unmasking contemporary social dynamics, educes a realism ostensibly antithetical to Gothic aesthetics and comparable to the appropriation of 'Gothic stylings' for urgent social critique by radicals like William Godwin and Mary Wollstonecraft.[36] This raises the crucial issue of the politics of the Gothic itself. In the introduction to the first trade-paperback collection of *Swamp Thing*, Moore poses the question of 'why an entire society should stand around engrossed, reading *Dracula* while up to our jugulars in blood'.[37] The implication that the Gothic could be an escapist distraction from reality aligns with Franco Moretti's argument that Gothic metaphors filter social threats and anxieties, dislocating 'the antagonisms and horrors evidenced within society to outside society itself' into the realm of the supernatural or a mystified past.[38] However, the inter-

Swamp Thing *and radical ecology* 55

textuality of 'American Gothic' highlights an awareness on the creators' part of the Gothic as a mode deeply embedded in modernity, marking 'a very intense, if displaced, engagement with political and social problems' of its time.[39] Other scholarship has alternatively cast it as a particularly subversive tradition, 'a gesture of defiance' threatening hegemonic certainties and the security of bourgeois subjectivity, and contravening restrictive rules of artistic verisimilitude and propriety, thereby inviting critical alarm and even censorship.[40]

Given the importance of form in this debate, and intersecting arguments about popular reception, the characterisation of the Gothic as a means of containing social antagonisms can be usefully aligned with consonant theories about mass culture, most notably by Frankfurt School theorists such as Theodor Adorno. Along with Max Horkheimer, Adorno elaborated a theory of the culture industry producing mass-cultural commodities that invoked masochistic consuming subjects distracted from the reality of capitalism's historical contingency, and socialised to authoritarian administration and passive conformity. For Adorno, any attempt to create oppositional work within the realm of instrumentalised mass culture would be attenuated by fundamental technical limitations and assimilation into the process of commodified consumption as a whole. In relation to comics, the standardisation and mythic repetition identified by Adorno as the fetishised characteristics of mass culture were located by Umberto Eco in the cyclical lack of causal progression and exchangeable sameness of superhero narratives, ultimately returning to and affirming the status quo (a factor Moore had himself identified in the early *Swamp Thing* strips).[41]

This recuperation of oppositional ideas through the commodity fetish, and the magical resolution of social threats through closure or mythical circularity, poses problems of agency and urgency, which, as noted above, are extremely germane to the radical ecological movement. The *Swamp Thing* story, 'The Nukeface Papers', offered a way of potentially overcoming this problematic and, as such, perhaps marks the most effective political intervention made by the series. In the two-part narrative Swamp Thing is killed by a radioactive hobo who feeds off toxic waste. Standing as an indictment of numerous Silver Age super-heroes who acquired their superpowers from benign radiation accidents, the horrific character Nukeface was created by the dumping of toxic waste in a disused mine situated near the ironically named

Blossomville. The artists' depiction of the town explicitly referred to the Three Mile Island nuclear power plant, site of the worst civilian nuclear accident in US history, in March 1979. The story of Nukeface's arrival in Louisiana, seeking waste freshly dumped in the swamp, is told through a Gothic montage of the cumulative accounts of multiple characters. The horror of Nukeface is rendered through his visibly decomposing face and even his speech balloons, which seem to corrode their own edges (see Figure 3.3). Unlike Swamp Thing he is completely discordant with his environment, emphasised by the fact that he is always surrounded and demarcated by a sickly blue glow and leaves luminous footprints on the ground. Most significantly, Nukeface is never defeated in the story. Having failed to dig the waste out of the swamp and poisoned Swamp Thing, the story ends with him merely departing to seek out further stashes of his favourite tipple, declaring: 'don't care if I gotta look in every state, every town ... every street dammit! I know it's there ... heads up, America ... here I come!' (see Figure 3.4).

The particular political resonance of this story was achieved by the fact that the creators included fragments of real newspaper clippings throughout, climaxing in the final full-page collage. These clippings were accounts of actual industrial accidents and discoveries of hazardous waste dumps, including the Three Mile Island incident and the Bhopal disaster of December 1984 in India. Toxic waste had been a key issue in the US environmental struggles of the 1970s, and had led to the Toxic Substance Control Act (1976) and the setting-up of the Superfund to cover the cost of emergency clean-ups. However, the Reagan administration, supported by a powerful alliance of businessmen and New Right think-tanks, attempted to reverse the move towards environmental protection. Reagan cut the budgets of government regulatory agencies, rolled back and tried to repeal environmental legislation and appointed notorious anti-environmentalists to key positions. As head of the Environmental Protection Agency, Ann Gorsuch 'spared countless corporate polluters from government action and forced the EPA to delay or scrap regulations on workplace chemicals, hazardous wastes and automobile emissions'.[42] In the face of such government complicity with corporate interests, a number of local activist groups emerged that particularly focused on radioactive waste and spent reactor fuel from nuclear power stations. These included the Clamshell Alliance, the Abalone Alliance and the Citizen's Clearinghouse for Hazardous Wastes.

3.3 Alan Moore, Steve Bissette and John Totleben, 'The Nukeface Papers Part 1', *The Saga of the Swamp Thing*, 35 (Apr. 1985), 19

3.4 Alan Moore, Steve Bissette and John Totleben, 'The Nukeface Papers Part 2', *The Saga of the Swamp Thing*, 36 (May 1985), 23

Such groups were often more confrontational and uncompromising than their predecessors and importantly drew in many women, minority groups and blue-collar workers who lived in the areas targeted as potential dumping sites. As a result, and drawing strongly from social ecology, these groups were an important catalyst for today's environmental justice movement.[43]

In some ways the inclusion of these newspaper clippings invoked the tendency of Gothic narratives to exaggerate their own fictionality through the use of different forms of writing, from letters and diary entries to the presentation of the narratives themselves as found manuscripts, framed by falsified editorial prefaces or notes on translation. Crucially, however, unlike the fake documents of the Gothic tradition, these were real. As a result, rather than serving to epiphemonalise the material world as a purely discursive construction through intertextual metafiction in a postmodern sense, the self-reflexivity of these issues points to a realist epistemology and more Brechtian aesthetic. The effect of these newspaper fragments was not to sublimate the horror through the restoration of boundaries either within the narrative, in terms of its own fictional closure, or through a cyclical and internalised self-referentiality, but to have it spill out of the confines of the work, concretely situated in material reality. With the final climactic collage, unframed by any panel border, what ultimately contains and limits the story of Nukeface is the much larger horror of actual events in the recognisable social world shared by the reader. Indeed, Nukeface is dwarfed by the overwhelming mass of clippings which frame him and fill the white space of the page. The audience is distanced from the story as a fictional construct and refused any satisfactory conclusion or facile resolution to the very real environmental problems raised in the narrative. Instead readers are compelled to take their own critical stance in relation to these issues and to seek redress and resolution through their own self-determined political action.

The issue received a significant response from readers, many recognising clippings from incidents local to them and providing further information. One of the most insightful letters revealed the success of this externalised orientation of the narrative, stating: 'the story was not sufficient to scare me ... No fiction can match the reality of what nuke waste ... can do.'[44] The reader, from Louisiana themselves, went on to urge 'all anti-nukes to get smart about nuke laws and unite', asserting the need for concerted action. Moore, Bissette and Totleben's *Swamp Thing* serves to both elaborate the Gothic scale of the threat of environmental destruction and to conceptualise an ecological sensibility of alternative attitudes and values less founded in the technocratic domination of nature; however, though these elements of the series are politically salient, the evocation of such critical and activist responses is perhaps the most significant aspect of the legacy bequeathed to contemporary radical social movements attempting to abate the destruction of our planet.

Notes

1. Alan Moore, Rick Veitch and Alfredo Alcala, 'Natural Consequence', *Swamp Thing*, 52 (Sept. 1986), 16.iii.
2. Richard Kerridge, 'Ecothrillers: Environmental Cliffhangers', in *The Green Studies Reader: From Romanticism to Ecocriticism*, ed. Laurence Coupe (London: Routledge, 2000), pp. 242–9 (p. 248).
3. Elizabeth K. Rosen, *Apocalyptic Transformations, Apocalypse and the Post-Modern Imagination* (Lanham, MD: Lexington Books, 2008), p. xii.
4. Lawrence Buell, *Writing for an Endangered World: Literature, Culture and the Environment in the United States and Beyond* (Cambridge, MA: Harvard University Press, 2001), pp. 1–29.
5. Fred Botting, *Gothic* (London: Routledge, 1996), p. 14.
6. Len Wein, cited in Dan Johnson, 'Wein and Wrightson: The Roots of Swamp Thing', *Back Issue*, 1:6 (Oct. 2004), 3–14 (p. 8).
7. Wes Craven (dir.), *Swamp Thing* (Swampfilms/Embassy Pictures, 1982).
8. Dan Johnson, 'Bissette and Veitch: Old Monster, New Tricks', *Back Issue*, 1:6 (Oct. 2004), 48–56 (p. 50).
9. John Totleben, 'John Totleben', interview with George Khoury, *Rough Stuff*, 1:4 (Spring 2007), 24–42 (p. 42).
10. Kirkpatrick Sale, *The Green Revolution: The American Environmental Movement 1962–1992* (New York: Hill & Wang, 1993), p. 58.
11. Timothy W. Luke, *Ecocritique: Contesting the Politics of Nature, Economy and Culture* (Minneapolis: University of Minnesota Press, 1997) p. 4.
12. Arne Naess, *Ecology, Community and Lifestyle: Outline of an Ecosophy*, ed. and trans. David Rothenberg, 8th edn (Cambridge: Cambridge University Press, 2001), pp. 166–7.
13. Sale, *Green Revolution*, p. 64. See Murray Bookchin, 'The Concept of Social Ecology', in *The Ecology of Freedom: The Emergence and Dissolution of Hierarchy* (Oakland, CA: AK Press, 2005), pp. 80–108.

14 Alan Moore, personal interview, 28 Nov. 2007.
15 John McCormick, *British Politics and the Environment* (London: Earthscan, 1991), p. 123.
16 Moore, personal interview.
17 Steve Bissette, 'A Monstrous Talent: An Interview with Steve Bissette', interview by Wellington Srbek: http://maisquadrinhos.blogspot.com/2008/05/when-i-think-about-which-comic-book.html.
18 Rosen, *Apocalyptic Transformations*, p. 5.
19 Alan Moore, 'Metamorphosis', *Prisoners of Gravity*, Season 3 (TVOntario: broadcast 3 Dec. 1992).
20 *Ibid.* The creators reference Hamlet in the dream sequence in which Swamp Thing comes to terms with the fact he never was human and engages in a conversation with a skull representing his lost humanity. Ultimately Swamp Thing finds and buries the skeleton of Alec Holland, guided by a spectral representation of the Wein/Wrightson version of the character, thereby putting the preceding continuity to rest; for discussion of further reference to Hamlet, see the discussion provided by Jochen Ecke in Chapter 4 below.
21 Steve Bissette, 'Growing up with Dinosaurs: An Interview with Steve Bissette', interview by David Ehrlich, *International Journal of Comic Art*, 4:1 (Spring 2002), 97–133.
22 For further discussion of *Swamp Thing*'s affinity to the Green Man tradition, see Colin Beineke, '"Her Guardiner": Alan Moore's Swamp Thing as the Green Man', *ImageText: Interdisciplinary Comics Studies*, 5:4 (Spring 2011): www.english.ufl.edu/imagetext/archives/v5_4/beineke/.
23 'A Chat with Alan Moore' (DC Comics/Lynn Vanucci Productions, 1985): www.youtube.com/watch?v=ze3rCvyilSA&feature=related.
24 Alan Moore, Stephen Bissette and John Totleben, 'Another Green World', *Swamp Thing*, 23 (Apr. 1984), 21.v.
25 Alan Moore, Stephen Bissette and John Totleben, 'Roots', *Swamp Thing*, 24 (May 1984), 13.ii.
26 Robert Mighall, 'Gothic Cities', in *The Routledge Companion to the Gothic*, ed. Catherine Spooner and Emma McEvoy (London: Routledge, 2007), pp. 54–62 (p. 59).
27 Alan Moore, *Alan Moore's Writing for Comics* (Urbana, IL: Avatar Press, 2003), p. 23.
28 Bissette, 'Growing up with Dinosaurs', p. 109.
29 Lawrence Buell, *The Environmental Imagination: Thoreau, Nature Writing and the Formation of American Culture* (Cambridge, MA: Harvard University Press, 1995), p. 85.
30 Alvise Mattozzi, 'Innovating Superheroes', *Reconstruction*, 3:2 (Spring 2003): http://reconstruction.eserver.org/032/mottazzi.htm.

31 Markman Ellis, *The History of Gothic Fiction* (Edinburgh: Edinburgh University Press, 2000) p. 8.
32 Bissette, 'Growing up with Dinosaurs', pp. 121–2.
33 Alan Moore, Stephen Bissette and John Totleben, 'Revelations', *Swamp Thing*, 46 (Mar 1986), 17.
34 Max Horkheimer, 'The Revolt of Nature', in *Green History: A Reader in Environmental Literature, Philosophy and Politics*, ed. Derek Wall (London: Routledge, 1994), pp. 235–7 (p. 236).
35 Teresa A. Goddu, 'American Gothic', in *The Routledge Companion to the Gothic*, ed. Catherine Spooner and Emma McEvoy (London: Routledge, 2007), pp. 63–72 (p. 65).
36 Mary Poovey, 'Ideology and the *Mysteries of Udolpho*', in *Gothic: Critical Concepts in Literary and Cultural Studies*, ed. Fred Botting and Dale Townsend, 2 vols (London and New York: Routledge, 2004), II, pp. 116–36 (p. 132).
37 Alan Moore, 'Introduction', in *Saga of the Swamp Thing* (New York: DC Comics, 1987), pp. 7–12 (p. 7).
38 Franco Moretti, *Signs Taken for Wonders: On the Sociology of Literary Forms*, trans. Susan Fischer, David Forgacs and David Miller (London: Verso, 1988), p. 84.
39 David Punter, *The Literature of Terror: A History of Gothic Fictions from 1765 to the Present Day*, 2nd edn, 2 vols (London: Longman, 1996), I, p. 54.
40 This phrase is used by Punter to express the perspective of Michael Sadleir's *The Northanger Novels* (Oxford: Oxford University Press, 1927); see Punter, *Literature of Terror*, I, p. 13.
41 Umberto Eco, 'The Myth of the Superman', in *The Role of the Reader: Explorations in the Semiotics of Texts* (London: Hutchinson, 1979), pp. 107–24.
42 Sale, *Green Revolution*, p. 51.
43 Buell, *Writing for an Endangered World*, p. 32.
44 Letter from J. P. Shannon, published in 'Southern Change', *Swamp Thing*, 41 (Oct. 1985), 25.

Part II

Gothic tropes

4

'Is that you, our Jack?': an anatomy of Alan Moore's doubling strategies

Jochen Ecke

The didactic doppelgänger

The double is everywhere in Alan Moore's work. In *V for Vendetta*, the elusive V is intent on turning working-class girl Evey into his doppelgänger by subjecting her to a simulation of the traumatic experiences of a woman known simply as 'Valerie', an early victim of the Larkhill Resettlement Camp who served as an inspiration during his own incarceration. The story of Valerie's life and death is delivered first to V and then to Evey in the form of a letter written on toilet paper and hidden in a hole in the wall of a prison cell. A reiteration of the found manuscript of early Gothic fiction, this missive instigates a double-doubling as Evey replicates V's replication of Valerie's suffering and perseverance. Similarly, the idea that Batman and the Joker are mirror images of each other is the premise of *The Killing Joke*, in which the mirroring of their acts, images and insanity reproduces the symbiosis of law and transgression. Timothy Hole, the protagonist of *A Small Killing*, meanwhile, is haunted by a small boy who not only looks uncannily like his own younger self, but also stands in for the son who might have grown from the aborted foetus sent to him by his ex-girlfriend. And in *Promethea*, protagonist Sophie Bangs turns into what could be conceptualised as a Platonic ideal version of herself by writing, a process of doubling that extends out into multiplicity as she comes into contact with a plethora of earlier Prometheas, and that culminates in a return to traumatic origins with the schism between the eastern and western versions of the goddess. These are but a few examples of doubles in Moore's oeuvre. As a matter of fact, once one opens the pages of any one of the writer's works, it is difficult *not* to find instances where a doubling strategy is at work.

Moore's doppelgängers largely appear in uncanny scenarios that borrow heavily from the Gothic tradition, and are themselves unsettling figures, both for the diegetic characters and for the reader. The key features of the Gothic motif of the doppelgänger are neatly illustrated in Sheridan Le Fanu's 1872 vampire tale, 'Carmilla', and it is notable that the function of the double in this Victorian novella closely corresponds with the deployment of doubling in Moore's work. The trauma associated with encountering a doppelgänger results largely from the destabilisation or confusion of identity, which nevertheless allows the writer to employ the trope to define identity in a neutral, or even a positive, sense as a process of negotiation defying any attempt at final synthesis. In the encounter with the double, both the characters and the audience are forced to acknowledge that which is repressed, abjected or denied, and once these unconscious processes have been brought to light, there is no return to former certainties. Fictions of the double thus exhibit a didactic dimension, initiating a reflection on identity by exposing what is 'excessive in what seeks to become absolute'.[1] In addition to their impact upon the depiction of subjectivity in both the nineteenth-century Gothic and in Moore's work, these doubling effects are similarly operative on the narratological and ideological levels. Indeed, a careful consideration of 'Carmilla' demonstrates that the double not only serves as a commentary on subjectivity, but on generic conventions as well, since the motif calls into question simplistic or conservative resolutions to narrative conflict. In short, the doppelgänger can equally be employed as a metafictional device without any immediate psychological implications, a feature naturally quite attractive to Moore, whose penchant for self-reflexivity is well documented.

Identifying four doubling strategies from the Gothic tradition

At the beginning of Le Fanu's 'Carmilla', the eponymous girl is introduced into the family of Laura, the first-person narrator. Very quickly, Laura bonds with Carmilla, and soon afterwards their relationship takes a turn towards the sexual, a development which Laura both abhors and welcomes:

It was like the ardour of a lover; it embarrassed me; it was hateful and yet overpowering; and with gloating eyes she [Carmilla] drew me to her, and her hot lips travelled along my cheek in kisses; and she would whisper, almost in sobs, 'You are mine, you *shall* be mine, you and I are one for ever.'[2]

As the quotation implies, a doubling strategy is at work in the tale; or rather, at least four separate doubling strategies, since the doubling of a character in most cases 'operates in tandem with a doubling of narrative structure'.[3] From the point of view of genre, 'Carmilla' is as much a Gothic tale as it is a confidence (wo-)man story in which Carmilla positions herself as Laura's doppelgänger in order to dissimulate her murderous intentions. Carmilla's line of attack also comprises the second doubling strategy, which takes place on a more subconscious level. As Laura puts it herself, 'the precautions of nervous people are infectious, and persons of a like temperament are pretty sure, after a time, to imitate them'.[4] In other words, the victim herself performs the brunt of the doubling work, identifying with Carmilla so thoroughly that her own personality dissolves. When, in a dream, Laura's dead mother warns her daughter to 'beware of the assassin' and Laura subsequently sees Carmilla 'standing, near the foot of [her] bed, in her white nightdress, bathed, from her chin to her feet, in one great stain of blood', she does not draw the logical conclusion that the blood is actually her own; instead, she is convinced that Carmilla is being murdered that very instant.[5] Laura's error is not the product of entirely irrational behaviour on her part. After all, Carmilla has functioned repeatedly as a representational figure for Laura's past suffering. In particular, by indulging in her 'deviant' sexual orientation, Carmilla has expropriated Laura's own repressed lesbian desires and thus staged a representation of Laura's sexual deprivation, uncannily rendering 'past absence present again'.[6] Crucially, though, Carmilla's strategy has been to suggest that the pain incurred by the repression of desire has been transferred from Laura to herself. Nothing could be further from the truth, but the confidence trick has worked in so far as Laura is now willing to believe that any harm coming her way will be equally deferred.

It is in Gothic tales like Le Fanu's that the motif of the doppelgänger is thus imported from such German works as Jean Paul's *Siebenkäs* and modified in a number of important ways. Paul himself famously defines the 'Doppeltgänger' [sic] as 'people who see themselves',[7] and thus supplies one of the distinctions between the uses of the motif in German Romanticism and in the Gothic. While the Gothic double is to some extent still a 'figure of visual compulsion',[8] a 'predominantly visual phenomenon',[9] characters in the Gothic tale or novel who undergo a traumatic doubling often do not see themselves 'duplicated as phantasm in such a way as to defy distinction'.[10] Instead, Laura encounters Carmilla as a completely distinct character from a narratological point of view. In other words, in what amounts to the third important instance of subversive doubling in the tale, Carmilla is both a separate character of her own *and* a manifestation of Laura's divided self, which – unlike the character Carmilla, who is ritually beheaded by a band of patriarchal males at the end of the tale – cannot be exterminated and will return compulsively.

Unlike Webber and Bär, though, I do not believe that this disparity between the double in German Romanticism and the British Gothic can be adequately described as a difference in the mimetic degree of 'the autoscopic, or self-seeing'.[11] Rather, I would suggest that the double in the Gothic is often bound up in a tradition of double address to the audience, a tendency which, Little has argued, is also central to Moore's work.[12] A tale such as 'Carmilla' very much upholds the surface appearance of what Todorov terms the genre of 'the fantastic'. For much of the story, the reader is held in suspense over the question of whether Carmilla truly is a vampire or not; in Todorov's words, Le Fanu aims to make the reader wonder whether Laura is 'the victim of an illusion of the senses ... or ... [whether] the [supernatural] event has taken place'.[13] Since Carmilla is revealed to be a vampire in the final pages of the tale, this 'duration of uncertainty' ends, and the story can be classified as being of the 'fantastic-marvellous' variety, 'the class of narratives that are presented as fantastic and that end with an acceptance of the supernatural'.[14] But this supposed resolution is actually only part of Le Fanu's authorial confidence trick, and represents less an acceptance of the supernatural than a fulfilment of a conservative reader's expectations, since Carmilla's sexuality is thus conveniently consigned to the realm of the fictional alongside the supernatural attributes of the vampire. The tale's apparent decision for one of the two genres bordering on the fantastic – that is, the marvellous and the uncanny – amounts to a reassurance of the audience, since the dialectical hesitation that characterised it is comfortably ended. Demonstrating that Le Fanu is not interested in such games of elimination is not a difficult task; one need only be reminded of the final paragraph of the tale in which Laura's double is described as waiting right outside the drawing room, ready to invade the sacred space of the Victorian upper middle class, to conclude that nothing at all is resolved at the end of the story:

> to this hour the image of Carmilla returns to memory with ambiguous alternations – sometimes the playful, languid, beautiful girl; sometimes the writhing fiend I saw in the ruined church; and often from a reverie I have started, fancying I heard the light step of Carmilla at the drawing-room door.[15]

In short, then, the uses of the double multiplied when British writers applied the concept to genre fiction – the trope became a tool for the subversion of generic conventions and their conservative ideological implications. At the same time, it retained all of its former potency, serving as 'an inveterate performer of identity' and helping to spread and explore the notion of subjectivity as an interminable 'process of enactments of identity always mediated by the other self'.[16] But on top of that, as in the case of Le Fanu's tale, Victorian society's repressive attitude towards homosexuality could now be framed in metafictional fashion as a conflict of genre conventions versus the(ir) double. This self-reflexive strategy on the level of genre I will designate as the fourth level of doubling in the tale.

But why, upon closer inspection, do doppelgänger fictions tend towards non-resolution, and how far is this of any importance to Alan Moore's work? E.T.A. Hoffmann speaks of the double as of a permanent illness – a 'chronic dualism'.[17] To Webber, this dualism is predicated on 'the element of misrecognition which inheres in the relationship between host and double' that 'always leaves the dialectical work in the reconnaissance of identity open ended',[18] as is the case in 'Carmilla': the double persists because Laura does not recognise her own homosexuality. To Webber, Laura would thus become a figure characterised by a profound sense of loss. But should we consider a tale in which the heroine and the reader are forced to acknowledge that mainstream Victorian society is repressive as merely communicating a sense of thwarted yearning for a stable identity? In other words, we need to frame the motif on more positive grounds. Dimitris Vardoulakis recognises this theoretical desideratum, and suggests instead that 'the reversal enacted by the *Doppelgänger* is all about a type of subjective relationality, not about what the subject is related to. It is about the *how*, not the *what*.'[19] He does so to counter what he identifies as 'the dialectic of loss' that is often implied in theoretical texts on the doppelgänger.[20] Instead, the fact that the double alerts its subject to excess – in Laura's case, repressed homosexual desires – where there seemingly was none, thus 'undoing occlusion',[21] points towards a wholly modern, performative view of identity.

Uncanny indeterminacy in *The Saga of the Swamp Thing*

The element of the irresolvably performative is of equally central importance to Moore's work. We need only to pause and consider which characters in Moore are (eventually) certain of their identity to realise that, in his work, to be absolutely certain of oneself is, more often than not, to be a mad sociopath. Adrian Veidt from *Watchmen* and William Gull of *From Hell* are prime examples of figures who are at the very least highly ambiguous, committing extreme acts of violence because they see themselves as 'self-appointed saviours' trying to initiate a 'utopian renewal and reordering of society'.[22] Karin Kukkonen considers this anti-monological attitude towards identity a fundamental principle of Moore's work, and she reads *Watchmen* as an example of Bakhtin's concept of polyphony at work, arguing that the comic presents a multitude of competing ideological 'frames of reference', but does not privilege any one of them.[23] In fact, this negotiation between competing voices, Kukkonen writes, should not be conceptualised as dialectic at all, since it

> does not result in a superior synthesis. In the same vein, Veidt's brave new world after the end of east-west dualism in chapter XII of *Watchmen* will not last: Rorschach's diary, which is set to reveal Veidt's plan, has already found its way into the inbox at the *New Frontiersman* newspaper.[24]

Where heroes and villains differ crucially in Moore's works, then, is in their reaction to polyphony; whereas the villains will attempt a definitive synthesis, the heroes will always refrain from this attempt.

When Moore took up the reins of DC Comics' *Saga of the Swamp Thing* from the previous writer Martin Pasko in 1982, he was faced with the task of revising a character that had gone through horror scenarios *ad nauseam*. In this respect, it is worth noting that Moore is among the first mainstream comics writers to recognise and actively reflect upon the fact that 'the principle of seriality almost inevitably demands an aesthetic that surveys its own history and thus creates ever new generic variations'.[25] In short, contemporary writers of serial fiction cannot avoid scouring the archives. But what Moore inherited in the case of Swamp Thing has often been characterised both in critical writing and by the author himself as merely a pseudo-Gothic narrative. Already on the pages of Swamp Thing's 1970s incarnation, a doubling strategy is used to define the hero character against a villain named Anton Arcane.[26] In a particularly poignant story, the villain has offered to exchange bodies with Swamp Thing, who as of yet does not know that Arcane is evil. The Thing is going to regain his human form, whereas Arcane is to enjoy the monster's physical prowess. As Swamp Thing comes to realise his mistake, he chooses to reverse the process by returning to his former monstrous state. There is nothing subversive about this doubling at all – it is merely a poor copy of the Gothic trope without any of the benefits of excess. Wein and Wrighton's Swamp Thing is monstrous only in appearance; to think of Arcane as a stand-in for some repressed aspect of Alec Holland's psyche seems far-fetched, and hardly any such suggestion is made throughout the story.

While Moore largely discards all the distinctive features of Pasko's convoluted and often troublingly misogynistic stories, he picks up on a number of elements from the bog monster's original Wein/Wrightson run (1972–73), of which the representation of Arcane as the Thing's double is the most important. The first issue written by Moore finds Swamp Thing confronted with what seems to be the definitive demise of Arcane. In a series of five panels which show the protagonist miming Rodin's statue 'The Thinker', a *Pietà* painting and Hamlet holding Yorick's skull, Swamp Thing muses about his relationship with the villain:

> You were my opposite. I had my humanity ... taken from me. ... You started out human ... and threw it all away deliberately.
> We defined each other, didn't we? By understanding you ... I came that much closer ... to understanding myself.
> And now... you're dead.
> Really dead.
> And what ... am I going to do now?

The sequence is suffused with irony in a number of ways. First, we need to take into account the references to works of high art. The sequence mocks Swamp Thing's self-importance by comparing his self-pity to actual instances of pathos in the history of art, but also by denouncing the Thing's identity crisis as clichéd. The series' original concept as devised by Wein and Wrightson is thus exposed as flat, bathetic and prone to definitive synthesis: what else do Swamp Thing's thoughts imply but the certainty of identity that the dialectic of Swamp Thing and Anton Arcane made possible?

It is in this sense that we should also interpret some of the formal strategies of the issue, such as the symmetrical *mise-en-page* of the entire chapter. Bissette makes ironic use of symmetry, since Moore's concept for *Swamp Thing* hinges on the *disruption* of harmony. In other words, the issue's symmetry signifies its own absence. Moore and Bissette also use a potent visual metaphor to announce this approach to the character. As the villainous Sunderland explains how he is going to capture Swamp Thing, he sets an office toy called a 'Newton's cradle' in motion, whose functioning is predicated on the preservation of energy between two steel balls on strings. The subsequent montage shows Sunderland's private army preparing for its capture operation and the steel balls swinging back and forth as would be expected of them; finally, in the page's penultimate panel, Sunderland abruptly stops one of the balls, disrupting the equilibrium with disastrous results. It is not particularly difficult to see how this metaphor encapsulates Moore's own anti-dialectical aims, especially as the page is framed on its outside edge by an image of Swamp Thing himself such that the black background of the cradle panels bleeds into his body.

This is not to say that Swamp Thing is not confronted with a double during this first issue in Moore's run. The doppelgänger is merely difficult to discern, since it is also characterised by an absence. To put it bluntly, Swamp Thing is his own double, a proposition that is thematised directly eight issues later, in 'The Burial', in which Swamp Thing is confronted with the spectre of his former self and haunted simultaneously by the ghost of Alec Holland, in human form, who cannot rest until his body is recovered and interred. Now that Moore has rejected the dialectical conception of the character, the question arises: what can be considered excessive in the monster's former incarnations? Moore sums up his own findings, which inform his work on the title:

as he sounds at the moment, the Swamp Thing is a largely nondescript character [. . .]. [I]t was obvious to even the slowest reader that Alec Holland – the Swamp Thing – was never going to find some way to turn himself back to Alec Holland because the moment he did, that would be the end of the series.[27]

Moore raises two important points here: his perception that the Swamp Thing's character is 'nondescript' and the indisputable fact that the series' dialectical foundations undermine its serial format. Instead of filling the void, Moore chooses to make the monster's lack of definition his theme. This is an important point to remember, since it is a strategy that we will also encounter in *From Hell*. With an almost perverse glee, the writer then declares the Swamp Thing even more of a blank slate in his and Bissette's second issue, 'The Anatomy Lesson', in which it is revealed that the Swamp Thing never was human to begin with but rather was 'a plant that *thought* it was Alec Holland!', a change that harbours significant ontological and political implications.[28]

This methodical emptying-out of the character can be characterised as uncanny in the Freudian sense, in that it turns a seemingly familiar character into a creature that *looks* entirely recognisable, but is nonetheless now alien both to itself and to the reader. As Bresnick puts it, 'the uncanny [. . .] would not merely be something a given subject experiences, but the experience that momentarily undoes the factitious monological unity of the ego'.[29] This is exactly what happens to the bog monster – in the encounter with its former incarnation(s), it permanently loses any sense of stable identity. This loss, however, is not momentary, but permanent, or in any case highly repetitive, as befits the serial nature of the story. And as in Le Fanu's 'Carmilla', it operates both on an intra-diegetic and a metatextual level as well as affecting characters and readers alike. For the reading audience, the Swamp Thing has thus been turned into an alienation machine which will not cease to produce uncanny effects. This understanding of the character should be helpful in defining its narrative purpose more clearly. The monster's very human function will be to serve as the reader's double, pointing out what is excessive and relative in the human condition under the cover of the supposedly 'non-human', the repressed or abject.

The sequence on pages 17 to 22 of 'The Anatomy Lesson' serves as a striking illustration of the consequences the emptying-out of the character entails. Here, the creature has finally been informed of its liminal status between man and plant. This revelation sends it into a murderous rage against Sunderland, who is responsible for the Thing's identity crisis. Significantly, the 'Newton's-cradle' motif recurs in this sequence. The toy can be seen on Sunderland's desk on page 17, and again on page 19, when the Swamp Thing destroys the desk, sending the balls flying in much the same manner as before. As the monster chases Sunderland through the corridors of his empty headquarters on page 20, the steel-ball motif recurs once more, with the notable difference that this time the balls can be seen suspended from the ceiling of the building in much magnified form (panel four). The dramatic irony is fairly clear – Sunderland has become the victim of his own disruptive act; he has emptied out the Swamp Thing and thus made this outbreak of violence possible within the domain where he thought himself safe. Again, the diegetic world mirrors the story's disruptive set-up metaphorically.

While the capacity for aggression partially has its origin in the amoral character of Sunderland, the sequence does not portray the villain as the Thing's double. Instead, here the doubling is suggested in the relationship of word and image. The verbal narrator of this sequence is Jason Woodrue, the villain also known as the 'Floronic Man', since his human appearance is only a camouflage concealing a plant body.[30] His propensity to serve as the Swamp Thing's *doppelgänger* is, in other words, quite apparent. Woodrue cynically provides verbal commentary to the visual narration, and he is able to predict the events down to the last detail. He says as much on the issue's first page:

> I'm thinking about the old man.
> He'll be pounding on the glass right about now . . .
> . . . Or maybe not now.
> Maybe in a while.[31]

Once again, the disruptive agency is put in the proximity of an authorial figure, since the Swamp Thing will act uncannily upon Woodrue's desire for destruction in the course of the issue by killing Sunderland.

The concept of Woodrue as partial author of the story can be substantiated in a number of ways, not the least of which can be gleaned from the final panel of the 'killing Sunderland' sequence on page 22 (see Figure 4.1). Here, the Swamp Thing can be seen in a *chiaroscuro* long shot, clutching his surrogate father Sunderland in a deadly embrace. The two figures are dwarfed by the rest of the *mise-en-page*, which shows the

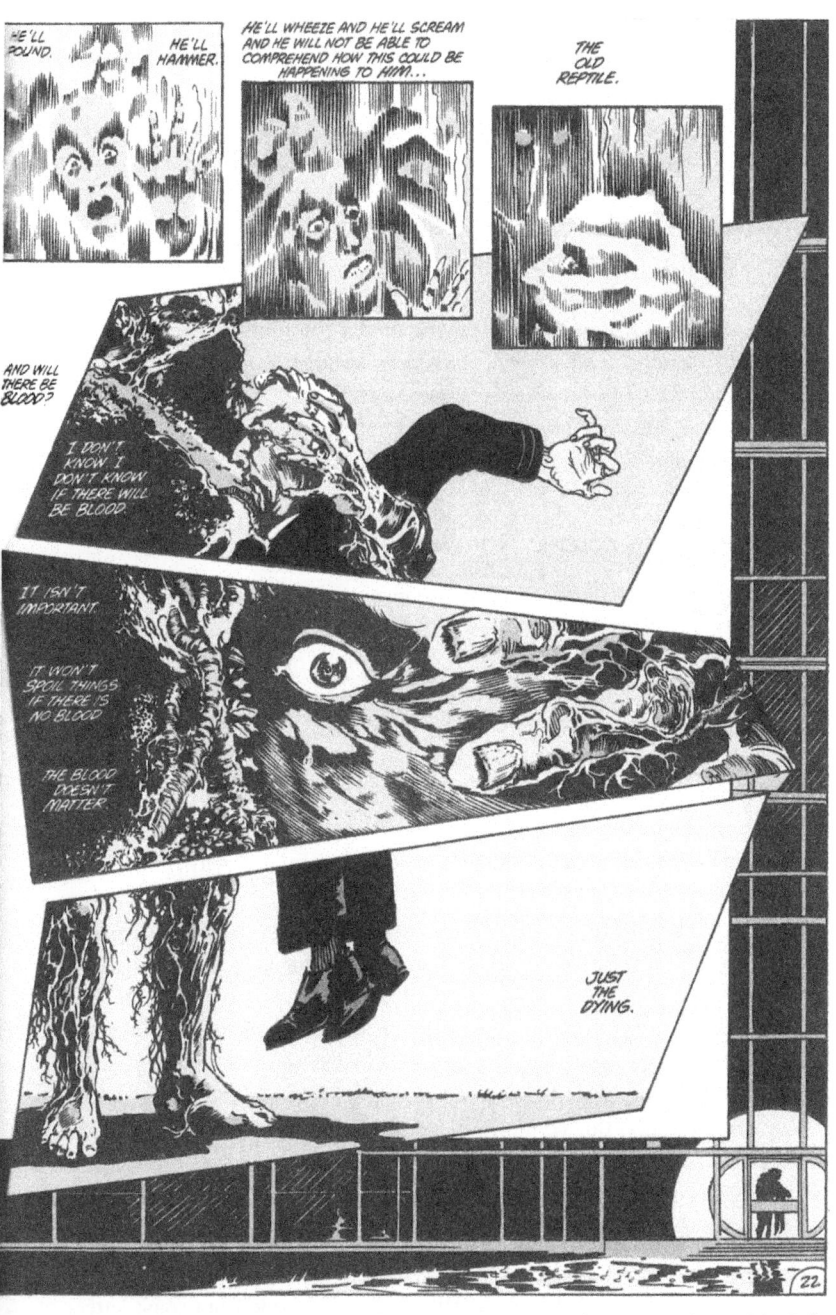

4.1 Moore, Bissette and Totleben, 'The Anatomy Lesson', *Swamp Thing*, 21 (Feb. 1984), 22

Swamp Thing at the climax of its rage. While the pathos of quasi-Frankensteinian patricide lends the scene some weight, the seriousness of this Gothic conflict is rendered questionable from the point of view of narrative perspective – after all, Swamp Thing is acting out an ironic Gothic scenario devised by Jason Woodrue. The true gravitas of these panels, then, lies in Swamp Thing's subjugation to the whims of his double, that is, the Floronic Man, a relationship also reflected in the *mise-en-page*: the rectangular shapes of the windows suggest that the character's actions have been plotted by another agency, since – especially in contrast to the oblique angles dominating the frames on the rest of the page – they are highly reminiscent of the conventional shape and spatial arrangement of comic-book panels.

The dystopian double: *From Hell*

While in the case of *Swamp Thing* the character's indeterminacy is eventually celebrated, Moore's thinly veiled *Bildungsromane* also have a dystopian potential. *From Hell* is an example of this tendency in the author's oeuvre. Here, we are again introduced to an uncannily indeterminate character in the guise of Dr William Gull, the historical figure chosen by Moore and Eddie Campbell to be 'their' Jack the Ripper. Many hints as to the character's emptiness are given throughout the book, most prominently in Chapter 2, 'A state of darkness', where Moore's use of doubling strategies becomes most apparent.

Although five years elapsed between the two works under scrutiny here, and despite the fact that *From Hell* is usually considered a work of a 'more literary' sensibility than *Swamp Thing*, there is, in fact, little to suggest that Moore's approach to Gull is fundamentally different. *From Hell* may be more radically self-reflexive, but that is merely a difference in degree; apart from that, the only major distinguishing feature is that Moore's account of the Ripper murders takes its inspiration from actual historical events. But while Moore never expresses any doubt as to the horrible suffering the five murdered women had to endure,[32] his notion of the murderer is considerably less rooted in corporeal reality:

> we cannot establish a real material physical identity for the being we call Jack the Ripper. [. . .] Jack the Ripper, in a very real sense, never actually had a physical existence. He was a collage-creature, made from crank letters, hoaxes, and sensational headlines. He exists wholly in Idea Space, looming

forward from our books of theory and our fictions, from our slasher films and our contemporary mythology of serial murder, from the pages and appendices of *From Hell*.[33]

In other words, much like Swamp Thing, Moore's Ripper is a creature of the archive. In approaching Gull, then, we need to distinguish between the same three interpretive levels as in the case of the bog monster: we must look at the doctor as a distinct diegetic character who, in the course of the biographical narrative, is shown to be obsessed with establishing his purpose in life; at Gull as the product of the comic's formal operations cueing the reader to imagine the character; and finally at the complex discursive construct 'Jack the Ripper' that has been created by generations of readers and writers.

The doppelgänger in its widest sense represents a useful tool for Moore in establishing these highly self-reflexive layers of the narrative. Again, it is helpful to differentiate between two different doubling strategies: intra-diegetically, the heteronymous Gull finds himself doubled in a variety of patriarchal male figures, including his father, his tutor Harrington, James Hinton and architect Nicholas Hawksmoor.

The reader, on the other hand, is practically forced to become Gull's doppelgänger through a variety of formal operations, the most prominent of which is a series of supposedly subjective points of view throughout many individual panels of the chapter. At first glance, therefore, the visual narrative seems to imply a complete doubling of the gaze. Indeed, that is the assertion made by Marc Bernard and James Carter.[34] But the question is a much more difficult one. For example, if one considers page II.4 closely, one will find that it is actually William's *left* arm reaching into the panel's diegetic space (see Figure 4.2). This effectively means that Gull is standing slightly to the right of the frame in off space. The panels on page 2 thus represent *nearly* his point of view, but not quite. The effect is one of deliberate confusion, for surprisingly, our gaze seems to be absolutely identical with William's on page II.5, only to return to the nearly-but-not-quite subjective point of view on later pages. This alerts us to the fact that we are witnessing two *different* narratives unfold on these pages: we construct William's biography out of the cues given by the comic book, and at the same time, William is fashioning his own biographical narrative.

How far, then, are the reader's and Gull's constructive activities and

4.2 Alan Moore and Eddie Campbell, *From Hell*, II.4.

their final results similar but different? To answer this question, it is important to consider that fatalism is pervasive in *From Hell*, which seemingly represents a complete reversal of attitude compared to *Swamp Thing*. While the latter delved into the archives in order to construct a more durable future for the eponymous character, *From Hell* is a completely fictional rendition of the past that will nevertheless produce a future we all know: in co-operation with the reader, it will construct a version of the fictional entity known as 'Jack the Ripper'. In short, then, the difference between the reader's and Gull's account of the doctor's life is anchored in historicity – our retrospective point of view allows us to refrain from the same catastrophic acts of synthesis that Gull commits. The comic book's 'fatalism', then, should not be confused with authorial pessimism vis-à-vis the human condition in general; rather, *From Hell*'s bleakness is shown to be the product of a dialectical process that, though inevitable for Gull, can still be rejected by his double, the reader.

The only task that remains is to explore the intra-diegetic doubling strategies at work. At the beginning of the chapter, Gull, as a child, utters the wish that God grant him 'a task most difficult' (*From Hell*, II.3.v–vi). Unfortunately, as the biographical narrative makes clear, this wish is not granted. Gull lives a typical middle-class Victorian life predicated on social heteronomy; even his choice of profession, that of a surgeon, is not a choice at all, but is decided upon by another male authority figure (II.6.ii, vi). Small wonder, then, that he later disappointedly exclaims, 'Father, I am almost seventy, and the lord has found me no special task' (II.25.vi). Like Swamp Thing, Gull craves certainty, but the chapter demonstrates that this is impossible to consolidate from the events of his life. The doctor does so anyway. Gull's ambiguous epiphany happens on pages 25 and 26 of 'A state of darkness', where he seems to suffer a stroke. In this moment of physical and mental crisis, all the important male doppelgängers of the chapter appear to him in a vision: first, in panel four, architect Nicholas Hawksmoor; then Gull's father, in panel six; and finally James Hinton, in panel seven, indicating to Gull that he should ascend to the cusp of the hill. It is important to note that Hawksmoor, Gull's father and Hinton represent a highly contradictory set of different ideologies, from the archaic to the patriarchal to the naïvely optimistic.

The apparition of this questionable male trinity points towards an irrational act of synthesis that Gull is about to commit. Indeed, in Chapter 2, page 26, we can see Gull dwarfed in front of yet another trinity, which is Jahbulon, the deity supposedly worshipped by the Freemasons. Jahbulon is introduced on page 17 as three deities shown in separate panels, just as Hinton, Hawksmoor and Gull's father are individualised on the previous page. The unified trinity represented on page 26 is therefore a synthesis of hitherto disparate parts. But it is not just a fusion of the deities' representations. In fact, to Gull, it seems that Jahbulon is largely made up of his father, Hinton and Hawksmoor. He thus makes unified meaning of the disparate and violent male ideologies that he has admired in his life, an act which will result in the Whitechapel murders. Finally, then, his 'task most difficult' has not been bestowed upon him by his father's Christian God, but by a doppelgänger deity he has created himself.

The question is, therefore, which excessive element characterises Gull's three-headed doppelgänger that may then chiasmically be bequeathed upon Gull? Drawing on Walter Benjamin's discussion of 'foundational violence', Quiring argues that *From Hell* represents London as a 'mnemonic device' that 'commemorates that its urban law and order was established by acts beyond the law, namely violent seizures of power'.[35] Gull comes to see himself as a 'builder of heavenly cities' who wants to repeat 'the foundational violence of London town' and thus ritualistically re-establish patriarchy.[36] In this manner, he aims to make use of the violent excess articulated in his doppelgänger relationship with Jahbulon; but Moore and Campbell never tire of pointing out that this plan cannot succeed. The excess of the double does not establish closure, but undoes it; Gull 'doesn't reinvigorate the old law but its sadly parodic mimicry',[37] and thus prefigures similarly catastrophic attempts at repeating foundational violence during the twentieth century, most prominently Hitler's, whose conception is depicted as an omen of the persistence of the double.[38]

The madwoman speaks

There remains one final doubling strategy at work in *From Hell*, which further complicates Moore's negotiations with the Gothic doppelgänger. Quiring hints at this manifestation when he writes that Gull and Moore's 'mission statements and working methods are remarkably similar'.[39]

Moore, in short, doesn't just liken the reader's gaze and cognitive processes to Gull's, but his own as well. The difference between the two figures, as in the case of the audience, lies in historical perspective, but also in the refusal of definitive synthesis.

What does this tell us about Moore's relationship with the Gothic? First of all, the writer's uses of the archive indicate that his authorial attitude is less iconoclastic than restorative. In encountering the ideologically contaminated Gothic permutations of American mainstream comics of the early 1980s, he chooses to return the doppelgänger trope to its former potency. And it is exactly the strength of the original pattern that enables him and his artists to bring out the utopian potential in the respective narratives. To reiterate, we might say that Moore sees the Gothic less as a tradition of mournful loss than as a treasure trove of potentially disruptive tropes to be used to constructive ends. Even the Victorian dystopia of *From Hell* thus gains a potential for renewal, as when the madwoman in Guy's Hospital cries out to Gull: 'Jack, is it you?' (II.11.ix). The question isn't just addressed to Gull, but to the reader as well. Do we dare recognise the similarities? Will we be able to avoid the lure of certainty on our personal quest for identity? Some might consider the bluntness of the inquiry not quite subtle enough. Moore himself might call this final directness, which only *seems* to run counter to the self-reflexive complexity of his narratives, 'cheerily vulgar',[40] a little bit like the Gothic itself.

Notes

1 Dimitris Vardoulakis, 'The Return of Negation: The Doppelgänger in Freud's "The Uncanny"', *Substance*, 110 (2006), 104.
2 Sheridan Le Fanu, 'Carmilla', in *In a Glass Darkly* (Oxford and New York: Oxford University Press, 2008), p. 264.
3 Andrew J. Webber, *The Doppelgänger: Double Visions in German Literature* (Oxford: Clarendon Press, 1996), p. 41.
4 Le Fanu, 'Carmilla', p. 277.
5 *Ibid.*, p. 283.
6 Webber, *Doppelgänger*, p. 14.
7 'So heißen Leute, die sich selber sehen.' Jean Paul, *Siebenkäs* (Berlin: Insel, 1987), p. 67.
8 Webber, *Doppelgänger*, p. 3.
9 'Vorzüglich ... als visuelles Phänomen.' Gerald Bär, *Das Motiv des*

Doppelgängers als Spaltungsphantasie in der Literatur und im deutschen Stummfilm (Amsterdam: Rodopi, 2005), p. 438.
10 Webber, Doppelgänger, p. 9.
11 Ibid., p. 3.
12 Ben Little, '2000AD – Understanding the "British Invasion" of American Comics', in Comics as a Nexus of Cultures: Essays on the Interplay of Media, Disciplines and International Perspective, ed. Mark Berninger, Gideon Haberkorn and Jochen Ecke (Jefferson: McFarland, 2010), p. 146.
13 Tzvetan Todorov, The Fantastic: A Structural Approach to a Literary Genre (Ithaca, NY: Cornell University Press, 1975), p. 25.
14 Ibid., p. 52.
15 Le Fanu, 'Carmilla', p. 317.
16 Webber, Doppelgänger, p. 3.
17 Cf. E.T.A. Hoffmann, Prinzessin Brambilla (Stuttgart: Reclam, 1986 [1820]), p. 17.
18 Webber, Doppelgänger, p. 6.
19 Vardoulakis, 'Return of Negation', p. 104.
20 Ibid., p. 105.
21 Ibid., p. 104.
22 Björn Quiring, '"A Fiction That We Must Inhabit" – Sense Production in Urban Spaces According to Alan Moore and Eddie Campbell's From Hell', in Comics and the City: Urban Space in Print, Picture and Sequence, ed. Jörn Ahrens and Arno Meteling (London: Continuum, 2010), p. 203.
23 Karin Kukkonen, 'Wie im Einstein'schen Universum der Relativität ... bilden die Perspektiven der Figuren Referenzrahmen, mit deren Hilfe sie ihre Welt konstruieren.' Neue Perspektiven auf die Superhelden: Polyphonie in Alan Moores Watchmen (Marburg: Tectum, 2008), p. 14.
24 'Der Dialog mündet in keine überlegene Synthese, ebenso wenig wie Veidts schöne neue Welt nach dem Ost-West-Dualismus in Kapitel XII von Watchmen Bestand haben wird: Rorschachs Tagebuch, das Veidts Plan enthüllt, liegt bereits im Eingangsstapel des "New Frontiersman".' Ibid., p. 17.
25 'Ein Blick auf die interne Dynamik populärer Kultur zeigt, dass v.a. das Strukturprinzip der Serialität nahezu zwangsläufig eine Ästhetik fordert, die ihre eigene Formengeschichte beobachtet und auf diese Weise immer weitere Variationen und Selektionen realisiert.' Daniel Stein and Frank Kelleter, 'Great, Mad, New: Populärkultur, serielle Ästhetik und der frühe amerikanische Zeitungscomics', in Comics: Zur Geschichte und Theorie eines populärkulturellen Mediums, ed. Stephan Ditschke, Katerina Kroucheva and Daniel Stein (Bielefeld: Transcript, 2009), p. 90.
26 Len Wein and Berni Wrightson, 'The Man Who Wanted Forever', Swamp

Thing [First Series], 2 (Jan. 1973); reprinted in Len Wein and Berni Wrightson, *Swamp Thing: Dark Genesis* (New York: DC Comics, 1991), pp. 38–62.

27 Alan Moore, 'Swamp Daze', in *The Extraordinary Works of Alan Moore*, ed. George Khoury (Raleigh, NC: TwoMorrows, 2008), p. 85.

28 Alan Moore, Stephen Bissette and John Totleben, 'The Anatomy Lesson', *Swamp Thing*, 21 (Feb. 1984), 49.

29 Adam Bresnick, 'Prosopoetic Compulsion: Reading the Uncanny in Freud and Hoffmann', *Germanic Review*, 71:2 (1996), 117.

30 For further information, see Scott Beatty et al., *The DC Comics Encyclopaedia: The Definitive Guide to the Characters of the DC Universe* (New York: Dorling Kindersley, 2004), p. 116.

31 Moore, Bissette and Totleben, 'Anatomy Lesson', 38.

32 See Alan Moore and Eddie Campbell, *From Hell: Being a Melodrama in Sixteen Parts* (London: Knockabout Comics, 2006), n.p.: 'This book is dedicated to Polly Nichols, Annie Chapman, Liz Stride, Kate Eddowes, and Marie Jeanette Kelly. You and your demise: of these things alone are we certain'; hereafter cited in the main body of the text.

33 'Correspondence: From Hell', correspondence between Alan Moore and Dave Sim, in *Alan Moore: Portrait of an Extraordinary Gentleman*, ed. Gary Spencer Millidge and Smoky Man (Leigh-on-Sea: Abiogenesis Press, 2003), pp. 303–45 (p. 321).

34 Marc Bernard and James Bucky Carter, 'Alan Moore and the Graphic Novel: Confronting the Fourth Dimension', *ImageTexT: Interdisciplinary Comics Studies*, 1:2 (2004), 20: www.english.ufl.edu//imagetext/archives/v1_2/carter/index.shtml.

35 Quiring, '"Fiction That We Must Inhabit"', p. 200.

36 *Ibid.*, pp. 210, 206.

37 *Ibid.*, p. 211.

38 Moore and Campbell, *From Hell*, V.1–V.3.

39 Quiring, '"Fiction That We Must Inhabit"', p. 210.

40 'The Craft', interview by Daniel Whiston, *Zarjaz*, 1:3–4 (24 May 2003); reprinted by *enginecomics.co.uk* (2005): www.enginecomics.co.uk.

5

'Nothing ever ends': facing the apocalypse in *Watchmen*

Christian W. Schneider

THE END IS NIGH
Life goes on.
Alan Moore and Dave Gibbons, *Watchmen*[1]

The intention was to try and make people feel a little bit uneasy about it.
Alan Moore[2]

Maybe it is all about transgression. According to Fred Botting's well-known definition of Gothic literature, the form is characterised by its inherently transgressive nature, constantly violating any set standard.[3] And if there is one text transgressing limits, breaking into new territory, then it is Alan Moore and Dave Gibbons's graphic novel *Watchmen*. Nominally still a superhero comic, the work subverted and deconstructed most of the genre's rules, creating something groundbreaking. As Douglas Wolk testifies, it was 'obvious from the front cover of the first issue alone ... that *Watchmen* was something revolutionary', with an incredible influence on comics as a medium and as an industry.[4]

Perhaps it is this revolutionary character, turning things upside down, which allows for a starting point to discuss Watchmen in the context of this volume. After all, at first glance, the comic does not follow common Gothic conventions. Obviously, it is Moore's best-known work, arguably his magnum opus. However, regarding the Gothic in his writing, it is not the title that comes to mind first. In contrast to many other of his works illustrated impressively by the chapters in this collection, *Watchmen* does not feature evidently Gothic settings or characters. Obviously, it is not a horror comic like *Swamp Thing* or *From Hell*, but works within the 'diametric opposite' conventions of superhero comics.[5]

Still, this volume demonstrates that there is a myriad of approaches to the Gothic and just as many potential Gothic readings of Moore's work. Given the appropriate perspective, it is certainly possible to comprehend *Watchmen* as a Gothic text. Scholars of the form have done so when extending the Gothic mode to comics, listing *Watchmen* among other Gothic texts and discussing its Gothic features.[6] David Punter thus notes its 'distinctly Gothic feel', presenting a Gothic angle to Moore's work beyond its status as a groundbreaking comic.[7] In identifying the elements responsible for this 'Gothic feel', Punter lists the text's '[s]elf-referentiality, a concern with personal and social terror, the shameless exploitation of the exotic and the disastrous'.[8] Indeed, these formal and thematic aspects indicate Gothic parallels to be found in *Watchmen*. On a structural level, there is Moore's 'tissue of referentiality', his complex assemblage of diverse texts alongside and within each other.[9] This evokes the fragmented Chinese-box structures of Gothic texts, often resembling 'a Frankenstein's monster, assembled out of the bits and pieces of the past'.[10] As *Watchmen* includes references to the past of comics as well as to the entire cultural realm, from Blake to Bob Dylan, Moore's typical tendency towards 'playing in somebody else's sandbox' shows a structural affinity to the Gothic.[11]

The most obvious of these intertextual references are to comics' very own Gothic past – the infamous horror comics of the 1950s, resurrected here in the alternative pirate comics tradition that replaces the superhero genre in Moore's uchronia. This resurgence of the horror comics – in the form of a narrative whose shipwrecked protagonist survives by building a raft from the bodies of his dead shipmates – represents an agonistic contest between traditions that is reflected in *Watchmen*'s own relationship with its precursors, an intertextual struggle that Klock reads in distinctly Gothic terms:

> The absorption of the dead, of tradition, requires a certain process or methodology [...] in order for the corpses of tradition to be properly 'incorporated'. [...] *Watchmen* is very concerned with being able to handle all of the dead it attempts to ingest [...]. It fears that the dead it attempts to handle will overwhelm it, and failing control it will perish, sinking down among them to be judged by a stronger vision above the waves.[12]

Beyond the text's reworking of the comics form, it is telling that in an alternative history in which actual superheroes exist in the world, comics focus on gruesome horror narratives, implying a surprisingly close connection between the genres. Indeed, Moore exposes the Gothic impulse inherent in the superhero genre itself, showing that the heroes' larger-than-life powers can be clearly linked to similar Gothic discourses and further exploring the consequences of this excess. In this respect, Moore's reflexive and more realistic presentation of the superhero parallels the representation of the Gothic hero that emerges in the post-revolutionary context of the 1790s: 'Alienated from society and themselves, Romantic-Gothic heroes undergo the effects of this disillusion, doubting the nature of the powers that consume them, uncertain whether they originate internally or from external forces.'[13] What is more, the moral imperative that compels superheroes to mask themselves and their true identities reflects the typically Gothic notions of the hidden, the unseen and the repressed. Focusing on its potential unsavouriness, Moore explores this notion of living double lives, in a manner that, as Andy W. Smith notes, is suggestive of a typically Gothic duality, and which shows that, in Julia Round's words, a 'Gothic fragmentation of identity is at the basis of . . . the superhero condition'.[14]

In *Watchmen*'s radical genre re-examination, this fragmented identity is far from being whole or wholesome; Rorschach, the most damaged character, notes rather hypocritically: 'Why are so few of us left active, healthy, and without personality disorders?' (I.19.iii). Progressing sociopathy, sadist tendencies, megalomania – the obvious psychological deficiencies among Moore's so-called superheroes are impressive, and indeed rather Gothic. Many of these problems have a disturbing sexual bent, the masks hiding – or embodying – assorted 'deviancies', sadism, fetishism and homosexuality.[15]

Still, the question remains whether these parallels justify the inclusion of *Watchmen* in a Gothic canon of graphic novels. While they are crucial in viewing the text as Gothic, they do not capture the essential factor identified by Punter, its overall Gothic feeling. Trying to grasp *Watchmen*'s 'feel', it is best to consult an approach to the Gothic which takes this factor into account, focusing on how a text's specifically Gothic atmosphere is created and conveyed to its audience. One can find this focus in Chris Baldick's often-quoted definition of the Gothic: 'for the Gothic effect to be attained, a tale should combine a fearful sense of inheritance in time with a claustrophobic sense of enclosure in space, these two dimensions reinforcing one another to produce an impression of sickening descent into disintegration.'[16] Baldick's formula provides us with a working definition of the Gothic, although his categories are too specific. Assuming a 'claustrophobic sense of enclosure in space' is not entirely appropriate, since Gothic texts are just as often characterised by spatial representations of infinity and greatness, the very opposite of enclosure, whether in *Frankenstein*'s impressive landscapes or the edificial grandeur of Otranto. Still, these situations account for a similar effect in the individual confronted with them – a feeling of being overwhelmed. The key feature of Gothic space is that it is unmappable for those trying to navigate it, filling them with confusion and helplessness. The same is true for the temporal component of Baldick's definition. While Gothic horror is indeed mostly connected to a threatening past, an unavoidable future can be just as dismaying; the significant aspect is the overall fearful effect of the temporal situation.

With these modifications, Baldick's definition suggests how the 'Gothic effect' – its feel – is created by texts. It emphasises the importance of the spatio-temporal dimensions constructed by the text and the specific situation of the individual within them. Furthermore, Baldick stresses the effect this situation has on the characters – and, in turn, on the readers. Constrained by the influence of space and time, one loses all control over oneself; this loss of control is the source of a Gothic text's atmosphere. Whether it means being overwhelmed by excessive passion, transfixed by a horrible spectacle, lost in inescapable dungeons or haunted by an alien presence – losing control, not being master of one's body and soul, is a topic surfacing repeatedly in Gothic texts, and may well be seen as a basic condition at the form's core. This loss of control has been a constituent feature of the genre since its inception, and is linked to Edmund Burke's location of the anticipation of a certain self-annihilation at the heart of the sublime via an encounter with the overwhelming transcendence of God's 'great and tremendous Being'.[17] While, on reflection, this divine omnipotence is tempered with the Christian virtues of mercy and compassion, its immediate effect is one of trepidation, for when confronted with the irrefutable proof of such power, 'we [...] are, in a manner, annihilated'.[18] In Burke's view, 'the sublime is a negative experience because it reinforces feelings of transience (our passing) and insignificance (our smallness)'.[19]

Nevertheless, as the sublime's ambivalence suggests, not all Gothic texts adhere fully to this patently negative notion, often depicting the individual overcoming or escaping his or her constrained position. However, the paradigmatic model of a Gothic world, in which the spatio-temporal environment severely undermines the subject's perception, knowledge and autonomy in general, can be applied to even more optimistic Gothic narratives and is ultimately responsible for the distinctly Gothic effect. This anxiety becomes more acute as the reassertion of divine harmony is withdrawn from the genre, leaving in its stead not only the Gothic's violent motifs and abject imagery, but also a collection of fragmented structures, whose gaps, ambiguities and repetitions disorientate and frustrate the reader, mirroring the characters' helplessness.[20] Here, the loss of control eventually becomes a loss of meaning – in the end, there is no regulative centre, no God. Indeed, while much early Gothic fiction invokes a divine order, depicting the apparent triumph of justice and stability over satanic turmoil, these happy endings often appear as no more than 'thin excuses'.[21] Uncertainty and unease are essential to the genre, and Andrew Smith notes that 'always in the Gothic, ambivalence is the central issue'.[22] With this all-encompassing uncertainty pervading every aspect of the text, the prototypical Gothic environments express a world-view that is not so much pessimistic as nihilistic, because all meaning remains provisional and uncertified.

This world-view is at the heart of *Watchmen*. At the narrative's outset, the reader is confronted with Rorschach's horrific vision of chaos overwhelming order. As the text progresses, this apocalyptic vision is linked to the vigilante's inability to extricate himself from a system of moral absolutism, but even in the opening lines it is clear that Rorschach's air of authority is tied to his attempt to assume a godlike perspective: 'Now the whole world stands on the brink, staring down into bloody hell, all those liberals and intellectuals and smooth-talkers . . . / . . . and all of a sudden, nobody can think of anything to say' (I.1.vi). In a way, this statement echoes the Gothic's challenge to an optimistic Enlightenment teleology, even as it anticipates the arrogance of the anti-hero Adrian Veidt. Rorschach's mental stability is questionable, but his aggressive nihilism has a point. Indeed, 'Moore presents nihilism as a psychological state shared by almost all the heroes in *Watchmen*.'[23] This attitude is hardly surprising, considering the circumstances with which the characters are confronted; 'nihilism is a natural fall-back position' in the world Moore and Gibbons construct, and all characters have to come to terms with it.[24] Watchmen's world is bleak, with its glaringly negative sides exposed, full of brutality, debauchery, urban decay and drug-fuelled gang delinquency; ultimately, it is not worth saving.[25] Its chaos, unfairness and viciousness drive Rorschach over the brink, into insanity and extreme nihilism. In a highly effective speech, he describes his dark epiphany to Malcolm Long, his attending psychologist:

> Looked at sky through smoke heavy with human fat and God was not there.
> The cold, suffocating dark goes on forever, and we are alone [.]
> Live our lives, lacking anything better to do. Devise reason later.
> Born from oblivion; bear children, hell-bound as ourselves; go into Oblivion.
> There is nothing else.
> Existence is random. Has no pattern save what we imagine after staring at it too long.
> No meaning save what we choose to impose. (VI.26.ii–iv)

Rorschach's nihilism is unsettling in its deranged rigidity, but its clarity is quite alluring.[26] It certainly affects Long, confronting him with the ugly side of human existence – not only the revulsion of death and violence, 'the fat, glistening grubs writhing blindly, squirming over each other', but facing a nihilistic horror: 'in the end, it is simply a picture of empty meaningless blackness. / We are alone. / There is nothing else' (VI.28.v–vii).

This declaration of futile existence in a meaningless world is shaped less by the cruelties and sufferings of life than by its imminent end. It becomes clear that a manmade apocalypse may have become unavoidable, since the danger of a nuclear war between the USA and the USSR becomes increasingly certain. In Watchmen's 1980s mindset, the logic of the Cold War's nuclear arms race is re-created within the context of superhero comics; Judgement Day could happen at any moment, as every character, superhero or not, realises. This is the prevalent trait of Watchmen's world; its 'overarching metaphor [...] is nuclear eschatology'.[27] More than any individual suffering, this apocalyptic situation causes a fundamentally pessimist outlook. The unavoidability of humanity's demise cannot seem to be altered or stopped, its devilish mechanisms removed from the sphere of human influence. Indeed, there is something distinctly mechanical about its unswerving advance; as Rorschach remarks, 'the future is bearing down like an express train', a statement pointedly accompanied by the image of a burning map of the USA (II.26.vii). Inescapably, the future will bring destruction, after which there will be no future.

This gloomy situation also traps the superheroes of *Watchmen* in its inexorability. According to the expectations of the genre, they are the world's saviours; yet, they cannot alter its fate either. Ultimately, they are in no better position than the rest of humanity, neither on a moral nor on an authoritative level. Indeed, it is striking how much Rorschach, Dr Manhattan and Ozymandias go beyond traditional superhero types and resemble the archetypal Gothic villain as filtered through the iconography of Lord Byron: 'arrogant, contemptuous of human beings, bad-tempered, overbearing, cold, ruthless, and emotionless'.[28] They are bound to fail in their transgressive hubris, no matter how powerful they are. In the case of superhuman Dr Manhattan, this notion is particularly pronounced; he is repeatedly described as a godlike being, seemingly all-powerful and all-knowing, triggering a 'feeling of intense and crushing religious terror' – in other words, a feeling of the sublime ('Dr Manhattan: Super-powers and the Superpowers', in *Watchmen*, p. 2). However, even he must acknowledge: 'We're all puppets, Laurie. I'm just a puppet who can see the strings' (IX.5.iv). He is 'paradoxically the most ineffectual' character, still helpless against the world's destructive course.[29] In the end, he is not God, and there is no other in *Watchmen*'s universe.

Discussing Grant Morrison's *The Invisibles*, Punter and Byron observe that 'like any Gothic hero, the protagonists are doomed by forces beyond their control, and even their self-awareness and scepticism cannot help them to escape from the horror of their position'.[30] This apt comment is even more applicable to *Watchmen*'s so-called superheroes; as Moore confirms, they are 'not in control of their world'.[31] Despite having literally world-changing abilities, they are trapped in a position of helplessness and despair. As Geoff Klock notes, 'Moore revives the horror comic book within the superhero comic book', not only by including *Tales of the Black Freighter*, but by portraying heroes that are similarly helpless within a horrific world.[32]

What becomes clear in examining the heroes' powerlessness in *Watchmen* is the role of time. Presenting the future as unavoidable presupposes a notion of time as unchangeable. This is best expressed in Dr Manhattan's warped perspective, where past, present and future exist simultaneously. From this position, time becomes preordained, denying the possibility of influencing one's fate: 'I can't prevent the future. To me, it's already happening' (IV.16.ii). Here, one can reflect again on the significance of the temporal for the Gothic; however, despite the importance of the past, it is principally the future exerting its influence in *Watchmen*. This is a key feature of one of the Gothic's most vigorous offshoots, science fiction, which as Botting notes has, since the work of H.G. Wells, departed from many of the uncanny devices from its parent tradition: 'while the irruption of terror from the past served as a way to evoke emotions that reconstituted human values, the future only presents a dark, unknown space from which horrors are visited'.[33] Even Dr Manhattan finds himself unable to obtain a clear vision of the future beyond vague impressions of a post-apocalyptic world – 'There are streets full of corpses. The details are vague' – such that the most powerful being in the world finds himself limited by obscurity and uncertainty: 'There's some sort of static obscuring the future, preventing any clear impression' (IX.17.ii, iii). Time inhibits the individual's possibilities in a truly Gothic way and the protagonists are trapped within the more abstract dungeons of history rather than in any spatial way, a notion fitting into Moore's often-formulated concept of the architecture of history.[34] In this arrangement, structures beyond human control – the logic of the nuclear arms race and the machinations of Ozymandias – progress as inevitably as time itself. Humanity is deprived of its autonomy, left with a nihilistic outlook on a world doomed for destruction.

This temporal confinement of *Watchmen*'s Gothic world is also represented formally, conveying its gloomy effect to the audience. Supported by Dave Gibbons's art, Moore's panel organisation emphasises and expands on the narrative; Thierry Groensteen is correct to state that 'everything in this work is sacrificed to the imperialism of an overwritten and minutely arranged story'.[35] The most obvious structure is the strict panel grid, a staple technique of Moore's comics. Most pages are subject to a matrix of 3 X 3 panels, with the larger panels also conforming to these preset measurements. This rigid structuring of the comic is a 'simple and striking way of organizing things from the view of perception'.[36] However, its effect on the reading experience 'can be almost stifling' – and that may be exactly the point.[37]

Watchmen's structural rigour distinctly lacks playfulness; Martin

Schüwer considers Moore's invariant panel structure downright merciless, presenting the reader with an inflexible system, simultaneously aiding and inhibiting their processing of the narrative.[38] This is mirrored by the characters' actions, which are also restrained by the limited action space within the layout. A striking example is the end of Chapter 5, when Rorschach is the victim of a set-up and is captured. Desperately muttering 'Been framed' (V.28.i–iii), he is right on more than one level – he has been framed from the beginning of the story within the unyielding structure of the panels.

What is even more important, however, is the temporal component of *Watchmen*'s page layouts, whose arrangements communicate the Gothic notion of time. Here, the medium's singular possibilities of expression emerge. Its basic units of communication, the panels, always express a temporal state, a certain situation in time. Generally, this is more complicated than simply presenting a clear-cut moment.[39] Various variables, the site, size and form of panels in restricted and general arthrology, give us cues regarding the temporal structure of the narrative world – albeit always as spatialised sections on a page.[40] As Scott McCloud states: 'in learning to read comics, we all learned to perceive time *spatially*, for in the world of comics, *time* and *space* are *one and the same*'.[41] This links seamlessly to our observations about the spatio-temporal interaction in creating the Gothic effect. There is no better medium to express Gothic confinement than the complex structuring of time on the comic page. In *Watchmen*'s case, its regular page layout presents a tight and persistent notion of time. 'Panels tick by like a metronome or a timebomb, counting down to midnight', substantiating the image of an unavoidable future.[42] There is no escape from this temporal grid, no ending the apocalyptic countdown. Just as within the textual world, there is no other course to follow, just the rigid progression predetermined by the panels' sequence.

Watchmen's regular page layout fosters further structural intricacies, as it 'strengthens the bonds between predetermined locations' within the panel system.[43] One strategy taking advantage of this is Moore's impressive use of structural symmetries.[44] Most prominent here is Chapter 5, whose completely symmetrical organisation is ordered around an astonishing central panel spanning two pages (V.14.iv–5.i). This formal symmetry again has an air of rigidity, of structure dominating characters.[45] It also creates a moment of ambivalence, in a literal

Facing the apocalypse in Watchmen

sense, connecting different sides in a common structure.[46] Ultimately, opposing principles, good and evil, hero and villain, justice and injustice, are associated and blended – ambiguity on yet another level, similar to the Gothic's often ambivalent ethics.[47]

Yet, Moore's structural intricacy does not stop there; it also interacts with the content of the panels. Much has been made of Moore's tightly spun web of references within the text, the keyword being 'tight'. Groensteen talks about *Watchmen*'s use of intratextual 'braiding'.[48] As he points out, the recurrence of certain iconographic motifs 'at essential moments in the story and/or naturally privileged sites by the book' is 'accompanied with a considerable symbolic richness'.[49] As an example, Groensteen mentions the recurring image of the circle and its 'symbolic connotations (perfection, eternal recommencement, etc.)'.[50] It is particularly prominent in the frequent appearances of the doomsday clock, a perfect illustration for time running out, and the associated smiley face. Another common symbol is the silhouette of the 'Hiroshima lovers', again an image of both symmetry and doom, repeated and linked to other symbolically charged motifs of symmetry (VI.27.iii). With all these connections, a close-knit structural network is generated, implying a 'palpable sense of suffocation';[51] the system constructed exists beyond the mere action sequence and therefore beyond the protagonists' sphere of influence.[52] While this structure is more about thematic configurations, the recurring images have symbolic connections to the notion of apocalypse.

In general, Moore and Gibbons's intricate form directs the reader's attention to the comic's structural configuration and its trans-sequential levels of communication. In order to describe such configurations, Martin Schüwer takes up Gilles Deleuze's concepts of the movement-image and the time-image. While the former is based on a rather conventional sequence of perception, affect and (re-)action,[53] the latter is expressed in more complex structures, pointing towards a notion of time existing beyond measurable and perceivable temporal succession.[54] Applied to the medium of comics, the movement-image is primarily realised in Groensteen's restricted arthrology; the panel sequence is easily processed by the reader, focusing on the content. The time-image, in contrast, surfaces whenever the reader pays attention to anything beyond the mere sequence, the structures and connections of Groensteen's general arthrology. Basically, Moore's trans-sequential arrangements can be seen as formal representations of the time-image, establishing a world beyond sequential action.

This notion can be connected to *Watchmen*'s Gothic feel. In visualising trans-sequential structures, Moore illustrates how the fates of the protagonists are shaped and influenced by configurations beyond their sphere of influence, invisible to them. Traditionally, superhero comics are very much dominated by clear-cut action sequences, allowing the protagonists to use their powers to perceive, act and react, while their actions have direct consequences, altering and advancing the plot. In *Watchmen*, however, the heroes are not in a position of control; they must subject themselves to the rule of time, mercilessly leading them and the rest of humanity towards the apocalypse. In the end, the comic evinces a prototypically Gothic bleakness, expressed thematically as well as formally.

And yet – this is not the end of it all. *Watchmen*'s complexity does support several readings since 'the meanings of almost every word, image, panel, and page are multiple – *obviously* multiple'.[55] This semantic polyvalence practically obliges the recipient to reread the text, deciphering new and often coexisting meanings. Nothing is simple in the world of *Watchmen*, not even the seemingly inescapable end of that world.

As demonstrated, the notion of catastrophe is central to the comic; but its evaluation and consequences are presented more ambivalently, starting with the ambiguous morality of Ozymandias's master plan. In a sense, he is the narrative's villain, his secret plan responsible for the death and pain of literally millions of people. Yet, at the same time, he is the one superhero who actually has some bearing on the world's fate – and can be seen as its saviour.[56] After all, he may have succeeded: the apocalypse might not take place. Obviously, there is a horrible catastrophe, shown with unflinching grimness (XII.1–6). However, this is not the end of the world; humanity survives and life goes on. 'Nothing ever ends', as Dr Manhattan tells Ozymandias, a highly programmatic judgement (XII.27.v). The image of the apocalyptic future bearing down on humanity without mercy might be not as fitting as previously thought.

This continuation beyond the apparent end is certainly not definite, and not a genuinely positive idea either. On the one hand, 'mankind might be faced with the intimidating prospect of dealing with a future', with yet another chance to fill the world with cruelty and unfairness.[57] On the other hand, the apocalypse is not averted beyond all doubt, as the very last page of *Watchmen* shows; it may only have been postponed. As Peter Paik remarks, Ozymandias's very name, 'in recalling Shelley's famous poem, unavoidably pronounces the ultimate futility of any human undertaking'.[58] However, in the very end, humanity's fate is no longer out of its hands. Ultimately, despite many limitations, human responsibility and control are affirmed by Moore. This is typical for his writing: 'if there is a central theme in Alan Moore's work, it is the appeal to the affirmation of the individual and individual responsibility. Taking full responsibility for their actions, including both successes and failures, nothing can stop individuals in their process of discovery, of their own identity and universal dimension.'[59] This notion is best expressed in *Watchmen*'s very last words, 'I leave it entirely in your hands' (XII.32.vii), another programmatic message. In any case, the final interpretation is entirely up to the readers.[60] This 'disconcerting openness' embodies the Gothic ambivalence of the text, denoting a lack of certainty and stability.[61] However, it is not the uncertainty of pessimism; in the face of bleak and seemingly inevitable doom, it is the uncertainty of hope.

In *Watchmen*'s narrative, the 'thermo-dynamic miracle' of human life proves to be full of possibilities (IX.27.i). Regardless of its deviousness, humanity is also capable of compassion, which is exemplified by Malcolm Long, whose marital difficulties stem from his inability to turn a blind eye to human suffering; Seymour, whose ketchup-stained hands hold the fate of the world; Bernie, the newspaper seller, trying to protect the boy next to him in the face of certain death (XI.28.vii–xii). Like them, every human being is, in Moore's own words, 'fantastic in what they can do and what they can be. [. . .] *That* is heroism.'[62] Despite its powerlessness, humanity can reclaim a modicum of control.

Although it seems paradoxical, one can reconcile these cautiously optimistic observations with the bleak picture painted before, the distinctly Gothic world-view without hope or trust in human agency. Indeed, there is one thing in *Watchmen*'s world still beyond humanity's influence: the inevitability of change. Humankind may be able to affect what the future holds in store, but it cannot prevent the future from happening. All things must change, which is not always a peaceful affair; the 'idea of change and clearing away the past often takes violent forms in *Watchmen*, but the effects can be seen as positive'.[63] To open up new ways and overcome the past, its prison walls have to be destroyed, however painful this might be.

Again, this notion is expressed formally. Despite the noted rigidity of Moore's page layouts, its regularity also leaves the 'possibility of sudden and spectacular ruptures from the initially given norm'.[64] Most panels breaking out from the grid depict acts of violence; Ozymandias's spectacular incapacitation of his would-be attacker in Chapter 5, or the first pages of the last chapter, detailing death and destruction after New York has been attacked. Disturbing the rigidity of the panel structure shows that the seemingly inexorable temporal construction is not indestructible; there is no unavoidable end, there will be a future, even if it requires the violent destruction of existing structures.

What becomes clear is that *Watchmen*'s ambivalent outlook on the world and its fate stretches beyond the text itself; the reader is intrinsically linked to the textual world, its ultimate constructor and addressee. Just like its Gothic atmosphere, *Watchmen*'s message of change and cautious optimism is structured to have a distinct effect on its recipient. As Mark Bernard and James Carter rightly remark: 'Moore's work with the fourth dimension and the space-time continuum is stimulating and empowering for his audience, but Moore can also use this aspect of sequential storytelling to shock and frighten his readers in new and unique ways.'[65] The empowerment mentioned is connected to the comic's ambivalence, forcing the readers to generate their own meaning from the multitude of impressions. Reading a comics page, its recipient has to master both sequence and synchronicity, experiencing the textual world beyond the limited sequential possibilities and perceptions of the characters. Despite Moore's regular panels ticking away, the reader is ultimately in control of the whole text, able to see several layers and to reread. Bernard and Carter have compared this to Dr Manhattan's position, describing him as 'a metaphor for ... the graphic novel experience'.[66] However, our power not only to perceive but to construct the comic's world freely makes us even more powerful, an empowerment generated by Moore's structuring.

These observations still leave us with a paradox: a graphic novel constructing a pessimistic Gothic world-view on several levels but subverting its own bleakness by allowing substantial instances of optimism and empowerment to subvert its atmosphere. We have already hinted at one way to grasp this paradox, the notion of change and its often radical consequences. This seems to be a fruitful path of thinking, which becomes even more convincing if one regards not only the text but also its cultural context, in this case, the context of 1980s graphic novels, with *Watchmen* as one of its foremost representatives.

Not only did many works at the time introduce sex, grim violence and controversial political issues into the often decisively naïve mainstream, but this thematic revolution also caused 'major institutional changes to the production, reception and marketing of comics for "mature readers"'.[67] In this framework, *Watchmen*'s often bleak outlook on the world can be understood not only in the context of the Cold War, but also from the perspective of the medium. Correspondingly, Julia Round remarks how *Watchmen* 'can be read as an extended metaphor for the failure of the comics industry to grow with and sustain the genre'.[68] Thus, Moore's message of the brutal inevitability of change is even more pointed from a contextual angle. Trying to counteract the stagnancy of superhero comics, Moore's uchronia introduces the notion of time into a notoriously unalterable world, showing us ageing and failing heroes, whose golden age lies in the past.[69] On yet another level, the importance of time in *Watchmen* is highlighted. The often horrifying implications of temporal rigidity can be easily interpreted as a message to the comic readers: you might not like it, but the times are changing.

In the context of this change, it is also possible to examine *Watchmen*'s Gothic ambivalence, which is not uncommon for graphic novels of the time. Abraham Kawa notes that Moore's ambiguous attitude was shared by other 1980s comic creators, using 'near-apocalyptic narratives' which 'end with a glimmer of hope for the future or, at least, an ambivalence as to whether Armageddon is coming'.[70] He also links this observation to the industry changes at the time, as 'creators were willing to use this new-found freedom with cultural signs to move away from pessimistic eschatology and into stories stressing the possibility of rebirth for the human race'.[71] The Gothic traits we observed are connected to the notion of thematic change, introducing provoking and therefore more 'adult' topics and motifs into a superhero setting, an act of unsettling Gothic inversion.

Yet, Moore and other graphic novelists of the 1980s did not want to terminate the medium, not even the superhero genre; as Kawa says, 'we never reach the end of everything'.[72] Ultimately, they aimed at renewing comics and widening their horizon; simply propagating a vision of bleakness would not do that. Hence, there is, however hesitant, optimism and hope regarding the future, for both the world of *Watchmen* and the comics world in general. In the end, one can argue that the Gothic traits revealed are Moore's way of helping the medium grow up, paradoxically turning to a form as historically maligned as comic books themselves. Thus, true to *Watchmen*'s message that nothing ends, we are back at the beginning, looking at the notion of transgressing standards – however, transgression beyond a bleak state of stagnation and negation, as Moore and Gibbons have cleared the path for new possibilities across the medium.

Notes

1 Alan Moore and Dave Gibbons, *Watchmen* (New York: DC Comics, 2005), II.2.iv; hereafter cited in the main body of the text.
2 Alan Moore, 'A Portal to Another Dimension', Alan Moore and Dave Gibbons interviewed by Neil Gaiman, *Comics Journal*, 116 (July 1987), 80–7 (p. 83); reprinted in *The New Comics: Interviews from the Pages of* The Comics Journal, ed. Gary Groth and Robert Fiore (New York: Berkley, 1988).
3 Fred Botting, *Gothic* (London: Routledge, 1996), pp. 6–8.
4 Douglas Wolk, *Reading Comics: How Graphic Novels Work and What They Mean* (Cambridge, MA: Da Capo Press, 2007), p. 236.
5 Geoff Klock, *How to Read Superhero Comics and Why* (New York: Continuum, 2002), p. 74.
6 See David Punter and Glennis Byron, *The Gothic* (Oxford: Blackwell, 2004), pp. xvii, 71–2; David Punter, *The Literature of Terror: A History of Gothic Fictions from 1765 to the Present Day*, 2nd edn, 2 vols (New York: Longman, 1996), II, pp. 147–8 and Andrew Smith, *Gothic Literature* (Edinburgh: Edinburgh University Press, 2007), p. xxiii.
7 Punter, *Literature of Terror*, II, p. 148.
8 Ibid., p. 147.
9 Ibid.
10 Maggie Kilgour, *The Rise of the Gothic Novel* (London: Routledge, 1995), p. 4.
11 Wolk, *Reading Comics*, p. 230. Here, Julia Round's concept of superscription – an intramedial form of intertextuality and a structural Gothic element of many graphic novels – applies; see Julia Round, 'Fragmented Identity: The Superhero Condition', *International Journal of Comic Art*, 7:2 (2005), 358–69.
12 Klock, *Superhero Comics*, p. 70.

13　Botting, *Gothic*, p. 93.
14　Andy W. Smith, 'Gothic and the Graphic Novel', in *The Routledge Companion to Gothic*, ed. Catherine Spooner and Emma McEvoy (London: Routledge, 2007), pp. 251–9 (p. 253) and Julia Round, 'Fragmented Identity', p. 366.
15　In the predominantly heterosexual world of superhero comics of the time, the suggestion that such figures might harbour non-normative sexual preferences retains a counter-hegemonic charge. Nevertheless, homoeroticism has been a constant companion of the medium since its inception, as for example in the relationship between Batman and Robin (for further discussion, see Chapter 8 below). In this respect, Moore finds himself working within a tradition that is tied to the hegemonic framework in a manner strikingly similar to that found in Gothic fiction, which 'often reproduces the conventional paranoid structure of homophobia and other moral panics over sex, and yet [. . .] can also be a raucous site of sexual transgression and excess that undermines its own narrative efforts at erotic containment'; Ellis Hanson, 'Queer Gothic', in *The Routledge Companion to Gothic*, ed. Catherine Spooner and Emma McEvoy (London: Routledge, 2007), pp. 174–82 (p. 176). While Superhero comics are nevertheless more muted than much Gothic fiction in this respect, it is notable that shortly after completion of *Watchmen*, Moore himself mobilised a number of the key writers and artists in mainstream and alternative comics to protest against institutionalised homophobia and celebrate the diversity of human sexuality; see Alan Moore et al., *AARGH!* [Artists Against Rampant Government Homophobia] (Northampton: Mad Love, 1988). Moore's contribution, together with an introduction outlining the political context of *AARGH!*, has been reprinted with illustrations by José Villarrubia as *The Mirror of Love*, intro. David Drake (Atlanta, GA: Top Shelf, 2004).
16　Chris Baldick, 'Introduction', in *The Oxford Book of Gothic Tales*, ed. Chris Baldick (Oxford: Oxford University Press, 1992), pp. xi–xxiii (p. xix).
17　Edmund Burke, *A Philosophical Enquiry into the Origin of Our Ideas of the Sublime and Beautiful: With an Introductory Discourse Concerning Taste, and Several Other Additions*, new edn (London: J. Dodsley, 1787), p. 117. The influences and occurrences of Burke's notions of the sublime within Gothic literature are well documented; see e.g. Smith, *Gothic Literature*, pp. 10–13.
18　Burke, *Philosophical Enquiry*, p. 119.
19　Smith, *Gothic Literature*, p. 12.
20　For further discussion see William Patrick Day, *In the Circles of Fear and Desire: A Study of Gothic Fantasy* (Chicago: University of Chicago Press, 1985), p. 43.
21　Botting, *Gothic*, p. 8.

22 Smith, *Gothic Literature*, p. 68.
23 Iain Thomson, 'Deconstructing the Hero', in *Comics as Philosophy*, ed. Jeff McLaughlin (Jackson: University Press of Mississippi, 2005), pp. 100–29 (p. 108).
24 *Ibid*. For an analysis of the characters' nihilistic positions, see J. Keeping, 'Superheroes and Supermen: Finding Nietzsche's Übermensch in *Watchmen*', in *Watchmen and Philosophy: A Rorschach Test*, ed. Mark D. White (Hoboken, NJ: Wiley, 2009), pp. 47–60.
25 Wolk, *Reading Comics*, p. 240.
26 Moore has lamented Rorschach's popularity: 'an awful lot of comics readers felt his remorseless, frightening, psychotic toughness was his most appealing characteristic – not quite what I was going for'; quoted in Jeff Jensen, 'Watchmen: An Oral History', *EntertainmentWeekly: EW.com* (21 Oct. 2005): www.ew.com/ew/article/0,,1120854_1,00.html.
27 Wolk, *Reading Comics*, p. 244.
28 Atara Stein, *The Byronic Hero in Film, Fiction, and Television* (Carbondale: Southern Illinois University Press, 2004), p. 2.
29 Keeping, 'Superheroes and Supermen', p. 57.
30 Punter and Byron, *Gothic*, p. 75.
31 Alan Moore, 'Portal to Another Dimension', p. 85.
32 Klock, *Superhero Comics*, p. 74.
33 Botting, *Gothic*, p. 163.
34 Alan Moore and Eddie Campbell, *From Hell: Being a Melodrama in Sixteen Parts* (London: Knockabout Comics, 2006), II.1.viii.
35 Thierry Groensteen, *The System of Comics*, trans. Bart Beaty and Nick Nguyen (Jackson: University Press of Mississippi, 2007), p. 100.
36 *Ibid.*, p. 97.
37 Wolk, *Reading Comics*, p. 234.
38 Martin Schüwer, *Wie Comics erzählen: Grundriss einer intermedialen Erzähltheorie der grafischen Literatur* (Trier: WVT, 2008), p. 220.
39 Scott McCloud, *Understanding Comics: The Invisible Art* (New York: HarperCollins, 1994), pp. 94–117.
40 Groensteen, *System of Comics*, p. 22. Groensteen's concept of arthrology includes the relations between panels in a linear sequence (restricted arthrology) and between panels in the whole of a page or even text (general arthrology).
41 McCloud, *Understanding Comics*, p. 100.
42 Paul Gravett, *Graphic Novels: Stories to Change Your Life* (London: Aurum, 2005), p. 82.
43 Groensteen, *System of Comics*, p. 97.
44 Wolk, *Reading Comics*, pp. 237–8.

45 The idea of a symmetrical order delimiting the individual harks back to William Blake's ideas, one of various connections between Blake's and Moore's work; see Roger Whitson, 'Panelling Parallax: The Fearful Symmetry of Alan Moore and William Blake', *ImageTexT: Interdisciplinary Comics Studies*, 3:2 (2007): www.english.ufl.edu/imagetext/archives/v3_2/whitson/.
46 Groensteen, *System of Comics*, p. 100.
47 Botting, *Gothic*, p. 9.
48 Groensteen, *System of Comics*, p. 22.
49 *Ibid.*, p. 155.
50 Ibid.
51 Peter Y. Paik, *From Utopia to Apocalypse: Science Fiction and the Politics of Catastrophe* (Minneapolis: University of Minnesota Press, 2010), p. 50.
52 Schüwer, *Wie Comics erzählen*, p. 248. Schüwer calls this, following Deleuze, world-memory; see Gilles Deleuze, *Cinema 2: The Time Image*, trans. Hugh Tomlinson and Robert Galeta (London: Athlone, 1989), p. 98.
53 Schüwer, *Wie Comics Erzählen*, pp. 201–3.
54 *Ibid.*, p. 210.
55 Thomson, 'Deconstructing the Hero', p. 103.
56 Paik, *Utopia to Apocalypse*, p. 36.
57 Abraham Kawa, 'What if the Apocalypse Never Happens?: Evolutionary Narratives in Contemporary Comics', in *Comics & Culture: Analytical and Theoretical Approaches to Comics*, ed. Anne Magnussen and Hans-Christian Christiansen (Copenhagen: Museum Tusculanum Press, 2000), pp. 209–24 (p. 211).
58 Paik, *Utopia to Apocalypse*, p. 36.
59 Pedro Mota, 'Alan on the Other Side of the Mirror', in *Alan Moore: Portrait of an Extraordinary Gentleman*, ed. Gary Spencer Millidge and Smoky Man (Leigh-on-Sea: Abiogenesis, 2003), p. 34.
60 Jeffrey Lewis, 'The Dual Nature of Apocalypse in *Watchmen*', in *The Graphic Novel*, ed. Jan Baetens (Leuven: Leuven University Press, 2001), pp. 139–43 (p. 143).
61 Paik, *Utopia to Apocalypse*, p. 35.
62 Alan Moore, in The *Extraordinary Works of Alan Moore: Indispensable Edition*, ed. George Khoury (Raleigh, NC: TwoMorrows, 2008), p. 119.
63 Lewis, 'Dual Nature of Apocalypse', p. 140.
64 Groensteen, *System of Comics*, p. 97.
65 Mark Bernard and James Bucky Carter, 'Alan Moore and the Graphic Novel: Confronting the Fourth Dimension', *ImageTexT: Interdisciplinary Comics Studies*, 1:2 (2004), 21: www.english.ufl.edu/imagetext/archives/v1_2/carter/.
66 *Ibid.*, p. 20.

67 Smith, 'Gothic and the Graphic Novel', p. 256.
68 Round, 'Fragmented Identity', p. 364.
69 Gravett, *Graphic Novels*, p. 77.
70 Kawa, 'What if the Apocalypse Never Happens?', p. 210.
71 *Ibid*.
72 *Ibid.*, p. 216.

6

Gothic liminality in *V for Vendetta*

Markus Oppolzer

Alan Moore and David Lloyd's *V for Vendetta* is not a Gothic novel – at least, if one were to rely on the ubiquitous 'narrative props' or 'stock features' that characterise the genre's early wave (1764–1820).[1] On the contrary, this graphic novel can best be described as a rich intertextual web that combines features of several different genres and engages with so many works of art, both explicitly and implicitly, that a neat label for this formal and literary experiment seems hard to come by. Lance Parkin praises the elusiveness of the work's genre affiliation, calling it 'a detective story, a futuristic thriller, an action adventure and a depiction of an ideological struggle'.[2] Most critics agree that it represents a dystopian science fiction novel in the tradition of Aldous Huxley's *Brave New World*, George Orwell's *1984* or Ray Bradbury's *Fahrenheit 451*, using a futuristic setting to comment on contemporary events, specifically Britain under Margaret Thatcher's government in the 1980s.[3] Within comics studies, *V for Vendetta* can be understood as 'an unconventional approach to the costumed superhero comic',[4] both in formal and conceptual terms. It dissolves the strict dichotomy of hero and villain which became a trademark of Moore's work in the 1980s. In 'Behind the Painted Smile' Moore explicitly names the *Batman* comics as the most relevant intertexts within the medium itself,[5] a title in which hero and villains are uncannily alike.

It is precisely this proximity to superhero comics that offers an ideal entrance point for a discussion of Gothic concerns in *V for Vendetta*. Both genres focus on traumatised characters who are forced – or choose – to act outside the law. Incarcerated in a concentration camp, stripped of his former identity, and subjected to medical experiments, V, the eponymous hero, is transformed into a superhero by this outrageous crime, committed and kept secret by the totalitarian state. The sins of the past begin to haunt the present in the person of V himself.[6]

This move to take the law into one's own hands is predicated on a deep mistrust of the authorities' ability to deal adequately with the misery suffered by individuals, especially if the law sides with the culprits. William Godwin's *Caleb Williams* and the creature's predicament in Mary Shelley's *Frankenstein* are interesting case studies of this moral ambiguity within early Gothic narratives. Feeling betrayed and abandoned by their 'fathers', they seek redemption and reintegration but compromise their chances by succumbing to hate and revenge. Although Gothic heroines are less likely to retaliate in a similar fashion, their victimisation is often equally cruel. Emily in Ann Radcliffe's *The Mysteries of Udolpho* or Ellena in *The Italian* lose everything and are constantly struggling to regain a foothold in their respective social environments, while their adversaries are keen to subject them completely to their own spheres of influence. Most Gothic characters have to face the threat of becoming permanently lost in the liminal sphere, a situation described by Victor Turner in his seminal study of the transitions from one social state to another:

> The attributes of liminality or of liminal *personae* ('threshold people') are necessarily ambiguous, since this condition and these persons elude or slip through the network of classifications that normally locate states and positions in cultural space. Liminal entities are neither here nor there; they are betwixt and between the positions assigned and arrayed by law, custom, convention, and ceremonial.[7]

To facilitate the transition at least in social terms, most societies have developed so-called rites of passage that accompany the major changes in human life. These consist of three stages: separation, transition and incorporation.[8] While liminality represents a transitional and voluntary stage in successful rites of passage, it threatens to become a permanent and involuntary state in Gothic narratives.

David Punter poses the liminality of Gothic characters, their structural invisibility and precarious existence, against the entrenched norms of the legal apparatus. In his preliminary definition of the law he talks of it in terms of a total order that finds its unity in the exclusion of contaminated matter and its purest expression in the written form.[9] For Punter, the law is an abstract ideal or system that rigorously shuts out the particular, the doubtful, the abject, or, simply, 'the other'. However, as a perfect order, it is haunted by those phenomena that do not – or are not permitted to – fit in, that exist in the liminal areas of society, in its crevices and folds. For the individual there is a basic need to be acknowledged as a legal subject, which serves as a fundamental prerequisite for official interactions within a particular culture. If the law is the only institution to which the individual can turn and appeal in a time of crisis, then the refusal of one's case to be heard and acted upon condemns the individual to remain in the liminal sphere. This is what the Gothic is essentially about: 'Gothic fiction . . . deals with those moments when we find it impossible, with any degree of hope, for our "case to be put".'[10] No matter how eager these characters are to plead their case and regain some foothold in the social order, the extraordinary circumstances of their lives – and especially their liminal and thus unofficial status – prevent such a proceeding.[11] This is equally true of Caleb Williams, Frankenstein's monster or Ann Radcliffe's heroines, whose personal testimonies and legal claims are overshadowed by more powerful narratives and ignored by institutions whose operations do not accommodate special circumstances easily.

V for Vendetta presents a particularly dystopian version of such a configuration, since the futuristic Britain of 1997 is ruled by a fascist regime that will not accept anything or anyone outside its all-encompassing order. Since the state exerts full legal and social control over what can officially exist within its classificatory system, any deviation from the established norms is severely punished. In the chaotic aftermath of a third World War, all the unwanted individuals – 'the darkies, the nancy boys and the beatniks' (B1.IV.4.vii) – were rounded up and quickly disposed of. At that time V was taken to Larkhill Resettlement Camp, where he was made to serve the regime in a particularly cruel way.

It is helpful to think of Larkhill and, by analogy, the fascist regime, as a total institution, as described by Erving Goffman: 'a place of residence and work where a large number of like-situated individuals, cut off from the wider society for an appreciable period of time, together lead an enclosed, formally administered round of life'.[12] The complete segregation of these institutions also manifests itself in physical terms. 'Their encompassing or total character is symbolized by the barrier to social intercourse with the outside and to departure that is often built right into the physical plant, such as locked doors, high walls, barbed wire, cliffs, water, forests, or moors.'[13] After the 'civil death'[14] of those deemed unfit to remain members of society, their daily routines of life are dictated by the new regime. 'Once the prepatient begins to settle down, the main outlines of his fate tend to follow those of a whole class of segregated establishments – jails, concentration camps, monasteries, work camps, and so on – in which the inmate spends the whole round of life on the grounds, and marches through his regimented day in the immediate company of a group of persons of his own institutional status.'[15] The 'transition from person to patient' is accompanied by an elaborate 'rite of passage' that is forced upon the inmate and described by Goffman in great detail.[16] In the process of institutionalisation V is stripped of his name, his belongings, his identity, and, most importantly, his rights as a citizen. He becomes part of the 'research stock', 'so weak and pathetic' that the chief medical scientist, Dr Delia Surridge, feels offended by the wretched state of the inmates which makes them appear 'hardly human' (B1.XI.2.iii, v). Nevertheless, she is eager to make good use of this 'heaven-sent opportunity' and 'get to work' on the inmates as soon as possible (B1.XI.2.iii–iv).

In its treatment of total institutions *V for Vendetta* is conceptually indebted to early Gothic fiction, such as Charles Maturin's *Melmoth the Wanderer*, which explores the effects of imprisonment on a variety of characters. All its narrative strands are powerful demonstrations of Goffman's thesis that institutionalisation threatens to transform inmates into those beings whose character traits are projected onto them by the authorities. In 'Tale of the Spaniard', Alonzo Monçada, 'a descendant of one of [Spain's] noblest houses', is separated from his parents at birth and 'kept in the most sordid privacy', living 'in a wretched house in the suburbs of Madrid with an old woman'.[17] At the age of 12 he is 'conveyed to a convent of Ex-Jesuits [...], where an agreement had been made for [his] board and education, and where [he] became an inmate that very day'.[18] This forced noviciation enables the monastery to determine every small detail of his future life – a key characteristic of total institutions. Unlike Ambrosio in Matthew Lewis's *The Monk*, Alonzo does not give in willingly to the indoctrination of the monks. For a long time, he struggles to keep his sanity and sense of self. Yet there is no escape. He feels physically transformed into a mechanical device by the mind-numbing routines of monkish life.[19]

Melmoth presents one of Gothic fiction's most interesting infringements on personal freedom by institutional power. Highly relevant to the present discussion is the parricide's description of the Catholic Church later in the tale. When Alonzo finally escapes from the monastery, having been imprisoned for the better part of his life, he is betrayed by a treacherous monk who kills his brother – Monçada's accomplice – and then delivers him into the hands of the Spanish Inquisition. There he conjures up a Kafkaesque vision of the Catholic Church as a global and total institution:

> 'And you dreamt,' he cried, 'in your temerity, you dreamt of setting the vigilance of a convent at defiance? Two boys, one the fool of fear, and the other of temerity, were fit antagonists for that stupendous system, whose roots are in the bowels of the earth, and whose head is among the stars, – *you* escape from a convent! *you* defy a power that has defied sovereigns! A power whose influence is unlimited, indefinable, and unknown, even to those who exercise it, as there are mansions so vast, that their inmates, to their last hour, have never visited all the apartments; – a power whose operation is like its motto, – one and indivisible. The soul of the Vatican breathes in the humblest convent in Spain, – and you, an insect perched on a wheel of this vast machine, imagined you were able to arrest its progress, while its rotation was hurrying on to crush you to atoms'.[20]

Not only does this passage represent a prime example of the melodramatic confrontation between individuals and total institutions, but it also highlights the power of rhetoric and propaganda: more important than the actual reach of the Church is the belief of the population in its complete dominance.

A similar mode of subjectification and control, operative on both the psychic and corporeal levels – is evident at Larkhill. At the hands of the authorities, 'seventy-five percent' of Surridge's patients die in the experiments (B1.XI.2.vii). Eventually, V, the person in room five, is the only survivor, permanently transformed by the drug. He is quickly diagnosed as suffering from 'some kind of psychotic breakdown' (B1.XI.3.ii). His very unaccountability becomes his greatest strength. In an act of defiance, V blows up the compound with the help of fertilisers that he was allowed to use for his little garden patch. By means of his escape – a dramatic rebirth through fire and destruction – he becomes a complete anomaly: he exists physically and legally outside the system, a ghostlike presence on the fringe of society into whose classificatory system he no longer fits. James R. Keller provides a pertinent assessment of V's new condition: 'As a result of the fires at Larkhill, V has no face, at least, no face that he is willing to reveal to the world, and certainly his unseen visage is without character or definition, as is common among those with extensive facial burns. His visage embodies the slipping signifier to which no stable meaning can be attached.'[21]

Contrary to the predominantly female victims of Gothic literature, who generally survive their ordeals morally intact, their male counterparts are frequently transformed by the experience. Their obsession to bring down a corrupt and unjust system lets them compromise their own integrity. Tellingly, the moral ambiguity of *V for Vendetta* is analogous to that expressed at the end of *Caleb Williams*. Against impossible odds, Caleb has succeeded in compelling the legal institution to recognise his innocence, bringing a successful charge of murder against his former master, Lord Falkland. However, rather than a return to freedom and normality, this restoration of his legal status is accompanied by the internalisation of that guilt which had previously been imposed on him, a severe sense of the disjunction between justice and law:

> [Falkland] survived this dreadful scene but three days. I have been his murderer. It was fit that he should praise my patience, who has fallen a victim, life and fame, to my precipitation! It would have been merciful in comparison, if I had planted a dagger in his heart. He would have thanked me for my kindness. But, atrocious, execrable wretch that I have been! I wantonly inflicted on him an anguish a thousand times worse than death. Meanwhile I endure the penalty of my crime. His figure is ever in imagination before me. Waking or sleeping I still behold him. He seems mildly to expostulate with me for my unfeeling behaviour. I live the devoted victim of conscious reproach. Alas! I am the same Caleb Williams that, so short a time ago, boasted, that, however great were the calamities I endured, I was still innocent.[22]

Unlike his contemporary Radcliffe, whose hero in *The Italian* emerges largely unscathed from imprisonment and interrogation at the hands of the Inquisition, Godwin demonstrates a distinctly modern sense that no one escapes the labyrinth of institutional power unscathed. Though Radcliffe's account of institutional terror anticipates, and indeed rivals, Maturin's, it is not until Kafka that Godwin's horrific vision of the total dissolution of the subject's character by the institution is taken to its extreme. Indeed, so extensive is Caleb's imputation of guilt that it exerts a metanarrative force that undermines the very origins of the text itself: 'I began these memoirs with the idea of vindicating my character. I have now no character that I wish to vindicate.'[23]

Though V, like Caleb, owes his very identity to the institutions that have oppressed him, his struggle is not for vindication but for vengeance. Given the fact that the very perpetrators of the crime now form the government, even the semblance of justice cannot be sought through official channels. As Keller notes: 'since the Norsefire Party is the prevailing and indeed the only power structure in the realm, V has no choice but to pursue a private vendetta'.[24] From the first moment of his new existence, V is beyond absolution, beyond the possibility of having his case put and his former identity restored. The liminal sphere thus becomes his home, his chosen base of operation: 'This place is the only universe I've got at the moment' (B1.VI.1.iv), he tells Evey. Since all possible rites of passage are closed to him, he sets out to reinvent first himself and then society at large.

In his years of isolation and re-education, V heavily relies on works of art for company. While the Shadow Gallery harbours an exclusive assembly of the greatest works, banned by the fascists, there is more to his interest in history and the fine arts. He is faced with the daunting challenge of reinventing himself completely by breathing new life into the artefacts of a dead culture. V especially cherishes those fictional heroes and historical figures that provide him with a blueprint for the person he might be, instrumentalising and recontextualising these narratives to serve his own agenda. Referring to V's collection of paintings, Keller stresses their central importance: 'So horribly disfigured that he must wear a mask, V lives vicariously through those activities captured in the multitude of frames surrounding him. Unable to live life directly, [...] V must settle for aesthetic stimulation and the ecstasy of retribution and gore that defines his monomaniacal pursuit.'[25]

V emulates his beloved narratives of revenge and retribution to such an extent that he becomes a 'real-life' epitome of the literary avenger.[26] Though his major source and greatest inspiration, the Guy Fawkes legend, adds a political tincture to his violence, the primary function of his iconic mask is to provide the means to perform his new identity. That this is a performance is made clear not only by the fact that he dresses up in the costume, but also by his propensity for grand gestures and speeches made in blank verse. His initial appearance in the book illustrates this flair for the dramatic, from costume, words and gestures right down to the stage lighting. He literally stands between the darkness and the light, a ghostlike presence seeming to emerge from nowhere, garbed in period dress and quoting *Macbeth*: 'The multiplying villainies of nature / Do swarm upon him'.[27] Shakespeare's lines serve as an emotional stimulant that prepares him for the task at hand, to save Evey from rape and perhaps worse at the hands of the secret police. Keller comments that 'V repeatedly quotes from Shakespeare's plays and often in such a way that it is clear he is shaping his behavior in conformity to literary paradigms.'[28] In this sense he is 'Hamlet's ideal revenger',[29] for although both start from a theatrical paradigm, it is V who successfully performs the role of the cold-blooded assassin. As Joachim Ecke notes in Chapter 4 of this collection, Moore would also rework Hamlet in his first issue of *Swamp Thing*, penned while he was still writing *V for Vendetta* for *Warrior*; however, while the Shakespearean intertext in the latter may veer towards melodrama, it steers clear of the sort of pastiche found in the Swamp Thing's meditation on the death of Arcane.[30] Free from irony, V's self-conscious literary inheritance does not so much open a gap between narrative and metanarrative as provide the materials to make sense of, and give purpose to, his liminal existence.

The narrative is constructed on a sustained analogy between the microcosm of the Larkhill Resettlement Camp and the macrocosm of Britain run by the Norsefire oligarchy. This reading is clearly supported by the visuals. The second panel on the very first page creates an unsettling blend between a street scene, in which workers are leaving their factory, and a prison camp with a high barbed-wire fence around the compound and closed-circuit television. This analogy suggests that the fascist state uses the very same strategies to exercise complete control over its subjects: constant surveillance, a strictly regulated life, rigorous punishment and incessant indoctrination. Lewis Prothero, the former commander of Larkhill, is now the Voice of Fate, the official spokesperson of the regime, whose broadcasts are revered as almost mystical expressions of the system's will and which represent a breakdown of communication in a dialogical sense. The Voice of Fate is presented as ubiquitous and authoritative, permeating public spaces and private homes. It is purely monological, the expression of a single will. Having studied the regime's propaganda machine in secret, V begins to publicly leave marks, from harmless graffiti (e.g. B1.III.2.v, B2.II.5.vii) to the destruction of the Old Bailey (B1.V.5.vii), and voice his own truth, culminating in a chapter-long television broadcast on the regime's main channel (B2.IV). Against the backdrop of a 'formally administered round of life',[31] V is putting on his own subversive show.

Mikhail Bakhtin's concept of the carnivalesque is highly relevant in this context.[32] While carnival, vaudeville and the theatre in general are usually public forms of liminality – a suspension and subversion of everyday rules within a fixed temporal and spatial frame – V's private liminality, his 'carnival', explodes out of its narrow boundaries and becomes a revolutionary or rather anarchic force. For Lewis Prothero, he re-creates Larkhill as an elaborate showpiece which includes the mock execution and incineration of Prothero's beloved dolls in the ovens of the concentration camp. Yet, the purpose of this grotesque 'game' is deadly serious: as intended, Prothero is driven mad.

V completely dissolves the boundaries between reality, re-enactment and fiction, between culturally defined spaces and the chaos lurking without. For him, life within the fascist regime is a vicious cabaret (see the 'Prelude' to Book Two), but it should not be forgotten that he himself is the director of his own théâtre macabre. His reaction to the regime's machinery of theatricality and pretence is not an open confrontation, but an even greater charade:

> *V*: Melodrama, Evey! Isn't it strange how life turns into melodrama?
> *EVEY*: That's very important to you, isn't it? All that theatrical stuff.
> *V*: It's everything, Evey. The perfect entrance, the grand illusion. It's everything.
> ... and I'm going to bring the house down.
> They've forgotten the drama of it all. You see. They abandoned their scripts when the world withered in the glare of the nuclear footlights.
> I'm going to remind them. About melodrama. About the tuppenny rush and the penny dreadful. You see, Evey, all the world's a stage. And everything else
> ...
> ... is vaudeville'. (B1.IV.2.iv–vii)

Secretly, V has become the master puppet player who has all the strings in his hands. It has taken him years to plan for this greatest of spectacles, and as any successful theatre director, he is very much aware of his audience, of 'the performativity of terrorist violence, the idea of power on display, a power advertised through public spectacle, combining the dire consequences of politics with the seemingly inconsequential practices of theater'.³³ Apart from the physical struggle, there is always the propaganda war: 'in many ways, V's fight with Fate is a battle over controlling communication. His terrorist activities are always communicative – either disrupting the communication between the tyrannical government and the people, or sending a message beyond the system and directly to the populace.'³⁴

Thus, V's arsenal of weapons closely resembles that of his enemy. He even rebuilds Fate in his underground compound to gain complete access to and control over the fascists' main instrument of power. He is so caught up in his ideological struggle and his self-fabricated world of heroic revenge, that he cannot see the larger picture. In his holy war against a regime built on mass murder and high-tech terrorism he feels justified in resorting to the very same measures. Despite all the surveillance gadgetry, V is as blind as they are.

When V rescues Evey, he appears to be genuinely interested in her fate and even finds the right words to calm her (B1.III.5.iv, B1.III.8.i–ii). By presenting this scene of compassion immediately following Evey's disturbing childhood memories, recalling the loss of her parents at the hands of the fascists, we are led to believe that V is capable of caring for her. An orphan who has lost everything and is now struggling to gain a foothold in a world that has gone mad, Evey resembles the typical Gothic heroine. Narrowly escaping the henchmen of the regime, she is now in the hands of a costumed hero, leading a liminal existence. Being very naive, Evey wants to help V and proposes a deal, trading her safety in his underground lair for assistance in his obscure plans, which V immediately compares to Dr Faust's contract with the devil (B1.VI.1.vii, B1.VI.2.ii–iii). Nevertheless, he begins to instrumentalise her for his own purposes. As a first step, he lets her dress up as a prostitute and sends her to Bishop Lilliman's residence to distract him long enough to gain access himself. What he has in mind for her, ultimately, is to erase her past life and rebuild her from scratch.

Imprisoned in the Shadow Gallery, Evey not only becomes the only other occupant in V's liminal sphere, but also finds herself at the epicentre of a dangerous conflict. Parkin comments that 'Evey is an everywoman who is tossed between equally brutal alternatives.'³⁵ From Horace Walpole's *The Castle of Otranto* onwards, the Gothic has consistently returned to questions of allegiance: to which social institution, political order or eternal principle are the characters willing to subordinate themselves – and, more importantly, at what cost? *Otranto* set a precedent in this respect by placing young characters between competing institutions. Due to the medieval setting of the narrative, there are only two centres of power: the feudal hierarchy represented by Manfred and the Church personified by Jerome, the Catholic priest. As Robert Miles demonstrates, the central focus of the novel is not the question of proper religion but the shaky basis of all authority: '*Otranto* is not about, is not a defence of, or an attack on, Catholicism. It is really about legitimacy, or rather the lack of it.'[36] In this context, Mark Canuel's remarks on the representations of the monastery explicate the Gothic's treatment of the Catholic Church as an institution:

> The Gothic presents monastic institutions as fascinating sources of danger, but not because the genre seeks to suppress Catholicism as a set of alien beliefs. Instead, even early examples of the genre by Horace Walpole and Clara Reeve frequently identify monasticism as a private and self-enclosed structure of confessional authority, visible in Britain itself, that the Gothic novel participates in dismantling and modifying.[37]

For such centres of power, individuality and independent thought are suspicious. Canuel observes that the 'competition between mirroring social organisations – between the castle and the church – plays out over the course of the novel as a competition over the allegiance of individuals'.[38]

Like the prototypical Gothic heroine, Evey desires reintegration in both the social and private spheres; however, the possibility of a comedic resolution to the narrative either through the rediscovery of a lost parent or through a happy marriage is precluded from the text. As Evey speculates about her relationship to V, questions of sexual desire – or, more accurately, V's apparent lack of desire – begin to surface. Dancing with V, beneath the whirling lights of a disco-ball, she broaches the topic of sexual and familial relations:

> *EVEY*: I mean, well, there could be lots of reasons . . . y'know, why you don't ever, y'know, sleep with me or anything.
> Perhaps there was some-body else. I'd understand if there was.
> Or . . . uh . . . perhaps you don't sort of fancy women. But, like, there's nothing wrong with that.
> Or perhaps . . .
> *V*: . . . Or perhaps I'm your father? (B2.I.3.v–ix)

What Evey does not understand, however, is that V's transformation at Larkhill put an end to his capacity to maintain any form of social relationship, and this is precisely what he has in mind for her: to sever all her social ties and re-create her in his own image. Evey, the first woman, should rebuild Britain, as soon as V is gone with the rest of the old regime. He sees in her a mirror image of himself who still has to undergo an important rite of passage. This entails overcoming both familial and sexual love – and indeed happiness itself – which, for V, represent forms of imprisonment. He insists that 'I didn't put you in a prison, Evey. / I just showed you the bars' (B2.XIII.5.ii).

V's imposition of a simulation of the ordeal to which he was subjected – and out of which his new subjectivity was formed – positions Evey within a cycle of violence in which she experiences another reiteration of the suffering inflicted on V himself; by provoking a resistance in Evey modelled on his own defiance, he believes he can purify her and, essentially, transform her into himself. Only now can he accept her as one of his kind. Only now can he express his love for her as a supreme expression of his own ideals:

EVEY: Oh, you tortured me . . .
V: Because I love you. Because I want to set you free. (B2.XII.2.vi–vii)

V's recourse to the language of love could be regarded as a perversion of Christian love. While Christ died and sacrificed himself so that others will not have to undergo eternal torment, V can only love Evey as soon as her personality is erased through the torturous experience of death and rebirth. It seems paradoxical that he wants to punish the regime for his own treatment, but then uses exactly the same procedure to transform Evey into a copy of himself. His cold-blooded revenge blinds him from the truth that he is not free, but a traumatised individual suffering from the delusion that he is and believing he could be Evey's saviour.[39]

Though Evey finally accepts V's insane measure as a liberating act, her rebirth as V's creature and clone dooms her to a life scripted by and for another, but one which she now assumes as her personal destiny: 'in anarchy, there is another way. With anarchy, from rubble comes new life, hope reinstated' (B3.X.7.iv). The unfettered masses may indeed take to the streets and beat their oppressors to death. Yet, who is going to rebuild the nation from the rubble? A costumed mass murderer?

In becoming V, she enters a cycle in which his madness is bound to repeat itself. She blows up Downing Street and takes an apprentice of her own. Although the novel seems to invoke the glorious tradition of a new superhero stepping in, donning her costume and finding her sidekick, this development still perpetuates a mad pursuit and prevents any kind of reconciliation or progress. Like *Watchmen*, *V for Vendetta* thus ends on a morally ambiguous note, raising questions that are not only central to Moore's work in the 1980s but also to Gothic fiction: to what degree are we willing to compromise to fit into the pre-existing subject positions offered by various institutions? How does a society deal with its liminal sphere, the unstructured space outside its classificatory system, where some individuals choose or are forced to exist? Where do the personal liberties of individuals end? *V for Vendetta* is as successful in activating the readers' active participation in negotiating these questions as the classics of Gothic fiction.

Notes

1 The noun phrase 'narrative props' is taken from Andrew Smith, *Gothic Literature* (Edinburgh: Edinburgh University Press, 2007), p. 3 (also see p. 4); the second phrase is from Fred Botting, *Gothic* (London and New York: Routledge, 1996), p. 2. See also Jerrold E. Hogle, 'Introduction: The Gothic in Western Culture', in *The Cambridge Companion to Gothic Fiction*, ed. Jerrold E. Hogle (Cambridge.: Cambridge University Press, 2002), pp. 1–20 (p. 2). In *Gothic Fiction: A Reader's Guide to Essential Criticism* (Basingstoke: Palgrave Macmillan, 2007), pp. 20–5, Angela Wright shows how such narrative 'recipes' were used by contemporary readers as a popular argument against the genre.
2 Lance Parkin, *The Pocket Essential Alan Moore* (Harpenden: Pocket Essentials, 2001), p. 30.
3 See 'Behind the Painted Smile', in Alan Moore and David Lloyd, *V for Vendetta* (London: Titan, 2009), pp. 267–76. In this 'making-of' article, included in the paperback edition and originally published during the book's first run in *Warrior* magazine, Moore explicitly names Orwell, Huxley and Bradbury as major influences (p. 270). Moore is also very explicit about the political subtext of the novel and has voiced his strong objections to Thatcher's policies in the 1980s in several interviews. See, e.g., George Khoury, *The Extraordinary Works of Alan Moore* (Raleigh, NC: TwoMorrows, 2008), pp. 54–79, where he particularly criticises the British government's anti-homosexual legislation (p. 75).

4 Gene Kannenberg, Jr, *500 Essential Graphic Novels* (New York: Collins Design, 2008), p. 375.
5 See Moore, 'Behind the Painted Smile', p. 270. It is important to note that Moore wrote *The Killing Joke* (1988), one of the most influential titles in the Batman universe of stories, at the time he was finishing *V for Vendetta*.
6 For discussion of this plot device in earlier Gothic fiction, see Botting, *Gothic*, p. 1, Hogle, 'Introduction', p. 2, Robert Mighall, *A Geography of Victorian Fiction: Mapping History's Nightmares* (Oxford: Oxford University Press, 2003), pp. 9, 17 and David Punter, *The Literature of Terror: A History of Gothic Fictions from 1765 to the Present Day*, 2nd edn, 2 vols (London: Longman, 1996), I, p. 47.
7 Victor Turner, *The Ritual Process: Structure and Anti-Structure* (New York: Aldine de Gruyter, 1997), p. 95.
8 See Arnold van Gennep, *The Rites of Passage*, trans. Monika B. Vizedom and Gabrielle L. Caffee (Chicago: Chicago University Press, 1960), pp. 11, 21 and Turner, *Ritual Process*, pp. 94–5, for a description.
9 See David Punter, *Gothic Pathologies: The Text, the Body and the Law* (Basingstoke: Macmillan, 1998), pp. 2–3.
10 *Ibid.*, p. 5.
11 See *ibid.*, p. 202.
12 Erving Goffman, *Asylums: Essays on the Social Situation of Mental Patients and Other Inmates* (Harmondsworth: Penguin, 1973), p. 11.
13 *Ibid.*, pp. 15–16.
14 *Ibid.*, p. 25.
15 *Ibid.*, p. 137.
16 *Ibid.*, pp. 130, 27; see more generally, pp. 24–40.
17 Charles Maturin, 'Tale of the Spaniard', in *Melmoth the Wanderer*, ed. Douglas Grant (Oxford: Oxford University Press, 1998), pp. 73–272 (p. 73).
18 *Ibid.*, p. 75.
19 See *ibid.*, pp. 99–100.
20 *Ibid.*, pp. 219–20.
21 James R. Keller, *V for Vendetta: A Critical Study of the Graphic Novel and Film* (Jefferson, NC: McFarland, 2008), p. 10.
22 William Godwin, *Caleb Williams* (Oxford: Oxford University Press, 1998), p. 325.
23 *Ibid.*, p. 326.
24 Keller, *Critical Study*, p. 140.
25 *Ibid.*, pp. 166–7.
26 By the time the book starts, he has already killed over forty people and reserves the leading members of Larkhill's staff – Lewis Prothero, Bishop Lilliman and Dr Delia Surridge – for a final showdown and elaborately

planned demise; see Moore and Lloyd, *V*, B1.XI.6.v.
27 William Shakespeare, *Macbeth*, ed. Kenneth Muir (London: Thomson Learning, 2003), 1.2.11–12. Quoted in Moore and Lloyd, *V*, B1.I.3.ix. For a sustained reading of this Shakespearean intertext, see Jessica McCall, 'V for Vendetta: A Graphic Retelling of Macbeth', *Popular Culture Review*, 20:1 (Winter 2009), 45–60.
28 Keller, *Critical Study*, p. 125.
29 *Ibid.*, p. 138.
30 For further discussion, see Chapter 4 above.
31 Goffman, *Asylums*, p. 11.
32 See Mikhail Bakhtin, *Rabelais and His World*, trans. Hélène Iswolsky, intro. Michael Holquist (Bloomington: Indiana University Press, 1984).
33 Keller, *Critical Study*, p. 39.
34 Jonathan Mills, 'V for Verbal Violence' (7 May 2001): www.ninthart.org/display.php?article=5.
35 Parkin, *Alan Moore*, p. 108.
36 Robert Miles, 'Europhobia: The Catholic Other in Horace Walpole and Charles Maturin', in *European Gothic: A Spirited Exchange 1760–1960*, ed. Avril Horner (Manchester: Manchester University Press, 2002), pp. 84–103 (p. 93).
37 Mark Canuel, *Religion, Toleration, and British Writing, 1790–1830* (Cambridge: Cambridge University Press, 2002), p. 7.
38 *Ibid.*, p. 68.
39 V and Evey remind me of Melmoth the Wanderer and Immalee. V and Melmoth are both morally and socially ambiguous characters: saviours, fathers, lovers, but also demonic tempters/manipulators. The girls, too, share certain similarities. But that would lead too far away from the present argument.

Part III

Inheritance and adaptation

7

'The Sleep of Reason': *Swamp Thing* and the intertextual reader

Michael Bradshaw

> At 5:32 this evening you will be impaled by a swordfish. There is nothing to be done. It is written. Selena has already decided not to buy the lawn furniture.
> Alan Moore, *Swamp Thing*[1]

The practices of intertextual allusion and pastiche have long been known to be intrinsic to Gothic writing;[2] and the complex textuality of the Gothic is customarily related to its propensity to disrupt unitary meaning, and challenge orthodox codes by generating the 'undecidable'. Judith Halberstam, for example, writes that Gothic manifests 'the breakdown of genre and the crisis occasioned by the inability to "tell", meaning both the inability to narrate and the inability to categorize'.[3] However, the need to negotiate a network of eclectic intertexts may also pose an overt challenge to the sophistication of a reader, and the experience of reading such a text functions as that reader's initiation into a set of specific ethical meanings; in this case, the 'telling' is a shared duty of author and reader – there are positions to be won and lines to be drawn. This chapter will investigate how Moore, as a self-aware practitioner of Gothic conventions, uses the intertextual energies of the tradition to fashion and nurture a politicised reader who will be worthy of the meanings of his text. In Moore's radical horror comic *Swamp Thing*, Gothic is not the breakdown of genre, but the multiplicity of genre and its manipulation.

Serious comics

Swamp Thing is still marketed as the series which changed comics permanently: 'From 1983 through 1987 [...] Alan Moore revolutionized the American comic book. His ground-breaking tenure on DC Comics' *Swamp Thing* set new standards for graphic storytelling and touched off a revolution in the medium that is still expanding today.'[4] Moore transformed his received subject matter from the undemanding horror of DC's creature comic into a psychologically and symbolically evolved narrative, rich in literary allusion. It was with his skill and taste in intertextual allusion to canonical literature that Moore signalled the maturity and intellectual credibility of graphic narrative to new constituencies of readers. The series also deepens comics' engagement with the Gothic genre. Murder, mutilation, haunting and black magic are certainly widespread in Moore's representation of 1980s America, but it is in the complexity of the protagonist Alec Holland/the Swamp Thing that the comic's generic sophistication really lies: as a protean, empathic creature of pure plant matter, Holland functions as humanity's connection to 'the green', a living conduit for the conscience and retribution consequent on ecological harm. Moore's 'green Gothic' anticipates the general raising of awareness on ecological themes in the UK and USA in the late 1980s, and uses the revenge-fantasy elements present in Gothic to direct opprobrium against those who harm the environment, as discussed in detail by Maggie Gray in Chapter 3 above. The story is a deep-Southern-US enactment of anti-Thatcherite politics, the periphery of the main plot littered with newspaper reports – both documented and fictional – of corporate greed, chemical pollution, the Iran–Contra scandal and campaign to re-elect Ronald Reagan.[5] Over the course of this elaborately structured series, Moore is also constructing a reader who will be worthy of the material: the literary allusiveness of the writing – sometimes signposted, sometimes submerged – becomes the gradual initiation of Moore's ideal reader into the text's great ethical theme: when the reader reaches the end of the series, perhaps, she is ready to begin reading.

Alec Holland's 'elemental' or 'swamp thing' is visually monstrous, and deliberately so. The artists working with Moore have maintained the ragged, dripping, vaguely humanoid colossus of the old DC Swamp Thing, this physical monstrosity now counterpoint to Holland's gentleness and moral goodness, in a fairly straightforward narrative paradox. In the cover image and first few pages of 'The Sleep of Reason', he and Abigail Cable play flirtatiously at 'creature from the black lagoon', the vulnerable beauty suddenly grabbed by a vile creature emerging from below, a humorous salute to the pulp horror of the comic's origins and simultaneously an assertion of having transcended them.[6] When Moore, Stephen Bissette and John Totleben took on *Swamp Thing* in 1983, the new team's first decision was to take him apart, examine his workings – biologically and, as it were, generically – before putting him back together on their own terms.[7] As Ramsey Campbell observes, this intervention was at once an audacious destruction of what they had inherited, and an inspired transcendence of its limitations.[8] In this episode, 'The Anatomy Lesson', Jason Woodrue ('the Floronic man') discovers the process by which the swamp creature has formed itself, after Holland was destroyed by fire:

> What about the plants in the swamp? The plants whose hungry root systems are busily ingesting the mortal remains of Alec Holland? Those plants eat him [...] and they become infected by a powerful consciousness that does not realize it is no longer alive! Imagine that cloudy, confused intelligence, possibly with only the vaguest notion of self, trying to make sense of its new environment ... Gradually shaping the plant cells that it now inhabits into a shape that it is more comfortable with. It remembers having bones, and so it builds itself a skeleton of wood. It remembers having muscle and constructs muscles from supple plant fiber ... It remembers having lungs, and a heart, and a brain ... and it does its best to duplicate them. You see, you were wrong, General. We thought that the Swamp Thing was Alec Holland, somehow transformed into a plant. It wasn't. It was a plant that thought it was Alec Holland.[9]

The physical embodiment of the creature is born of a collision between human and plant, technology and nature, reason and instinct; it is also a myth of origin which predestines the creature's simultaneous tragic alienation from both worlds and comic power to mediate, heal and unify. The trope of the anatomy lesson is loaded with irony as well as lurid horror: having discovered the truth at a cellular level, Woodrue and Sunderland both misinterpret the lesson's broader implications, the former becoming radicalised as the enemy of humankind, the latter retreating into anthropocentric denial.

Intertextual monsters

Moore's method in *Swamp Thing* may be described as self-aware intertextual Gothic. There are various forms of intertextual effect, including the kind of semi- or subconscious formation of texts from a network of other texts first proposed by Julia Kristeva. At the other end of the spectrum is the deliberate, strategic deployment of literary allusion which is apparent in all of Moore's major work: his favoured source material is British Romantic poetry, Victorian fantastic fiction and classic American and British horror films. More than probably any other British comics writer, his work is associated with the maturation and legitimisation of 'comics' as a literary mode with intellectual as well as aesthetic credibility, appropriate for adult readers; and the deployment of literary intertexts is one way that he has achieved this shift in the perception of his chosen form. One effect of reading a graphic narrative which references Blake's *Songs of Experience* or Coleridge's 'The Rime of the Ancient Mariner' is an awareness of literary credentials, and a greater receptivity to the serious ideas the author may wish to advance.[10] Another effect is political: the transposed intertext, such as a Romantic poem from the 1790s now situated in a 1980s popular cultural context, brings with it original connotations which are transformed by its new setting, releasing political meaning.

An example of this is the Swamp Thing's descent into hell in order to rescue Abigail, in 'Down Amongst the Dead Men' (from *Swamp Thing Annual*, 2), in which his psychic journey resembles and maps onto that of Dante in all major respects – in the quest with both personal and ethical dimensions; in the graduated testing encounters with various levels of demons; in the meeting with those known in life and now enduring their punishment (Sunderland, Arcane); and above all in the accompaniment by an expert guide, in which DC's 'the Stranger' and Deadman replace Dante's Virgil. True to the spirit of the original *Inferno*, both are forced to turn back after a certain point, unable to penetrate the further reaches of hell. Moore's invocation of Dante in *Swamp Thing* is as much a case of Romantic intertextuality as his more familiar fascination with Coleridge. Romantic-era readers were the first generation to value Dante's religious epic as much for its thrilling aesthetic power as for its edifying moral theme.[11] The Swamp Thing's journey is a simultaneous pop-cultural rewriting of two great myths, in fact – not only

Dante's *Inferno*, but also the myth of Orpheus's search for his wife in the underworld; one is a sacred quest for the guidance of the heavenly Beatrice, the other an uxorious/artistic quest for reunion with Eurydice as the source of song. The Swamp Thing's descent into hell is part of the developing love story of the series, and asserts his moral goodness. The erotic relationship between the Swamp Thing and Abigail, a plot which develops over a great many chapters, has had a certain inevitability about it since the beginning of Moore's tenure on the title; the symbolic mating of the Swamp Thing and Abigail can be read as a kind of 'chymical wedding', which seals the tolerant symbiosis between plant and human that the Swamp Thing recommends to the radical Woodrue in 'Roots': 'And what ... will change the oxygen... / ...back into ... the gases that ... we ... need ... to survive ... / ... when the men ... and animals ... are dead?'[12] It was left to Rick Veitch, when he took over the writing as well as the art of the series, to make the symbiotic point fully explicit, as the lovers share a mutually sustaining kiss: 'the intoxicating whisper of carbon dioxide ... / ... for the exhilarating rush of purest oxygen'.[13] However, the intertextual reader also values the grotesque comedy of Moore's enthusiastic demonology, and the inventive punishments of Abigail's tormentor Anton Arcane:

>ARCANE: Huh— how many years have I buh— been here?
>SWAMP THING: Since yesterday.[14]

The episode demands to be read as a subtle combination of moral seriousness and playful generic experimentation, a divided perspective which centres on the hybrid creature himself.

In 'Abandoned Houses', Abigail encounters Cain and Abel in a dream vision, retaining traces of secret knowledge on waking; her attempt to jot down its substance and meaning is interrupted by a telephone call – Moore's allusion to Coleridge's 1797 anecdote on the origin of Kubla Khan and the arrival of the notorious 'person on business from Porlock': '"I cannot remember the ..?" What did I write that for? Oh, well, that's life ... full of little mysteries.'[15] Coleridge reappears periodically in Moore's writing, most famously in the reworking of 'The Ancient Mariner' in *Watchmen*. In the rich middle period of Moore's writing, there are signs that he was deliberately assembling a corpus of work which invited and would reward rereading and cross-reference: witness the Swamp Thing's exile on the alien planet in the classic episode 'My Blue Heaven', when his reconstruction of Abigail's Louisiana town of Houma with manipulated plant matter foreshadows Dr Manhattan's fantastical structures on Mars during his turning-point conversation with Laurie in Chapter 9 of *Watchmen*.[16] The whole origin narrative of John/Dr Manhattan is in fact a self-aware rewriting of the genesis of the Swamp Thing: in each case, the original human is completely destroyed, and an arrangement of sentient matter consolidates around an imprint of his consciousness. The Swamp Thing is not Alec Holland, although Abigail always chooses to call him 'Alec'; he is a being of pure plant matter who is, in his own words, 'heir to [Holland's] limitations'.[17]

The use of Gothic tropes and allusions in the *Swamp Thing* series is from the outset strikingly self-aware. The overarching narrative of numbers 37 to 42, which represents the first stage of the 'American Gothic' story-arc, is the psychic preparation implemented by the Native American witchcraft cult 'the Brujería', for their assault on heaven. The Brujería themselves distort a comfortable liberal assumption on the benevolent eco-consciousness of Native American cultures – they do not so much consider themselves guardians of the earth as its malevolent 'owners';[18] their undeniable close kinship with the earth is combined with the most disturbing horror motifs, including rituals of mutilation and cannibalism. As John Constantine explains, they will deploy all the conventional nightmares of the supernatural in order to soften up earth's human populations and create a receptive climate of suitable credulousness and terror:

> The story will get bigger in the telling. [. . .]
> Before you know where you are, everybody within fifty miles believes in vampires a little bit more . . .
> . . . just as they planned it.
> [. . .] They're planning something very big, but they need the right sort of atmosphere to make it happen.[19]

There are, in fact, several parallel initiations into horror going on in this sequence, including the Brujería's manipulation of the human imagination, Constantine's brutal education of the Swamp Thing as he prepares him to play a part in their defeat, and also the conditioning of Moore's horror-literate reader to accept the Swamp Thing into the pantheon of Gothic film and fiction. The use of classic Gothic paraphernalia in *Swamp Thing* is offered, then, in a reflexive spirit – a horror story about the persistent human susceptibility to horror stories. On this horror tour of the USA, the Englishman John Constantine acts as a figure of the controlling author, who delays a full revelation until the time suits him, while the slow-to-catch-on swamp creature resembles a reader with no appetite for horror who nevertheless gets repeatedly drawn into the story. In this case, it is appropriate that Moore has chosen the most mainstream of Gothic figures, giving each a clear ideological dimension: the vampire (predatory but peace-loving, a moral indictment of Holland's pro-human willingness to exterminate them); the werewolf (the feminist wolfwoman raging at the persecution that is justified by ancient myths of menstruation); the zombie (revenge from beyond the grave for the Deep South's guilty legacy of slavery and racist atrocity); and the ghost (unquiet spirits from the history of casual killing that 'won' the American West). The array of monsters deployed in this story-arc is deliberately conventional, then, and also politicised; a cinematic rather than literary form of popular Gothic is invoked. The classic instance where these two traditions coincide is of course Mary Shelley's *Frankenstein*; aside from a brief cameo from Frankenstein's monster in a narcotic hallucination in 'Windfall', the most celebrated of all Romantic monsters is reserved for the much later return of Abigail's father Gregori Arcane.[20]

At the culmination of this tour of American horror, the Swamp Thing pursues a serial killer through the bayou until he panics and drowns in quicksand; the Swamp Thing meditates:

> Another monster dead . . .
> How many more?
> How many more . . . before this country . . . has been squeezed dry . . . of nightmares?
> Constantine . . . led me through the badlands . . . promising me knowledge . . . but delivering only horror . . . after horror . . .
> [. . .]
> I struggle . . . to impose a structure . . . that has meaning . . . on the madness that churns . . . within this continent [. . .]
> But tonight . . . I looked into a man's eyes . . . and glimpsed the abyss . . . And I fear . . . that it may be . . . bottomless.[21]

Constantine's explanation of the looming crisis is offered in a long scene of dialogue between the sorcerer and the swamp creature in 'Revelations':

I only showed you the trouble spots I thought you could learn from.
Each incident has increased the general belief in the paranormal by degrees, until the whole psychic atmosphere is like a balloon ripe for bursting.
Belief is power ...
... And the Brujería intend to use that power to accomplish something monstrous.[22]

As the full horror dawns on him at last, the Swamp Thing screams with his head in his hands; in the surrounding collage, he is seen running, fleeing before a backdrop of a melting Stars and Stripes, red peering eyes, decaying monsters: the moment is camp horror masquerading as tragedy. On the following page, the conversation resumes, a lengthy exposition staged in the deepening shadows of the swamp, Constantine puffing his trademark cigarettes, trench-coat collar up, detective-style. The storytelling is unusually wordy for Moore, and Bissette's postures and close-ups explicitly melodramatic. The promised narrative climax begins to appear camp and trivial; but the episode is effective in spite of this, due to its self-referential energy. Constantine – a brilliant creation – has many narrative functions, and one of them is to perform the unstable connection between the Swamp Thing and the intertexts of Gothic horror.

Green Gothic

The patterns of intertextuality enhance and enable the development of Moore's political theme in *Swamp Thing* – green activism and an ecological critique of the free-market Reagan-Thatcher years. The habit of Romantic allusion is highly appropriate to the development of a green politics in the intertextual dimension of Moore's narrative. As Jonathan Bate observes, 'in Romantic poetics, poetry is to be found not only in language but in nature; it is not only a means of verbal expression, it is also a means of communication between man and the natural world'.[23] Like *Swamp Thing*'s distinctive form of self-referential Gothic, the green politics of the series is constructed intertextually. The reader is positioned in an anxious middle state between 'green' and 'red' worlds. There is a parallel 'educational' theme: Constantine teaches the Swamp Thing all of his signature powers – abandoning and rapidly regrowing bodies and thus transporting himself through 'the green' to anywhere in earth's biosphere, his self-awareness as an 'earth elemental', and his introduction to the Parliament of Trees; Moore is also at work giving his reader a similar initiation, conditioning her ethical response to the story. The ethical construction of Moore's reader, however, is also a question of disorientation, the subversion of the reader's implied liberalism by making her complicit with the mainstream human world while fully aware of the harm it is doing to the environment.

In the first major story-arc, the Swamp Thing plays the liberal, inclusive reformer to Woodrue's militant extremist. This moderate role is abandoned by the Swamp Thing in 'Natural Consequences' and 'The Garden of Earthy Delights', when he holds Gotham City to ransom, demanding Abigail's release from police custody. It is when the Swamp Thing is provoked personally beyond endurance by the persecution of his lover that he finally becomes what could be construed as an 'eco-terrorist'. The narrative in these two chapters suggests a growing hubris in the Swamp Thing, by consistently referring to him as 'the swamp god', rather than the more familiar 'creature' or 'elemental'. Arriving in Gotham intent upon making war against humanity, he senses another mind in the green, and goes to visit Woodrue in Arkham Asylum, where he lives as a fellow inmate of Harvey Dent and the Joker. Woodrue greets him as a divinity, and the Swamp Thing grants him forgiveness for his crimes against the green, the uncomfortable religious discourse indicating to the reader that the protagonist is losing his appealingly human traits of humility and compassion – that in fact the mission to rescue Abigail which epitomises his goodness is also a masculine rage to claim back what belongs to him, the most savage and unappealing light in which we have seen him. Concerned, it seems, lest the reader grow too accustomed to accepting the Swamp Thing as a benign, gentle green giant, Moore takes us back periodically to his identity as avenging monster: for example, in 'Loose Ends (Reprise)', the Swamp Thing visits a series of elaborately sadistic executions on the corrupt government agents responsible of robbing him of his connection to the green and thus exiling him from Earth/Abigail – strangulation with rose thorns, suffocation with peach-blossom petals, abandonment in a maze of long grass, and killing his final victim by growing inside him from some salad leaves until his body is ripped apart in a bloody explosion, leaving a huge grinning treelike growth draped with the man's suit and tie.[24] Episodes such as this invite a queasy moral ambivalence in the reader: Moore is at pains to make the victims as revolting as possible, and yet we are left with a sense that it is not their ruthlessness or corruption that provokes these executions so much as their crime of coming between the Swamp Thing and his mate. Paradoxically, the Swamp Thing is also at his most human in indulging this ruthless revenge upon his enemies; he embraces the aggression of the covetous human, rejecting the advice he has received from of the Parliament of Trees: 'Power? Power is not the thing. To be calm within oneself, that is the way of the wood. / Power tempts anger, and anger is like wildfire. Avoid it.'[25] Moore's manipulation of genre, then, achieves its complexity not by completing a 'legitimate' transcendence of naive comics, but by remaining hospitable to his creature's roots in pulp horror.

It was not until September 1988 that Margaret Thatcher made her famous speech to the Royal Society raising awareness of ecological issues, and asserting her government's commitment to combating the 'greenhouse effect' and acid rain.[26] Throughout her first two terms in office there had been few signs of environmental awareness or policy-making, and initial responses to this sudden conversion from media commentators were sceptical. At the time when Moore and his creative team took on the *Swamp Thing* title, the British Green Party still operated as its predecessor the 'Ecology Party', and played a very minor part in the 1983 General Election, when the triumphant Thatcher trounced the still-Socialist but confused Labour Party, led by Michael Foot, whose Manifesto was called 'the longest suicide note in history'.[27] For Moore to develop so assertive and coherent a green politics in 1983, long before it became part of the mainstream lexicon of British politics, shows great confidence.

As Gray argues in Chapter 3 above, 'The Nukeface Papers'[28] is the episode which seals the environmental message of the series, its polemic against the corporate hubris of the Reagan-Thatcher years. It also effects a decisive twist in the creature's identity: the Swamp Thing is utterly destroyed by toxic waste, causing him to regrow his body for the first time; enter John Constantine to instruct him of his powers and responsibilities, assisting his self-discovery as earth's remaining plant elemental, as opposed to the biological accident he had believed himself to be. The Swamp Thing's disappointing first encounter with the Parliament of Trees evolves Moore's use of 'the green' into something more closely resembling the 'Gaia' theory of geo-sentience first proposed by the ecologist James Lovelock in the late twentieth century.[29] But modern philosophical environmentalism has also repeatedly asserted a validating history for itself that looks back to Romantic and post-Romantic writers of the eighteenth and nineteenth centuries, figures such as William Wordsworth, John Clare and Henry David Thoreau. In interpreting Moore's 1980s 'green Gothic', therefore, we should take serious notice of his consistent habit of Romantic intertextual allusion. The moral authority of the Swamp Thing, as he mediates between a raging, technophilic human history and the sentient non-human world of 'the green', conceivably owes as much to the pantheist nature-mysticism of Coleridge as to the Gaia hypothesis of Lovelock. Gothic and Green aspects of the narrative (both of them profoundly connected to 'the Romantic') are fully interlocked, and catalyse each other throughout.[30]

'The Sleep of Reason'

To negotiate this complex of generic and political ideas while consuming a comic is no mean task: Moore is demanding of his implied ideal reader, and, it seems, he is very willing to subvert, criticise and provoke. The reader is required to be in command of allusions to Coleridge, Dante and Shelley, as well as the DC heritage, and must fashion a coherent reading experience from a multiplicity of genres. Even more disconcertingly, perhaps, the reader is constructed as an anxious inhabitant of the borderline between swamp and city, 'green' and 'red' worlds, Romantic instinct and classicist reason. Suspected, perhaps, of a naive susceptibility to the moral certitudes of the DC superhero, Moore's readers are never allowed to grow comfortable in their assumptions about what the comic is 'telling'. Moore himself has indicated the 'absurdities' of setting his horror comic in the teeming DC universe, and thus having to allow for the presence of the Justice League superheroes, along with that latent kiss of death to any narrative tension – Superman.[31] And yet his accommodation of the superhero to his narrative is astute, and ironically promotes the singular identity of the Swamp Thing. The Justice League gaze down impotently from their shiny space station as Jason Woodrue holds the planet to ransom, fast running out of ideas; they turn up at the end merely to cart Woodrue, already humbled by the Swamp Thing, off to the asylum. The superhero for Moore, as for his successor Veitch, represents a complacent, judgemental morality combined with a highly problematic glamour.[32] Certainty does not have a good reputation in this discourse, and the reader is required to sustain an ethical awareness by embracing purposeful ambiguity.

The uncertainty of Moore's implied reader in response to questions of nature and reason is epitomised by the early story, 'The Sleep of Reason', which references Francisco Goya's drawing *El sueño de la razón produce monstruos*.[33] This issue provides an apt case study for exploring the formation of Moore's reader, in that a Romantic intertext is invoked and its political connotations transplanted into new ground. The episode contains Romantic themes of instinct versus reason, as well as the Gothic-Romantic theme of nightmares from the subconscious breaking into the waking world.

El sueño de la razón produce monstruos, printed as an aquatint in *Los Caprichos* in 1799, is one of a sequence of images satirising the vanity of contemporary Spanish society, and promoting the values of reasoned education. It depicts an artist – thought to be a sketch of Goya himself, although the face is concealed – asleep at his desk, surrounded by nocturnal creatures looming from the deeply shaded background – bats, owls and a lynx. The benighted creatures – representing moral blindness and stupidity rather than evil – roam abroad when Goya loses consciousness. The image suggests the question of whether the artist should remain alert and vigilant, in order to exclude these creatures from the world, or whether they are actually the source of his creativity and the visionary passivity of his sleep a necessary sort of 'negative capability' to activate their power.[34] The print became *Capricho* 43, roughly in the middle of the sequence of 80 satirical images, having first been intended for the frontispiece; it is thought that Goya took a tactical decision to demote the image's importance, owing to its contentious affinity with some images from Rousseau's *La Philosophie* (1793). The historical reception of *Los Caprichos* tends to emphasise Goya's antipathy to superstition and irrationality; and yet the overall stylistic impression of the volume, with Goya's gnomic matching of moral mottoes to images, is teasing and cryptic, and a peculiar ambiguity surrounds this, the volume's most celebrated image. *Sueño*, most often assumed to be synonymous with 'sleep', may be alternatively translated as 'dream'.

Like Rousseau, Goya is a figure of the European Enlightenment who has become at least as important as a direct influence on the Romantic movements which superseded it. *El sueño de la razón* may be said to stand at the very cusp of Enlightened and Romantic views of imaginative creativity: does it promote the primacy of the reasoning faculty in keeping monsters of the unconscious at bay? Or does it celebrate the ingress of instinctual sensations into the conscious world, in which 'reason' itself may after all be a self-deluding and complacent dream? By invoking – and reproducing several times – this visual intertext, Moore and Bissette place themselves also in the narrative, strategically occupying this ambiguous fulcrum which impels the story, the sensations of suspenseful terror and gratuitous horror that it produces, and also the reader's unresolved reflections on the dialogue between imaginative and rational faculties. Carrying a strong charge of this ambiguity into its life as intertext in Moore's narrative, the importance of the image might be summarised as follows: to think ethically about the environment is to accept the pre-rational world of the green, but this relaxation of the controlling reasoning faculty is also the welcoming portal of demons into the conscious world. Ambiguity is an integral feature of the politics of the series, for all its polemical gestures: for example, the wilderness that the Swamp Thing unleashes on Gotham is morally ambiguous – on the one hand, a purging of the urban corruption and return to a verdant Eden, but on the other, a radically permissive environment in which predatory new forms of culture will inevitably prosper.[35]

In 'The Sleep of Reason' a 'devil' named Jason Blood arrives in Houma, Louisiana, and checks into a cheap hotel, after visiting a head shop, where he inspects a Ouija board and buys a poster of Goya's picture. He intends to find out how a certain demon has 'clawed its way through into the world of sanity and reason'.[36] The 'monkey king' has in fact been summoned by an accidental incantation on a similar Ouija board, and has slaughtered the parents of Paul, a troubled autistic boy living in the care home where Abigail is about to begin work. The monkey king likes Paul and wants to be his friend. The last page of this chapter has the diminutive white monkey leaving Paul's bedroom and loping along the corridor, visiting each of the sleeping children and feasting on their terror. Bissette's final image of the monkey licking its chops with a sticky blue tongue appears alongside another reproduction of Goya's *capricho*, printed in bright red. It is a chilling combination of images, drawing much of its power from the managed clash of visual genres, arranged on either side of a diagonal division (see Figure 7.1). The sense of a menacing, uncanny transfer of matter from the subconscious centres on the intensely logical and unsocialised perspective of the autistic boy; in another brilliant panel, Paul stares in terror at his hand that has been kissed by the monkey, conveying fracture and self-alienation.[37] In using this image from Goya as part of the devil's manipulation of plot and character, Moore reiterates one of the founding paradoxes of (reading) horror: in order fully to engage with the genre, the reader must remain equally alive both to a sense of societal moral repugnance, and also to the greedy amoral pleasure of the text.

The chapter stands as one of the most successful passages of sustained Gothic styling in Moore's *Swamp Thing*; the baroque demonology of later chapters is feeble in comparison with the brutal economy here. 'The Sleep of Reason' shows Moore's intertextual Gothic at its visceral best; and yet it has little contribution from the protagonist himself. Jason Blood investigates the killing of Paul's parents, prophesies the freak accident that despatches Harry Price, the loft-insulation salesman, and makes contact with Abigail Cable. Abigail begins her new job at the children's home, and is introduced to Paul and his nightmares. Matt Cable again begins to dabble in black magic as an expression of his jealous alienation from Abigail. At the auction at Paul's parents' house, Selena prefers the mummified swordfish to the lawn furniture, and seals the fate of the philandering salesman. Meanwhile, the eponymous Swamp Thing is largely inactive. In the next chapter, it is true, he plays an active role in trying to rescue the children from the demonic invasion. But in 'The Sleep of Reason' he spends a whole chapter just hanging out with Abigail in the swamp, and brooding on autumnal (constructed) memories of Alec Holland's death by fire. His is not a conventional hero's role;[38] he often functions more as a catalyst of the actions and transformations of human characters who orbit around him. Already exhibiting the wise passivity of an 'earth elemental', the Swamp Thing sometimes stands motionless in the epicentre of horror plots; as a constant, empathetic and often silent presence, he is of course exactly what Abigail needs in a partner. The Swamp Thing's greatest resentment is reserved for Constantine, who disturbs his peace and forces him repeatedly to take futile violent action without knowledge or understanding, imposing on him the role of anthropocentric, aggressive

7.1 Alan Moore, Steve Bissette and John Totleben, 'The Sleep of Reason', *The Saga of the Swamp Thing*, 25 (June 1984), 23.iv–vii

superhero. Each monster he defeats is a moral indictment of the 'red world' of humanity – the werewolf driven to distraction by the weight of historical misogyny, the almost pastoral separatism of the aquatic vampires. As an 'elemental', with the guardian's role of mediating between vegetable and human worlds, this self-alienation is clearly the Swamp Thing's appointed lot; the more he is compelled to act violently, the more strongly is felt his innate condition of passivity and watchfulness. This quality of 'negative capability' in the main character is also crucial to the way the reader is being fashioned throughout the series: the acceptance of ambiguity in the dreaming green world is the growth and preparation of Moore's ideal reader; the politicised ecological awareness that we finally take away from the series may be imagined as a timely 'waking' from this slumber.

At the outset of 'The Anatomy Lesson', which is Moore's second issue on the series and which represents the morning after he has tied up the narrative loose ends of his predecessors, the bewildered plant who believes he is Alec Holland wakes up to find himself lying in a coffin-like freezer, having been the object of a post-mortem dissection; he effects his own resurrection and, like Mary Shelley's creature before him, goes in search of some answers. From this initial monster lurching from the slab to do bloody murder, to the final ecstatic reunion of the civilised elemental with his human mate, Moore's *Swamp Thing* constitutes an epic journey of self-alienation and self-discovery. It is no less the 'anatomy lesson' of Moore's reader, a creature haunted by countless texts, a highly literate political activist who wakes from a dream in which she was just enjoying a comic.

Notes

1 Alan Moore, Stephen Bissette, John Totleben, John Constanza and Tatjana Wood, 'The Sleep of Reason', *Swamp Thing*, 25 (June 1984), 1.vi.
2 See, e.g., Jacqueline Howard, *Reading Gothic Fiction: A Bakhtinian Approach* (Oxford: Clarendon Press, 1994), on the phenomenon of 'heteroglossia' in Gothic fictions.
3 Judith Halberstam, *Skin Shows: Gothic Horror and the Technology of Monsters* (Durham, NC: Duke University Press, 1995), p. 23.
4 This account of Moore's accomplishment is included on the back-cover blurb of the most recent hardcover reprints of *Swamp Thing*; see, for example, Alan Moore, Rick Veitch, John Totleben and Alfredo Alcala, *Saga*

of the Swamp Thing: Book Six (New York: DC Comics, 2011).
5 The *Swamp Thing* series overlapped substantially with Moore's sustained critique of Thatcherism in *V for Vendetta* (1982–85), which is set in the UK.
6 Moore, Bissette and Totleben, 'Sleep of Reason', 3–4.
7 See also Maggie Gray's discussion of the artistically liberating implications of the creature's redefinition as pure plant matter in Chapter 3, above.
8 Ramsey Campbell, 'Foreword', in Alan Moore, Stephen Bissette and John Totleben, *The Saga of the Swamp Thing* (New York: DC Comics, 2009), pp. 9–11 (pp. 10–11).
9 Alan Moore, Stephen Bissette and John Totleben, 'The Anatomy Lesson', *Swamp Thing*, 21 (Feb. 1984), 11–12.
10 Examples include the title of chapter five of *Watchmen*, 'Fearful Symmetry', which references Blake's lyric 'The Tyger', while the comic-within-a-comic, 'Tales of the Black Freighter', references Coleridge's poem in its story of a cursed voyage and crew of corpses.
11 For example, see the account of how Dante's religious allegory was accommodated to Romantic notions of the sublime provided in Ralph Pite, *The Circle of our Vision: Dante's Presence in English Romantic Poetry* (Oxford: Clarendon Press, 1994), pp. 14–17.
12 Alan Moore, Stephen Bissette and John Totleben, 'Roots', *Swamp Thing*, 24 (May 1984), 14.iii.
13 Rick Veitch and Alfredo Alcala, 'Widowsweed', *Swamp Thing*, 81 (Holiday 1988), 1.iv.
14 Alan Moore, Stephen Bissette and John Totleben, 'Down Amongst the Dead Men', *Swamp Thing Annual*, 2 (1985), 32.iv–v.
15 Alan Moore and Ron Randall, 'Abandoned Houses', *Swamp Thing*, 33 (Feb. 1985), 20.v–vi: a crumpled piece of paper resembling the face of Swamp Thing is discarded in a litter bin.
16 See Alan Moore, Stephen Bissette and Rick Veitch, 'My Blue Heaven', *Swamp Thing*, 56 (Jan. 1987) and Alan Moore and Dave Gibbons, *Watchmen* (New York: DC Comics, 2005), XI.
17 Rick Veitch's words, rather than Alan Moore's: Veitch and Alfredo Alcala, 'The Thinker', *Swamp Thing*, 75 (Aug. 1988), 5.iii.
18 Alan Moore, Stephen Bissette and John Totleben, 'Revelations', *Swamp Thing*, 46 (Mar. 1986), 18.iv.
19 Alan Moore, Stan Woch and Ron Randall, 'Fish Story', 22.iii–iv.
20 Alan Moore, Stan Woch and Ron Randall, 'Windfall', *Swamp Thing*, 43 (Dec. 1985). In a story written by Bissette from a plot devised by Moore in collaboration with the other creators on the series, Gregori returns to his daughter in the form of a rapidly unravelling Frankenstein's monster, a hallucinatory journey inspired by his reading of Shelley's novel to the child

Abigail (Moore, Bissette, Totleben, Veitch and Alcala, 'Reunion', *Swamp Thing*, 59 (Apr. 1987).
21 Moore, Bissette and Totleben, 'Bogeymen', *Swamp Thing*, 44 (Jan. 1986), 20.ii–v.
22 Moore, Bissette and Totleben, 'Revelations', 17.ii.
23 Jonathan Bate, 'From "Red" to "Green"', in *The Green Studies Reader: From Romanticism to Ecocriticism*, ed. Laurence Coupe (London and New York: Routledge, 2000), pp. 167–72 (p. 169).
24 Alan Moore, Rick Veitch and Alfredo Alcala, 'Loose Ends (Reprise)', *Swamp Thing*, 63 (Aug. 1987), 20–1.
25 Alan Moore, Stan Woch and Ron Randall, 'The Parliament of Trees', *Swamp Thing*, 47 (Apr. 1986), 18.iii.
26 Margaret Thatcher, speech to the Royal Society (27 Sept. 1988), *The Margaret Thatcher Foundation*: www.margaretthatcher.org/speeches/displaydocument.asp?docid=107346.
27 This epithet was delivered by Gerald Kaufman in 1983; for Kaufman's recollection of the affair, see 'Michael Foot: Brilliant but wrong, wrong, wrong', *The Times* (4 Mar. 2010).
28 Moore, Bissette and Totleben, *Swamp Thing*, 35–6 (Apr.–May 1985).
29 The theory first addressed a wide audience in 1979 in *Gaia: A New Look at Life on Earth* (Oxford: Oxford University Press); see Moore, Woch and Randall, 'Parliament of Trees'.
30 Romantic pantheism is most fully explored in Thomas McFarland, *Coleridge and the Pantheist Tradition* (Oxford: Oxford University Press, 1969).
31 Alan Moore, 'Introduction', in *The Saga of Swamp Thing*, p. 8.
32 Veitch's continuation of the title after 1987 has a tendency to make explicit themes implied by Moore, and the superhero problem is an example of this; see Rick Veitch and Alfredo Alcala, 'The Thinker', *Swamp Thing*, 75 (Aug. 1988), 10.ii.
33 Moore, Bissette and Totleben, *Swamp Thing*, 25 (June 1984). Later in the series, Moore alludes to another Romantic visual text in Henry Fuseli's painting *The Nightmare* (1781): Swamp Thing, returning to Louisiana to find Abigail gone, muses on a picture in her empty house: 'Framed upon her wall . . . an incubus . . . squats upon . . . a sleeping woman's chest . . . and leers knowingly'; Moore, Veitch and Alcala, 'Home Free', *Swamp Thing*, 51 (Aug. 1986), 18.iv. Fuseli's most famous image – something of a Gothic cliché – deals in similar themes to the Goya drawing, but its image of vulnerable femininity threatened by monsters also provides a missed clue to Abby's disappearance: she is in custody in Gotham, awaiting prosecution under obscenity laws for her relationship with a non-human creature.
34 Keats's celebrated meditation on poetic creativity: letter to George and

Tom Keats (1817), in *The Letters of John Keats: A Selection*, ed. Robert Gittings (Oxford: Oxford University Press, 1970), p. 43.
35 See Moore, Veitch, Alcala and Totleben, 'Natural Consequences' and 'The Garden of Earthly Delights', *Swamp Thing*, 52–3 (Sept.–Oct. 1986).
36 Moore, Bissette and Totleben, *Swamp Thing*, 25 (June 1984), 18.v.
37 *Ibid.*, 22.i.
38 Geoff Klock argues that *Swamp Thing* has only an accidental relationship with the superhero cycles of the DC universe; *How to Read Superhero Comics and Why* (New York and London: Continuum, 2002), p. 18.

8

Madness and the city: the collapse of reason and sanity in Alan Moore's *From Hell*

Monica Germanà

> This mundus tenebrosus, this shadowy world of Mankind, is sunk into Night; there is not a Field without its Spirits, nor a City without its Daemons, and the Lunaticks speak Prophesies while the Wise men fall into the Pitte.
> Peter Ackroyd, *Hawksmoor*[1]

The tragic events associated with the archetypal serial killer known as Jack the Ripper were, as Darren Oldridge has commented, 'above all, a media event'.[2] The unprecedented coverage of the events fed the nascent appetite for the type of modern sensationalist press that would prove to be as long-lived as the legacy left by the elusive perpetrator of the Whitechapel murders. Jack the Ripper, as is well known, takes his name from the 'Dear Boss' letter – likely to have been written by a journalist – received by the Central News Agency on 27 September 1888. The sensationalist response to the murders raised questions about the effects on the general public of such an uncontrollable proliferation of theories, accusations and, most importantly, the commercial gain that the gruesome details of such murders generated. *Punch*, the satirical magazine, for instance, commented on the media-induced hysteria associated with the endemic spread of such narratives, be they visual or textual:

> Is it not within the bounds of probability that to the highly-coloured pictorial advertisements to be seen on almost all the hoardings in London, vividly representing sensational scenes of murder, exhibited as 'the great

attractions' of certain dramas, the public may be to a certain extent indebted for the horrible crimes in Whitechapel? We say it most seriously;– imagine the effect of these gigantic pictures of violence and assassination by knife and pistol on the morbid imagination of unbalanced minds. These hideous picture-posters are a blot on our civilisation, and a disgrace to the Drama.[3]

Some important points emerge from this comment. To begin with, there is a clear awareness of the entertainment factor that such crimes created in the city of London; as Oldridge notes: 'even before Chapman's death, sightseers were gathering at the location of Polly Nichols's killing and by late September a sideshow on Whitechapel Road was displaying wax models of the murdered women.'[4] The subsequent murders – and particularly, if the humour can be forgiven, the 'double bill' produced on 30 September when the murderer struck Liz Stride and Catherine Eddowes to death – increased the interest of the general public, as testified by this news item published on 1 October 1888:

> Terror and amazement were depicted in almost every face that one met in the streets of that now notorious district. [. . .] Trains, trams, and omnibuses disgorged their hundreds of passengers, who wended their way to the two localities, which have, for the moment, put Buck's-row and Hanbury-street into the shade.[5]

Given the monstrous rhetoric associated with the crimes, it may not be too far-fetched to relate the general public's interest in the Whitechapel murders to other kinds of weird spectacles the city of London had offered to its visitors in the past. As Roy Porter remarks, in the eighteenth century 'provincials up in town would tour Bethlem, together with other shows in London such as the lions in the Tower or Bartolomew Fair';[6] linking displays such as the mental asylum of Bethlem (Bedlam) and the sites of the Ripper murders is the collective fascination with deviancy, aberration and abnormality. In fact madness, on many levels, becomes the primary discourse in the interwoven narratives about the Whitechapel murders, and the article in *Punch* draws attention to the impact that sensationalist media may have on 'the morbid imagination of unbalanced minds'. Significantly, the address ends on a pessimistic note reflecting on the state of 'our civilisation', suggesting that, rather than the crimes themselves, it is the uncontrollable responses to them that question its rational foundations.

This chapter proposes a reading of Alan Moore's retelling of the 1888 Whitechapel murders in relation to its treatment and representation of madness. The principal argument of this analysis is that in *From Hell* the Ripper murders embody the collapse of logos at the end of the nineteenth century and thus expose the rise of a problematic anxiety about modernity. In doing so, the nature and context of the crimes point to the uncanny pervasiveness of insanity within the city. As pathologies of the mind constitute a significant strand in Gothic literature from Robert Louis Stevenson's *Dr Jekyll and Mr Hyde* to Daphne Du Maurier's *Rebecca*, so the reason/madness opposition underpins, at various levels, Moore's complex retelling of the murders. In destabilising the fixed boundaries within the binary opposition, however, the graphic novel points to a much more complex, discursive view of the city's psyche and history, which, haunted by demons past and future, appears to be quintessentially informed by madness.

In engaging with the most infamous of London's historical revenants, *From Hell*, which takes its title from a letter the alleged Ripper sent, along with half a human kidney, to the Chairman of the Whitechapel Vigilance Committee on 16 October 1888, insanity emerges on many levels. As the story revolves around the Royal physician William Gull, whom the reader knows from Chapter 4 to be responsible for the murders, it is contextualised within nineteenth-century medical and scientific discourse around pathologies of the mind and concurrent changes in the treatment and institutionalisation of mental health. On a different level, however, Queen Victoria's alleged request to 'silence' the five Whitechapel prostitutes aware of Prince Eddie's affair with a working-class girl is manipulated by Gull to suit his own 'mission': that of restoring the masculine/Apollonian/rational principle through the suppression of its opposite counterpart, the feminine/Dionysian/irrational principle, by taking the five women's lives in a series of highly ritualised murders. Madness, therefore, produces two important areas of investigation: first, it interrogates Victorian notions on the relation between women – and their sexuality – and hysteria. Secondly, it exposes the city's occult powers, which, Gull explains, embody the dialectic between reason and madness that in turn drives its history forward. As Moore acknowledges in the 2006 edition of the graphic novel, the royal conspiracy plot derives from Stephen Knight's *Jack the Ripper: The Final Solution*,[7] but the notion of Gull's engagement with the dark energy of the city draws significantly from Iain Sinclair's psychogeographical representation of the city in *Lud Heat* and *White Chappel, Scarlet Tracings* ('Appendix I', p. 11).

As Scott Brewster has noted, 'Gothic does not merely transcribe disturbed, perverse or horrifying worlds: its narrative structures and voices are interwoven with and intensify the madness they represent.'[8] As suggested earlier, in various ways, the discourse of madness emerges strongly from the narrative responses to the Whitechapel murders, as this passage from *The Star* published on the day of Annie Chapman's murder exemplifies: 'London lies today under the spell of a great terror. A nameless reprobate – half beast, half man – is at large, who is daily gratifying his murderous instincts on the most miserable and defenceless classes of the community.'[9] Across the press, the murderer is repeatedly referred to as 'a madman', 'a murderous lunatic', 'a monster', 'a homicidal maniac', 'a ghoul' and 'mad Cain', amongst other epithets;[10] specific types of madness, too, are listed, such as 'sexual insanity', as repeatedly proposed by the *Star* and the *Evening News*, as well as religious mania, referred to, amongst others, by Dr G. Savage in an article on 'Homicidal Mania'.[11] As Andrew Smith has observed: 'the sensationalist language runs together the unreal (the ghoul) with the real (a more prosaic xenophobia concerning Indians), and this bringing together of the fantastic with social and racial prejudice develops one anxiety of the time: the image of the city overrun with foreigners.'[12] Besides its literal xenophobic subtext, there is a definite emphasis on the uncanny foreignness of the events, as testified by the references to patterns of repetition, imitation and cross-fertilisation between the fictional and historical past of the city of London, and the current menace threatening the order, status and authority that the centre of the British Empire, at this stage, struggles to keep. Consider, for example, this extract from an article published in the *East London Advertiser* after Annie Chapman's murder:

> If, as we imagine, there be a murderous lunatic concealed in the slums of Whitechapel, who issues forth at night like another Hyde, to prey upon the defenceless women of the 'unfortunate' class, we have little doubt that he will be captured.[13]

The reference to Stevenson's character is significant: since the publication of his novella, Mr Hyde quickly grew to embody the savage other; at the time of the murders, an excellent performance by American actor

Richard Mansfield gave life to Jekyll/Hyde on the West End stage; he would also, at the time, be suspected of the murders; most importantly, however, the analogy reveals other speculations that a different kind of outsider could be responsible for the crimes: a member of the medical profession. A series of professional statements and opinions were, in this respect, published in *The Lancet*. Against the widely spread consensus in relation to the state of insanity affecting the serial killer, Dr Henry Sutherland commented instead that 'he or they are of perfectly sound mind';[14] to this, Dr L. Forbes Winslow responded that

> Homicidal lunatics are cunning, deceptive, plausible, and on the surface, to all outward appearances, sane; but there is contained within their innermost nature a dangerous lurking after blood, which, though at times latent, will develop when the opportunity arises.[15]

Such a response was in line with his previous letter published in *The Times*, where he stated that 'The whole affair is that of a lunatic, and as there is "method in madness," so there was method shown in the crime and in the gradual dissection of the body of the latest victim.'[16] But it was precisely the method deployed to mutilate the victims that inspired the theory that the person responsible for the murders must have some kind of medical/anatomical knowledge. Anxieties surrounding such speculations emerged, once again, in *The Lancet*: 'the public mind – ever too ready to cast mud at legitimate research – will hardly fail to be excited to a pitch of animosity against anatomists and curators, which may take a long while to subside'.[17] The truth was that the mutilations suffered by the victims drew attention to the practice of dissection and the fine boundaries separating medical practice from the violence perpetrated by the Whitechapel murderer. As Smith suggests: 'the question was whether this apparently pathologised autopsy indicated the signs of madness or implied something that was central, but concealed within, models of the "norm".'[18] The crucial issue, which, as Smith proposes, derived from the self-reflective questions medical practitioners were forced to ask when confronted with the uncannily dissected bodies of the Whitechapel victims, was the message that these bodies concealed in relation to the norm.

From Hell engages with the shifting boundaries of madness and reason and exposes the precarious foundations of normative ideology supporting definitions of mental sanity on many levels. The graphic novel is framed by a narrative situated within a later chronological period: both the Prologue and the Epilogue are set in September 1923, 35 years after the events that unravelled in Whitechapel. In the first section, we learn that the visions that would have supported the Royal conspiracy theory and William Gull's charge of the Whitechapel murders were an invention of the self-proclaimed psychic Robert Lees. Hence *From Hell* unfolds as an intricate plot of errors and red herrings that, in a sense, pre-empts the aim of every Ripperologist speculation; instead of leading the readers to the revelation of a clear, linear solution to the unsolved mystery of the Ripper murders, *From Hell* follows a trajectory which, from the start, interrogates the foundations of rational knowledge and logic. Beside Lees, other characters experience visions throughout the narrative: William Gull suffers a vision masqueraded as the result of a stroke (II.26); the vision would, apparently, underpin his belief in a divine call behind the murders; Abberline is caught daydreaming and reminiscing about his father (VI.1.i–iii); Klara, the future mother of Adolf Hitler, has an ominous vision of a Jewish massacre in the proximity of Christchurch at the time of Polly Nichols's murder (V.2.ii–vii); Polly Nichols *believes* she has the vision of the Indian divinity Ganesa, impersonated by Joseph, or, as Moore would have it, John Merrick (aka 'the Elephant Man'; V.28.iv–vi, V.29.i, iii). Whether induced by actual premonitions – as with Klara's omen of the Holocaust – or staged – as is the case with Ganesa's apparition – these notions are, like Lees's fake psychic visions, graphically visible in the drawings that accompany the text; aware of the forgery behind some of these visions, the reader is therefore forced to question the authenticity of each one, while the narrative progressively deconstructs any faith in the powers of logical deduction conventionally attached to a crime novel. Rather than throwing light onto the unsolved mystery, the narrative appears to be caught up in a web of self-fabricated, self-reflective lies.

That Moore's reworking of the Whitechapel murders ambiguously plays with visibility is also made clear by the other visions experienced by Gull, which implicate the novel's resistance to linear time. A significant instance of anachrony occurs after the murder of Liz Stride, when Gull's memory looks back on the concurrent event from a future perspective: 'I remember now . . . / This is the one I didn't finish, isn't it?' (VIII.33.iv–v). Later, in the same chapter, and the same historical night, Gull has another ahistorical vision of a tower block sublimely erected on the site of Catherine Eddowes's murder, Mitre Square (VIII.40). As Alexandra Warwick has suggested, 'events, such as murder, are produced not only out of a past, but also out of a future'.[19] The narrative anachronies suggest the necessity to read the narrative with a sense of its simultaneous implications, which, in turn, expose the palimpsestic structure of the city that accommodates the events. With Michel Foucault's notion of heterotopia in mind, it could be suggested that London, and Whitechapel in particular, embody several of the qualities pertinent to the quintessentially 'other' space of Foucault's theory; like the archive and the museum,[20] in relation to time, *From Hell* presents a city that exists outside linear chronology, a view supported by the repeated references to Howard Hinton's theory of time as a fourth dimension: 'time is a human illusion' (II.14.ii), history has 'an architecture' (II.15.iv). In the architecture and the topography of London, past and present coalesce with the future: 'all times coexist in the stupendous whole of eternity' (XIV.12.iii).

Thrust in a perpetually anachronic state, the city is also deviant because of its inherent subversion of cultural normativity. This is apparent in various forms of subversion staged in the narrative of *From Hell*. The theory adapted by Moore allows the narrative to focus on the management of mental illness in nineteenth-century Britain/London. The historical William Gull was an eminent representative of the medical profession, who contributed to the developing stages of psychiatry with studies on anorexia nervosa as well as myxodoema, which he linked to women's insanity in his paper 'On a Cretinoid State Supervening in Adult Life in Women'.[21] The fictionalised application of Gull's theory allows him to perform an operation on Annie Crook, who is, as a result, reduced to a state of permanent and irreversible insanity: when Walter Sickert sees her, she confuses the reference to her baby Alice with the fictional character of another Victorian text concerned with the permeable boundaries of reason and madness, Lewis Carroll's *Alice's Adventures in Wonderland*. The process is suggestive of the mismanagement of mental illness and the role played by normative medical discourse in the construction of madness. In order to stop her affair with Prince Eddie, Annie Crook is forcibly taken to the Lunatic Ward of Guy's Hospital, where she is treated without her consent; she is accused of being a lunatic on the grounds that she is not able to understand her situation, having been deceived into thinking that Albert was a common fellow; when she says, 'They took my Albert away, and they called him "Your Highness"', James Hinton comments to Gull, 'poor woman, I see what you mean about her condition' (II.31.ii). Before her operation, Gull reinforces this point: 'less than a thimble-full of iodine divides the intellectual from the imbecile. / of which phenomenon I shall forthwith attempt a demonstration' (II.32.vi). What the witnesses do not know is that the process will affect Annie the other way around: the (mad) doctor will induce her insanity by manipulating her thyroid.

Although Gull's professional misconduct is entirely fictional, it also reflects the biased approach that was common practice in Victorian psychiatric treatment of female insanity. As Elaine Showalter unveiled in her seminal work *The Female Malady*, a gender bias emerged strongly in the alternative treatments of mental illness in male and female patients. The study of mental illness was, in relation to women, always linked to female sexuality, with consequences on the treatment of such patients that bordered on – and in some cases exceeded – torture: the most infamous instance is perhaps that of Dr Isaac Baker Brown, who mutilated his patients' genitalia in the attempt to treat their mental problems,[22] as he expounded in his medical essay *On the curability of certain forms of insanity, epilepsy, catalepsy, and hysteria in females*.[23] Significantly, Gull is referenced in one of the case studies reported by Baker Brown.[24] It is hardly surprising, in the light of this, that at the time of the Whitechapel murders, members of the medical profession could be accused of crossing the fine line that separated treatment from torture and reason from madness. Moore makes this point clearly with his intertextual reference to William Hogarth's painting *The Reward of Cruelty*, part of a four piece-set called *Four Stages of Cruelty* and depicting medicine as a form of mutilation inflicted on criminal bodies (IX.176.vii). While, on one level, the satire is directed at criminals, it can be suggested that the inhumane practice of dissection also emerges in Hogarth's depiction, as Roy Porter notes of his work: 'folly was the idiom of satirists, and Hogarth engraved mankind's madness in a crazy upside-down world in which London and Bedlam formed an ironic tale of two cities'.[25] Similarly ambiguous links are established with the most gruesome of the Ripper murders, that of Mary Kelly, on 8 November 1888: here the inclusion of panels depicting Gull's role as a lecturer in an anatomy laboratory blurs the boundaries between medical autopsy and the pathological autopsy performed by the murderer in the adjacent panels (X.14.iv).

As Smith has noted of the narrative produced by post-mortem autopsies on the Whitechapel victims, there seems to be a (subconscious, perhaps) tendency to find natural causes for the victims' deaths in the evidence provided by their bodies. In other words, there is a search for clues that would identify the women's physical weaknesses, as demonstrated by statements such as Dr Timothy Killeen's in relation to Martha Tabram's autopsy: 'the heart, which was rather fatty, and that would have been sufficient to cause death'.[26] Though an autopsy would include, even today, a report on the state of all organs, evidence from press reports supports the view purported by Smith that 'there was an additional narrative which was looking for signs of disease [...] and general indicators of social deprivation which could, at least theoretically, render the victim complicit with their fate'.[27] Consider, for instance, this statement made about Liz Stride:

> Her features are pinched, like those of one who has suffered want, but her expression is not unpleasant. [...] Her hair is auburn, her lips thick, the upper one especially so, with that sort of double fold often noticed in lascivious women. [...] As she lies in the mortuary her dress is open over her bosoms, but her stays have not been undone.[28]

While the voyeuristic gaze can hardly be suppressed in this post-mortem description of the victim's body, the reference to Stride's lasciviousness, combined with a notion of social deprivation, lead to the assumption that somehow she was responsible for her own murder. Gull delivers a similar message in *From Hell*: after mutilating Kelly's body beyond recognition – to the extent that some still doubt whether she was the fifth canonical victim – Gull suffers a vision of late twentieth-century Britain as a soulless place where computers seem to have replaced human communication; in this 'sick' context, Gull justifies his actions, addressing the victim: 'you'd have all been dead in a year or two from liver failure, men or childbirth' (X.23.i). An article published in *The Times* after Kelly's brutal murder seems to contain the same subtext: 'it had been noticed that the deceased woman was somewhat addicted to drink, but Mr M'Carthy [keeper of 13 Miller's Court] denied having any knowledge that she had been leading a loose or immoral life'.[29] The victims' deprivations and their alleged fallen status seemed, in other words, to shift the emphasis from the sickness of the murderer to the sickness of the victims. To an extent, this would have been influenced by post-Darwinian theories of evolution and a medical approach that saw degeneracy as the combination of hereditary traits and habit. Consider, for instance, this reference to the 'skull' of the Whitechapel murderer in an article published in the *Daily News*:

> The police have to find for us one of the most extraordinary monsters known to the history of mental and spiritual disease, a monster whose skull will have to be cast for all the surgical museums of the world.[30]

In *From Hell*, Gull exposes similar views on physiognomy, when he comments on the 'usefulness' of Netley's features to the medical student: 'I'd undoubtedly find your remarkably shallow brow and closely-spread eyes indispensable' (II.29.vi), which echo the biological determinism of the atavistic *stigmata* exposed in Cesare Lombroso's *Criminal Man*. Organic causes and symptoms became central to the early detection – and construction – of mental illness, as Showalter reminds us:

> Whereas at least some early Victorian reformers deplored the social problems that had brought so many wretched people to the asylums, Darwinian psychiatrists sternly maintained that hereditary organic taint compounded by vicious habits caused madness.[31]

That mental instability may be a sign of degeneracy is also made clear by the particular interest in the abnormal characters of the Victorian Gothic: the apelike, stooping, savage-looking Hyde is perhaps the most iconic example that springs to mind; as noted by Rosemary Jackson: 'recidivism and regression to bestial levels are common post-Darwinian fantasies'.[32] The lunacy of the Whitechapel murders is conjoined with notions of endemic degeneracy and social deprivation in the famous *Punch* cartoon, 'Nemesis of Neglect' (29 September 1888), depicting a shadowy monster armed with a butcher's knife and accompanied by the parody of a Gothic poem; significantly, the menacing figure haunting the 'Dank roofs, dark entries, closely-clustered walls' and the 'Murder-inviting nooks, death-reeking gutters' of Whitechapel is, like Stevenson's Mr Hyde, 'unerect': stalled or underdeveloped in its evolutionary trajectory, the Whitechapel murderer is an aberration and, most threateningly, the living proof that human evolution may in fact point backward.

In their public display of aberrant lunacy the Whitechapel murders manifested the endemic degeneracy of British civilisation, on whose moral (and racial) supremacy the Empire rested. Press reports made this point repeatedly: 'THE series of atrocious murders in the East-end of London is a fresh and terrible reminder of the capacity of humanity for evil, and of the facilities which our congested centres of population offer to the commission of the wildest crimes', commented the *Evening News* in the wake of Annie Chapman's murder.[33] Moreover, following the unveiling of sexual scandals and campaigns to 'rescue' the fallen women of Whitechapel, which culminated in the publication of the 'Maiden Tribute of Modern Babylon' in the *Pall Mall Gazette* in the summer of 1885, the East/West London social divide had been exposed in relation to the corruption displayed by the growing appetite of West-London gentlemen for East-London girls. As Judith R. Walkowitz has observed:

> To middle-class observers, Whitechapel was an alien place, a center of cosmopolitan culture and entrepôt for foreign immigrants and refugees, whose latest wave consisted of poor Jews escaping the progroms of Eastern Europe in the 1880s.[34]

In *From Hell*, Gull makes similar remarks about the anarchic heterotopia that Whitechapel has represented in London throughout its history:

> The Huguenots who settled Spitalfields, their independence bordering on Anarchy, were massacred by soldiers barracked here in Hawksmoor's church. [. . .]
> The only populations that are constant hereabouts, untouched by passing centuries, are those perpetual multitudes of beggars, criminals . . .
> . . . and whores. (IV.32.iii–iv)

Abberline's musings, too, draw attention to the uncivilised, uncontrolled terrain of Whitechapel, when he tells his wife that 'Whitechapel's not society at all, it's something else. The people there, you can't control 'em' (XI.37.ii). Following the murder of Annie Chapman, the critique of the police inadequacy and the hidden hypocrisy of the wealthy London society emerged strongly on the pages of sensationalist dailies such as the *Star*:

> In the East a thousand slaves – as ignorant, as hopeless, as corrupt as were the slave-rowers in a Spanish galleon – toil to keep the West in all the trappings of finery, to make Jubilee dresses, ball-room costumes, and all the rest of the 'property' for the great sensual show we call 'society.' Of course 'society' does not know the cost at which its Juggernaut is kept up. It is only

idly and stupidly selfish, with a cotton-wool kind of callousness, out of which it will only awake by the help of such a thunderous sermon as the Whitechapel murders. [...] Will the West conclude that all its mad pursuit of wealth, its senseless craving after luxury, its ennui, its cruel indifference to the gospel of the religion it patronises, its neglect of all the teachings of history – is a mistake, and a fatal one?[35]

Significantly, the West End's frivolous shallowness is expressed in terms of 'madness', 'senselessness', 'callousness' and 'ennui': the discourse is, once again, that of insanity, suggesting that the lunacy of Jack the Ripper, the anarchy of Whitechapel and the obsessive appetite of the West End are all intricately interconnected in the same invisible pattern that the Whitechapel murders had been tracing. The initial section of Chapter 5 in *From Hell* makes this point distinctly with the juxtaposition of panels depicting the luxurious, comfortable quarters of Regent Street and Cavendish Square where Gull's residence is situated next to the unsanitised squalor of the East-End slums: the softer edges of the West-End depictions give it a somewhat dreamlike quality, hinting perhaps that the 'real' London is enshrouded in the sharp-edged darkness of Whitechapel.

But the Whitechapel murders – and their reading in *From Hell* – suggest something more than the radical critique of social unfairness. Violence and crime were familiar to Victorian London, particularly in the overcrowded slums of Whitechapel. Yet the apparent lack of a plausible motive, together with the particular nature of the mutilations, spoke of a kind of violence that exceeded the boundaries of the human; in *From Hell*, this is expressed by Abberline's struggle to decode the pattern that links the crimes:

> Smith was raped and tortured. That's *cruelty*. I can understand cruelty. Tabram was killed by frenzied and repeated stabbing. That's *rage*. I understand that too.
> This one's more ... methodical. Someone near enough did surgery on this woman. I don't understand that at all. (VI.12.v–vi)

Abberline's words here echo the historical Winslow's claim that 'there is "method in madness"' quoted earlier, and it is precisely on this paradox that *From Hell* defines the triumph of insanity over reason as the primary force running through the Whitechapel murders; moreover, what this crisis of rational principles implies is the indissoluble marriage of metropolis and madness. Madness, the text seems to suggest, cannot be eradicated from the metropolitan space of London, which Gull sees as the negotiation of a historical continuum deeply rooted in the Dyonisiac foundations of its architecture, concealed in the occult hot points which Moore identifies in specific London locations, following the footsteps of Sinclair's *Lud Heat* and Peter Ackroyd's *Hawksmoor*. The secretive core of Dyonisiac architecture thus rests upon the paradoxical basis of the irrational: 'they knew the unconscious was the inspiration whence their towers of reason sprang. Thus, HARNESSING its power symbolically was their sublime accomplishment' (IV.23.iv). Madness threatens reason and the social order apparently based on the rational principles of civilisation.

Yet, in *From Hell* Gull seems to suggest something entirely different: civilisation cannot exist without madness. Simultaneously, in order to maintain power, and to counteract the subversive forces represented by the concurrent uprisings of the socialist and feminist movements at the end of the nineteenth century, reason must accommodate the irrational force of madness. As Gull explains: 'sometimes an act of social magic's NECESSARY; man's triumph over woman's INSECURE, the dust of history not yet SETTLED. / Changing times erase the pattern that constrains society's irrational, female side' (IV.30.ii). The mission proposed by Gull, therefore, is seemingly that of suppressing the power of subversive madness embodied by the fallen women of Whitechapel through the ritualised sacrifice of their bodies in order to propitiate their Goddess, Diana. Upon killing Polly Nichols, Gull remarks the significance of the location: Buck's Row signals a reference to 'Diana's sacrificial beast' (V.30.vii).

The theory of Gull's mystical involvement in the Whitechapel murders is also explored by Sinclair's *White Chappel, Scarlet Tracings*; here Gull explains his vision in a similar vein as he does in *From Hell*:

> I would leave a city of female cretins if I could absolutely erase the work that I have done. [. . .] I have done what was required of me. [. . .] I acted out the description of an act that was always there. And in doing this I erased it. I freed that space. It could not be left to madmen, prophets, millennial tremblers.[36]

Though fighting against madness, in Sinclair's version of the story, as in *From Hell*, Gull is ultimately expelled from the Masonic lodge on the grounds of his lunacy, to which accusations Gull responds with the ambiguous tones of self-accusation:

> I have a Gold Medal in Lunacy; I am Lecturer in Lunacy; Fullerian Professor in Lunacy; Fellow of the Royal College of Lunatics; Resident Madman to Guy's Hospital; Baronet and Mooncalf Extraordinary to Her Majesty the Queen. I rave in my chains; I rattle.[37]

The mad-doctor becomes simply the mad doctor, in an inversion that reflects Foucault's understanding of the shifting relationship between psychiatric doctors and their patients: 'the madman tends to form with the doctor, in an unbroken unity, a "couple" whose complicity dates back to very old links'.[38] The inversion is exemplified by the circular structure that sees Gull erroneously locked up in an Islington mental asylum, just as he had, at the beginning of the story, been responsible for Annie Crook's fake diagnosis. His defenceless position against the authority of the mental institution, and the system behind it, is well captured by one of the masons: 'I suppose it wouldn't matter WHAT he claimed if he were thought *insane*' (XII.24.vii).

The mutilations on the women's bodies, and particularly the removal of their wombs, also raises questions about the social function of madness. Associated with hysteria, the womb embodies the feminine principle of irrationality. In Sinclair's version of the story, Gull makes this point clearly when he claims to 'have hacked out an infected womb that would have bred monsters'.[39] In *From Hell*, too, the repetitive, methodical pattern of the mutilations conveys this notion of enforced rational, masculine control over irrational, feminine madness; the almost uninterrupted sequence of same-size panels used to depict the lengthy mutilations performed on Mary Kelly's body may suggest the regular pattern of a lucid mind: there is indeed method in madness (X.2–13). Yet, previously, the ambivalent response to Polly Nichols's organ suggests a different message; Gull's admission that 'she was full a light' interrogates the equation woman = madness = darkness. In his commentary, Moore suggests this is a reference to the spectral light emanating from the woman's death and part of London lore since the murder ('Appendix I', p. 21). While this could be also, arguably, a reference to Nichols's pregnant condition, the emphatic reference to the light represents an inversion of the sun/moon, masculine/feminine hierarchical oppositions (V.33.vii).

The graphic novel clearly refutes the binary oppositions of West/East, reason/madness, Man/Woman in favour of the pervasive acceptance of a principle of madness operating at all levels and in all sectors of the metropolis. In Sinclair's work, Gull eventually admits his failure and recognises the overwhelming force of the new myth his actions have created:

> But my acts failed. I did not see that they would themselves form the shape of a new myth, and that in removing the outline of the old fear I was planting a spoor of heat that would itself need to be brought to earth, chilled to immobility, stopped.[40]

In *From Hell*, too, the lunacy of Whitechapel gradually turns into a larger conspiracy, an all-encompassing infectious condition that affects the city at all levels: the series of illustrations in Chapter 9 depicting a range of random people – including a religious minister, a drunken working-class man, a journalist and two youths – seems to suggest the notion of a pervasive virus, deeply rooted in the dark underworld of London captured in the last panel of this series (see Figure 8.1). Just as Hyde is incestuously related to all characters in Stevenson's novella, so is Jack the Ripper the sick essence of London's psyche: 'I am not man so much as syndrome', declares Gull in the last visionary episode before his death (XIV.17.iii). Madness and excess, Gull suggests, are fundamental elements of metropolitan life; without them, the individual is lost in a pattern of meaningless repetition, which, as Gull fears and foresees, threatens the alienated identity of modern England: 'these mean-spirited and ugly English rooms. They speak of an ugly English future. / [...] / Furnishings and ornaments no doubt produced in thousands' (XIV.19.ii–iii). Modernity is relentless reproduction and urban life a 'real' threat to individual subjectivity.

In Moore's complex vision, then, madness functions as an ambiguous kind of discourse in relation to the city that has accommodated the longest-running murder-mystery story: exposing a pathologised version of normativity, the story challenges the supremacy of reason to argue for the necessary function of madness – viewed as deviancy from established order, subversion of authority as well as spectacle and object of repressed desire – in the construction of metropolitan subjectivity. In this sense, it could be argued that Moore reflects the theory exposed by Georg Simmel on the psychic life of the metropolis; arguing that the city

8.1 Alan Moore and Eddie Campbell, *From Hell*, IX.36.i–vi

privileges a kind of objective life that threatens individual autonomy and sense of identity, Simmel claims that 'the individual is reduced to a negligible quantity'.[41] To the threat of a loss of identity posed by the metropolis, the individual will react, Simmel argues, by accentuating idiosyncratic behaviour: 'this results in the individual's summoning the utmost in uniqueness and particularization, in order to preserve his most personal core. He has to exaggerate this personal element in order to remain audible even to himself.'[42] In his vision of a future office space after Kelly's murder, Gull laments the predicament of 'a culture grown disinterested even in its own abysmal wounds' (X.22.i). In this light, the Ripper becomes, paradoxically, a reminder of the human and the saviour of the metropolitan psyche, embodying with its excessive lunacy, the vital drive of the city:

> Below the skin of history are London's veins that pulse and glisten with significance. That course with energy and meaning.
> And I am that Meaning.
> And I am that energy. (XIV.10.vii–ix)

Notes

1. Peter Ackroyd, *Hawksmoor* (London: Penguin, 1993), p. 101.
2. Darren Oldridge, 'Casting the Spell of Terror: The Press and the Early Whitechapel Murders', in *Jack The Ripper: Media, Culture, History*, ed. Alexandra Warwick and Martin Willis (Manchester: Manchester University Press, 2007), pp. 46–55 (p. 46).
3. *Punch*, 15 Sept. 1888, p. 130.
4. Oldridge, 'Casting the Spell of Terror', p. 54.
5. 'The Reign of Terror in Whitechapel', *Evening News*, 1 Oct. 1888, p. 1.
6. Roy Porter, *Madmen: A Social History of Madhouses, Mad-Doctors and Lunatics* (Stroud: Tempus, 2004), p. 129.
7. Alan Moore and Eddie Campbell, *From Hell: Being a Melodrama in Sixteen Parts* (London: Knockabout Comics, 2006 [1989–96]), 'Appendix I', p. 1; hereafter cited in the main body of the text.
8. Scott Brewster, 'Seeing Things: Gothic and the Madness of Interpretation', in *A Companion to the Gothic*, ed. David Punter (Oxford: Blackwell, 2000), pp. 281–92 (p. 281).
9. 'Horror Upon Horror. Whitechapel is Panic-Stricken at Another Fiendish Crime', *Star* (8 Sept. 1888), p. 2.
10. See, for instance, 'The Whitechapel Horrors', *Evening News*, 10 Sept. 1888, p. 2; 'The Whitechapel Murder', *East London Advertiser*, 8 Sept. 1888, p. 5;

'The Fourth Whitechapel Murder', *Daily News*, 10 Sept. 1888, p. 5; interview with Sir James Risdon Bennett (physician), *Evening News*, 1 Oct. 1888, p. 3 and 'What We Think', *Star*, 10 Sept. 1888, p. 1.
11 G. Savage, 'Homicidal Mania', *Fortnightly Review*, 50 (1888), 448–63.
12 Andrew Smith, *Victorian Demons: Medicine, Masculinity and the Gothic at the Fin-de-Siècle* (Manchester: Manchester University Press, 2004), p. 70.
13 'The Whitechapel Murder', *East London Advertiser*, 8 Sept. 1888, p. 5.
14 Henry Sutherland, letter, *The Lancet*, 22 Sept. 1888, p. 603.
15 L. Forbes Winslow, letter, *The Lancet*, 22 Sept. 1888, p. 603.
16 L. Forbes Winslow, letter, *The Times*, 12 Sept. 1888, p. 6.
17 'The Whitechapel Murders', *The Lancet*, 29 Sept. 1888, p. 637.
18 Smith, *Victorian Demons*, p. 83.
19 Alexandra Warwick, 'Blood and Ink: Narrating the Whitechapel Murders', in *Jack the Ripper*, ed. Warwick and Willis, pp. 71–87 (p. 82).
20 Michel Foucault, 'Of Other Spaces', trans Jay Miskowiev, *Diacritics*, 16:1 (Spring 1986), 22–7 (p. 26).
21 William Gull, 'On a Cretinoid State Supervening in Adult Life in Women', *Transactions of the Clinical Society of London*, 7 (1873/74), 180–5.
22 Elaine Showalter, *The Female Malady: Women, Madness and English Culture, 1830–1880* (London: Virago, 1991 [1985]), p. 75.
23 Isaac Baker Brown, *On the curability of certain forms of insanity, epilepsy, catalepsy, and hysteria in females* (Hardwicke, 1866), pp. 9–10.
24 See ibid., p. 6.
25 Porter, *Madmen*, p. 26.
26 'The Murder in Whitechapel', *The Times*, 10 Aug. 1888, p. 12.
27 Smith, *Victorian Demons*, p. 80.
28 Description of Liz Stride in 'The Whitechapel Horrors', *Evening News*, 1 Oct. 1888, p. 2.
29 'Another Whitechapel Murder', *Times*, 10 Nov. 1888, p. 7.
30 'The Fourth Whitechapel Murder', *Daily News*, 10 Sept. 1888, p. 4.
31 Showalter, *Female Malady*, p. 104.
32 Rosemary Jackson, *Fantasy: The Literature of Subversion* (London: Routledge, 1981), p. 116. See also David Punter, *The Literature of Terror: A History of Gothic Fictions from 1765 to the Present Day*, 2nd edn, 2 vols (London: Longman, 1996), II, pp. 1–6.
33 'The Whitechapel Horrors', *Evening News*, 10 Sept. 1888, p. 2.
34 Judith R. Walkowitz, 'Jack the Ripper and the Myth of Male Violence', *Feminist Studies*, 8:3 (Autumn 1982), 543–74 (p. 547).
35 'What We Think', *Star*, 19 Sept. 1888, p. 1.
36 Iain Sinclair, *White Chappell, Scarlet Tracings* (London: Penguin, 2004 [1987]), p. 177.

37 *Ibid.*, pp. 174–5.
38 Michel Foucault, *Madness and Civilisation*, trans. Richard Howard (London: Routledge, 2007 [1959]), p. 260.
39 Sinclair, *White Chappell*, p. 177.
40 *Ibid.*
41 Georg Simmel, 'The Metropolis and Mental Life', in *Simmel On Culture*, ed. David Frisby and Michael Featherstone (London: Sage, 1997), pp. 174–85 (p. 184).
42 *Ibid.*, p. 184.

9

'I fashioned a prison that you could not leave': the Gothic imperative in *The Castle of Otranto* and 'For the Man Who Has Everything'

Brad Ricca

> We're near the Straits of Otranto and the castle of the same name, empty since the 18th century, when it was plagued by apparitions, which included a giant helmet covered with black plumage.
> Alan Moore, *The League of Extraordinary Gentlemen*[1]

In his frequent practice of exploring the further adventures of established literary characters in works such as *The League of Extraordinary Gentlemen* and *Lost Girls*, Alan Moore appropriates and adapts a wide range of canonical and non-canonical works, revisiting well-known characters, extending or re-examining popular stories, exploring and forging new intertextual connections and celebrating latent or repressed elements from his source material. In many cases, the allusions are specific enough to allow readers familiar with the earlier works to trace and reflect upon these connections. A prime example of this occurs in the miscellanea appended to issues of *The League of Extraordinary Gentlemen*, which taken together chart a fictional world that combines a vast range of discrete literary and non-literary sources. It is in this context that Horace Walpole's *The Castle of Otranto* appears overtly in Moore's oeuvre, as a single item in a long list recorded by 'The New Traveller's Almanac', a fictitious compendium documenting notable sites from *The League*'s heterocosm. Otranto here appears nestled between the Arcadian Tunnel from Jacopo Sannazaro's *Arcadia* and Portiuncula from *Die Reise Nach Portiuncula* by Stefan Andres,[2] but the function of Walpole's castle is limited to filling in the imaginary topography of *The League*'s diegesis, less significant than Jules Verne's 'Arabian Tunnel leading to the Red Sea, its existence proved by Nemo' – a major character in the first two volumes – and of a completely different order from the Blazing World, which is a key locus of action in the subsequent instalment of *The League*, *The Black Dossier*.[3] In this sense, then, *Otranto*'s appearance in *The League*, while it demonstrates Moore's awareness of Walpole's work, does not register as an adaptation understood, in Linda Hutcheon's terms, as 'an extended intertextual engagement'.[4]

But this is not the end of the story. Over a decade before Moore began work on *The League*, he wrote a one-off story, 'For the Man Who Has Everything', for the *Superman Annual*, 11, illustrated by future *Watchmen* collaborator Dave Gibbons and published in June 1985, midway through his run on *Swamp Thing*. Though Walpole's work does not appear by name, 'For the Man' employs narrative devices that clearly parallel – in both form and function – those found in *Otranto*, elements which Frederick S. Frank has identified as the 'imperative features' of the Gothic revival inaugurated by Walpole: unrewarded virtue, claustrophobic containment, subterranean pursuit, fluctuating psychosexual peril and the possibility of actually losing to the bad guys.[5] Moore's story can also be seen as addressing Walpole's larger project, which is 'an attempt to blend the two kinds of romance, the ancient and the modern. In the former all was imagination and improbability; in the latter, nature is always intended to be, and sometimes has been, copied with success.'[6] My claim in what follows is not that Moore is producing a conscious adaptation or appropriation of Walpole's work and it is not dependent upon his familiarity with *Otranto* specifically, though it would be very surprising if he had not encountered it directly, given his prodigious reading and self-professed interest in magic, fantasy and the supernatural.[7] That said, reading *Otranto* alongside 'For the Man' allows us to perceive the ways in which the latter work draws on a set of narrative resources proffered by the Gothic in order to provide an uncanny adaptation of Superman. Specifically, Moore's text adapts Walpole's 'blend' of the ancient and modern to investigate parallel superhero conventions differentiated by imaginative improbability (the 'ancient' Silver Age of comics) and a more modernised psychological realism. The result is a nostalgic, ironic glance at what Walpole might term the 'fluffy' romance of the Silver Age, in order to realise Moore's own imperative that the practical silliness of the superhero may yet offer great capacity for hermeneutic interrogation. Without claiming that 'For the Man' is a deliberate adaptation of Walpole, it is nevertheless possible to discern a set of structural and thematic parallels between the two works that suggests an underlying intertextual relation between them. As a foundational work in the genre, *Otranto* provides a template for the first generation of Gothic novels, laying the groundwork of a tradition that 'For the Man' mines, consciously or unconsciously, to adapt Superman into a character that is as susceptible to emotional duress and desire as to Kryptonite.

Moore's presentation of the Man of Steel in *Superman Annual, 11* is a new work of interpretive fiction, adhering to Hutcheon's description of adaptation as 'an act of appropriation or salvaging [. . .] a double process of interpreting and then creating something new', producing 'a manifestly different interpretation' of Superman.[8] In the process, 'For the Man' calls attention to the abject material of the superhero genre, the repressed other of the public-facing hero to which Moore would return in 'Whatever Happened to the Man of Tomorrow?', written to mark 'the end of the character that had been around since the end of the '30s'.[9] What both stories demonstrate is that it is not the elements most commonly taken to characterise the dark and gritty turn of comics in the mid-1980s – that is, explicit violence and transgressive sexuality – that represent the abject of superheroism, but rather a desire for mundane domesticity. In this sense, then, 'For the Man' mirrors and thus reverses the relationship between transgression and desire in the eighteenth-century Gothic novel by positioning domestic harmony as the antithesis of, rather than a metonym for, social cohesion.

The castle of Superman

The so-called 'first' Gothic novel, *Otranto* begins with a dark turn for a birthday, introducing social disharmony through a domestic tragedy:

> Young Conrad's birthday was fixed for his espousals. The company was assembled in the chapel of the Castle, and everything ready for beginning the divine office, when Conrad himself was missing [. . .]. The Princess Hippolita, without knowing what was the matter [. . .] swooned away. Manfred, less apprehensive than enraged at the procrastination of the nuptials, and at the folly of his domestic, asked imperiously what was the matter? The fellow made no

answer, but continued pointing toward the courtyard; and at last, after repeated questions put to him, cried out, 'Oh! the helmet! the helmet!' [...][Conrad was] almost buried under an enormous helmet, an hundred times more large than any casque ever made for human being, and shaded with a proportionable quantity of black feathers.[10]

The plot of *Otranto* is *de rigeur* Gothic. Conrad, the infirm young prince, dies on the day of his wedding to the lovely Isabella, crushed by the mysterious giant helmet. The wedding itself had been planned in haste because Conrad's father, Manfred, fears a mysterious prophecy and is anxious for a long line of heirs. Unhinged by his son's death, Manfred vows to divorce his wife Hippolita and marry Isabella himself in order to produce more hearty offspring. A strange peasant named Theodore helps Isabella escape, instigating a prototypical series of Gothic chases, secret churches, mysterious strangers and shocking revelations about parentage. Near the end of the story, Manfred accidentally slays his own daughter, Matilda, whom he mistakes for Isabella. In the end, Theodore is revealed to be the true lord of the castle and marries Isabella as Manfred seeks forgiveness. The novel is, in other words, convoluted, tense and slightly ridiculous.

'For the Man Who Has Everything' is an almost completely self-contained story. Its narrative occasion and initial tone are predicated upon a period in comics history known as the Silver Age, which began in *Showcase*, 4 where editor Julius Schwartz introduced a new version of the Flash and 'kicked off the great superhero revival'.[11] Silver Age stories, especially Superman's, were usually marked by silly, often domestic plots designed to uncover his secret identity. Moore's story, though grounded in a similar Silver Age conceit (Superman's birthday), quickly escalates into something more serious for the reader. Batman, Robin and Wonder Woman all happily arrive at the Fortress of Solitude for the celebration, but they are not the first guests to arrive. To their shock, they discover that Mongul, an evil galactic conqueror, has incapacitated Superman with the aid of a bizarre alien flower called a Black Mercy. While Batman tries to solve the mystery of Superman's imprisonment, Wonder Woman engages in a brutal slugfest with the alien despot. Finally freed, the Man of Steel pays Mongul back in kind. But in the end, it is the unlikely Robin who saves the day.

Both stories are quite different, but there are striking similarities, especially in *Otranto*'s opening scene of Conrad's demise. The occasions of both stories are birthdays, Conrad's and Superman's. And though Conrad dies (Superman does not), they are both attacked by large, very strange objects that immobilise both victim and onlooker and contain a type of 'plumage'. There is also *Otranto*'s Princess Hippolita, who shares a name with Wonder Woman's mother. Manfred, though hardly Batman, does exhibit the Caped Crusader's predilection of analysing notes, threats and prophecies. What distinguishes Moore's story beyond *Otranto* – and beyond the superhero 'team-up' premise common in comics – is Superman's narrative during his period of psychic captivity. The Black Mercy's huge mass of roselike tentacles attaches to Superman's chest and forges a symbiotic bond with his mind, creating a completely believable dreamscape in which the plant gleans its victim's fondest wish and grants it in the form of a vivid hallucination that serves as the perfect prison – having been granted his 'heart's desire', Superman has no wish to escape.[12] While his super friends fight Mongul on the plane of continuity throughout the echoing halls of the Fortress, Superman is powerless. Unlike the helmet that crushes poor Conrad to death, the psychic assault acts as another sort of helmet, enclosing Superman's mind within his own deepest fantasy. Armitt describes this very common Gothic action as occupying 'an interior dream- (or rather nightmare-) space'.[13]

Gothic comics

As with much of Moore's work with literary characters, there is an undercurrent of nostalgia in his treatment of superheroes. This extends to his use of standardised, almost ironic, Gothic elements throughout 'For the Man', from screams echoing throughout the Fortress and bizarre creatures that wait around corners, to ritual celebrations, mute statues and even portraits that appear to move – all situated in a cold, isolated castle in the middle of nowhere. This Romantic locale – like the polar framing of Shelley's *Frankenstein* and the ocular starkness of Friedrich's *Arctic Shipwreck* – borders on the sublime, and thus shifts the traditional superhero narrative towards a more formulaic Gothic tale, causing the reader's expectations to waver. As E.J. Clery notes of the history and power of the Gothic in the eighteenth century:

For much of the century, 'gothic' was a term used synonymously for 'uncouth' or 'barbaric' when referring to art or manners [but] the gothic age, precisely because of its relative barbarity, was especially conducive to the free play of imagination.[14]

The imaginative situations of the Gothic are facilitated through imperatives of the genre that develop out of Walpole's 'extraordinary positions'.[15] As Frank summarises, these include subterranean pursuit, claustrophobic containment, unrewarded virtue, the failure of reason and fear of the triumph of evil, and fluctuating psychosexual emotional states.[16] It is hard to imagine superheroes in anything other than 'extraordinary positions', but 'For the Man' goes beyond this and explicitly satisfies each of Frank's imperatives, allowing for a more explicit understanding of the story as firmly situated in the same tradition as *Otranto*.

In *Otranto*, there is much movement into lower, more secretive layers. Isabella follows a stranger down 'some stone steps descending into a vault totally dark'[17] as Manfred follows her, resulting in a 'confused noise of voices [. . .] through the distant vaults'.[18] The chase leads to a secret chapel, barred and protected by hidden doors and causeways. Matilda's attendant Bianca also later hears something and remarks: 'I am sure I heard a voice. Does any body lie in the chamber beneath?'[19] There is also, of course, a series of caves where Theodore and Isabella hide in 'the secret recesses of this labyrinth' reported 'to be haunted by evil spirits'.[20] Finally, the prophecy that undoes the House of Manfred is founded on 'an enormous sabre' which is finally discovered after digging at a secret spot to 'the depth of six feet'.[21]

In the Superman story, similar subterranean pursuits take place as Wonder Woman chases the powerful Mongul through several levels of the Fortress, with both characters smashing the other through walls, floors and ceilings in acts of penetrative display. The further they go, the more mysterious it becomes to Batman and Robin, who initially remain on the floor of the Fortress proper, perhaps symbolically so, given their deductive, non-superpowered states. Robin remarks: 'He knocked her though the far wall, and, and [. . .] Bruce, what's happening in there?'[22] This violent, interior retreat signifies not only darker secrets, but higher levels of sexual danger. Wonder Woman barely holds her own as Mongul teases and taunts her: 'You're a female, I think' (18.ii), causing her to lose her usually disciplined composure: 'Go to Hell!' (18.v). At the same time, in his dream reverie, Superman goes down into the 'Kandor crater' (a tragedy that he obviously was not able to prevent) as his imaginary son Van exclaims: 'Th-there isn't much out here. / I don't like it' (22.ii). This Gothic descent into what, following Paglia, we can term a 'chthonian darkness'[23] gets stranger and stranger. Weird animals from Superman's extraterrestrial zoo begin to wander and scream like children and 'three sentient puddles' become 'over-excited'.[24] And the more punishment Wonder Woman receives from Mongul's powerful fists, the more the possibility raises itself that she might lose this fight. The lower they descend, the farther Superman lapses into his psychological prison, and the more doubt begins to cloud the mind of the comics' reader who has been normalised to denouements of Truth, Justice and the American Way in the Silver Age Superman. The physical signifiers of the story correlate directly with effect, placing the reader in a position, as Holland and Sherman note of the Gothic experience, 'hover[ing] between radical exploration and a familiar, conservative ending'.[25]

Moore's adaptation of Gothic devices in 'For the Man' facilitates an uncanny explication of the psychological content normally repressed by Superman, but allowed free play within his state of physical imprisonment. In *Otranto*, although most of the subterranean locations are imprisoning, the main object of imprisonment is the bizarre fallen helmet that engulfs Conrad and comes to symbolise the repressed crime of the novella's patriarch. The Black Mercy is smaller than the helmet, but the metaphorical fit is the same. Once the servant sees the fallen helmet, he turned, 'eyes staring, and foaming at the mouth. He said nothing, but pointed to the court. The company were struck with terror and amazement.'[26] This scene appears mirrored precisely in 'For the Man', when Batman, Robin and Wonder Woman first enter the Fortress and see an equally mute Superman, uncharacteristically frozen, his head tilted slightly back, oblivious to the world around him (4.i). This Superman is at the mercy of our gaze – he neither returns nor ignores our astonished scrutiny. Here, Superman – a man wearing a cape and tights – is presented as the hermeneutic focus rather than exciting the unreflecting, outwardly exclamatory gestures – such as 'Look! Up in the sky!' – more commonly associated with his appearance. Because superheroes tend to be figures of action – punching, flying, fighting – rendering them physically motionless within the narrative tends to promote a focus on their psychological aspects. Once the hero is inert, he or she ceases to be a physical signifier of action. Just as the Gothic retreats into the dark, the static hero signifies a withdrawal from outer experience.

Robbed of his position in the physical world, Superman's status as an exemplum of unrewarded virtue can also be explored through an examination of his desires rather than those of his villains or love interests. In *Otranto*, the young hero is killed on a day of social and personal significance – his birthday. Though sickly, 'and of no promising disposition', Conrad is 'the darling of his father' and certainly does not deserve his exceedingly strange death, especially on his birthday *and* wedding day to the lovely Isabella.[27] Manfred certainly has no virtue, but he deems himself worthy of reward: his imminent departure from leadership makes him wish for not only heirs, but the life his son will never have. As Conrad's father and ruler of the castle, Manfred believes he is worthy of his own reward. Superman's dream demonstrates a similar dynamic. After all, superheroes are seldom rewarded, as they sacrifice a normal life for one of uncomfortable costumes and nightly patrols. But within the psychological grip of the Mercy, Superman experiences the reward he (apparently) thinks he deserves: he is on a yet-intact Krypton, married to an actress named Lyla, and father to a son and daughter. In superhero comics, where the normal conventions are flying, invulnerability and secret origins, the idea of marriage and children is far more unbelievable than fighting Braniac on Pluto. It is thus somewhat like Manfred's delusion – selfish but desirable. Unsaid but importantly, Kal-el is not Superman in his fantasy, indicating that he not only desires domestic bliss, but also a life free of public responsibility. The uncaped Kal does very un-Supermanlike things such as getting stuck in traffic, being short of change for the telephone and having sex with his wife. This is a somewhat romantic fantasy for a superhero, but why is it terrible? Why is it Gothic? It is Gothic because the desire felt by Superman transgresses the bounds of his primary character. The untwisting of his fantasy is that, family or not, and even on an intact Krypton, Superman is still Superman – though he is not a hero, he is a geologist who is still investigating the Kandor problem. He has no powers, but he still strives to be good. Initially, the Mercy dream is wondrous, funny and somewhat nostalgic, but it quickly changes. Superman begins to put these clues together and shake himself out of the hallucination, abjecting the familial in order to reassert the diegetic logic of the superhero genre. In the crater with his son, he explains:

> Van, it's this feeling I . . . Oh, Dear Rao, am I going mad? I keep thinking that . . .
> Van, please, I know this won't make sense, but . . . You're my son. I was there at your birth and I'll always love you. Always. But . . . But, Van, I . . .
> . . . I don't think you're real. (22.iv–vi)

The possibility exists that the dream itself has simply become too much, as Jor-el is now a leader of a Klanlike zealot group. But his words 'think' and 'real' suggest that up until this moment, these two notions have been separated, as he has only accepted what is real instead of thinking about it. Although from within the dream the growing realisation that this world is an illusion accompanies the breakdown of its function as wish-fulfilment, from the perspective occupied by those outside – both the other characters in the story and the reader – this deterioration of familial bliss represents a reassertion of a superhero logos in which the life of the nuclear family becomes not simply unbearable but unthinkable.

The Gothic failure of reason is readily apparent throughout *Otranto*'s wild and woolly plot, which indeed, Walpole claimed, 'originated in a dream', and which revolves around the violation of family bonds.[28] In many ways, the narrative of 'For the Man' is set up from the start as the failure of reason. The first we see of the invincible Man of Steel is as a defeated prisoner, which within the Superman tradition is a ludicrous image. In the words of Grant Morrison, Superman enters the Western mythos as a reinvention of 'Apollo, the sun god, the unbeatable supreme self'.[29] 'For the Man' not only offers an immobilised Superman, but one who has succumbed to an irrational phantasy of domesticity which calls into play the dialectic between the Apollonian and the Dionysian that Moore would later address directly in *From Hell*. The representation of Batman further emphasises the impotence of reason. While in *The Killing Joke*, published three years later, Moore would present Batman and the Joker as 'a couple of psychopaths' whose 'psychoses are a mirror image of each other',[30] in 'For the Man' Batman performs his identity – or rather fails to perform his identity – as the World's Greatest Detective. He initially shows bravado – 'Really, it's just a matter of putting the pieces together' – but this quickly devolves into a simple, desperate plea: 'We're in serious trouble, old friend. You've got to wake up' (19.vi). As Morrison notes, Batman enters the nascent DC universe as the 'hero of the night' whose original artistic presentation is characterised by a 'Gothic woodcut effect and weirdly distorted anatomy';[31] however, in 'For the Man', as in his appearances in *Swamp Thing* the following year, Batman appears as a straightforward agent of the law forced to acknowledge – and with varying degrees of success to regulate – the disruptive obtrusion of desire in the world of light and truth.

According to Frank, the deepest trenches for readers are the 'fluctuating psychosexual emotional states',[32] which traditionally provide the lurid appeal of Gothic fictions. In *Otranto*, this is Manfred's desire to marry his son's intended bride, Isabella. When this fails, Isabella marries Theodore simply because she understands his loss. Sexuality is certainly pursued in *Otranto* in the characters of Isabella and Matilda, but love is not very romantic; it is doomed, royal and convenient. Superheroes also traditionally exhibit very little variance as to their desires, which usually run a rigid continuum from strict moral platitudes and driving justice to feelings of unrequited love, which is rarely sexual. 'For the Man', however, exhibits a strange amount of similarly untraditional psychosexual states in the form of desires that are more akin to the Gothic fiction of the late eighteenth and early nineteenth centuries, which was feared for its 'transgressive sexuality and behavior, criminal activity, and fallen reputations'.[33] In Moore's story, one such transgressive moment occurs when Robin shows an overt sexual interest in Wonder Woman. When they meet on the tundra outside the Fortress, Robin ogles her star-spangled costume as she walks away from him, prompting Batman to flash a knowing smile and whisper, 'Think clean thoughts, chum' (2.v). The diction of 'chum' hearkens back to the televised Dynamic Duo, as well as their Silver Age counterparts who shared a bed and drew eyebrow-raising questions from Wertham for displaying a 'subtle atmosphere of homoeroticism'.[34] But Batman doesn't scold Robin, he merely offers some fraternal tips; he brings Robin back to the superhero mindset, but the transgression has already occurred. Moore locates and acknowledges the realm of desire as being clearly in the eye of the reader who is watching comics transgress their genre and transplants it to the tyro Robin, who is fumbling at meeting the larger-than-life Superman.

As expected, the central moment of transgressive desire in the story takes place in Superman's wish-dream, which both he and the reader 'see'. As expected, Superman's wife, who is an actress (and decidedly neither Lois nor Lana), is not only a good wife and parent (she puts on a birthday party for him), but she lowers herself to his class status (he is a geologist) by giving him the sexual power in their relationship. Kal-el asks her, 'Why did you ever give up acting for this'? and she replies, 'I don't know, Kal. / Remind me' (6.v–vi), as Gibbons shows a quiet Kryptonian tower gone dark. Psychosexual issues also may be assigned to Kal-el's new problems with his dream-father. In the real continuity of Superman comics, the lost Jor-el is heroically idealised and two-dimensional, partly because of his absence. But in the fantasy, Jor-el becomes almost an enemy. He is overweight, uses a cane and is a fringe political leader rather than a brilliant scientist. He also has little love for Kal and doesn't even know the names of his grandchildren. Like Manfred, he seems to conspire against his family, as political radicals attack Superman's cousin Kara and confine her to hospital. Superman's feelings of abandonment in the main continuity are magnified here as Jor-el has also, in a way, somewhat replaced him. Though an extremist, Jor-el is bent at reforming a Krypton that has become corrupt and crime-ridden while Kal-el is left to fumble with rocks.

The 'Ideal presence' of the Gothic

Finally jolted from his dream-state, Superman adopts a stance that differs substantially from his usual hands-on-hips expression of embodied justice. Instead, Superman desires personal vengeance. He towers over a frightened Robin and screams: 'Who ... did this ... to me?' (25.v). Superman then rockets towards Mongul as an incoming force of powerful speed lines (26.iv). Mongul 'hears a voice like Armageddon shouting his name' (26.v) as Superman slams into him like 'a steam hammer as big as the world' (27.iv). Just as the Gothic imperatives affect desire by heightening sexual response, they also affect Superman's temper. What prompts such powerful, focused rage is not Superman's concern for his friends, but what Mongul hints at as a deeper register to his planned attack: 'I fashioned a prison that you could not leave without giving up your heart's desire. / Escaping it must have been like tearing off your own arm' (29.ii).

Mongul's villainous plan is fairly simple: to trap Superman in an ongoing fantasy that is so wonderful he would never wish to leave. Mongul wants Superman to experience the pain of escaping; in fact, he takes delight in it, as we see with the smile that greets both Superman's return and the raw viciousness the hero displays as payback. Superman has been emotionally hurt by the vision; not by leaving the fantasy behind, but by what the desire for it suggests – though he is inimitably Superman, he wishes he were not. As Veeder notes of the Gothic genre more generally, 'it is not truth that produces pleasure but rather pleasure that produces truth'.[35] What Superman experiences while under the influence of the Mercy is phantasmic, it is only a spectral experience. But because Gibbons uses an identical artistic style, an approach to lighting and modelling that gives 'the feeling of weight and bulk and substance' to characters in both worlds,[36] the dream produces an immersive effect for both the reader and Superman. Like the magic-lantern shows that were popular during the eighteenth and nineteenth centuries with their projected visions of ghosts, devils and planets, the Black Mercy reveals a Gothic illusion that is so eerily realistic it calls into question the observer's subjectivity. These lantern shows also dealt in forbidden desire: 'the lantern illuminated dreams and fantasies, not only supernatural, ghastly, and spectral, but naughty fulfillments of desire [including] "What the butler saw" jokes and keyhole glimpses of girls undressing'.[37] Moore and Gibbon's similar adaptation of the Gothic into the visual medium of comics allows more verisimilitude; as Hutcheon notes, 'some media and genres are used to *tell* stories (for example, novels, short stories); others *show*'.[38]

Through psychosexual transgression and supernatural elements, Gothic fiction tends to break down the apprehension of the expected narrative to reveal some forbidden secret. But it is never fully realised; it is often seen through a keyhole rather than an open space. As Gentile argues of *Otranto*: 'Walpole's sublime and supernatural effects work to confound and deceive rather than to terrorise.'[39] This can be seen in Chapter 4 when Manfred, 'guided by an imperfect gleam of moonshine that shone faintly through the illuminated windows', creeps up to Theodore and Matilda and, thinking her Isabella, accidentally stabs her.[40] This type of deceptive signifier is repeated throughout novels with Gothic elements in them, from the strange rumblings in Rochester's attic, the flickering candle of *The Mysteries of Udolpho* and the scraping tree branch of *Wuthering Heights*. Even Wonder Woman has her doubts about the Black Mercy's nature: 'I think it might have some magic in it' (5.ii). The Gothic disrupts the subjectivity of the reader by confusing their sense of things, thus demanding a more active, hermeneutic response that has something to do with identity: Who is that? Who am I? Kastbjerg connects this to Butler's discussion of gender performance: 'The hyper-theatrical exterior focus in Gothic – and Goth – on performance, show, costume, disguise, drag and stylization identifies through exaggeration and defamiliarisation the staged and highly unnatural nature of gender and self as a chain of performative citations and quotes, "a persistent impersonation that passes as the real".'[41] The concept of the 'persistent impersonation' can, I think, be helpful in understanding the precariousness of superhero identity in 'For the Man'. After all, the 'persistent impersonation' of being a superhero is an elaborate act of visuality – a disguise – predicated on ornamentation, costume and social transgression (wearing bright colours, gold bustiers and underwear on the outside) divided between the binaries of hero and secret identity. Coming out of the vision, even Superman questions his own sense of self-identity; his scream is both interrogative and desperately assertive: 'ME?' (25.v).

Otranto ends with Theodore revealed as the legitimate heir to the throne; that is, the tale concludes with new knowledge that changes the status quo of the narrative. This shift, which usually involves character and identity, does not have to be a pleasant one. As Gross notes: 'the Gothic journey offers a darkened world where fear, oppression, and madness are the ways to knowledge and the uncontrolled transformation of one's character the quest's epiphany [. . .] the Gothic quest ends in the shattering of the protagonist's image of his/her social/sexual roles and a legacy of, at best, numbing unease'.[42] In Moore's story, the new knowledge that Superman gains through his harrowing vision is also tied to his sense of self. He learns that his forbidden desire is really to not be Superman. Though there are certainly nostalgic nods to him continuing to be heroic in the Mercy narrative (he still strives to save Kandor and to protect his family), these are only nominal beats; he is initially more concerned about his father's attention, his wife's interest in him, and himself. What Superman learns as a result of his dream is what Theodore does in finding out that he is a prince: he has a secret identity of which he has been previously unaware. So while Superman may have always thought of himself as really being Clark Kent, his experience with the Black Mercy gives him a brand-new self to consider. Granted, Superman succeeds in fighting off the dream, but the accurate source of his painful desire is his self-knowledge of what lies in his own unconscious rather than the loss of false, spectral figures. The Mercy dream invites horror not because it shows him a life he cannot have, but because it shows him that the life he thought he loved – with Smallville, Metropolis, the *Planet*, Batman, Robin, Wonder Woman and Lois – is not his heart's desire at all. His real life, then, is like the Superman identity itself – a complete performance.

By the end of the story, nothing really has changed that will alter the series' continuity, but Superman's own self-knowledge does shift. So when Wonder Woman later gives him a thoughtful gift that he already has (a replica of the Bottle City of Kandor which she thinks has been restored), he uses super-speed to lie to her and quickly hide (in a closet) the actual city so she does not see it and think her gift spoiled. He then does the only thing 'Superman' can – he smiles. The Black Mercy is not just a trap; it releases Superman into the prison of his identity as a superhero. Superman, thought to be 'The Man Who Has Everything', is not truly living his heart's desire and it is a shattering experience, but he must keep up appearances. Earlier, Mongul explains the Mercy's powers: 'It's telepathic. It reads them like a book, and it feeds them a logical simulation of the happy ending they desire. Of course, its victims could shrug it off ... / They just don't want to' (11.vi).[43]

What Superman realises is that part of the pain of unrewarded virtue for a superhero is the loss of social and personal identity owing to the dominance of a façade-like public identity. After defeating Mongul, Superman tries briefly to alter this identity. In addition to his uncharacteristic fit of rage, after Wonder Woman gives him the replica of Kandor, the unthinkable happens as she and Superman actually kiss, with Batman and Robin as startled onlookers. Superman asks: 'Mmm why don't we do that more often'?, to which Wonder Woman replies: 'I don't know. Too predictable?' – Superman reluctantly agrees: 'You're probably right' (39.iii). The Gothic may be designed to trick, but it is so tied to genre that it becomes predictable. Were Wonder Woman and Superman to get together, it might as well be the Mercy dream all over again. Though Superman gives into his own desire only for a moment (before their kiss, his S-symbol is momentarily reflected as being contained in the bottled-up Kandor; 39.1), Moore holds out hope that superheroes do not have to be fixedly tied to genre. Superman, because of his moral apex and corporate ownership, is one of the most predictable characters in all of fiction. But by adapting a Superman plot to Gothic conventions, Moore can tell an unpredictable, transgressive story that, though resolved at story's end, remains unsettling.

Superman's traditional never-ending battle in this story is not about defeating Mongul or even celebrating his own birthday, it is, instead, about his interior struggle of 'fear, oppression, and madness'.[44] Superman's fantasy of desire is Moore's statement that there are deep psychological layers to what is largely considered a flat character. The Last Son of Krypton should fight Lex Luthor, not have father issues and wallow in an inferiority complex. But these are exactly what Moore gives him. Robin provides the impetus for using the Gothic to explore Superman: 'I mean, I met Superman before, but I still don't really, uh, know him that well. / This is a big place, isn't it? I bet there's some scary stuff in here' (3.ii). The 'scary', 'big place' is Superman's unconscious mind – his fears, motivations and forbidden desires are revealed by his own personal fortress in a move that conflates place with psychology in a manner that would become increasingly important in Moore's subsequent works like *From Hell*. More immediately, 'For the Man' acts as a thumbnail sketch for the longer 'Whatever Happened to the Man of Tomorrow?',[45] which would be published a year later and definitively end the era of the Silver Age Superman. In this story, Moore has Superman's villains exploit his desire for transgressive domesticity by attacking those closest to him. In the end, though, Superman's Mercy-dream is finally realised after he earns, through horrible bloodshed, a peaceful life as a disguised suburban husband.

Of *Otranto*, Watt argues that Walpole 'was surely in control of the fact that his appeal to the rhetoric of genius and sublimity was a spurious one' and that the novel contains 'playful excess and frivolity'.[46] This is a familiar argument about superhero comics as well, especially those of the Silver Age, whose adventures usually included heroes being transformed into babies, being split into two or other such nonsense. As Moore's reflections on 'Whatever Happened' suggest, part of the appeal of the superhero genre is the ease with which the sublime intermingles with the ridiculous:

> It's difficult to see anything but my love for the Silver Age and the often silly comic book concepts that typified that era. I'd got everything in there –

Krypto and Bizarro – all of those things that I had loved, because they seem to me to be just full of imagination and energy. They were wonderful, strange ideas.[47]

Even though the Silver Age ended around the early 1970s, it subsists in our adaptive apprehension of iconic superheroes and how we view them: Flash is fast, Green Lantern has a ring and Superman can fly. Moreover, although 'Whatever Happened' represents Moore's response to the invitation 'to write the "final" issues in the fifty-year run of both *Action Comics* and its sister title, *Superman*',[48] and though Moore's work is often identified with the darker, grittier turn in the superhero genre, the wonderful strangeness of the Silver Age continued to haunt and delight Moore's subsequent work in the genre, underpinning titles such as *Supreme* and *Tom Strong*. Both of these later series, the first published by Image and the second by Moore's America's Best Comics imprint, can be read as adaptations of the Superman template, confirming the sense that for Moore this figure is not so much an ideal composition as an adaptable fiction.

To understand how and why Moore adapts Walpole, I would like to conclude with Lord Kames's theory of the ideal presence, which was, according to Miles, 'the dominant model of eighteenth-century aesthetic response',[49] and thus important to understand not only Walpole's plan, but how Moore adapts it to elicit a Gothic reader response. In his *Elements of Criticism*, Kames speaks to, according to McInnis, 'that state of enchantment which so perfectly captivates the subject that their mind is dominated by the imagination, and reason has no opportunity to interject and evaluate the situation'.[50] This is not only the experience of reading the Gothic, but also of superheroes, who are unreasonable constructs themselves. As Kames himself states:

> In contradistinction to real presence, ideal presence may properly be termed *a waking dream*; because, like a dream, it vanisheth the moment we reflect upon our present situation: real presence, on the contrary, vouched by eye-sight, commands our belief, not only during the direct perception, but in reflecting afterward upon the object.[51]

Gothic fiction, like a magic-lantern show, barely stands up to intellectual reason, but its impact in those brief seconds is powerful because of its sensory, striking and often sexual transgression. Moore seeks to achieve this same experience for his readers in the Gothic Superman's 'waking dream', made allowable through Otrantoesque conventions, allowing the character to transgress the rigidity of being a performative 'ideal' superhero to see past the 'ideal presence' of his life as a character in the comics.

My argument here is that Moore adapts the conventions of the Gothic genre as exemplified and inaugurated by *Otranto* to produce a Superman who is slightly removed from his own ideal presence as an imaginative superhero, thus unsettling his readers. Moore uses the Gothic as not only a rich resource for adaptation, but also a parallel genre to comic books. As Fred Botting notes:

> On one hand, transgression enables limits and values to be reaffirmed, terror and horror eliciting rejection and disgust; on the other hand, it draws eyes and imaginations, in fascination, to peep behind the curtain of limitation in the hope of glimpsing illicit excitements made all the more alluring in the hope for bearing the stamp of mystery or prohibition.[52]

Even though Superman returns to his narrative core by the issue's end, Moore's Gothic exploration yields new, 'fascinating' results. 'For the Man' does not repeat *Otranto*, but adapts its key elements. By understanding Gothic conventions and the 'waking dream' of the Black Mercy, Moore's readers can finally begin to not only understand the process of the author as he writes an icon, but be led to investigate the larger possibilities of a modern Superman who doesn't just fight, punch and fly, but may brood, worry and love.

Notes

1. Alan Moore and Kevin O'Neill, 'The New Traveller's Almanac', in *The League of Extraordinary Gentlemen, Volume II* (La Jolla, CA: America's Best Comics, 2000), p. 12.
2. Jess Nevins, *A Blazing World: The Unofficial Companion to the League of Extraordinary Gentlemen Volume Two* (Austin, TX: MonkeyBrain, 2004), pp. 114–15.
3. The Arabian Tunnel and the Blazing World appear on pp. 12 and 7, respectively, of 'The New Traveller's Almanac'.
4. Linda Hutcheon, *A Theory of Adaptation* (New York: Routledge, 2006), p. 8.
5. Frederick S. Frank, 'Glossary', in Horace Walpole, *The Castle of Otranto and the Mysterious Mother* (Peterborough, ON: Broadview Press, 2003), p. 345.
6. Horace Walpole, *The Castle of Otranto* (Oxford: Oxford University Press, 1996), p. 9.

7 For further discussion of Moore's early – and longstanding – interest in the occult and supernatural, see 'Alan Moore Interviewed by Eddie Campbell', *Egomania*, 2 (2002), 1–32 (pp. 18–22). For further discussion of his sense of the significance of the Gothic revival in the history of Western culture more broadly, see 'Dracula Reborn', interview by David Bogart, in *The Best of Vampirella: Lost Tales*, ed. David Bogard and Bon Alimagno (New York: Harris, 2008), n.p.
8 Hutcheon, *Adaptation*, pp. 20, 8.
9 Alan Moore interviewed by George Khoury, *The Extraordinary Works of Alan Moore: Indispensable Edition*, ed. George Khoury (Raleigh, NC: TwoMorrows, 2008), p. 120.
10 Walpole, *Otranto*, pp. 18–19.
11 Randy Duncan and Matthew J. Smith, *The Power of Comics: History, Form and Culture* (New York: Continuum, 2009), p. 177.
12 Alan Moore and Dave Gibbons, 'For The Man Who Has Everything', in *Superman: Whatever Happened to the Man of Tomorrow*, deluxe edn (New York: DC Comics, 2009), 11.ii–v; hereafter cited in the main body of the text. Pagination follows that in the original magazine publication rather than the collected volume.
13 Lucie Armitt, 'The Magical Realism of the Contemporary Gothic', in *A Companion to the Gothic*, ed. David Punter (Oxford: Blackwell, 2000), p. 309.
14 E.J. Clery, 'Introduction', in Horace Walpole, *The Castle of Otranto* (Oxford: Oxford University Press, 1996), p. xi.
15 Walpole, *Otranto*, p. 10.
16 Frank, 'Glossary', p. 344. I have slightly altered Frank's wording and order here to sharpen his larger definition into a more incisive application and to perhaps update his nomenclature.
17 Walpole, *Otranto*, p. 30.
18 *Ibid.*, p. 33.
19 *Ibid.*, p. 43.
20 *Ibid.*, p. 75.
21 *Ibid.*, p. 81.
22 Moore and Gibbons, 'For The Man', 19.ii.
23 Camille Paglia, *Sexual Personae: Art and Decadence from Nefertiti to Emily Dickinson* (New York: Vintage, 1991), p. 265.
24 Moore and Gibbons, 'For The Man', p. 41.i.
25 Norman Holland and Leona Sherman, 'Gothic Possibilities', in *Gender and Reading: Essays on Readers, Texts, and Contexts*, ed. Elizabeth A. Flynn and Patrocinio P. Schweickart (Baltimore: Johns Hopkins University Press, 1986), p. 225.

26 Walpole, *Otranto*, p. 18.
27 *Ibid.*, p. 17.
28 *Ibid.*, p. vii.
29 Grant Morrison, *Supergods* (London: Jonathan Cape, 2011), p. 15.
30 Alan Moore interviewed in George Khoury and Friends (eds), *The Extraordinary Works of Alan Moore* (Raleigh, NC: Two Morrows, 2003), p. 123.
31 *Ibid.*, pp. 17–18.
32 Frank, *Otranto*, p. 344.
33 Marilyn Brock, 'Introduction', in *Wollstonecraft to Stoker: Essays on Gothic and Victorian Sensation Fiction* (Jefferson, NC: McFarland, 2009), p. 5.
34 Frederic Wertham, *Seduction of the Innocent* (Toronto: Rinehart, 1953), p. 190.
35 William Veeder, 'The Nurture of the Gothic, or How Can a Text Be Both Popular and Subversive?', in *American Gothic: New Interventions in a National Narrative*, ed. Robert K. Martin and Eric Savoy (Iowa City: University of Iowa Press, 1998), p. 28.
36 'Dave Gibbons: Pebbles in a Landscape', interview by Bhob Stewart, *Comics Journal*, 116 (July 1987): 97–103 (p. 99).
37 Marina Warner, *Phantasmagoria* (Oxford: Oxford University Press, 2006), p. 156.
38 Hutcheon, *Adaptation*, p. xiv.
39 Kathy Justice Gentile, 'Sublime Drag: Supernatural Masculinity in Gothic Fiction', *Gothic Studies*, 11 (May 2009), 17.
40 Walpole, *Otranto*, p. 108.
41 Kristine Kastbjerg, '"Dressed up in the body of an old woman": Gothic Conventions in Ingemann, Andersen, Blixen and Høeg', *Scandanavian–Canadian Studies*, 18 (2009), 36; Kastbjerg quotes Judith Butler, *Gender Trouble: Feminism and the Subversion of Identity* (London: Routledge, 1990), p. viii.
42 Louis Gross, 'Redefining the American Gothic: From Wieland to Day of the Dead', *Studies in Speculative Fiction*, 20:1(1989), 1–2.
43 In contrast, for the few panels that Batman is subjected to the Black Mercy, he is described in no uncertain terms: 'He is content' (25.ii.). His parents still alive, young Bruce Wayne actually smiles, which is the ultimate reward for the dark hero. Why can Batman enjoy his fantasy while Superman cannot? It would seem that Batman views his mantle as a necessity more than a want. The guise of Batman is also, many posit, his complete identity after his parents are killed. Wonder Woman is not subjected to the Mercy.
44 Gross, 'Redefining', p. 2.
45 In *Superman*, 423 (Sept. 1986) and *Action Comics*, 583 (Sept. 1986).

46 James Watt, *Contesting the Gothic: Fiction, Genre and Cultural Conflict 1764–1832*. Cambridge: Cambridge University Press, 1999), p. 29.
47 'Alan Moore Reflects on Marvelman: Part 1', interview by Kurt Amacker, *Mania* (3 Sept. 2009): www.mania.com/alan-moore-reflects-marvelman_article_117413.html; quoted in Gary Spencer Millidge, *Alan Moore: Storyteller* (Lewes: ILEX, 2011), p. 120.
48 Millidge, *Storyteller*, p. 120.
49 Robert Miles, 'Introduction: Gothic Romance as Visual Technology', *Gothic Technologies* (Dec. 2005): www.rc.umd.edu/praxis/gothic/intro/miles.html.
50 David McInnis, 'Mind-Travelling, Ideal Presence and the Imagination in Early Modern England', *Early Modern Literary Studies*, 19:7 (2009), 8.
51 Lord Kames (Henry Home), *Elements of Criticism* (London: A. Millar, 1765), p. 82.
52 Fred Botting, 'Preface: The Gothic', in *The Gothic*, ed. Botting (Cambridge: D.S. Brewer, 2001), 1–7, p. 2.

10

Radical coterie and the idea of sole survival in *St Leon, Frankenstein* and *Watchmen*

Claire Sheridan

> *Dave Gibbons*: I don't consider *Watchmen* to be a pessimistic book – on the contrary, it's very positive about the human condition.
> *Alan Moore*: I believe that with *Watchmen*, if we've achieved anything in terms of the moral aspect of it, I don't believe that optimism is possible without looking very long and very hard at the worst possible case [...]. So if we have any optimism in the series it'll be valid optimism because it won't simply be based on ignoring the nasty facts of life. To me, just in that last panel, in Godfrey's last line 'I leave it entirely in your hands' – that's talking to the reader as well . . . I leave it entirely in your hands, how do we sort out this Gordian Knot? If the question is 'who makes the world?' then if there's an answer it is that everybody does.[1]

Optimism is not high on the list of characteristics one would immediately associate with Alan Moore and Dave Gibbon's *Watchmen*. A series that begins with the words 'dog carcass in alley this morning' (I.1.i), does not bode well. Nevertheless, I want to propose that *Watchmen* can be viewed as belonging to a tradition of Gothic that had its first flourishing as a result of the optimistic, egalitarian philosophical theories of the 1790s. By looking in particular at Gothic novels that deliberately engage with the moral questions of that era, I want to show that *Watchmen* is an heir to what has been called 'the philosophical Gothic' in a strain of British radical fiction. I want to consider it specifically in relation to William Godwin's *St Leon* and Mary Shelley's *Frankenstein*.[2]

Avowedly political novels in the Godwinian school have sometimes been regarded as marginal contributors to the Gothic tradition. Critics have even felt that the presence of a radical agenda disqualifies a work from being considered 'Gothic'. Jerrold E. Hogle answers the charge that *Frankenstein* is 'counter-Gothic' by suggesting that this is only 'made possible by how extremely Gothic it is [...] the Godwin-Shelley circle [...] redeployed the Gothic mode on the basis of the most basic presuppositions underlying the Gothic itself'.[3] Writing about the influence of the French Revolution on Gothic novels, Ronald Paulson concludes that Godwin's Gothic fiction is instrumental in 'blurring [...] the old black-white morality of earlier Gothic fiction'.[4] Other writers on the Gothic have eschewed the idea that radical politics are anathema to the mode and have identified Godwin as a central figure in the development of 'an apparently radical and progressive Gothic, which attempts to use the tools of the past against themselves'.[5] For Ellen Levy, 'Godwin's flexible treatment of Gothic motifs' in *St Leon* enacts a 'textual alchemy that mirrors the necromantic activity of the protagonist'.[6] Marie Roberts and Maggie Kilgour both make Godwin's *St Leon* central to their arguments. For them, St Leon's status as an immortal alchemist makes him a particularly Gothic figure, associated with occult alienation, and, in Roberts's case, secret societies like 'the brotherhood of the Rosy Cross'.[7] The link with secret societies provides a sinister, Gothic reflection of the less sinister notion of coterie that will be discussed in this chapter. Both conceptions of the select group – as cabal and as coterie – are applicable to the discussion of *Watchmen* in relation to *St Leon* and *Frankenstein*.

Features of *Watchmen* mark it as a modern descendant of what Pamela Clemit has identified as 'The Godwinian novel'.[8] At the end of her study, Clemit acknowledges that the Godwinian model had only a limited influence on nineteenth-century fiction: 'there is a loss of the selective, theoretical and intensely imagined treatment of political issues in the Godwinian first person narrative. Finally the major significance of the Godwinian novel rests apart from its contribution to mainstream fiction.' This may be the case, but in *Watchmen* can be found a resurgence of precisely those qualities that Clemit regards as 'the historically specific achievement of the Godwin school'.[9] *Watchmen* comprises devices beyond the 'first person narrative', but it does make masterful use of this perspective. Vijay Mishra locates 'the Gothic sublime' in Godwin's *Caleb Williams* in its construction 'around competing discourses whose demarcations remain visible',[10] a description that can be transferred to the serial, literally 'visible' medium of *Watchmen*. Moore's narrative ethic, and his commitment to anarchism, also suggests connections to the Godwinian tradition. Here he is discussing *V for Vendetta*:

> And the central question is, is this guy right? Or is he mad? What do you, the reader, think about this? Which struck me as a properly anarchist solution. I didn't want to tell people what to think, I just wanted to tell people *to* think.[11]

Godwin, 'the founder of philosophical anarchism',[12] who referred to 'the universal exercise of private judgement' as 'a doctrine so unspeakably beautiful',[13] might have said the same.

Watchmen shares certain strategic elements with the work of Godwin and Mary Shelley. But the work also has in common with *St Leon* and *Frankenstein* a preoccupation with the question of what action to take in a world where popular optimism has failed. *St Leon*, *Frankenstein* and *Watchmen* can all be regarded as post-revolutionary works, their authors reacting to reactionary government – whether Pittite, Jenkinsonian, Thatcherite or Reaganist. A worry about how to address the sense that the radical ship has sailed pervades each of the works I want to consider. Throughout *Watchmen*, as well as in *St Leon* and *Frankenstein*, the characters show a continuing consciousness of coterie as an arena for social activism. On the surface, this is not the way that we are invited to read the group in *Watchmen*: it is more tempting to interpret the loose collocation of masked adventurers as a band of alarming bullies. 'Yes, we were crazy, we were kinky, we were Nazis, all those things that people say', Hollis declares.[14] Yet their personal and political partialities are varied enough to have a curbing, salutary effect on each other. As the work progresses, there are signs that the masked heroes are becoming 'a mutually monitoring community'[15] in an open, relational sense rather than the clandestine, hermetic one implied by Hollis Mason's surname. It is not the sectish, but the more discursive form of sociability – which this chapter designates coterie[16] – that appears to offer a way out of the pessimistic possibility that collectively negotiated change belongs to the past. The antithesis to this idea is the notion of having solely survived the coterie, which is a recurring theme in *St Leon* and is given subtle and complicated consideration in *Watchmen,* underscored by the inset narrative from *Tales of the Black Freighter*. Despite the bleak outlook and wrongheadedness of *Watchmen*'s Rorschach, and a similar scenario for the monster in *Frankenstein*, these characters are redeemed from their worst excesses by their wish to be connected to others in a way that gives their lives use and meaning. The persistence of an idea of coterie represents the kind of bottom-line optimism that Moore and Gibbons note in the round table discussion cited above. For Godwin, coterie is a necessary step in his vision of the perfectible society: people can gradually do away with government, but only if, for the meantime, smaller collectives are formed whose members can check one another's mistakes.[17] The state cannot be replaced all at once by 'a solipsistic riot of private judgement';[18] characters like St Leon, Victor Frankenstein and Adrian Veidt are a testament against this proceeding. The dynamic coterie, however flawed, is a better vehicle for change than party politics or the despotic individual. In each of the works discussed here, truly nihilistic consequences ensue from the desire to be, or conviction of being, last of the coterie.

There is a possible homage to *Caleb Williams*, William Godwin's first 'thesis' novel with Gothic propensities, encoded in Veidt's veneration for Alexander the Great, which is also one of the defining qualities of Caleb's nemesis Ferdinando Falkland. Falkland can be regarded as a template for a whole series of characters in Godwin and Mary Shelley's fiction: refined types, full of feeling but fatally flawed in their elitist devotion to reputation.[19] In some places Veidt's eulogium of Alexander reads like an updated paraphrase of Falkland's. In *Caleb Williams* we read:

> The death of a hundred thousand men is at first sight very shocking; but what in reality are a hundred thousand such men more than a hundred thousand sheep? It is mind, Williams, the generation of knowledge and virtue that we ought to love. This was the project of Alexander; he set out in a great undertaking to civilise mankind.[20]

From Veidt we get:

> Ruling without barbarism! At Alexandria, he instituted the ancient world's greatest seat of learning.
> True, people died ... perhaps unnecessarily, though who can judge such things? Yet how nearly he approached his vision of a united world. (XI.8.vii)

If Veidt is Falkland then Rorschach, curious to a fault, is Caleb. The opening murder of Edward Blake, and Rorschach's subsequent detective work leading to the discovery of Veidt's culpability, is reminiscent of Caleb's discovery of Falkland's murder of Tyrrel. *Watchmen* also contains further plots that pay tribute to Romantic-era Gothic forbears. The story for 'Marooned', the edition of *Tales of the Black Freighter* that Bernard, the teenager at the newsstand, is reading, recalls Coleridge's 'The Ancient Mariner'. Moreover, the *Black Freighter* mariner's memorable act of binding the bloated corpses of his shipmates together to make a raft is a Frankensteinian one, and one in which community is symbolically sacrificed to one individual's fixed idea. Just as suggestive are the echoes of *Frankenstein* at the denouement of *Watchmen*. The action may take place at the wrong pole, but the image of Rorschach and Nite Owl on their hoverbikes in Antarctica, in pursuit of Veidt (whose horrifying project of creation and reanimation also leagues him with Mary Shelley's protagonist), evokes associations with the arctic conclusion of Mary Shelley's novel, and reminds us of Victor Frankenstein sledging after the monster on the ice.

The character in *Watchmen* who regards an associational, group life in the most positive terms is Dan Dreiburg. His conversation with Laurie in his basement reveals that his conception of an elite community draws on codes of honour from an age of chivalry, of the sort that 'conservative' Gothic novels, infused with 'nostalgia for a lost feudal past',[21] have traditionally been seen to valorise:

> LAURIE: What got you into this business in the first place?
> DREIBURG: Well, I was rich, bored, and there were enough other guys doing it so I didn't feel ridiculous ...
> I guess Hollis was my hero. He was retiring when I was starting out, so I wrote and asked if I could carry on his name.
> I remember visiting his garage, that first time. I was awestruck.
> I mean ... there I was, hanging out with a real hero, being his friend and everything.
> Being a crimefighter, y'know? Like part of a brotherhood or something ...
> That's why I sort of regretted the crimebusters falling through back in sixty-whenever-it-was.
> It would have been like joining the knights of the round table; being part of a fellowship of legendary beings. (VII.8.i–iv)

Perhaps if there is a further reference to Godwin in *Watchmen* it is here: Dreiburg writing to his hero is like the young Percy Bysshe Shelley sending a letter to the author of *Political Justice*. Like Shelley, Dreiburg ends up in a relationship with the daughter of two leading figures from the controversial set of the previous generation.[22] Regardless of whether this moment in *Watchmen* resembles the Godwin–Shelley story by coincidence or otherwise, the important feature of Dreiburg's musings is in his conception of the group. Here, then, is what he calls elsewhere that 'adolescent, Romantic thing' (VII.7.vi). Dreiburg's reference to the Romance tradition evokes an ancestor that the Gothic and comic books have in common. But beneath Dreiburg's idealisation of the past is a comprehension of community with more progressive implications. Dreiburg apprehends that his identity can only realise its full scope in a situation where the same is true for a number of others. For Dreiburg, paradoxically, it is the act of being part of something that confers a special, unique status back to the participant: individuality is not erased, but fulfilled, by communicative association. Legendary beings are only legendary together; without 'other guys doing it' they are 'ridiculous' – being 'leftover' (V.10.vii) is therefore not a position to which one should aspire. This is also a point raised by Hollis in *Under the Hood*: 'You see, if you're the only one who'd bothered to turn up for a free-for-all in costume, you tended to look kind of stupid' (p. 12). In the end, being the only costumed hero will come to be associated with worse things than looking stupid.

Even if, as discussed above, *Caleb Williams* is used directly in *Watchmen* and *St Leon* is not, it is the distinctly retrospective flavour of *St Leon*, its 'valedictory tone',[23] that is closer in spirit to *Watchmen*. *Caleb Williams* appeared at a point when reform might still, just, have carried the day. *St Leon* bears the impression of avenues having been shut down. The hero of *St Leon,* who dooms himself to a perpetual search for reformist community, enacts the drama of belatedness that is also a powerful theme in *Watchmen*. In *St Leon* we find a struggle to reinforce philosophical, anarchist idealism in a post-revolutionary climate where neither individuals nor governments seem as amenable to improvement as they once did.

St Leon is a historical tale whose protagonist, Reginald de St Leon, is persuaded by a mysterious stranger to accept the secrets of the elixir of life and the philosopher's stone, on the condition that he communicate this information to no other person, not even his wife. The rest of the novel portrays the ruinous consequences of this pact, locating St Leon's downfall in the selfishness necessitated by secrecy. St Leon's belief that the situation of independence conferred by immortality and infinite wealth will allow him to execute numerous schemes of philanthropy and benevolence, proves totally misguided. As Kilgour argues, 'St Leon imagines himself, as his descendant Victor Frankenstein will later, as the source of immense good in the world, who will use base means to effect high purposes.'[24] We may also think of *Watchmen*'s Veidt here, and his self-justificatory remark, 'I'm trying to improve the world, like when I started out' (XI.18.ii). Instead of improving the world, St Leon's actions destroy his family and other innocents, and find him frequently imprisoned in dungeons. The novel concludes with St Leon lamenting his pointless, infinite life and the associated impossibility of engaging in society.

Like *Caleb Williams*, *St Leon* is a fictional project containing social lessons. The primary means by which *St Leon* conveys its message is by indicating that coterie, an adversarial association of equals, has the potential to be a corrective to solipsism and is the unit through which the world can be changed for the better. In *St Leon*, the well-being found as a member of a community is contrasted with the fraught and ineffectual existence resulting from the individual's egotistical quest for glory. As a development of anarchist ideas, the novel attempts to establish the meaning of properly balanced self-government. There is a difference between eschewing party and obedience to live well by your own lights, and living in a way that denies others the same rights. St Leon's refusal to acknowledge criticism shows him denying others the liberty he assumes for himself. It is this warping of notions of individual freedom that we also see illustrated in *Frankenstein* and *Watchmen*. In the wake of the Terror in France, and the resulting repression instituted by the British government, *St Leon* brought new sophistication to the anarchist treatment of Gothic tropes that Godwin had initiated with *Caleb Williams*. It is this sophistication, and its influence on Mary Shelley's *Frankenstein*, that offers an instructive heritage for *Watchmen*.

The protagonist of *St Leon* experiences greatest personal content as a member of a community. An early experience of this kind of belonging takes place during St Leon's time as a soldier: 'I was delighted with the society and friendship of my brother-officers. They honoured me; they loved me. I seemed to feel what sympathy was; and to have conscious pleasure in making one in a race of beings like myself.'[25] The terms have parallels with those Dreiburg reaches for in his basement. Indeed, the chivalric values that St Leon implies with regard to his martial brotherhood, and those Dreiburg invokes to describe his youthful idealism, indicate the imperfectness of these versions of coterie. The chivalrous coterie may be an improvement on the megalomaniac individual, but the limited system of values at its foundation will render it ineffective before long.

St Leon becomes alienated from later scenes in which he could make a difference to the well-being of the group, due to 'the opinion that fame was the first of all human possessions'.[26] In the novel, immortality becomes a symbol of the outcome of this view. As soon as St Leon has access to eternal life, he becomes divorced from the lived moment. His ability to survive his own age as well as subsequent generations separates him from the world of human endeavour in which he envisages taking a leading part. The elixir of life disqualifies him from coterie membership, which divorces him from the only role he values. Sole survival prevents progress:

> I found myself alone in the world. Must I for ever live without a companion, a friend, any one with whom I can associate upon equal terms, with whom I can have a community of sensations, and feelings, and hopes, and desires, and fears? [. . .] I could have been well content to be partaker with a race of immortals, but I was not satisfied to be single in this respect.[27]

In *Watchmen*, Veidt condemns himself to total isolation through a series of choices which similarly lead away from communal conversation into private soliloquy. Whilst several of the characters leave the disastrous inaugural 'Crimebusters' meeting of '66 to try to forge new relationships, Veidt makes his exit, taking Nelson's phrase 'someone's got to save the world' to apply to him alone (XI.19). This decision will ultimately lead him to the same kind of total alienation foreseen by St Leon. Veidt's complaint to Jon about not being understood shows him in a comparable state, occupying a position which leaves him cut off from humanity, only able to discuss it with the godlike Jon – and even then, lapsing into inarticulateness:

> I've made myself feel every death, by day I imagine endless faces. By night . . . Well, I dream, about swimming towards a hideous . . . no. Never mind. It isn't significant . . .
> What's significant is that I know. I know I've struggled across the back of

murdered innocents to save humanity ... but someone had to take the weight of that awful, necessary crime. (XII.27.i–ii)

In the words of Mary Shelley's Victor Frankenstein: 'no creature had ever been so miserable as I was; so frightful an event is single in the history of man'.[28] This is an expression of superlative misery, like Veidt's, that is itself a symptom of egotism.

Vijay Mishra notes of *St Leon's* influence, 'the line of descent is from Godwin's *St Leon* through *Frankenstein*'.[29] A literal genealogy exists between *St Leon* and *Frankenstein*: the novels are parent and child like their respective authors. But we can also detect a figurative relationship between those two novels and *Watchmen,* supporting the critical view that 'the Gothic is an extremely allusive form that is self-conscious of its own literary relations'.[30] The family resemblance between these works can be gauged via the peculiar treatment of the 'extremely Gothic' trope of sole survival.[31] In Godwinian Gothic, the condition of being 'last' is a consequence of individuals' misinterpretation of their own freedom and that of others, and entails the end of the progressive hopes that initially inspired the protagonist's actions. The coterie embodies optimism; outliving it indicates a slide into an opposite condition which has more affinities with a Gothic solipsism than with enlightenment.

In *Watchmen*, the ultimate condition of Veidt, and that of the mariner from the inset *Tales of the Black Freighter*, both of whom come to find that singular survival signifies moral desertion, is foreshadowed by a number of provisional scenes of solitary survival. In *The Black Freighter* narrative, prior to the events that truly isolate the seafaring narrator, he tells us: 'I alone survived upon my remote atoll / [. . .] / and in the terrible silence I understood the true breadth of the word "isolation"' (III.18.ii, ix). But it is not really until the end of the story that he understands this. *St Leon*'s eponymous protagonist also endures successive 'false' survivals, looking forward to his final, conclusive apartness. Early in his story he fights in a battle, which concludes with his comrades 'weltering in their blood', and St Leon remarking, 'when I recovered, and looked around me, I found myself in entire solitude'.[32] The hyperbolic terms of solitude through survival in both *Black Freighter* and *St Leon* are akin to those in '*The Rime of the Ancient Mariner*':

> The many men, so beautiful,
> And they all dead did lie!
> And a million million slimy things
> Liv'd on – and so did I.[33]

Coleridge's poem offers a glimpse of possible redemption. By contrast, the early isolations of St Leon, the *Black Freighter* mariner, and Veidt merely give way to a worse kind of isolation which it is impossible to assuage. True sole survival in the Godwinian mode is distinct from other Romantic varieties because the protagonists bring about this predicament by their abuse of anarchist prerogatives. They fail to take the individualism of others into account when wielding their own. Moreover, by doing so, they become excluded from their cherished projects of social improvement. Bypassing discussion in order to achieve change is a move that undermines itself by removing the element that makes change possible. It is this relationship to coterie and progress – you can't have the latter without the former – that makes sole survival in works with a Godwinian lineage different to other treatments of the Faustian or hubris theme.

In another of *Watchmen*'s fictionally non-fiction (meta)texts – this time a chapter from *Treasure Island: Treasury of Comics* – the significance of the character's isolation in *Black Freighter*'s 'Marooned' is made explicit, and we will need to remember this for the light it will shed on the conclusion of *Watchmen* as a whole: 'the mariner, though he has escaped from his island, is in the end marooned from the rest of humanity in a much more terrible fashion' (61). In case we have been inattentive readers, Moore is on record stating the importance of the narrative of 'Marooned' for an understanding of the larger arc in *Watchmen*: 'when you get right to the end of the story, in No 12, it becomes very clear that the story was about Veidt all the time, that the mariner is Veidt'.[34] In both cases the notion of solely surviving the group is key. The mariner's sense that he is the last of his comrades liberates him from a shared morality, allowing him to use and abuse corpses, seagulls and sharks, and later, to strangle passers-by in the delusional belief that they are in league against him. Veidt, meanwhile, engineers a situation in which he will become sole representative of coterie, and the fruition of his grand plan is conditional upon this.

Like the mariner of 'Marooned', Veidt interprets those who might challenge his belief system in a productive way as threats to his sovereignty. During the revelation scenes with Dreiburg and Rorschach, he discusses the means by which he has fended off his crime-fighting colleagues – beginning with Edward Blake, for whose murder he has just claimed responsibility:

> After Blake I neutralized Jon. Stolen Psychiatric reports indicated his mental withdrawal. The cancer allegations made it physical.
> By then, Rorschach's mask killer hunt needed stopping. My own 'assassination', confirming his erroneous theory, placed me beyond suspicion.
> I'd hired my own killer through a third party. When I fed him the cyanide capsule, perhaps he realized this.
> I knew only triumph. Nothing now stood between me and my goal. Humanity's fate rested safely in my hands. (XI.26.i–ii)

'We know that you prefer to be alone down here', one of Veidt's servants tells him. 'Yes, that's right, all alone . . . just me and the world' (X.8.iv–v), Veidt replies. Liking to be alone is a signifier, in the radical Gothic tradition this chapter traces to Godwin, not of outright villainy but of morally erroneous decisions. In *Mandeville*, Godwin's gloomy novel of 1817, we read: 'he that spends his days in solitude, and is seldom corrected in his determinations by the collision of another, has almost always an overweening opinion of himself.'[35] St Leon persuades himself to accept the secrets of eternal life and wealth, and the devastating consequences, by reasoning in the following manner:

> A man can never be respectable in the eyes of the world or in his own, except so far as he stands by himself and is truly independent. He may have friends; he may have domestic connections; but he must not in these connections lose his individuality. Nothing truly great was ever achieved, that was not executed or planned in solitary seclusion.[36]

Here, Godwin is allowing his protagonist to misapply the anarchist idea of self-reliance. In fact, Godwin's works, and his anarchism, develop the idea that the individual's ability to govern themselves is a mutual process, depending on other individuals having, or being given, the wherewithal to do the same. Moore's own recent summary of Godwinian proto-anarchism identifies this as its distinct innovation: 'William Godwin wrote his *Political Justice*, advocating that the individual act according to his or her individual judgement while allowing every single other individual the same liberty.'[37] St Leon is missing the distinction between moral autonomy and arrogance.

Victor Frankenstein, too, finds that 'company was irksome to me; when alone, I could fill my mind with the sights of heaven and earth'.[38] But solitaries and sole survivors are slightly different quantities; solitaries choose to be alone, sole survivors find themselves in this position through a conspiracy of circumstances – frequently of their own making – that robs them of the possibility of a social existence. St Leon, Victor Frankenstein and *Watchmen*'s Adrian Veidt all experience careers that have their beginnings in sociable coterie, their middles in solitary ambition and their ends in sole survival, although at the conclusion of *Watchmen* Veidt has yet to realise this. Indeed, he has courted not only solitude but sole survival of coterie – like *Black Freighter*'s mariner, using the bodies of his cohorts as a means to an end – failing to grasp that this makes him irrelevant to the new world created by his intervention. Immortality and riches make impossible the things for which St Leon wanted them, and Frankenstein's neglect, for ambition's sake, first of his domestic coterie and then of his creation leaves him isolated and unknown. The allegorical mariner from 'Marooned' describes this process as it applies to Veidt, in a way that is also applicable to the older Gothic protagonists: 'the world I'd tried to save was lost beyond recall' (XI.23.i).

The way to save the world, in *St Leon, Frankenstein* and *Watchmen*, is not to attempt, single-handedly, to be the one who can say, as Veidt does, 'I did it', but to be part of the world. It is to partake in the 'adolescent, Romantic thing' that Dreiburg identifies. But that does not necessitate the aspiration to the status of legend that he imagines. Brotherhood does not always occur most successfully within the circle of extraordinary, costumed heroes after all. In *Watchmen*, the fellowship that Dreiburg imagines ensuing upon initiation into a select group is actually happening – literally – on the streets. Rorschach's psychiatrist, Malcolm Long, argues with his wife moments before the explosion. Her view of social action has been adumbrated earlier in the series: 'You got a nice life, I got a nice life. Nobody else matters' (VI.8.v). Malcolm's delayed reply to this takes place several chapters later, in the critical moments before the end:

> In a world like this . . .
> I mean, it's all we can do, try to help each other. It's all that means anything
> [. . .]

It's the world . . .
I can't run from it. (XI.20.viii–ix)

This, in turn, is an upbeat version of the downbeat message that Long has heard from Rorschach. Long is making good the questionable aspects of Rorschach's imperative conception of duty:

> Once a man has seen [man's capacity for horrors], he can never turn his back on it. Never pretend it doesn't exist.
> No matter who orders him to look the other way.
> We do not do this thing because it is permitted. We do it because we have to.
> We do it because we are compelled. (VI.15.v–vi)

This is an important rhetorical moment for Rorschach, who is not a character remarkable for his eloquence. The use of anaphora in the last three sentences creates a sense of climax. This is matched by the retrospective illustration of Rorschach walking away from an alleyway, in which he appears to have beaten up a graffiti artist and left him on the ground, with discarded newspapers which proclaim 'Keene act passed: Vigilantes illegal', an order to look away that we know Rorschach has not heeded. We can see that the half-finished graffiti behind the beaten-up man was to read 'Who watches the watchmen?' – the Juvenalian tag that features throughout *Watchmen*.

It is not clear what we are to make of Rorschach's identification of the collective compulsion to do 'this thing'. For him it seems to involve murdering, maiming, the reading of right-wing magazines – and beating up graffiti artists, a rather bathetic act to be coupled with the resounding statement of what it is to feel called to action. The panel which depicts Rorschach's announcement of this manifesto therefore also contains a warning about him in his unilateral mode. Veidt picks off, 'neutralises' and otherwise distracts his colleagues and competitors, and the monster in Frankenstein causes the deaths of all the significant others in his creator's life. The ensuing stagnation of Veidt and Victor Frankenstein is the correlative of their unmediated decisions to act, in which they behave as if untrammelled by relationships to other human beings. Rorschach seems to labour under the same affliction: his role as the only independently practising vigilante (the rest have retired, or become 'government sponsored weirdos'; I.4.v) sees him disregard the fetters of other people's good opinion. 'Rorschach never retired, even after him and his buddies fell outta grace. / Rorschach's still out there somewhere' (I.4.vi). He can do as he pleases, and the results are not pretty.

After Rorschach's arrest, Malcolm Long writes in his notes, 'I've never met anyone quite so alienated' (VI.2.v). But there are features of Rorschach's alienation that make it distinct from the type endured by either Victor Frankenstein or Veidt: in both of those cases the final irremediable alienation is a reflection and consequence of an earlier, voluntary one. Rorschach continues to practise in a manner that suggests he consistently regards himself as a member of the group; it is, after all, the plural pronoun he uses in his 'we do it because we are compelled' speech. He is continually upbraiding others for giving up. Unlike Veidt, he is a surprisingly reluctant solitary. The early chapters of *Watchmen* see him visiting all his old associates, as if keen to effect a reunion. Later, as fraternal feeling is reignited in Dreiburg, Rorschach brings himself to tell him: 'you are . . . a good friend. / I know that. / I am sorry . . . that it is sometimes difficult' (X.10.viii). Regarding the workings of the group, not just as moral graft, or even 'brotherhood', in Dreiburg's high-minded phrase, but as the activities of a group of friends, links Rorschach with the more 'ordinary' figures in *Watchmen*. We may think in particular of Bernard the news-vendor, who, for all his early bluster about being 'a survivor' (III.2.vi), turns out to be seeking meaningful interaction: 'I took this job to meet people, y'know' (XI.23.iv). The hat-and-name-sharing relationship he has with Bernard the teenager could be regarded as another of the 'thermo-dynamic miracles' that Jon allows to be the redemptive feature of humanity (IX.26.v). This pattern of the dangerous or unreliable solitary rehabilitated, at least in idea, by their longing for community has an important forebear in Frankenstein's monster: 'If any being felt emotions of benevolence towards me, I should return them an hundred and an hundred fold; for that one creature's sake, I would make peace with the whole kind!'[39]

William Godwin's *St Leon*, Mary Shelley's *Frankenstein* and Alan Moore's *Watchmen* are all highly politicised texts, and for all three the 'flexible treatment of Gothic motifs'[40] reinforces this. Each of them depicts discursive modes of association and contrasts them with despotism, indicating that only through the former can true individuality and reform be achieved. In these works we learn that giving in to the attraction of charismatic solitude is not the way to regain lost ground in a post-optimistic world, while coterie – the achievement of tolerant, diverse togetherness – is. The perception of being, like Gothic remains, 'left over' from a golden age when change could be effected should not be indulged too far, since it is a self-fulfilling prophecy.

Notes

1. Round table discussion with Alan Moore and Dave Gibbons, first pub. in *Fantasy Advertiser*, 100 (Mar. 1988): www.johncoulthart.com/feuilleton/2006/06/24/watchmen/.
2. Ellen Levy, 'The Philosophical Gothic of St Leon', *Caliban*, 33 (1996), 51–62.
3. Jerrold E. Hogle, 'Frankenstein as Neo-Gothic: From the Ghost of the Counterfeit to the Monster of 'Abjection'', in *Romanticism, History and the Possibilities of Genre*, ed. Tilottama Rajan and Julia M. Wright (Cambridge: Cambridge University Press, 1998), pp. 176–210 (p. 178).
4. Ronald Paulson, 'Gothic Fiction and the French Revolution', *English Literary History*, 48:3 (1981), 532–54 (p. 539).
5. Maggie Kilgour, *The Rise of the Gothic Novel* (London: Routledge, 1995), p. 39.
6. Levy, 'Philosophical Gothic', 54–6.
7. Marie Roberts, *Gothic Immortals: The Fiction of the Brotherhood of the Rosy Cross* (London: Routledge, 1990), p. 1.
8. Pamela Clemit, *The Godwinian Novel: The Rational Fictions of Godwin, Brockden Brown, Mary Shelley* (Oxford: Clarendon Press, 1993).
9. *Ibid.*, p. 219.
10. Vijay Mishra, *The Gothic Sublime* (New York: State University of New York Press, 1994), p. 134.
11. 'A For Alan', interview with Heidi Macdonald, *The Beat* (1 Nov. 2005): web.archive.org/web/20070305213808/http://www.comicon.com/thebeat/2006/03/a_for_alan_pt_1_the_alan_moore.html.
12. Mark Philp, 'Godwin, William (1756–1836)', *Oxford Dictionary of National Biography*, ed. H.C.G. Matthew and Brian Harrison: www.oxforddnb.com/view/article/10898.
13. William Godwin, *An Enquiry Concerning Political Justice*, 2 vols (London: Robinson, 1793), I, p. 129.
14. Alan Moore, 'Under the Hood', in Alan Moore and Dave Gibbons, *Watchmen* (New York: DC Comics, 2005), p. 8; hereafter cited in the main body of the text.
15. Victoria Myers, 'William Godwin and the Ars Rhetorica', *Studies in Romanticism*, 44:3 (2002), 415–44 (p. 420).
16. The use of this term here is indebted to work by Gary Kelly, such as

'Politicizing the Personal: Mary Wollstonecraft, Mary Shelley and the Coterie Novel', in *Mary Shelley in her Times*, ed. Betty T. Bennett and Stuart Curran (London: Johns Hopkins University Press, 2000), pp. 147–59. See also Myers, 'Ars Rhetorica', esp. pp. 439–40.
17 Myers, 'Ars Rhetorica', p. 443.
18 Paul Hamilton, 'Coleridge and Godwin in the 1790s', in *The Coleridge Connection: Essays for Thomas MacFarland*, ed. Richard Gravil and Molly Lefebure (New York: St. Martin's Press, 1990), pp. 41–59 (pp. 45–6).
19 See Clemit, *Godwinian Novel*, p. 90.
20 William Godwin, *Caleb Williams* (Oxford: Oxford University Press, 1998), p. 111.
21 Duncan S. Miall, 'Gothic Fiction', in *A Companion to Romanticism*, ed. Duncan Wu (Oxford: Blackwell, 1999), pp. 345–54 (p. 346).
22 Alan Moore gives an account of Godwin's relationship with Wollstonecraft, and their daughter Mary's elopement with Shelley, in 'Frankenstein's Cadillac', *Dodgem Logic*, 4 (June–July 2010), 2–11 (3).
23 Levy, 'Philosophical Gothic', 51.
24 Kilgour, *Rise of the Gothic Novel*, p. 103.
25 William Godwin, *St Leon: A Tale of the Sixteenth Century*, ed. William Brewer (Ontario: Broadview, 2006), p. 67.
26 *Ibid.*, p. 244.
27 *Ibid.*, pp. 188–9.
28 Mary Shelley, *Frankenstein: The 1818 Text*, ed. Marilyn Butler (Oxford: Oxford University Press, 1993), p. 167.
29 Mishra, *Gothic Sublime*, p. 175.
30 Kilgour, *Rise of the Gothic Novel*, p. 39.
31 Hogle, 'Frankenstein as Neo-Gothic', p. 178.
32 Godwin, *St Leon*, p. 72.
33 Samuel Taylor Coleridge, 'The Rime of the Ancient Mariner', in *Lyrical Ballads, with a Few other Poems* (London: J. & A. Arch, 1798), p. 22.
34 'Watchmen', round table discussion with Alan Moore, Dave Gibbons et al. {*feuilleton*} (24 June 2006): www.johncoulthart.com/feuilleton/2006/06/24/watchmen/; reprinted in *Fantasy Advertiser*, 100 (Mar. 1988).
35 William Godwin, *Mandeville*, ed. Pamela Clemit (London: Pickering & Chatto, 1992), p. 91.
36 Godwin, *St Leon*, p. 167.
37 Alan Moore, 'Fear of a Black Flag', *Dodgem Logic*, 2 (Feb.–Mar. 2010), 2–5 (4).
38 Shelley, *Frankenstein*, p. 131.
39 *Ibid.*, p. 119.
40 Levy, 'Philosophical Gothic', p. 56.

11

Reincarnating Mina Murray: subverting the Gothic heroine?

Laura Hilton

The character of Mina Harker née Murray has played a recurring, influential role in a variety of media, including film, television, stage, prose, comics, manga and videogames.[1] This chapter will compare the presentations of Mina in three different media: the original incarnation of Mina in Bram Stoker's *Dracula,* the interpretation of Stoker's Mina by Alan Moore and Kevin O'Neill in Volumes I and II of *The League of Extraordinary Gentlemen*[2] and the reinterpretation of *League*'s Mina in Stephen Norrington's film adaptation, *The League of Extraordinary Gentlemen*. The field of Adaptation Studies will be an important context for this study, and issues surrounding the translation of Mina from textual description to two-dimensional illustration and finally to moving picture, alongside the significance of what is added and/or removed from each characterisation of Mina, will be revisited throughout the discussion. The aim of this chapter is to explore how the process of adaptation, or reincarnation, relates to both Moore's contribution to *The League* in particular and the wider Gothic tradition more generally.

Significant connections can be drawn between adaptation, the Gothic tradition and the comics industry in terms of reception. Linda Hutcheon notes that 'an adaptation is likely to be greeted as minor and subsidiary and certainly never as good as the "original"' and that adaptations are often negatively described as 'derivative' and lacking in creative qualities.[3] Both Gothic fiction and the comics industry have received similarly limited levels of critical acceptance in the past: Fred Botting notes that the Gothic has frequently been 'marginalised' and 'excluded from the sphere of acceptable literature' because of 'concerns about its poisonous effects on young and undiscriminating minds',[4] while the comics industry has experienced several similar attacks, such as Dr Frederic Wertham's *Seduction of the Innocent*, which denounced American crime, horror and superhero comic books and resulted in the development of the Comics Code Authority to regulate the content of comic books through the establishment of stringent censoring measures. A clear connection can thus be traced between the dismissive attitude frequently directed towards adaptations and the negative reception often experienced by both Gothic fiction and the comics industry.

The representation of women and sexuality represents one key nodal point in anxieties over both comics and the Gothic. As a site which can concentrate attention on cultural progressiveness or conservatism, a consideration of the representation of Mina in each of these works provides a productive focus for considerations of adaptation more broadly. The role of the Gothic heroine itself has attracted considerable attention within literary scholarship; for example, Coral Ann Howells observes that she is 'constantly threatened by emotional and physical assault';[5] Fred Botting adds that she is often depicted as 'passive and persecuted' and 'presented as an image of loss and suffering';[6] and Chloe Chard argues that Gothic heroines 'are frequently presented ... as emblems of oppression'.[7] These observations provide an argument for viewing the Gothic heroine as a representation of what several critics have termed the 'victim-heroine',[8] which Dani Cavallaro suggests also alludes to 'the Victorian stereotype of woman-as-child',[9] with the result that both heroines and children in Gothic literature are 'alternately construed as passive and innocent on the one hand, and criminally disruptive on the other'.[10] This concept of the Gothic heroine as an innocent, passive victim-heroine with the potential to be corrupted might describe some elements of Stoker's Mina but, like many Gothic heroines, including those in early Gothic works by authors such as Ann Radcliffe, Matthew Lewis and Charlotte Dacre, Mina retains the capacity for independence and even transgression. As such, the ambiguities of Mina's position in Stoker's novel, as well as how these ambiguities are expressed in later adaptations, will be particularly relevant to this discussion, and in order to explore the extent to which Mina reflects and/or deviates from the Gothic heroine, reference will be made to the late Victorian emergence of the iconic New Woman which complicates representations of the passive victim-heroine.

The novel

Dracula is a novel plagued by the theme of duality: the civilisation of London is juxtaposed against the unknown horror of Transylvania, the concept of the vampire blurs the boundaries between life and death, and – in addition to the threat of changing from human to vampire – the identity of the central female protagonist is divided between the conservative Victorian woman and the controversial New Woman. Indeed, despite her reserved demeanour and expressed desire to become a dutiful, submissive wife, Mina's independence, intelligence, journalistic skills and ability to master new technology serve to associate her with the New Woman. Angelique Richardson and Chris Willis argue that although 'the New Women themselves did not always define their goals clearly', some common features have emerged, including the New Woman's 'perceived newness, her autonomous self-definition and her determination to set her own agenda in developing an alternative vision of the future'.[11] Despite the fact she was defined as either 'a beacon of progress or beast of regression, depending on who was doing the naming', the New Woman ultimately 'represented a threat not only to the social order, but also to the natural order' owing to the common belief 'that the development of a woman's brain induced infertility by causing the womb to atrophy'.[12] This belief, in addition to the 'very real fear that she may not be at all interested in men, and could manage quite well without them',[13] led to a common fear that the New Woman could place the future of the human race at risk. Ultimately, the New Woman's desire to gain autonomy and independence was greeted with varying degrees of acceptance.

Several critics have discussed how Stoker's female vampires can be interpreted in relation to the New Woman. As Glennis Byron notes, the 'anxiety caused by [the New Woman's] desire to reject traditional roles is one of the most pervasive anxieties in *Dracula*', and this anxiety is exemplified by the vampire Lucy's 'rejection of maternity' and her 'preference not for feeding but rather feeding *on* the child'.[14] Sally Ledger describes Lucy's behaviour as 'an horrific infanticidal inversion of maternal nurturance',[15] and Bram Dijkstra argues that even before she becomes a vampire, Lucy unknowingly 'bears the degenerative stamp of the New Woman' owing to her desire to marry more than one man.[16] Furthermore, Dijkstra reads the novel as a whole as 'a very carefully constructed cautionary tale directed to men of the modern temper, warning them not to yield to the bloodlust of the feminist, the New Woman embodied by Lucy'.[17] In this way, Stoker's female vampires can be read as a negative representation of the autonomy, independence and sexual equality sought by the New Woman.

In this respect, Stoker's Mina demonstrates an interesting combination of conventional woman and New Woman, with the threat of her potentially becoming a corrupted vampire created when Dracula bites her and forces her to drink his blood. As a conventional, Victorian woman, Mina is caring, loving, accommodating and is accordingly described by Dr Seward as a 'wonderful wife'.[18] She selflessly loves both her husband and Lucy, her closest friend, and often makes personal sacrifices for them. She looks after Lucy whenever she begins to sleepwalk, and when Dracula lures Lucy from her house she pursues her friend alone, at night, with no thought for her own safety. Additionally, when Mina learns that Jonathan is in a hospital in Buda-Pesth, she travels alone from Whitby by train and boat in order to nurse him back to health. These examples demonstrate Mina's conventionally selfless, loving and devoted personality whilst also emphasising key traits of the New Woman: independence, self-reliance and autonomy.

Mina's sacrifices for the health of Lucy and Jonathan are not the only actions which combine the Victorian Woman with the New Woman. Mina works throughout the novel to better herself and learn new skills so that she might support Jonathan by 'keep[ing] up with [his] studies',[19] thus combining traditional devotion with autonomous self-development:

> I have been practising shorthand very assiduously . . . When we are married I shall be able to be useful to Jonathan, and if I can stenograph well enough I can take down what he wants to say in this way and write it out for him on the typewriter, at which also I am practising very hard.[20]

Mina also keeps a journal and explains that her intention is to be of further assistance to Jonathan by trying to emulate 'lady journalists' by 'interviewing and writing descriptions and trying to remember conversations. I am told that, with a little practice, one can remember all that goes on or that one hears said during a day.'[21] Mina's knowledge of shorthand and her increasingly accurate and reliable memory may stem from a dutiful desire to 'be useful' to her husband, but both become of instrumental value when planning the destruction of Dracula. Indeed, Dr Seward recalls that without Mina having transcribed his cylinders they 'never could have found the dates' they were searching for, and Jonathan notes that 'it is due to [Mina's] energy and brains and foresight that the whole story is put together in such a way that every point tells'.[22] Therefore, despite the fact that the motivation behind the development of such skills was initially to support her husband, Mina consequentially becomes learned in areas which were previously reserved for men, and thus embraces another key trait of the New Women; as Nina Auerbach wryly observes, Mina's 'almost occult secretarial competence endows her with the metamorphic potential of the New Woman; she repeatedly saves the day by knowing some bit of mystic lore about office work'.[23] Stoker's characterisation of Mina, therefore, presents an ambiguous combination of both the conservative Victorian woman and the progressive New Woman.

The comics

In the ongoing comics series, the League itself is a secret government organisation, founded to investigate and eliminate threats to British security. In its fin-de-siècle incarnation, the League consists of Mina Murray, Allan Quatermain from H. Rider Haggard's novels, Captain Nemo from Jules Verne's *Twenty Thousand Leagues under the Sea*, Hawley Griffin from H.G. Wells's *The Invisible Man*, and Jekyll and Hyde from Robert Louis Stevenson's *The Strange Case of Dr Jekyll and Mr Hyde*. In addition to the presence of these five central characters, countless references are made to literary and cultural products throughout the series in an intricate combination of adaptation, appropriation and allusion.[24] Straightforward examples of adaptation can be identified, such as the retelling of H.G. Wells's *The War of the Worlds* in Volume II, but perhaps the term bricolage, defined by Julie Sanders as 'those texts that assemble a range of quotations, allusions, and citations from existent works of art' in a 'purposeful reassembly of fragments to form a new whole',[25] provides the most useful description of the briefer and more subtle references that occur throughout the entire narrative.

The reincarnation of Mina presented in *The League* further develops the elements of the New Woman originally presented in Stoker's Mina, creating a character that often appears confident, independent and autonomous, experiencing only rare moments of despair at her perceived 'ridiculous female naiveté'.[26] Mina is the only central female character in the series and the League's predominantly strong and effective leader, despite the fact that some of the other members of the League have superhuman abilities and all of them are men. The status of Mina's leadership thus provides a clear example of her position as an autonomous New Woman.

Mina is initially introduced through a meeting with her superior, MI5 agent Campion Bond, where she is depicted in a long-sleeved, high-necked, corseted, full-length dress with a bright, blood-red scarf that we later learn conceals the scars from Dracula's attack. Mina appears in similar dresses throughout the series and on the front covers of the trade paperbacks (see Figure 11.1), except for occasions where a different outfit is necessary for her undercover operations, and thus presents a visual mixture of propriety through her dress and corset,[27] and the suggestion of transgression through her scarf and the scars it hides. In addition to her visual presentation, Mina's dialogue swiftly identifies her desire to be treated formally and professionally: she refuses Bond's invitation to speak informally and requests that she be addressed as 'Miss Murray' at all times (V1.I.2.i). Mina's actions here present an intriguing attempt to subvert traditional conservatism, with the formality of 'Miss Murray' adhering to Victorian conventions of address whilst also communicating two controversial pieces of information in that she is no longer married and has reverted to her maiden name, a fact which, Bond observes, must have left Jonathan 'mortified' (V1.I.3.i). She also promptly rejects any implicit invitation for a romantic relationship, suggesting a desire for both professionalism and the avoidance of any situation that might place her in a position of inferiority. Mina's unwillingness to appear inferior or weak recurs throughout the narrative and she refuses to ask for assistance despite the frequency with which she is placed in dangerous circumstances. For example, she refuses Jekyll's assistance when climbing out of a hot-air balloon floating high above London and she deliberately aggravates Hyde and faces his wrath alone (V1.VI.10.ii, V1.VI.12.ii). Mina is thus depicted as keen to embrace a strong and independent presence at all times.

Mina is also very protective of her leadership position, often introducing the League with statements such as 'I am Wilhelmina Murray, and these gentlemen are my associates' (V2.III.4.iv), a declaration that

11.1 Alan Moore and Kevin O'Neill, *The League of Extraordinary Gentlemen: Volume I*, cover image (cropped)

resonates with the New Woman's demand for 'inclusion in political life'.[28] In a further expression of her authority, Mina walks front and centre when the League travels together, sits at the head of the table during meetings and does not refrain from expressing her displeasure when decisions are made without her approval (V2.I.23.iv, V1.III.2.i, V1.V.14.i). She also smokes in the company of men (V1.III.1–2), demonstrating her embracement of 'another emblem of the New Woman – the cigarette'.[29] Furthermore, Mina's leadership presents one of the central divergences from Stoker's Mina through the opposition of the 'patriarchal hierarchy' of *Dracula* due to her position as 'a ruling woman' in the League. Her forthright and assertive behaviour during her leadership, however, is often treated with disdain by others. For example, when Mina voices her displeasure over Bond's behaviour, he responds: 'a waspish tongue, Miss Murray, is to my mind but one of the many unattractive features of the modern suffragette' (V1.II.9.i). Furthermore, in accordance with the common opinion that the New Woman was inherently 'associated with homosexuality',[30] James Moriarty, the villain of Volume I of the series, assumes that Mina's leadership naturally indicates that she is a lesbian (V1.VI.16.iii).

Despite Mina's position of leadership, she goes beyond simply issuing orders and consistently plays an active role in undercover projects. As a result, arguably in a progression of her trip to central Europe in Stoker's text, Moore's Mina travels alone to Cairo in search of Allan and is almost raped as a result; she forsakes propriety when posing as a prostitute in order to attract and ultimately capture Jekyll/Hyde; and she enters the den of the Lord of Limehouse with Allan and knocks a guard unconscious whilst scathingly announcing: 'I'm not incapable, you know!'(V1.I.5–9, V1.I.19–23, V1.IV.15.vi). Whilst characters such as Bond and Moriarty contemptuously dismiss her actions, her active and apparently fearless approach is appreciated by characters such as Auguste Dupin, who tells Mina reverentially: 'You're very brave' (V1.II.6.iv).

Griffin demonstrates a specific dislike of Mina's independence and capabilities, resenting her ability to outsmart and capture him in Volume I and exacting his revenge in a violent attack in Volume II (V1.II.18.iii, V2.III.16–17). Griffin's attack could be interpreted as an attempt to generate a position of gender-based power through the combination of a violent physical attack and a kind of psychological rape, as indicated

through the dialogue, including Mina's begging, 'No, don't . . . / Please
. . .' (V2.III.16.vii) and 'Listen, please . . . / Please don't' (V2.III.17.ii),
and Griffin's degrading and sexualised verbal abuse: 'Look at you, you
stuck-up little tart. / What are you? Say it!' (V2.III.17.v). Griffin's
attack marks the first occasion where neither Mina nor her companions
are able to stop a perpetrator, and Mina only survives Griffin's attack
because Griffin himself allows her to do so. This attack, therefore,
presents a pivotal moment in the narrative which forces Mina to
acknowledge that, despite her self-reliance and independence, she is still
vulnerable in the contexts of her human mortality, her lack of superhuman powers and her connection here to the female Gothic heroine, who
is often described as 'constantly threatened by emotional and physical
assault'.[31]

In addition to this example of vulnerability, Mina forsakes a proportion of her independence by embarking upon an emotional and physical
relationship with Allan Quatermain, which develops throughout the
narrative. In Volume I, Mina is clearly unnerved when she must
introduce Allan as 'my, uh, husband, Mr. Murray' for the sake of an
undercover investigation, and the use of Mina's maiden name for their
fabricated married surname further emphasises Mina's desire to retain
control over the situation (V1.II.12.ii). Later in the volume, Mina is
furious when Allan pretends to kiss her in order to prevent them from
being discovered in Limehouse (V1.III.21.iv–ix). The first suggestion
that a romantic relationship might develop is indicated towards the end
of Volume I, when Mina begs a shocked Allan to hold her as they face
death whilst plummeting to the ground in a hot-air balloon
(V1.VI.21.ii–iii). Here, Mina is illustrated with tears streaming from
her eyes as she holds Allan's surprised face close to hers, with the
suggestion rather than confirmation that Allan and Mina actually kiss. In
Volume II, we learn that Mina's attraction to Allan was not simply the
result of a potentially fatal situation, and a deeper relationship begins to
develop. For example, Mina uses Allan's surname rather than her own
for their undercover assignment in the country and, in response to
Allan's complaint about sleeping on the floorboards, Mina replies, 'it is
entirely up to you where you sleep, Mr. Quatermain, I am quite sure',
marking the beginning of a sexual relationship in which Mina often takes
the dominant role (V2.IV.8.v, V2.IV.19.i–ii).[32] During and immediately
following Mina's first sexual encounter with Allan, reference is made to

Dracula's attack through her desire to be bitten during sexual intercourse and Allan's discovery of the scars on her neck (V2.IV.22–3, V2.IV.24), thus evoking the potential sexuality and transgression in Stoker's characterisation of Mina. Mina's physical relationship with Allan thus distances her from the virginal passivity of the traditional Gothic heroine whilst once again connecting her to the depiction of the New Woman as 'interested in and familiar with sexual feeling', 'sexuality' and 'sexual frankness'.[33]

The fact that most New Women were described as 'pessimistic about their chances of finding New Men to share their lives'[34] may seem to problematise the prospect of Mina finding a permanent partner, but Allan's adventurous past experiences appear to provide a common ground between them. However, their relationship is compromised at the end of Volume II and the narrative closes with Mina's declaration of an intention to leave London for 'Coradine', a ladies' commune in Scotland because, as she explains, 'I need time by myself' (V2.VI.25.vii, V2.VI.26.i). Whilst this move might be interpreted as an inability to cope with the events she has experienced, which would seem to undermine her fortitude, it could alternatively be read as a significant divergence from Mina's actions in *Dracula*. Indeed, Stoker's Mina marries in accordance with the common convention for Gothic heroines,[35] but Moore's Mina instead embraces independence and autonomy in reflection of the New Woman, as she does throughout a large proportion of the *The League*.[36] She thus embodies the autonomous potential of the New Woman whilst only occasionally adhering to the limitations of conventional Victorian conservatism and the traditional Gothic heroine. As such, Moore's Mina transgresses several of the boundaries that so often restrict Stoker's Mina in order to present a progressive female character who is often capable of thriving in a patriarchal society.

The film adaptation

The 2003 film adaptation compromises a significant proportion of the autonomy of the New Woman embodied in Moore's Mina. A number of plot and character changes can be identified in this loose adaptation of Volume I, such as Allan Quatermain's role as the leader of a League that now also includes Dorian Gray and Tom Sawyer, and Mina's reduction to a relatively marginalised figure who bears little resemblance to the character found in the comics.

As adaptation theorists often stress, fidelity to an original text is rarely the central motivation behind the creation of an adaptation,[37] and 'it is usually at the very point of infidelity that the most creative acts of adaptation and appropriation take place'.[38] However, a comparison of the comics and the film adaptation does raise the question of why Mina's character is changed so dramatically and what comment this makes about contemporary cultural issues surrounding the relationship between gender and power. If, as Sanders argues, adaptations comment on a source text 'most often by offering a revised point of view from the "original", adding hypothetical motivation, or voicing the silenced and marginalized',[39] then what is the significance of the film's refusal to present a controversial, independent and powerful female as the leader of a group of men, and what might this suggest about wider issues of representations of women in the film industry?

Mina is introduced to the other members of the League with the following words: 'Gentlemen, Mrs. Wilhelmina Harker. Mina's prior acquaintance with a reluctant League member [. . .] may prove useful.' Two key issues are evident: Mina's retention of her married name and the indication that her value for the group rests in her connection with a man, Dorian Gray, rather than being useful in her own right. Dorian himself draws attention to this second fact, describing Mina as 'nothing more than an enticement', and we might argue that Mina functions as both an enticement to convince Dorian to join the League and an enticement to widen the potential audience of the film. Indeed, the official promotional poster and DVD artwork present Mina in a low-cut outfit that contrasts strikingly with O'Neill's illustrations of Mina throughout the majority of the *League* series. In addition to presenting images of the main cast, the promotional poster also describes each member of the League with a single word, and Mina's description, which is placed fourth after the descriptions of Allan, Nemo and Tom Sawyer, is simply 'vampire'. Despite the fact that O'Neill himself has confirmed that Mina is not a vampire in the comics series,[40] Mina's status as a vampire becomes her sole textual signifier in the promotional material for the film, suggesting that it is by embodying the monstrosity of the figure associated with anxieties over female sexuality in Stoker's novel, rather than by virtue of her independence or leadership qualities, that she qualifies as a suitably 'extraordinary' member of the League.[41]

Dorian is not alone in belittling Mina's role, and Allan also shows little respect towards Mina. After her introduction, Allan begs, 'Please tell me this is Harker's wife with a sick note', and when he realises that Mina herself has been invited to join the League, he tells M: 'I'm waiting to be impressed.' Allan continues to show disdain towards Mina and soon after declares: 'I've had women along on past exploits and found them to be, at best, a distraction.' Mina responds by accusing Allan of unfairly judging her on the basis of her appearance alone, but her serious point is somewhat undermined by her informal and potentially flirtatious use of the greeting 'Mr. Q', a phrase never used in the comics series. Allan assumes that Mina's conversation automatically implies that she is attracted to him, and he patronisingly adds: 'My dear girl, I've buried two wives and many lovers . . . and I'm in no mood for more of either.' Mina's relationship with Allan thus begins with his open dismissal of her and any potential liaison with her, and it only progresses to a begrudging acceptance that 'the vampire lady' may be able to offer some assistance when he and Tom are under attack later in the film. This dismissive behaviour here presents a striking contrast with Allan's acceptance, in *The League*, of Mina in both her professional and personal capacities.

Overall, Mina plays a much less prominent role in the League's activities in the film adaptation. For example, rather than directly contributing to the capture of Hyde, Mina is left behind whilst Allan and Tom herd him towards Nemo's submarine with their guns. After Hyde's capture, Mina mockingly imitates Allan in order to repeat a conversation that would appear to have taken place earlier: 'This hunt's too dangerous for a woman, even one such as you. Leave it to me', in an echo of the recurring narrative device of the Gothic heroine who is restricted within 'the imprisoning house of [. . .] patriarchy',[42] which here takes the form of Nemo's submarine. The rare occasions in which Mina is presented as self-sufficient and powerful in the film adaptation are predominantly related to her status as a vampire, implying that as a mere human she would lack the ability to protect herself; moreover, Mina's demonstrations of her vampiric abilities are regarded with varying levels of acceptance by her colleagues. In the scene where her powers are revealed, which begins with a gunfight at Dorian Gray's house, Mina is immediately pulled behind a bookcase by Nemo and she takes no active role in the fight. Since she is virtually invincible, she could have been a useful aid to her colleagues; however, at this point in the film she has yet to reveal her status as a vampire and she only reappears on screen to scream Dorian's name when he is shot, but she is unable to help him and is instead manhandled back behind the bookcase by an assailant. She reappears only after the gunfight is over, in response to Dorian's enquiry as to where she is, which draws increased attention to her lack of involvement in the fight. Allan dismissively replies that 'she's probably hip-deep in some sort of trouble', and although Mina's slightly ruffled appearance suggests that she might have been involved in some behind-the-scenes skirmish, this is merely implied rather than represented on screen in a potentially empowering display of physical capability. Furthermore, Mina is almost immediately taken hostage and held at knifepoint by another assailant who believes that Mina's colleagues will not attack him for the fear of harming Mina, but as her eyes turn red Mina informs him, 'That's your biggest mistake, thinking that I need them to protect me', and she proceeds to kill him by biting his neck and drinking his blood. The other members of the League move backwards from the scene in surprise and begin to reach for their weapons, suggesting that they now view Mina as a threat. They exchange wary glances before returning their incredulous gazes towards Mina, collectively subjecting her to a predominantly disapproving male gaze. When the victim falls to the ground, Mina jumps on top of him to continue feeding, and when she has finished she enthusiastically licks her lips and her fingers. Nemo exclaims the word 'extraordinary' once the event is over, reinforcing the implication that her vampiric powers are the reason why she has been included in the League.

This incident can be read as empowering since Mina is able to demonstrate that she is not a typically passive, Gothic 'victim-heroine' and is able to act as her own rescuer, but her empowerment is undermined by the reactions of the other members of the League and how she responds to them. Under their collective, disapproving gaze, Mina immediately turns away from the rest of the group and locates a mirror in order to restore her dishevelled appearance. Only Tom attempts to diffuse the tension of the situation through joking that Mina has 'missed a spot' whilst cleaning the remaining blood from her face, and Mina's response is to ask Tom to 'excuse' her. In a conversation that closely follows this scene, Allan refers to Mina's vampiric attack and implies that he now views her in a similar way to how he views Hyde: 'like some kind of animal', creating a striking contrast with Allan's acceptance of Mina's scars and her connection with Dracula in the comics series (V2.V.4–7). Therefore, this scene presents a combination of power and suppression in relation to Mina's vampiric powers that is commensurate with the disapproving reactions to the New Woman in the late Victorian period. In according her the strength of the vampire, the film effectively ties her power to a metaphor of fallen and bestial sexuality such that it becomes a source of shame to be hidden rather than a point of pride to be maintained.

In the comics, Mina uses her leadership and intelligence to develop plans and undertake undercover investigations to discover information that can aid the League's quests, but the film adaptation removes many such scenarios in favour of action sequences. Mina is only able to defend herself and other members of the League through her vampiric powers, such as when she transforms into a group of bats who protect Allan and Tom from several snipers and when she heals herself during her battle with the traitorous Dorian Gray. Removing the threat of Dorian is in the best interests of the League as a whole, but this public good is reduced to an act of personal revenge on an ex-lover who has exploited her emotional vulnerability to steal her blood. Mina is featured in a fetishised, fitted leather outfit with an accompanying floor-length leather coat, and several of Dorian's lines include sexual innuendoes such as, 'We'll be at this all day. The bedroom, Mina, does it give you memories or ideas?' and 'I hoped I'd get to nail you one more time. I didn't think it'd be literally.' Additionally, both Mina and Dorian fight with knives, evoking the imagery of sexual penetration, and Dorian attempts to kill Mina by stabbing her through her heart and causing her to fall lifelessly onto his bed. However, once Dorian removes the blade she revives and proceeds to stab him, pinning him to the wall before destroying him by forcing him to finally look at his painting. Mina's success in eliminating Dorian certainly moves away from the traditional Gothic heroine and towards the powerful New Woman, and the fact that she is capable of stabbing as well as being stabbed also suggests a level of sexual equality. As such, elements of this scene can be interpreted as offering a rare occasion in which Mina is able to demonstrate the independence and autonomy of the New Woman. After this scene, however,

Mina disappears from the narrative, only reappearing in the last sequence of the film for Allan's funeral, and there is thus no opportunity for this potential embracement of the New Woman to be further developed.

Sanders notes that 'as the notion of hostile takeover present in a term such as "appropriation" implies, adaptation can also be oppositional, even subversive. There are as many opportunities for divergence as adherence, for assault as well as homage.'[43] In this context, the film's substitution of many autonomous and progressive elements of Mina's characterisation in both the comics and the novel with characteristics including passivity, persecution, suppression and sexual shame, marks a distinct divergence from its source texts. Norrington's Mina does exhibit a transitory position of power owing to her vampiric abilities, but this power is repeatedly undermined by the disapproving gaze of other members of the League and the dismissive attitude of the League's new leader, Allan. Furthermore, Moore's Mina commands the respect and obedience of the other members of the League for the majority of the narrative, even though she is human, which Norrington's Mina fails to do even with her added superhuman powers. The broader statement this makes in relation to contemporary reincarnations of the Gothic heroine in the film industry is bleak, and we can only hope that future visions of Mina embrace her intriguing potential for subversion and transgression.

Notes

1 In addition to the three examples discussed in this chapter, adaptations of Mina's character have appeared in film (e.g. F. W. Murnau's 1922 *Nosferatu*, Todd Browning's 1931 *Dracula* and Francis Ford Coppola's 1992 *Dracula*), television (e.g. Philip Saville's 1977 *Count Dracula*, Stewart Harcourt's 2006 *Dracula* and Shine Productions' 2009 *Demons*), stage (e.g. Hamilton Deane's 1924 *Dracula*), prose (e.g. K. J. Anderson's 2003 *League of Extraordinary Gentlemen* and Dacre Stoker and Ian Holt's 2009 *Dracula the Un-dead*), comics (e.g. Leah Moore, John Reppion and Colton Worley's 2010 adaptation, published by Dynamite Entertainment; see also Marvel's 1973–75 *Dracula Lives!*), manga (e.g. Kouta Hirano's 1997–2009 *Hellsing*), and videogames (e.g. Sony's 1993 *Bram Stoker's Dracula*).

2 Mina features in every *League* publication to date, but the analysis here will focus on her presentation in Volumes I and II, which depict events taking

place between May and September 1898. The justification for this decision is that these volumes are set in the same Victorian Gothic era as both Stoker's original novel (published in 1897) and the film adaptation (set in 1899) and thus can be usefully discussed from within the same temporal context. More recent *League* publications are set in a later time period, such as *Black Dossier* (partially set in 1958) and *Century* (set in 1910, 1969 and 2009) and are thus outside both the scope and the discursive aims of this chapter.

3 Linda Hutcheon, *A Theory of Adaptation* (New York, London: Routledge, 2006), p. xiii.
4 Fred Botting, *Gothic* (London: Routledge, 1996), pp. 15, 79.
5 Coral Ann Howells, *Love, Mystery, and Misery: Feeling in Gothic Fiction* (London: Athlone, 1978), p. 9.
6 Botting, *Gothic*, p. 131.
7 Chloe Chard, 'Introduction', in Ann Radcliffe, *The Romance of the Forest*, ed. Chloe Chard (Oxford: Oxford University Press, 1999), pp. vii–xxiv, xvii.
8 E.g. Elizabeth A. Fay, *A Feminist Introduction to Romanticism* (Malden, MA: Blackwell, 1998), p. 130 and Helen Wheatley, *Gothic Television* (Manchester: Manchester University Press, 2006), p. 119.
9 Dani Cavallaro, *The Gothic Vision: Three Centuries of Horror, Terror and Fear* (New York, London: Continuum, 2005), p. 144.
10 *Ibid.*, p. ix.
11 Angelique Richardson and Chris Willis, 'Introduction', in *The New Woman in Fiction and in Fact: Fin-de-Siècle Feminisms*, ed. Angelique Richardson and Chris Willis (Basingstoke: Palgrave Macmillan, 2001), pp. 1–38 (p. 12).
12 Lynn Pykett, *The 'Improper' Feminine: The Women's Sensation Novel and the New Woman Writing* (London: Routledge, 1992), pp. 137–40.
13 Sally Ledger, *The New Woman: Fiction and Feminism at the Fin de Siècle* (Manchester: Manchester University Press, 1997), p. 5.
14 Glennis Byron, 'Introduction', in Bram Stoker, *Dracula*, ed. Glennis Byron (Peterborough, ON: Broadview, 1998), pp. 9–24 (p. 17; original emphasis).
15 Ledger, *New Woman*, p. 104.
16 Bram Dijkstra, *Idols of Perversity: Fantasies of Feminine Evil in Fin-de-Siècle Culture* (Oxford: Oxford University Press, 1986), p. 344.
17 *Ibid.* p. 348.
18 Stoker, *Dracula*, p. 271.
19 *Ibid.* p. 86.
20 *Ibid.* p. 86.
21 *Ibid.* p. 86.
22 *Ibid.* pp. 264, 287.
23 Nina Auerbach, *Our Vampires, Ourselves* (Chicago, London: University of

Chicago Press, 1995), p. 87.
24 For a detailed description of these references throughout the *League* series, see Jess Nevins's valuable encyclopaedic volumes: *Heroes & Monsters: The Unofficial Companion to* The League of Extraordinary Gentlemen (London: Titan, 2003), *A Blazing World: The Unofficial Companion to* The League of Extraordinary Gentlemen *Volume Two* (Austin, TX: MonkeyBrain, 2004) and *Impossible Territories: An Unofficial Companion to* The League of Extraordinary Gentlemen The Black Dossier (Austin, TX: MonkeyBrain, 2008).
25 Julie Sanders, *Adaptation and Appropriation* (London, New York: Routledge, 2006), p. 4. For further discussion of bricolage – and the development of this term through the works of Claude Lévi-Strauss and Jacques Derrida – see Chapter 1 above and Chapter 14 below.
26 Alan Moore and Kevin O'Neill, *The League of Extraordinary Gentlemen: Volume I* (La Jolla, CA: America's Best Comics, 2000), V1.V.21.iii; hereafter cited in the main body of the text.
27 As Christine Bayles Kortsch notes: 'Corsets fashioned a figure that embodied social etiquette and class status'; *Dress Culture in Late Victorian Women's Fiction: Literacy, Textiles, and Activism* (Farnham: Ashgate, 2009), p. 59. Interestingly, Mina later describes her corset as 'this wretched thing' in Moore and O'Neill, *The League of Extraordinary Gentlemen: Volume II* (La Jolla, CA: America's Best Comics, 2003), V2.IV.19.v., suggesting a connection to many New Women's desire to challenge the use of corsets due to the argument that they functioned as a 'symbol of women's societal restrictions' (Kortsch, *Dress Culture*, p. 57).
28 Pykett, *'Improper' Feminine*, p. 139.
29 Richardson and Willis, 'Introduction', p. 22.
30 Ledger, *New Woman*, p. 5.
31 Howells, *Love, Mystery, and Misery*, p. 9.
32 For an example of Mina's sexual dominance see V2.IV.22.ii–iii.
33 Pykett, *'Improper' Feminine*, pp. 140, 200.
34 Elaine Showalter, 'Introduction', in *Daughters of Decadence: Women Writers of the Fin de Siècle*, ed. Elaine Showalter (London: Virago, 1993), pp. vii–xx (p. xvi).
35 Diane Long Hoeveler, *Gothic Feminism: The Professionalization of Gender from Charlotte Smith to the Brontës* (University Park: Pennsylvania State University Press, 1998), p. 36.
36 In *Black Dossier*, Allan and Mina are described as reuniting less than one year after Mina initially leaves for Coradine (XII.1), suggesting that this example of Mina's independence is temporary.
37 Hutcheon, *Theory of Adaptation*, p. xii.
38 Sanders, *Adaptation and Appropriation*, p. 20.

39 *Ibid.*, pp. 18–19.
40 'Kevin O'Neill reveals the secrets of *The League of Extraordinary Gentlemen* and *Marshal Law*', interview by Owen Vaughan, *TimesOnline* (25 Feb. 2009): http://entertainment.timesonline.co.uk/tol/arts_and_entertainment/books/fiction/article5767132.ece.
41 The depiction of Mina as a vampire here might also be read as a deliberate evocation of the sexual and social transgressions of Stoker's female vampires in general and Lucy in particular.
42 Chris Baldick, 'Introduction', in *The Oxford Book of Gothic Tales*, ed. Chris Baldick (Oxford, New York: Oxford University Press, 1992), pp. xi–xxiii (p. xxii).
43 Sanders, *Adaptation and Appropriation*, p. 9.

Part IV

Art, magic, sex, other

12

'These are not our promised resurrections': unearthing the uncanny in Alan Moore's *A Small Killing, From Hell* and *A Disease of Language*

Christopher Murray

Alan Moore's early work in the 1980s, such as *Captain Britain*, *Marvelman* and *Swamp Thing*, earned him a reputation as a clever innovator, producing reinventions of old characters, subverting their histories, remoulding them as 'realistic' or adding shades of characterisation uncommon in comics. In this sense he was a 'resurrection man', bringing defunct or ailing properties back to life. These characters were haunted by what would be a key element in Moore's work – a profound sense of alienation, disappointment and loss. With these characters Moore rehearsed the elements that would mark his mature work, texts such as *Watchmen*, *A Small Killing* and *From Hell*, and the spoken performance pieces *The Birth Caul* and *Snakes and Ladders*, which were adapted into comics by Eddie Campbell and later collected as *A Disease of Language*. In these works Moore explores the relationship between alienating environments and minds pushed to the brink of madness by violence and fear.

The notion that Moore draws much from the Gothic is supported by the fact that his resurrection of defunct or unfashionable characters itself seems like a process of unearthing the pleasures of childhood, rediscovering the past, but it is a version of the past and childhood now tainted with adult anxieties and concerns, including violence, sex and frustration. The relationship between past and present, as well as the way in which the past intrudes upon the present, is a key theme of the genre, while Gothic literature is, as Jerrold E. Hogle points out, very much like

Frankenstein's creature, stitched together from 'different types of previous writing'.[1] The same is true of the superhero genre, of which Moore's early work is undoubtedly a part. Indeed, superhero comics can be described as a kind of 'super-genre', amalgamating western, crime, romance, science fiction and horror. A case could also be made that superhero comics are a version of the medieval romance narratives that were so influential on early Gothic fiction, in which heroic questing characters, usually knights, undertook fantastic adventures, often drawn from myth and legend. Both Gothic literature and superhero comics are therefore conglomerate, hybrid entities, and Moore's transposition of Gothic themes to the superhero narrative seems a natural move, drawing together various threads that exist in both, with the coexistence of the supernatural and the scientific, elemental chaos and social order and the past and the present in an attempt to reveal the ornate, complicated and contradictory state of human nature and the universe. Another way in which Moore weaves Gothic concerns into his comics is on a formal level. He is interested in the mutability of time and space, and the way the past haunts the present; one of the ways he exploits this Gothic concern is by relating it to the formal operation of the comics page, playing to one of the key strengths of the medium, its ability to represent time *as* space.[2] In a sense the comics page, with its arrangement of panels in a sequence, is like a broken mirror through which past and present, reality and imagination, self and other, can all be mapped in a single composition, the uncanny tensions of which are perfectly suited to Gothic themes. Finally, both genres are dominated similarly by sensation and excess. In Moore's stories the kinds of sensation and excess traditionally seen in superhero comics becomes inverted into the kind usually seen in Gothic literature.

In this respect, Moore is part of a contemporary formation that draws on the older Gothic tradition in a manner suggested by Andrew Smith, William Hughes and Diane Mason in their introduction to *Fictions of Unease* (2002):

> It was once popular cliché that all authors at some time or another attempted a foray into the genre of ghost fiction. Today it might be said with more accuracy that most others, consciously or not, make recourse to the generic conventions of the Gothic, and seldom in a manner which may be described as slavish or imitative. The Gothic as allusion, as backdrop and as a fruitful source for plot and characterisation, thus permeates, mobilises and

influences the postmodern world as much as it did that of Walpole, Radcliffe and Mary Shelley.[3]

Given this, it is unsurprising that there are several other comics writers (especially British ones) who use Gothic tropes, such as Neil Gaiman (*The Sandman*) and Grant Morrison (*Arkham Asylum*, *The Invisibles*).[4] In their comics these writers are responding to the established literary tradition of Gothic as well as its contemporary and popular manifestations.

The trick that Moore pulls off with his revisions is that he performs a kind of alchemy with Gothic tropes, the superhero genre and the comics form, blending the themes of the literary Gothic with its shadow self, the sensational, schlock Gothic that exists in popular culture. The tensions between literary Gothic and other modalities of the genre are described by David Punter, who notes that the Gothic encountered in art and literature is often very different to the stereotypical images of haunted castles and damsels in distress that have been taken from traditional Gothic texts by popular culture; however, the one thing that unites all these kinds of Gothic is the exploration of fear.[5] This is noteworthy, as the one thing that superhero comics traditionally do not contain is fear. The villains may be drawn from horror fiction and film, but the victory of the superhero is always assured, as is the inviolability of the superheroic body. Moore inverts this, making superheroes feel fear, making them vulnerable, and spectators, or even perpetrators, of extreme violence. In doing this he unleashes themes that are implicit in the mainstream comics, adding fear to the equation and 'displaying the underside of Enlightenment and Humanist values',[6] of which the superhero is an exemplar, standing up for reason and justice.

As discussed elsewhere in the present collection, the attempt to make superhero comics Gothic is evident in most of Moore's work up to and including *Watchmen*, but following difficult experiences Moore retreated from mainstream comics, and to a certain extent, began to divorce himself from the genre, seeking particular distance from superheroes. At this time his interest in the literary side of the Gothic became more pronounced, seeing the creation of some of his most sophisticated work, including *A Small Killing*, *From Hell*, *The Birth Caul* and *Snakes and Ladders*. This was also the time when Moore proclaimed himself to be a magician, and when his ideas about art as magic were frequently articulated in his comics.[7] What emerges from these texts is a sublime sense of the interconnectedness of all things, inner and outer worlds, literature and popular culture, past and present, which brings a powerful apprehension of the uncanny, something that is very clear in *A Small Killing*.

'The Imp of the Perverse': childhood and guilt in *A Small Killing*

A Small Killing, with artwork by Oscar Zarate, was published by VG Graphics (an imprint of the book publisher Victor Gollancz) and tells the story of an advertising executive, Tim Hole, whose success with a large contract prompts long forgotten feelings of guilt. As he travels from New York back to his home in England he is apparently pursued by a strange child, who seems to be an imp or a demonic presence. The child, who looks tellingly familiar to Tim, follows him relentlessly, taunting him, and Tim in turn starts to pursue his tormentor. Tim eventually learns the truth – that the boy is in fact an imagined version of himself, and that the trauma that has created this doppelgänger comes from an incident in the past, when Tim, as a child, buried insects in a jar, leaving them to die. When recalling the incident over the years Tim has lied to others, and to himself, saying that he felt remorse and ran back to release the insects. This realisation brings Tim back to the spot where he buried the jar years before only to find it now swollen to monstrous proportions. When he takes off the lid grotesquely huge insects pour out, overpowering him with their monstrous physicality and their insect otherness (Figure 12.1). At this point the boy appears and the two fight, resulting in a rather ambiguous conclusion. This is linked to a back story in which Tim refuses to take responsibility for an abortion procured by his girlfriend, leaving her to decide for herself what to do. This psychodrama enacts the horror that Tim feels towards his first knowingly destructive act (the killing of the insects), reverberating through time and memory, touching on his other destructive acts and selfish behaviours such that in one reading the imp is the imagined aborted child, or the guilt associated with this incident. The resulting repression creates the split within Tim's personality which brings the imp into being, festering in his unconscious like the bodies of the dead insects in the jar or the aborted child sent to him by his then ex-girlfriend (the small killings of the title).

2.1 Alan Moore and Oscar Zarate, *A Small Killing*, p. 84

A Small Killing draws much from Franz Kafka, especially 'Metamorphosis' and *The Trial*. As Fred Botting notes, 'some of the most disturbing Gothic images of the twentieth century appear in Kafka's work, writings which vacillate between subjective and objective positions, between the horrors of individual alienation and self-loathing and the grotesquely distorted images of everyday family and social life'.[8] In this story Moore moves beyond transposing Gothic elements into superhero comics and pursues a more personal project, responding directly to the Gothic tradition of Kafka, Robert Louis Stevenson and Edgar Allan Poe – in particular Poe's stories 'William Wilson' and 'The Man of the Crowd', with their themes of the doppelgänger and the *flâneur*. The impulse towards self-destruction also recalls another Poe story, 'The Imp of the Perverse', in which a man who commits murder and gets away with it is compelled to confess, feeling that he is being tormented by an imp or a fiend who induces him to reveal his secret. The intertextuality of *A Small Killing* is revealing. From Kafka comes the revulsion and alienation associated with the body, from Stevenson the conflict with an alter ego and from Poe comes the sense of estrangement and doubling.

The Gothic elements of *A Small Killing* do not only spring from the literary sources, however; the artwork by Zarate is surreal and uncanny, offering a series of mirror images and reflections that represent the theme of doubleness and grotesque caricatures which unsettle the protagonist. The crowd scenes in particular are claustrophobic and oppressive, with the cacophony of dissonant voices being unnerving, and to the protagonist, clearly annoying, as he struggles to retain his composure in a world that is continually pressing in on him. Tim, as always, is aloof and distant, and struggles to connect with others. The story shows the gradual erosion of his sense of restraint and he comes into closer contact with his dark other self. The theme of a long-buried secret being uncovered with horrific consequences is a fundamentally Gothic one, as is the depiction of the return to the scene of the crime, which takes in the atmosphere of a graveyard, with a dark tree laden with ravens and run-down houses evoking medieval ruins. This is a suitable setting for the conclusion of *A Small Killing*, which sees Tim and the child embroiled in a brutal fight to the death, overlaid with Tim narrating stage directions in captions as he rehearses the pitch of his campaign to his clients. His latest success is counterpointed with his original sin, his first failure, and the two are directly related. The killer instinct, that dark impulse to achieve victory, no matter the cost, even if it means one's own soul, is the power that Tim has cultivated to achieve success in corporate America as an advertising executive, but such power comes with a price.

In the end it is a newly resurrected Tim who walks away from the conflict, with the strong suggestion that it is the imp who survives within Tim's body. It leaves Tim's spectacles behind and buys a Vimto (the child's favourite drink) and a newspaper, scanning the 'situations vacant' page, looking for a new job and a new start. The last page is unusually intense, with vivid colours, and takes on a dreamlike quality as the morning sun shines down, casting long shadows. All the previously inert symbols of mobility, the bicycle, the taxi, the train and the aeroplane burst into new life, representing the enormous weight that has lifted, as this resurrected Tim '[slips] from the scene of the crime'.[9] In this reversal of 'William Wilson' it is the doppelgänger who kills the protagonist. The ending seems to dispel the dark Gothic imagery that has characterised the final pages, but even though the images bustle with new energy and possibility, the sense of excess and implicit violence remains, making the ending eerie and uncanny, with the familiar becoming suddenly alien and forbidding, full of portent and mystery, as if an occult ritual had taken place, transforming the imp into Tim. As with *Swamp Thing*, memory is very closely related to place in *A Small Killing*, and this is informed by Moore's interest in psychogeography, which is even more obviously delineated in *From Hell*.

'Motive is implicit in the brickwork': *From Hell* and 'I Keep Coming Back'

From Hell, which started in the short-lived *Taboo* magazine published by Mad Love, was a long and exhaustively researched examination of the Jack the Ripper case. Of all of Moore's work this is the one that is most obviously Gothic. Here London becomes an erotic body, bound and violated, with the violence towards women encoded onto the urban environment. Physical symbols of phallic power (churches and towers) and oppression (the weight of bricks and mortar bearing down on the earth) act as manifestations of the control of nature made possible by 'male' endeavours (imperialism and the commemoration of the glorious past enacted through architecture).[10] The killer, Gull, is motivated by a pathological desire to enact a ritual using the city itself as an instrument, with architect Nicholas Hawksmoor's Christ Church playing a key part, along with Cleopatra's Needle, and other locations. In the tour that Gull and his coachman Netley take round London, Gull's explication of his goal is unsettling, especially when the importance of the city and its symbols becomes clear. The influence of psychogeography via Iain Sinclair and Peter Ackroyd is also evident. In Iain Sinclair's Poem *Lud Heat* and Peter Ackroyd's novel *Hawksmoor* it is postulated that Hawksmoor's churches and obelisks are designed to channel dark energies. This ties into Moore's interest in psychogeography, which argues that the consciousness of a people is partly determined by environment.[11] As Moore says in an interview with Eddie Campbell in *Egomania*, 2:

> Psychogeography [...] led me to consider what exactly it is that constitutes the reality of a place. Obviously there is more to our experience of a place than the bricks and mortar. Our reaction to various locations seems to me to be dependent upon the richness of the web of associations that we connect with those sites.[12]

Moore, like Sinclair and Ackroyd, adds an occult dimension to this, presenting London as the site of a demonic ritual and exploring the after-effects of violence, how it imprints itself on places, and on the collective unconsciousness, reverberating through history, touching on the Holocaust, the Moors murderers, the Kray Brothers, the Yorkshire Ripper and other murderers.

The idea that space can become a repository of memory is particularly interesting to Moore as it ties into his notion of 'Ideaspace', and this is especially relevant to comics, which manipulate space and time. From a certain point of view the panels of the comics page have an architectural function, structuring space, building not just in the two dimensions of the page, but through the illusion of perspective and the introduction of time, which is created by the sequence of panels, creating different time frames on the page, adding another dimension. In this sense the comics page constructs a continuum which can be entered through imagination. Moore finds this to be magical, and through detailed research both he and Campbell construct a world that is historically convincing yet malleable, given to distortion, or, in a word – uncanny.

2.2 Alan Moore and Eddie Campbell, *From Hell*, VII.24

The uncanny nature of the world that Campbell and Moore create is seen when the madman Gull lures one of his victims down an alleyway (Figure 12.2). As the viewpoint alternates in each panel a sense of the claustrophobic environment is established and a dread anticipation of the impending act of violence creeps in. Suddenly Gull sees a man pulling a curtain, revealing the interior of a room lit by an electric light bulb, an anachronism in 1888. As the killer and the man in the room gaze at one another across time other anachronistic elements become clear, including a television set, and a photograph of Marilyn Monroe in her famous pose, standing on an air vent, her skirt blown up around her thighs. The sexual nature of this pose, and the more liberal culture that produced it, astound Gull, showing him a world alien to him, but in its sexual objectification of the feminine it can be perceived that perhaps this is the world that his ritual has brought about – the fulfilment of his vision. This realisation is unsettling and provocative. The formal construction of the page, using the nine-panel grid, is conservative and restrained, matching Gull's calm veneer and his chillingly methodological approach towards the murders. However, the alteration of viewpoint and the shift in time, or the blurring of boundaries, serve as a counterpoint to this, as if the mask of order and restraint is about to slip, which we know, in terms of the murders, is indeed the case. The sense that the comics page measures time steadily but subjectively is something that Moore perfected with Dave Gibbons in *Watchmen*. Moore and Campbell replicate this effect, drawing the reader into Gull's world and positioning them as a voyeur and accomplice, but whereas the artwork and page composition in *Watchmen* had the structural and stylistic precision of a metronome, Campbell's style offers no such comfort, despite the formal similarity. This scene is one of the many instances of the uncanny in the story, and as Gull's mind unravels he is granted further visions of the future, the world of the twentieth century that he has 'delivered', as he terms it, conflating the abdominal mutilations he performs with a sort of assisted birth of a new vulgar era in which the feminine is bound and contained by his ritualised sacrifice. As his violence and madness soak London in blood his consciousness becomes part of the place; madness becomes mapped onto the environment, distorting it forever. More uncomfortable, though, is the growing realisation that the world he has brought into being is the one in which we live.

This theme is continued in 'I Keep Coming Back', an often overlooked companion piece to *From Hell*, with artwork by Zarate, which appeared five years after their collaboration on *A Small Killing* and features in a collection of short 'London Noir' graphic stories, *It's Dark in London* (1996), edited by Zarate. The story is told from Moore's perspective (literally, we see through his eyes), or at least this is the obvious implication, and Moore has since said that the events in this story are 'almost completely true to life'.[13] The reader/protagonist/Moore is involved in a documentary about Nicholas Hawksmoor's Christ Church in Spitalfields, London, which, as already noted, plays a prominent part in *From Hell*. Taking a break from the filming of the documentary, Moore visits the Ten Bells public house, which is strongly associated with the Ripper murders, as it is the pub which his victims frequented. Moore passes some time with the film crew as an exotic dancer strips. The environment remains soaked with blood and associated with sex and its commercialisation. The character of Moore is drawn into an uncomfortable act of voyeurism; then, as the alcohol takes effect, he drifts towards thoughts of sex and violence:

> Of course, I'd never use a woman like that. It's just an interesting scenario. I take her to her flat. She pays her babysitter.
> Take her face between, one thumb stroking her chin, the other following her lip line; dipping in, she shuts her eyes.[14]

Gradually, this fantasy develops into envisioning a sordid encounter with the dancer in an alley, a blurring of imaginative lines that finds visual expression on the page, for as the woman dances the image of her pubic hair blurs, almost unrecognisably. This distortion is an effect of alcohol, but also a violent rending of the feminine by the male gaze. Ultimately, Moore's narration of the protagonist's imagined sexual encounter mirrors one of the Ripper murders, climaxing as he imagines reaching into his pocket, presumably finding a weapon there:

> Wait till she clocks off. Walk her home. We find a sidestreet somewhere. Maybe Hanbury. Facing the fence, she moans. I reach into my pocket. Maybe I should leave. (93.i)

But he does not leave; he waits till the dancer goes home, watching her walk down the dark streets from the shadows as the Gothic architecture of Christ Church looms over him. He ponders 'ancient anatomical imperatives', noting that 'motive is implicit in the brickwork' (94.ii).

The environment remains saturated with the violence that the Ripper perpetrated, and it seeps into the consciousness of those who are drawn to the area, but as he notes, 'I keep coming back' (94.iii). This is a territory that haunts Moore's consciousness, his memory and his imagination, compelling him to retrace the steps of a killer, imagining the world from the killer's perspective. This story is, like *From Hell*, explicitly Gothic, and the claustrophobic effect of the text is achieved by immersion in the psyche of the protagonist. The first-person narrative and point of view draw the protagonist, and the reader, into uncomfortable proximity with the Ripper, and the ripples of violence that still emanate from his acts:

> During the 'seventies, the pub adopted the name of the area's only true celebrity. Feminists grumbled. The original sign was retrieved from the cellar. I think that shows a degree of sensitivity to women's feelings. (87.iii)

Interestingly, 'I Keep Coming Back' is one of the few stories in which Moore writes autobiographically, although it has a notable companion in this respect, *The Birth Caul*, in which he once again focuses on psychogeography, this time more closely associated with his personal history. *Snakes and Ladders*, on the other hand, traces Moore's thoughts about creativity and magic through a psychogeographical reading of Red Lion Square in London and the biographical details of those historical figures and artists who were in some way connected to it. What links *The Birth Caul* and *Snakes and Ladders*, beyond the fact that they are both derived from performance pieces, is Moore's modified use of the Gothic, which is liberated from his use of it to destabilise the generic conventions of superhero comics, becoming bound up with psychogeography and magic.

'Whose is all this blood?': *The Birth Caul* and *Snakes and Ladders*

At around the time of writing *From Hell* Moore was in the process of formalising his ideas about art and magic. In 1993, on his fortieth birthday, he announced that he was a magician, and since then much of his work has commented on his beliefs about magic and art being the same thing, arguing that everyone can perform magic through acts of will and imagination. This interest in magic is evident in his 'workings',

The Birth Caul and *Snakes and Ladders*, both of which are spoken-word pieces performed by Moore and his collaborators in *The Moon and Serpent Grand Egyptian Theatre of Marvels*.[15] These are place-specific, again showing the influence of psychogeography and the occult, and include ritual and music to respond to the history of the location. Eddie Campbell, Moore's collaborator on *From Hell*, adapted the text of these performances into comic versions of both *Snakes and Ladders* and *The Birth Caul*, which were collected together under the title *A Disease of Language* (named for Aleister Crowley's famous description of magic).[16]

The Birth Caul ruminates on language and identity, moving in and out of memory and autobiography. It considers the birth caul (a membrane that covers the face of some children at birth) to be a metaphor for the veil of language that orders perception. Moore recounts how following his mother's death he goes through her possessions, finding his grandmother's birth caul. There is the suggestion that those who enter the world 'masked' by a caul perhaps perceive more easily than others that life is a performance and that we all wear masks, playing many parts before our final exit. In one sequence Moore is shown at the age of 20 wearing a clown mask, as well as the masks of other 'teenage dreamselves', before burying them 'at night beneath the patio'.[17] The collision of memory, repression, guilt and domestic detail recalls *A Small Killing*, but unlike Zarate's artwork Campbell offers a world not of caricature and expressionism, but of collage and mixed media, with different artistic styles, photographs, typographical manipulation, and on this page, an allusion to Roy Lichtenstein, with his stylised pop-art image of a brushstroke, which is itself an imitation of an imitation. Taken together these elements create an unstable world in which various masks keep slipping off, revealing a multilayered text. In visual terms this is perhaps more Campbell's doing than Moore's. While Moore is famous for copiously detailed scripts, *The Birth Caul*, like *Snakes and Ladders*, was not written as a comic but as a performance piece. Freed from Moore's usual habit of providing scripts that detail the significance and import of each panel, Campbell works instead from the transcript of Moore's spoken performance, finding his own visual equivalences in the creation of the comic. Perhaps for those reasons the comic seems less overly Gothic in its conception than it might have been had Moore been steering things more directly, but the Gothic elements creep out in other ways, notably through the anxiety and brooding malleability of the narrative, its return to the past, to childhood and even the moment of conception, which is treated with a simultaneous sense of foreboding, even revulsion, but tempered by awe and a sense of the sublime.

There are certainly Gothic elements in *The Birth Caul*, but they are in tension with the autobiographical elements, and overall the effect is more towards the uncanny than horror. However, the presence of the past in the present and a sense of monstrous knowledge predominate. As Moore says, imagining the moment of his conception from the perspective of sperm and egg, 'Somewhere now above in giant chambers full of light and unthinkable emotions, gods and goddesses fuck, and there amidst the sweat and stench of the taboo, is light uncanny and profound' (47.ii). The power of *The Birth Caul* comes from its excavation of memory and the backwards tumble through time, marked by a collapse in the narrator's vocabulary (and the typography), returning to a state of childhood, and beyond, ending with the aforementioned return to the moment of conception, which in the final pages spirals out to a portrait of the evolutionary process and the creation of the universe, which are all part of the same moment of creation, and the same primordial unveiling, the ripples of which are still to be felt (and Moore might locate them in Ideaspace). This is very much the same territory that Moore negotiates in *Snakes and Ladders*.

In *Snakes and Ladders* Moore uses the metaphor of the children's game to trace psychogeographical relationships between historical figures such as Cromwell, the artist and poet Dante Gabriel Rossetti, writer Arthur Machen and Francis Crick, co-discoverer of the structure of DNA, as well as numerous other figures associated with Red Lion Square. It links the snake of the garden of Eden with the double helix of DNA, and the game, Snakes and Ladders with evolutionary and spiritual progress. The work moves from the beginning of the universe (imagined like an orchestra tuning up) to the horror of Cromwell's disinterment ('Lank Hair, fused now with the fraying scalp') and Rossetti recovering his poetry from the grave of his beloved ('Lizzie Siddall hauled like Cromwell from her grave in order to retrieve the poems that he's buried with her').[18] The piece then culminates in Machen's visionary wanderings in Syon, the imagined world created in his madness, which Moore sees as the dreaming world, the collective unconscious, or, to put it another way, Ideaspace (Figure 12.3). As Moore notes, place and memory play an important role in this text:

2.3 Alan Moore and Eddie Campbell, 'Snakes and Ladders', *A Disease of Language*, 9

As with all of the site based works, *Snakes & Ladders* and its specific nature grew out from my reading of the site itself [Conway Hall in London's Red Lion Square]. The disinterment of Oliver Cromwell and Elizabeth Siddell [sic]; the visionary nature of Arthur Machen's experiences after the death of his first wife and their relation to the lunar and solar spheres of the Kaballah; the musings about DNA (which is pretty much all about death and reproduction) ... all of these things seemed to have a whiff of resurrection about them, tying them together. Love, death, art, resurrection, dreams, visions, heartbreak, romance ... these seemed to be the predominating colours of the landscape, that gave the place its individual soul and character.[19]

The tone of *Snakes and Ladders* as a performance piece is eerie and somewhat mystical, aided by Tim Perkins's music and Moore's gruff, unmistakable Northampton accent, which is counterpointed with the linguistic complexity and ironic juxtapositions of the imagery of this poem. As in *The Birth Caul*, in Campbell's comic version some of this is lost, and the abundance of text he has to find space for is sometimes a problem, but in most instances he works the text into the compositions in ingenious ways. What is lost in atmosphere is more than compensated for by the power of the images and the uncanny quality Campbell creates, with a complex topography of photographs, sketches over photographs, maps, documents, reproductions of artwork and an archive of other artefacts. Added to this is the relationship between the various art styles and mediums he employs, with pen and ink, watercolour wash, oils and collage. The effect is a malleable, multilayered text which achieves a visual equivalency to the atmosphere created in the performance.

The themes of *Snakes and Ladders* are creation, reproduction, the mythology of the Fall and the gradual ascent to enlightenment, which is mapped onto the game, Snakes and Ladders. In addition to the serpent in the Garden of Eden and the twisted helix of DNA, the snake becomes the Roman god, Glycon, who was alleged by the satirist Lucian to be a hoax perpetrated by the Greek prophet Alexander of Abonoteichus. The cult was alleged to be a con, and the 'god' a glove puppet.[20] Part of Moore's 'coming out' as a magician was to announce that he worshipped this false god, clear in the knowledge that all gods are false, while asserting that the gods, like all myths, undeniably have power in the realm of the imagination, where they can unlock hidden potential. A key point in the text has the muse (Imagination) dance with a snake puppet, showing how imagination can lend power and divinity to mundane things, with faith and belief fleshing out the improbable. While both *The Birth Caul* and *Snakes and Ladders* employ the same Gothic architecture of alienation, madness and doubt as Moore's earlier work, bringing the past into the present, counterpointing synchronicity with chaos, and using the environment to stand in for the unconscious, these texts move away from the Gothic angst of earlier works, transmuting fear into creative possibility and repression into self-knowledge. In these texts contradictions resolve and a fresh perspective on fear and limitation is made possible. It would appear that Moore's magic trick, his sleight of hand, is to turn his Gothic concerns into a fusion of occult magical thinking and scientific and spiritual enlightenment, showing that in Ideaspace, through magic and imagination, there exists a world of possibility and hope. Like a birth caul being removed, or a snake shedding its skin, Moore peels away the Gothic, leaving the world 'luminous with sense'.[21] This, then, is the evolution of Moore's use of the Gothic, ascending from primordial fear, embracing the madness and the uncanny, marrying them to science and finding an amalgamation of all these elements through the alchemy of imagination.

Conclusion

In Moore's early work the reader is continually shown moments of artistic creation which result in contact with Eternity, or with the sublime, yet transcendence is always just out of reach, the promised resurrection or transfiguration always being too radical, only able to be hinted at, something we must crawl towards, up the spiritual and evolutionary chain. This reveals the Gothic themes of overreaching and the dangers of self-transformation. However, in Moore's later work, and in its delineation of space and environment as psychic space (Ideaspace), he allows for the possibility of contact with such power. Therefore, while the concerns of the Gothic are central to Moore's world-view, and evident in almost all of his writings, it would seem that where he relied on it in his earlier genre work to give an atmosphere of dread and terror commensurate with the changes in characterisation he was enacting, in later more personal works he shows the reader a means to pass through Gothic concerns such as unease and fear and a way to embrace the uncanny.

Moore exploits the ability of comics to collapse time and space together, turning the page into a stage upon which the enactment of madness and trauma are linked to a complex treatment of psychogeography that inextricably links the outer world of bricks, mortar and bodies to an interior architecture of memory and fear, hope and imagination. If Moore is a resurrection man it is not simply a matter of his ability to reconstitute old characters as more 'realistic' versions of themselves, it is his ability to provide them with this complex inner world of feelings, desires and flawed humanity. The characters he unearths are not given their 'promised resurrections' into a new world, but are dragged briefly into the light to show us the rotting corpse; but, tangled in that still bright shining hair, we may find a book of long-lost poetry. In his view magic and creativity blend to become one thing, revealing both illusion and truth as two sides of the same coin. For Moore art is terrible in its power, yet a guiding light, even for the mad and the monstrous (perhaps especially for them), offering the possibility of a luminous assent, or a perilous Fall, but ultimately 'it's all just snakes and ladders' (*Snakes*, 100.iv). In his mature work the reader encounters a writer fully aware of his influences, yet also striving to unravel the puzzle of how one can gain the power to overcome fear and turn dark impulses into a new formulation of power capable of freeing itself from the corruptions of the past. Moore's most recent returns to Lovecraft, together with his related meditations on the works of Kenneth Grant and others, suggest that while art can be redemptive and rejuvenating, it can also be coopted by a magic whose effects are violent and repressive; however, in linking retellings of the Gothic to his practice of magic and his explorations of Ideaspace, he nevertheless presents a powerful vision which suggests that, through a celebration of the power of the uncanny, it is possible to obtain a transformative comportment towards fear and limitation.

Notes

1 Jerrold E. Hogle, 'Introduction: The Gothic in Western Culture', in *The Cambridge Companion to Gothic Fiction*, ed. Jerrold E. Hogle (Cambridge: Cambridge University Press, 2002), pp. 1–20 (p. 6).
2 Scott McCloud, *Understanding Comics: The Invisible Art* (New York: HarperPerennial, 1994), p. 100.

3 Andrew Smith, William Hughes and Diane Mason, 'Introduction', in *Fictions of Unease: The Gothic from Otranto to The X-Files* (Bath: Sulis Press, 2002), p. 3.
4 Moore is a huge influence on these younger writers, and in some ways their use of the Gothic derives from him.
5 David Punter, *The Literature of Terror: A History of Gothic Fictions from 1765 to the Present Day*, 2nd edn, 2 vols (London: Longman, 1996), I, p. 2.
6 Fred Botting, *Gothic* (London and New York: Routledge, 1996), p. 2.
7 'Alan Moore interviewed by Eddie Campbell', *Egomania*, 2 (2002), 1–32 (pp. 2–7); reprinted in Alan Moore and Eddie Campbell, *A Disease of Language* (London: Knockabout Comics, 2010), pp. 110–40.
8 Botting, *Gothic*, p. 160.
9 Alan Moore and Oscar Zarate, *A Small Killing* (London: VG Graphics, 1991), 93.i.
10 For more on this in relation to comics see Björn Quiring, '"A fiction that we must inhabit" – Sense Production in Urban Spaces According to Alan Moore and Eddie Campbell's *From Hell*', in *Comics and the City: Urban Space in Print, Picture and Sequence*, ed. Jörn Ahrens and Arno Meteling (London and New York: Continuum, 2010), pp. 199–213; see also Chapter 7 above.
11 See Guy Dubord's *Society of the Spectacle* (New York: Zone Books, 1999 [1967]) and Merlin Coverley's *Psychogeography* (Harpenden: Pocket Essentials, 2006).
12 'Moore interviewed by Campbell', p. 7.
13 'The Story behind the stories', Alan Moore interviewed by William Christensen, in *Yuggoth Cultures*, ed. William Christensen (Urbana, IL: Avatar, 2007), pp. 105–15 (p. 115).
14 Alan Moore, with art by Oscar Zarate, 'I Keep Coming Back', in *It's Dark in London*, ed. Oscar Zarate (London: Serpent's Tail, 1996); reprinted in *Yuggoth Cultures*, pp. 83–94 (p. 92.ii); hereafter cited in the main body of the text.
15 Other happenings/performances include *The Moon and Serpent Grand Egyptian Theatre of Marvels*, *The Highbury Working: A Beat Séance* and *Angel Passage*, which was based on the poetry and artwork of William Blake.
16 'Moore interviewed by Campbell', p. 4.
17 Alan Moore and Eddie Campbell, *The Birth Caul* (Paddington, QLD: Eddie Campbell Comics, 1999), 13.v–vii; reprinted in *A Disease of Language* (London: Knockabout Comics, 2010), pp. 5–56.
18 Alan Moore and Eddie Campbell, *Snakes and Ladders* (Paddington, QLD:

Eddie Campbell Comics), 8.iv, 9.vii; reprinted in *A Disease of Language*, pp. 57–108.
19 'Moore interviewed by Campbell', p. 126.
20 'Moore interviewed by Campbell', pp. 4–5.
21 Alan Moore and Eddie Campbell, *Snakes and Ladders*, 47.i.

13

Medium, spirits and embodiment in *Voice of the Fire*

Julia Round

Alan Moore's debut novel *Voice of the Fire* is a lyrical and poetic collection of prose stories set within the same ten-mile radius (of the Northampton township), in the month of November, over five thousand years of history. Each chapter is narrated by a different character at a different point in time, although the lines between past and present quickly become blurred as echoes of characters and events resonate between the stories. This chapter will use Gothic and psychogeographic theory to examine the construction of Moore's novel, linking *Voice*'s bodily symbols to the Gothic trope of abjection and relating its circular structure to the Ouroboros and the pattern of birth and life. It also discusses the role of hallucination in constructing *Voice*'s haunted chronology and relates this to the Gothic questioning of perception and authenticity, arguing that Moore makes exceptional use of the prose medium in this way to quite literally embody the spirit(s) of Northampton.

Haunted bodies

Annalisa De Liddo quotes Jay Babcock's definition of psychogeography as 'a means of divining the meaning of the streets in which we live and pass our lives, and thus our own meaning' – the process of exploring cultural and historical resonances and memories, which creates a fictional map that makes up the basis of one's own identity.[1] In a discussion of *Big Numbers*, Di Liddo notes 'the quasi-archeological investigation of English spaces that has frequently appeared in Moore's work, especially from the nineties onwards',[2] and location also dominates some of Moore's notable earlier works, such as *Swamp Thing*, *From Hell* and *V for Vendetta*.[3] Psychogeography is at the core of *Voice*, as its series of historical narratives are shown to make up Northampton's identity as their recurring patterns inform its day-to-day life.

Moore's atypical narrative succeeds, in part, due to the strong sense of thematic unity that runs through the book. As Neil Walsh comments:

> None of the stories are what you would call pleasant. They deal with violence, madness, death, mutilation, betrayal, loss of faith, and other such unhappy subjects. Most of them, however, have moments of agonizing brilliance. Ultimately, the book is about the myth and magic of story. Images and events from one tale recur in later one[s], so that each contains echoes of the others. Finally, all the themes are loosely brought together in that last, authorial-voiced story.[4]

All these themes have a peculiarly Gothic sense to them. While some (violence, death, mutilation) emphasise the corporeal, the other three (madness, betrayal, loss of faith) belong to the psychological realm. This division between (physical) horror and (emotional) terror is apparent in the earliest Gothic texts (for example, Matthew Lewis versus Anne Radcliffe); however, Steven Bruhm identifies an overarching drive towards the corporeal in the Gothic, arguing that it is, above all, a 'discourse of the body' as sense perception validates feeling.[5] Walsh's above summary thereby defines *Voice*'s themes as Gothic by merging such opposed elements ('agonizing brilliance') into a single, mutual list.

This dichotomous structure (of physical versus psychological) can be linked more clearly to the Gothic through cryptomimesis. Jodey Castricano's model defines the crypt as internal yet external; and cryptomimesis as 'a writing practice that, like certain Gothic conventions, generates its uncanny effects through the production of what Nicholas Rand might call a "contradictory 'topography of inside out'" (*topique des fors*) (lxviii)'.[6] Bruhm's above arguments regarding the inseparability of the physical and the perceptual in our experience of pain[7] can certainly be read according to this model as, although the brain contains the mind, the psyche can simultaneously be considered so much more than mere biological and electrical impulses. *Voice* as a whole sustains this kind of divide in other ways too; while its focus could be described as external (the locality of Northampton dominates, and each tale contains at least one shocking event), it is also internal, as first-person narrators expound on their thoughts, feelings and visions.

Voice uses a series of metaphors, similes and images to link body and land in a variety of ways, both explicit and implicit. Personification of the land is used from the very first chapter, whose narrator (the Pig Boy) muses after burying his mother, 'Dirt suck on I's foot. Old dirt, he gleans I is not putting mother's foot to he and wants he's due, for there is one foot due he yet, and take he I's foot to make good for it.'[8] Here the land itself is given human motivations and abilities.

Moore also uses visual symbols to enhance this parallel. The Torso Garden (a display of the mutilated remains of lawbreakers in 'The Cremation Fields') is itself a phrase that combines the corporeal and the horticultural. The garden's lopped torsos are compared by the narrator to 'giant, severed heads, sex-mouthed and nipple-eyed, each with a plume of meat-flies trailing in the breeze. Ant freckles moving, out the corner of my eye' (p. 95). Here, cut-up bodies are transformed into faces, with insect life making up some of their features. This individual and interchangeable nature of body parts echoes 'Hob's Hog', whose narrator describes burying his mother a piece at a time, fragmenting her body with his words: 'dirt fall in she's eyes, in mouth, in belly-hole, and now she's face is go, and now she's arms and titties go, and now is she but one white foot stand out, which puts I dirt a-bout, and push it soft and grey to toes of she' (p. 19).

Fragmented bodies reappear throughout the book, and in his final chapter Moore comments on the 'curious proliferation of both injured and completely missing legs' which he states 'emerged unbidden' alongside the severed heads that are 'a starker, more insistent motif' (p. 308). The initial image of the Pig Boy's mother's foot emerging from the grave and the Boy's injured leg are followed by a series of characters that recall this: the crippled nun Alfgiva dragging herself on her elbows ('November Saints'), the lame knight Simon de Senlis ('Limping to Jerusalem'), John Clare's bad foot ('The Sun Looks Pale upon the Wall'), the burned-through leg in 'I Travel in Suspenders' and, finally, Uncle Chick and Big John Weston ('Phipps' Fire Escape'). Similarly, Moore lists:

> The minted head of Diocletian or the more substantial one of Mary Tudor. Francis Tresham, Captain Pouch, and the mysterious head revered by the

Knights Templar. Ragener, and Edmund with a black and snarling Cerberus. Heads are the soft and staring eggs from which the fledgling skull hatches. (*ibid.*)

To this list can be added the wartime injuries to head and leg received by Alfie Rouse ('I Travel in Suspenders', p. 272) and the Corby murder victim whose missing head was discovered underneath a hedge, retrieved by a black dog some weeks later ('Phipps' Fire Escape', p. 315). Again, this synecdoche is linked with nature, and life. Although the majority of these mutilations reference death, Moore's egg metaphor reminds us of its antonym (life); and the stories can also be said to bring his characters to life.

In a similar vein, the Torso Garden simile ('like giant, severed heads') also aligns the personification of land with something sexual, as the features of these 'faces' are composed of sex organs. This imagery also features in other chapters, as in 'Angel Language', whose narrator (Judge Augustus Nicholls) uses phrases more suited to the natural world to describe his masturbation, for example, 'I would no longer suffer the relentless elbow-cramping visitations of these succubi, that mapped the foam-splashed shorelines of my passion; penned their snail cartographies upon my sheets and clouded my good sense with humid, feverish distractions' (pp. 202–3). This sentence combines corporeal awareness ('elbow-cramping') with marine and natural imagery – and also links the same to stories and writing, through its description of 'penned [...] snail cartographies'. In this way, motifs of life and stories and landscape and sex are linked throughout the book. The judge in fact comments explicitly on this when he reflects on a dream he had in which John Dee 'was moved to reassure me that all would be well if he and I were but to have our wives in common, though he may have said not wives but lives' (p. 220).

Suffering and sacrifice also appear as key themes, as implied by Walsh's discussion above. Olun, the shaman of 'The Cremation Fields', wears a map of his village tattooed on his skin, and his body becomes indelibly linked to the suffering of the village, as he complains, 'This willage is too much a part of me. Its sicknesses are mine. If there are beetles in the grain down at the southfields, then it gnaws my vitals here' (p. 77). This suffering extends to the village's inhabitants as well: 'when Jebba Broken-Tooth takes mad and kills his woman and their child, then is there seeping from my ear' (p. 77). Although the narrator initially disbelieves Olun, by the end of the tale she has changed her mind and it seems consistent with the themes of *Voice* to take Olun's story as truth. Both people and land make up the 'willage', and the lives of both become part of the shaman's body: a Gothic intersection that (as David Punter argues) paradoxically defines the body as vulnerable and fragile, yet also an excessive and overdetermined signifier.[9] Later, Caius Sextus, the Roman general suffering from toothache, muses that 'perhaps we are so much a part of Rome that we grow sick as she does; some peculiar bond, some sympathy of flesh and land' (p. 141). Textual and visual metaphor and overt statements are used throughout *Voice* to link body to land, and these images are frequently sexualised and fragmented. They also contribute to the magical realist impulse that underlies *Voice* by allowing the reappearance of ghostly figures and stories to exist at the level of the uncanny: a questioning of fact and fiction that again seems peculiarly Gothic.

Along similar lines, the structure of the book can also be likened to a body, as layer upon layer builds up its skin and substance. Rebecca Scott comments:

> If *Voice of the Fire* has a protagonist, it must be Northampton itself, because this is the story of the formation of the mythology of that place. It is a geological study of the strata of the collective unconscious of the area. Each of its twelve chapters is the first-person story of an individual who crystallized into the forming stones in the hill of tales, whose bodies fed its grass and trees. Their histories wind through that of the land, bringing us closer and closer to the present day.[10]

Gothic themes such as the abject are relevant here. Julia Kristeva defines the abject as that which exists outside the symbolic order, and which directly embodies the duality of self-other, confronting us with the knowledge that our living bodies are also objects of otherness:

> A wound with blood and pus, or the sickly, acrid smell of sweat, of decay, does not *signify* death. In the presence of signified death – a flat encephalograph, for instance – I would understand, react, or accept. No, as in true theater, without makeup or masks, refuse and corpses *show me* what I permanently thrust aside in order to live. These body fluids, this defilement, this shit are what life withstands, hardly and with difficulty, on the part of death. There, I am at the border of my condition as a living being.[11]

The dead narrators of *Voice* confront us with this knowledge as they represent both self and other: the immediacy of their first-person narratives being combined with the distance of fiction and time. As noted, there is a Gothic tendency in these stories that combines tropes of spirituality and gross physicality. For example, the nun Alfgiva receives spiritual and religious visions, but they are described in the most physically horrifying terms: 'In Hel's Town was my brother Edmund flayed first from his neck to his loins [. . .] lying spread as if garbed in a bloodshirt that Ingwar's men folded back, shewing the red, stinking harp there beneath' (p. 151). Alfgiva also speaks of a woman who 'is possessed of a spirit, and vomits up animal beings like little white frogs' (p. 150). Other narrators offer a similar juxtaposition of the ethereal and corporeal, such as the 'stale putrefaction' (p. 192) of Francis Tresham's disembodied (but nonetheless sentient) head, decorated with bird shit (p. 193). Blood, vomit, rotting flesh and excrement are all argued by Kristeva to provoke the abject which (because it exists prior to the self-other divide) is summoned by any substance that crosses corporeal boundaries.

Abjection (as the pairing of ethereality and gross corporeality) can therefore also perhaps be seen as another cryptomimetic trope: as Margaret Shildrick notes, 'It is through the dynamic of abjection that the subject must distinguish both between inside and outside the body, and between one body and another.'[12] In this context, the binary pairs found in *Voice* seem significant, and a further duality of purification and pain is noted by Santala in her discussion of fire:

> By telling twelve tales centered around the element of fire, Moore has embraced the myriad potential meanings it evokes in the reader's imagination. After all, it's just the matter of a jump-cut from the fire beneath a cauldron to the burning pyre of a witch hunt, or from the purifying white light of Pentecost to the tormenting flames of hell. Indeed, this contrary pairing of the extreme states of purification and torment seems to be something that Moore is aiming at in *Voice of the Fire*: to relay in prose the white heat of life.[13]

Voice articulates an oxymoronic 'abhuman identity'[14] that exists at this point of trauma and exhilaration, like the feelings of recoil and jouissance Kristeva finds in abjection. As Francis Tresham concludes, 'the burning and the song are one' (p. 201). By layering stories and using the tropes and symbols of abjection and bodily and sexual metaphor, Moore brings forth an image of the land as haunted body, and the voice of the fire as the medium (in both a spiritual and textual sense) through which its tales are told.

Haunted chronology

Although the narration begins at 4000 BC and ends in AD 1995, it can be argued that, rather than a linear history, Moore creates a circular, cyclical narrative. Neil Gaiman's introduction quotes Moore's statement that 'one measures a circle starting anywhere' (itself a quotation from Charles Fort, used in *From Hell*) and describes *Voice* as 'a carousel ride, not a race' (p. 11), encouraging readers to 'start where you like: the beginning and the end are both good places, but a circle begins anywhere, and so does a bonfire' (p. 13). In support of this idea, there are clear links between the novel's start and end points, which are both first-person, present-tense narratives based around strikingly similar symbols and themes. Moore's narrative concludes with these words:

> These are the times we dread and hunger for. The mutter of our furnace past grows louder at our backs, with cadence more distinct. Almost intelligible now, its syllables reveal themselves. Our world ignites. The song wells up, from a consuming light. (p. 316)

This seems similar to those images that bookend the Pig Boy's narrative, which opens, 'A-hind of hill, ways off to sun-set-down, is sky come like as fire, and walk I up in way of this, all hard of breath, where is grass colding on I's feet and wetting they' (p. 15). The Pig Boy's chapter concludes with his ritualistic murder, of which the Pig Boy narrates 'say of fire is come through I, and rise, and rise, with grits of bright, in neath of old black sky' (p. 60). The metaphorical furnace that is behind Moore seems similar to the sunset in front of the Pig Boy, and the 'say of fire' that overtakes the Boy at his death can only be the consuming song Moore wants us to hear. All these stories come from the voice of the fire: 'We stand and speak our piece in our own moment, and about us fires of time and change fan out unchecked. Our words ignite upon our lips, no sooner spoken than made ash' (p. 314).

Another theme that these two chapters share is the exploration of truth and lies: the Pig Boy is taught how to lie in his account ('one may say of thing while thing is not'; p. 33), whereas Moore's focus is on not lying: 'this final chapter is the thing. Committed to a present-day first-person narrative, there seems no other option save a personal appearance, which in turn demands a strictly documentary approach: it wouldn't do to simply make things up. This is fiction, not a lie' (p. 293). Despite the extremely limited vocabulary of the first chapter (which has 'only one tense, one form of any pronoun, one word for both *food* and *thought*, and a most peculiar grammar'),[15] such idiosyncrasies call our attention to the similarities between the two accounts. Moore elects to not use the words *I*, *me* or *mine* in his final chapter, which, Di Liddo argues, erases his own presence and universalises his narrative persona, 'in order to help the reader start his/her own psychogeographical experience'.[16] However, this lack-of-self also means that his chapter can be read as an antonym of the first, which uses the word *I* to refer to all aspects of the self. This emphasis links the two chapters by contrast, but similarities can be also seen: for example when, speaking of black dogs and shagfoals, Moore writes, 'some time, thing change and come like other thing' (p. 312), this voice clearly evoking the Pig Boy's.

Extending this analysis, it can even be proposed that *Voice*'s narrative constantly expands and contracts as its narrators only occasionally let in other characters or refer to previous events in the past or imperfect tense. The Pig Boy is the only one to speak in his chapter, which is entirely in the present tense – the speech of the girl is only ever reported to us. Subsequently, 'The Cremation Fields' expands the narration by not only containing direct speech from other characters, but also including flashbacks and allowing the narrating voice to comment on other featured voices. This tendency continues throughout the book, whose first-person, present-tense narratives let in flashes of past conversations and other voices. In 'I Travel In Suspenders', narrator Alfie Rouse even incorporates his audience; addressing us directly – 'Do you ever get that?'(p. 281) – and indicating where he expects us to react – 'There now, you see? Another laugh' (p. 268).

The corporeal symbols I have noted and the amount of deaths that organise the text lead me to suggest that this pattern of expansion and then contraction might represent birth. As such, I propose that the structure of *Voice* can be best understood using the symbol of the Ouroboros, the snake consuming itself. This shape appears many times in the text, which is permeated by circles, from the fancybeads that identify the narrator of 'The Cremation Fields' to the round temple in which Sir Simon must 'circle, circle round, forever round beneath an empty sky' (p. 184). Further, the stories as a whole are contained within a geographical circle of a ten-mile radius, or (in more literal and visual terms) the horizon surrounding Northampton. Johnston also identifies this circular theme, stating that the text is a warning, imploring us 'to dream again lest we be trapped forever in ever-decreasing circles of superficiality'.[17]

The Ouroboros represents cyclicality, especially in the sense of something constantly re-creating itself, and primordial unity. The 12 chapters (perhaps representing a year, a complete cycle of the earth around the sun – although all are set in November) also support this interpretation. The Ouroboros also symbolises self-reflexivity, and this is also apparent in the text's content, for example as Moore describes himself sitting at his computer, narrating 'The author types the words "the author types the words"' (p. 290). Jung's interpretation of the Ouroboros as one of the archetypes of the human psyche (signifying our assimilation of the other and rebirth) also seems relevant here. Peter Barreda argues:

> In the purity of the continuous cycle depicted by Ouroboros we can see the process of our essential nature – we form, we disintegrate, we re-assemble as something else. Whether or not our personality survives, our innate sense of self, there is no doubt that the basic elements of [the] matter that comprises us has witnessed the origin of the Universe and will continue to live on for near eternity in an amazing variety of forms. Rebirth is inevitable, and so we are truly eternal.
> Here the symbol of Ouroboros represents the continuity of life as a persistent process in the universe.[18]

This can be seen in the symbolic embodiment of land that has been noted in *Voice*: which merges people and their stories, just as their material bodies will ultimately decompose into the land.

Echoes of events and characters

The cyclical (rather than linear) nature of the chapters is enhanced by their content, which frequently prefigures or revisits past and future characters. The methods used to do this are extremely evocative of the

Gothic and include dreams, hallucinations and visions. Both Caius Sextus and Sir Simon de Senlis dream of the other narrators and other characters encounter them at times of great stress or unbearable pain, such as when the aged nun Alfgiva is being flogged and her identities merge with past and future narrators: 'I lie on a smouldering pyre with my throat cut, and cook, in a great skull of iron or bound to a post, and I rot as the head of a traitor hung high on the gates of this town. I am child. I am murderer, poet and saint' (p. 162). The contexts of these visions place them in the Gothic realm of the hallucinatory.

However, they are also simultaneously evidenced as true, as they contain representations that cohere with the stories we have already read, or fill in gaps in the tales. The rotting head of Francis Tresham dreams of talking with the torso of the treacherous narrator of 'The Cremation Fields', and we believe in this vision (rather than dismissing it as hallucination), not least since our knowledge of her trickery means we have assumed that the Torso Garden was probably her fate. Tresham states, 'we hatch a plan between us to combine our best resources, with my head to be somehow set up on her ragged neck. She tells me, grumbling through her loins, that she has heard of legs and feet that may elect to join with our conspiracy' (p. 191). The same metaphor is used in both chapters ('sex-mouthed'/'grumbling through her loins') and the book's continued focus on feet and legs create paradigmatic links between these narratives, which pull from the same shared imagery. Again, this revisited imagery acts as a kind of evidence of authenticity.

However, there are also meetings claimed to take place in reality: John Clare meets gypsies in the wood who speak of a banished pigboy and his buried mother and also encounters the narrator of 'The Cremation Fields'. Here, truth and fiction are impossible to separate as reality and dreams are now being used interchangeably. The dubious reliability of our narrator (who has just left an asylum) also contributes to this and can be considered an additional trope, of both magical realism and the Gothic. Unreliable narrators feature in many Gothic tales (such as Charlotte Perkins Gilman's 'The Yellow Wallpaper', Henry James's *The Turn of the Screw* and August Derleth's 'The Lonesome Place') and Jack Morgan notes that the obscuration of truth is frequently a condition of the terror that the Gothic inspires,[19] quoting Edmund Burke: 'when we know the full extent of any danger ... a great deal of the apprehension vanishes.'[20] Magical realists such as Angela Carter

(*Wise Children*) also use such narrators, juxtapositioning a reminder that memory is fallible against exquisite detail that belies this.[21] The effect, when used at the most intimate and internal points in the narrative, is to jerk us back into the awareness that this is fiction and we are external to the narrative – arguably another cryptomimetic trope, and one that allows Moore to not only achieve a sense of the uncanny, but also to remind us that his prose is part of our 'real' world.

For in *Voice* the crossing-over between dreams and reality and the prefiguration and revisitation of characters and events does not simply demonstrate these as false or supernatural. Rather, it has the effect of flattening time and evidencing the coexistence of all these lives and stories; a notion Moore has explored extensively in his other work.[22] Characters move at will between different periods as they join the voice of the fire. The witches Elinor and Mary burn at the stake, saying, 'I see my fellows in the flame, the unborn and the dead. I see the gash-necked little boy. I see the ragged man that sits within a skull of blazing iron. I almost know them, almost have a sense of what they mean, like letters in a barbarous alphabet' (p. 238). Entombed in fiction, their narrative slips between the years of their lives: 'Soon, only the idea of us remains. Ten years ago in the laburnum field we look into each other's eyes and hold our breath. A beetle ticks, down in the grass. We're waiting' (p. 249). These time slips within chapters and the reference to literature ('letters in a barbarous alphabet') stress the power of lives-as-stories.

Authenticity and the Gothic

As mentioned, authenticity (or lack thereof) is a key trait of the Gothic, which frequently problematises notions of a simple true/false dichotomy, for example by presenting supernatural tales as historical truth, and introducing extratextual evidence (such as testimonies, letters, appendices and innumerable footnotes) to support the most outrageous claims. Paradoxically, it is only through this process that the question of veracity is brought to our attention, and the fact that the striven-for authenticity is generally disbelieved is a further fiction of the Gothic.

These processes pervade traditional and contemporary Gothic texts, from Horace Walpole's *The Castle of Otranto* to Mark Z. Danielewski's *House of Leaves*, and Richard Davenport-Hines notes the legacy of the former as 'a prototype for many later Gothic stories which were presented as taken from medieval manuscripts and were prefixed with proofs of antiquity and authenticity'.[23] This performative structuring and layering of stories again recalls Castricano's cryptomimetic structure: invoking Derrida's notion of the crypt as 'a place comprehended within another but rigorously separate from it [...] sealed, and thus internal to itself'.[24]

Voice is no exception; as Gaiman comments, 'nothing in this book is true, not the way you're thinking, even if it happened [...]. Or to put it another way, *Voice of the Fire* is truth, of a kind, even if its truths are historical and fictional and magical' (p. 13). These paradoxical claims support a Gothic reading of the text and alert us to the fact that history, as a narrative, can also be claimed to be Gothic in this sense. Moore comments that 'history, unendingly revised and reinterpreted, is seen upon examination as merely a different class of fiction' (p. 306), a point noted by Antony Johnston: '*Voice of the Fire* is a tale of lost myths, of history's subjective nature. As history must always be written by survivors, is any man's history more "real" than another's? Who is to say?'[25]

The subjectivity that underlies philosophical notions of truth is addressed by Moore in the content of the book, whose characters reflect on this at various points. One example of this comes from 'The Drownings', whose narrator tells us:

> they say [the Hob-fields] is haunted by a murdered boy. Once I told Salka that I'd seen him, standing on the mound there with his throat all cut, his hair all burned. She knew I'd made it up, and yet she made as if she thought it true, and clung to me and let me feel her gilly there inside her breeks. (p. 130)

Again, fiction is sexualised and truth and falsity are interrogated, as our reading of 'Hob's Hog' evidences that the murdered boy did indeed have his throat cut and his hair burned. 'Story' in this case, does not necessarily equal 'lie' – as Alfie Rouse concludes, 'I've told so many stories I can't tell myself which ones are true and which ones I've invented. Do you ever get that? No?' (p. 281). Here, Moore explores the ways in which language constructs reality (informing his own self-description as a magician) by exploring its darker side. Taught to lie, the Pig Boy becomes victim and sacrifice; Caius Sextus loses everything through believing the Roman Empire's lie of wealth; and Rouse is a liar, murderer and philanderer who was ultimately hanged.

Moore also explores the linguistic construction of reality by tracing the continual adaptation and reinterpretation of events. The murder of the Pig Boy is first an event, but 1,500 years later has become a village ceremony where an effigy of a boy with a face flayed from a pig is burnt (also foreshadowing Guy Fawkes Night). The Pig Boy then becomes a ghost story before finally reappearing as the local saying, 'well you thought wrong like Hob's Hog' (p. 263). The translation of life into custom into story into proverb demonstrates the move from life to language through oral storytelling traditions.

This translation helps to demonstrate how the events and characters of *Voice* are shown to be beyond the human perception of time. In one sense these narratives are eternal and unchanging: they make up the voice of the fire that lies behind everything. However, constant adaptation and reiteration also sustain these stories, as traced above. In this way the prose medium becomes essential to *Voice*. As Scott observes, 'this is a text novel, not a graphic novel, and the words are the things. Very fine words they are, too: "Trust in the fictive process, in the occult interweaving of text and event must be unwavering and absolute. This is the magic place, the mad place at the spark gap between word and world."'[26] As Moore is, of course, best known for his work on comics, this may provide a reason for his use of prose. *Voice* is about the translation from world to word: 'The text, predictably, melts into the event' (p. 306). The use of José Villarrubia's illustrations in the Top Shelf edition of the book succeeds admirably where the comics medium might well have failed. Santala argues that Villarrubia's illustrations 'do not attempt to subvert the reader's imagination by somehow presenting a more "authoritative" visualization of Moore's suggestive prose',[27] which it seems probable that a comics narrative would have done. Narratologists have long debated the question of view, of vision, noting the 'tension between seeing and writing [. . .] in contemporary narratology'[28] where seeing overrules the authority of verbal narrative.[29]

Mark Currie notes further that writing is seen as a 'fall from presence'[30] and its existence invokes questions of origin – referring to the moment of speech when the signifier was uttered, uniting sign, signifier and even the signified (by invocation). The very oral nature of Moore's prose (first-person, present-tense) goes some way to countering this. His voices are distinct and realised; utterly separate in tone from each other, from the wry and disdainful narrator of 'The Cremation Fields' to the verbose and jocular salesman of 'I Travel in Suspenders'. The authentic feel of these voices is particularly apparent in 'The Sun Looks Pale upon the Wall', the narrative of John Clare, which exploits the absence of punctuation that characterised Clare's poetry. Clare also used the Northamptonshire dialect in much of his work, and it therefore seems significant that it is his chapter which includes the saying 'you thought wrong like Hob's Hog'.[31]

Spelling, writing and conjuring: a conclusion

In selecting this critical approach to *Voice*, and owing to limitations of space, this chapter has necessarily had to overlook many of the text's other significant features. The appearances of black dogs, supernatural shagfoals and a mysterious horned figure certainly seem relevant to the Gothic tradition in their evocation of the magical and pagan. Perhaps this demonic figure is Herne, the horned English forest god, or another version of the Gaulish deity Cernunnos, or the Graeco-Roman god Pan.[32] Despite their lack of discussion in this piece, the presence of these motifs further support a view of *Voice* as a spiritual and mystical text, a feature which fits well with Moore's much publicised view of the writer as magician.

Moore refers to this book in these terms, reflecting on 'this attempted wedding of the language and the life; this ju-ju shit' (p. 306) in his final chapter.[33] As this chapter has tried to demonstrate, *Voice* is an exceptional kind of psychogeographic text wherein both words and stories are embodiments of its landscape. Moore refers to himself as a shaman, like Olun, whose tattoos

> become a part of him so that he might in turn become the town, a magic of association with the object bound up in the lines that represent it: lines of dye or lines of text, it makes no difference. The impulse is identical, to bind the site in word or symbol. Dog and fire and world's end, men and women lamed or headless, monument and mound. This is our lexicon, a lurid alphabet to frame the incantation; conjure the world lost and populace invisible. Reset the fractured skeleton of legend, desperate necromancy raising up the rotted buildings to parade and speak, filled with the voices of the resurrected dead. (p. 313)

This paragraph most obviously recalls the Gothic aspect of conjuring and evidences Moore's belief in the magic of storytelling. He has spoken many times of writing as a magic power, and the definition of magic as 'art', as well as the dual meanings of words such as 'spelling' and 'curse', which link literature and linguistics to magic.[34] It therefore may not be too much to propose that, in its rejection of linearity and the trans-temporal links it draws between eras, *Voice* is a revolution in storytelling, an argument that can perhaps be best illustrated using Saussurean linguistics.

Ferdinand de Saussure transformed linguistics by proposing the synchronic study of language (that is, considering it as a complete system at a given moment) alongside its diachronic study (examining the changes which take place over time). A chess metaphor is often used to illustrate this, as Saussure argues that, in chess, a person joining a game's audience mid-way through requires no more information than the present layout of pieces on the board and who takes the next turn. They do not benefit from knowing how the pieces came to be arranged in this way. For this reader, Moore's text incorporates both a synchronic and diachronic narrative, as its voice(s) come from a dual position from both inside and outside the human narrative cycle. It illustrates that, while knowing how the chess pieces got to their present position may not help us win the game, this knowledge is nonetheless essential to understand the game's narrative and the significance – and sacrifices – behind some positions. In so doing it offers a new model for fiction, one that is not simply linear or plot-driven, but instead a deeper combination of poetics and prosody.

As Johnston notes, *Voice* 'is a tale of witchcraft and magic; from the first "Hob-Men," through Elizabethan court magicians, and finally ending with only myth'.[35] Rebecca Scott takes this further, stating 'this book is a work of magic' whose writing 'both presaged and paralleled a change in Moore's consciousness during the five years in which he worked on it' studying magic and mysteries.[36] While its content certainly includes the elements noted by Johnston, and it is possible the research Moore conducted inspired his own belief system, *Voice* seems magical on another level. Its town is made up of a 'web of joke, remembrance and story' which is the 'vital infrastructure on which the solid and material plane is standing. A town of pure idea, erected only in the mind's eye of the population, yet this is our only true foundation' (p.

313). Moore himself describes the book as 'a bridge, a crossing point, a worn spot in the curtain between our world and the underworld, between the mortar and the myth' (p. 302) and (if 'bridge' is taken literally) the analogy of place to page is again prominent here. By merging landscape and language, *Voice* literally conjures its people, stories and places into eternal life. To read it as a 'crossing point' between words and worlds creates a truly Gothic experience, fraught with the dark magic of creation and transgression.

Notes

1. Annalisa Di Liddo, *Alan Moore: Comics as Performance, Fiction as Scalpel* (Jackson: University Press of Mississippi, 2009), p. 127.
2. *Ibid.*, p. 126.
3. For further discussion, see Julia Round, 'London's Calling: Alternate Worlds and the City as Superhero in Contemporary British-American Comics', *International Journal of Comic Art* (ed. J. Lent), 10:1 (Spring 2008), 24–31.
4. Neil Walsh, 'Voice of the Fire', *SF Site* (2004): www.sfsite.com/12b/vf190.htm, n.p.
5. Steven Bruhm, *Gothic Bodies* (Philadelphia: University of Pennsylvania Press, 1994), p. 5.
6. Jodey Castricano, *Cryptomimesis* (London: McGill-Queen's University Press, 2001), p. 6.
7. Bruhm, *Gothic Bodies*, p.8.
8. Alan Moore, *Voice of the Fire* (Atlanta, GA: Top Shelf, 2009), p. 27; hereafter cited in the main body of the text.
9. David Punter, *Gothic Pathologies: The Text, the Body and the Law* (Basingstoke: Macmillan, 1998).
10. Rebecca Scott, 'Alan Moore, *Voice of the Fire* (Top Shelf, 2003)', *Green Man Review* (2003), n.p.: www.greenmanreview.com/book/book_moore_voiceofthefire.html.
11. Julia Kristeva, *Powers of Horror: An Essay on Abjection*, trans. L. S. Roudiez (Chichester and New York: Columbia University Press, 1982 [1980]), p. 3.
12. Margrit Shildrick, *Embodying the Monster* (London: Sage, 2002), p. 81.
13. Ismo Santala, 'Voice of the Fire', *The Modern Word* (2004), n.p.: www.themodernword.com/reviews/moore_fire.html.
14. Kelly Hurley, *The Gothic Body: Sexuality, Materialism, and Denigration at the Fin de Siècle* (Cambridge: Cambridge University Press, 1996), pp. 30–1.
15. Scott, 'Alan Moore', n.p.

16 Di Liddo, *Alan Moore*, p. 130.
17 Antony Johnston, 'Alan Moore: Voice of The Fire', *Spike Magazine* (2008), n.p.: www.spikemagazine.com/0399voiceofthefire.php.
18 Peter Patrick Barreda, 'Ouroboros: The Serpent in the Spirit', *The Mandala Zone* (2004), n.p.: www.mandalazone.com/essay-0407.html.
19 'Apotropaion and the Hideous Obscure', in Jack Morgan, *Biology of Horror: Gothic Literature and Film* (Carbondale: Southern Illinois University Press, 2002), pp. 200–23.
20 Edmund Burke, *A Philosophical Enquiry into the Origin of Our Ideas of the Sublime and Beautiful: With an Introductory Discourse Concerning Taste, and Several Other Additions*, new edn (London: J. Dodsley, 1787), p. 99.
21 Susan L. Deefholts, 'Hazarding Chance: Reading Angela Carter's *Wise Children*', *Margin* (2003), n.p.: www.angelfire.com/wa2/margin/nonficSLD3.html.
22 For further discussion of nonlinear time in Moore's oeuvre, see Julia Round, 'Gothic and the Graphic Novel', in *A New Companion to the Gothic*, ed. David Punter (London: Blackwell, 2012), pp. 335–49.
23 Richard Davenport-Hines, *Gothic: Four Hundred Years of Excess, Horror, Evil and Ruin* (New York: North Point Press, 1998), p. 137.
24 Jacques Derrida, '*Fors:* The Anglish Words of Nicolas Abraham and Maria Torok', in N. Abraham and M. Torok, *The Wolf Man's Magic Word: A Cryptonymy* (Minneapolis: University of Minnesota Press, 1986), pp. xi–xlviii (p. xiv).
25 Johnston, 'Alan Moore', n.p.
26 Scott, 'Alan Moore', n.p.
27 Santala, 'Voice of the Fire', n.p.
28 Mark Currie, *Postmodern Narrative Theory* (Basingstoke: Macmillan, 1998), p. 127.
29 For further discussion, see Julia Round, '"Be vewy vewy quiet: we're hunting Wippers." A Barthesian Analysis of the Construction of Fact and Fiction in Alan Moore and Eddie Campbell's *From Hell*', in D. Hassler-Forest and J. Goggin (eds), *The Rise and Reason of Comics and Graphic Literature: Critical Essays on the Form* (Jefferson, CA: McFarland, 2010), pp. 188–201.
30 Currie, *Postmodern Narrative Theory*, p. 82.
31 Clare's story seems especially suited to *Voice* as his early work is characterised by a focus on nature and the cycle of the rural year (such as *Winter Evening* or *Haymaking*), and a similar focus on nature can also be found in many of Edward Thomas's writings (including 'Lob').
32 See Richard Lowe Thompson, *The History of the Devil, the Horned God of the West* (London: Kegan Paul, Trench, Trubner & Co., 1929) and Michele Morgan, *Simple Wicca* (Newburyport, MA: Conari, 2000).

33 'Ju-ju shit' may also reference abjection by invoking the psychological/physiological.
34 See, e.g., *The Mindscape of Alan Moore*, dir. DeZ Vylenz (London: Shadowsnake Productions, 2003) and 'Magic is Afoot: A Conversation with Alan Moore about the Arts and the Occult', interview by Jay Babcock, *Arthur*, 4 (May 2003), n.p.: www.arthurmag.com/2007/05/10/1815/; reprinted in *Yuggoth Cultures*, ed. William Christensen (Urbana, IL: Avatar, 2007), pp. 117–38.
35 Johnston, 'Alan Moore', n.p.
36 Scott, 'Alan Moore', n.p.

14

A darker magic: heterocosms and bricolage in Moore's recent reworkings of Lovecraft

Matthew J.A. Green

> You men know that those Whateleys were wizards – well, this thing is a thing of wizardry, and must be put down by the same means. I've seen Wilbur Whateley's diary and read some of the strange old books he used to read; and I think I know the right kind of spell to recite to make the thing fade away. Of course, one can't be sure, but we can always take a chance.
> H.P. Lovecraft, 'The Dunwich Horror'[1]

> Might not the entire of Magic be described as traffic between That Which Is and That Which Is Not; between fact and fiction? If we are to speak of Magic as 'The Art', should we not also speak of Art as Magic?
> Alan Moore, 'Beyond Our Ken'[2]

Since the early 1990s, Alan Moore's creative activities have been closely bound up with his development as a magician, and the Gothic strands of his inheritance provide perhaps the most obvious threshold linking these pursuits. Alongside the wide range of works explored elsewhere in this collection, since the early 1990s Moore has returned specifically to the works of H.P. Lovecraft in a series of short stories, prose poems and, most recently, a comics mini-series. These smaller-scale projects are unique across Moore's corpus in positioning themselves explicitly in relation to a sole author, with other intertextual elements being woven within a Lovecraftian frame. Lovecraft – who can himself best be viewed as a bricoleur combining elements from preceding and contemporaneous authors – offers Moore an opportunity to explore the possibilities of intertextuality developed most famously in his work with Kevin

O'Neill on the ongoing *League of Extraordinary Gentlemen* series, which itself contains an extended homage to Lovecraft in the form of a stand-alone short story.[3]

The violence inherent in bricolage is mirrored,[4] in Lovecraft's work, by representations of forces capable not only of violating bodies, but of bursting through the very fabric of time and space; the only hope resides in a careful negotiation of textual bodies – either the careful curtailing of knowledge or, as in the case of 'The Dunwich Horror', the strategic reiteration and recombination of texts in a form of scholarship akin to wizardry. Thus, Lovecraft provides a set of tools and materials – images, terms, concepts and textual forms – with which Moore can explore the darker aspects of magic, laying bare the latent violence in the very imaginative and sexual freedoms that he elsewhere imbues with a messianic potential.

Magic and fiction are for Moore both concerned with the creation and manipulation of worlds, a process which is itself a constituent feature of bricolage, which, 'in the best of cases', provokes the recognition that the most radical and inventive 'are surprised and circumvented by a history, a language, etc., a *world* [. . .] from which they must borrow their tools, if only to destroy the former machine'.[5] *The League* exemplifies Moore's practice of adapting, reworking and combining the heterocosms of other writers and artists. Defined by Linda Hutcheon as 'literally an "other world" or cosmos', a heterocosm includes all 'the stuff of a story – settings, characters, events, and situations'.[6] Lovecraft's work, which has been reformatted across a variety of media, has a long history of this sort of adaptation; however, Moore's reworkings of Lovecraft differ from those of his predecessors not only because they tend to be more self-reflexive, incorporating a metanarrative dimension that alerts the reader to their status as fictions, but also because they allow Moore to work through the darker implications of his understanding of art as magic. If art can allow human beings to imagine alternate worlds and if apocalypse can be understood as the process of bringing such worlds into being on a wider scale, then Lovecraft provides the materials for a case study of what might happen when such imaginative endeavours give themselves over to cruelty and chaos.

The fecundity that Moore finds in Lovecraft appears due in part to the latter's often ambiguous and ambivalent position within both the Gothic tradition and the contemporary magic scene. Though Lovecraft's writing has been adapted and appropriated more than perhaps any other Gothic writer from the twentieth century,[7] his position within Gothic scholarship is complicated by a pervasive sense that his written style lacks quality and substance (a perception perhaps related to the fact that his primary literary output was in the form of short stories for pulp magazines), by the racist and elitist ideology often encoded by his works[8] and by his development of a pseudo-mythology – the Cthulhu mythos – that places considerable demands upon first-time readers. Nevertheless, as David Punter argues, Lovecraft's work shares a structure common to the original Gothic literature, 'in that it hinges on an unassimilable fear of the past, and in that primal crime is symbolised in terms of unholy aspiration after forbidden knowledge'.[9] The danger – and the promise – of knowledge in Lovecraft is that it 'will lead to revelations that will forever change humanity's view of the universe and its place in it'.[10] For Lovecraft himself, this involved developing a mythos that could communicate a doctrine of 'cosmic indifferentism' grounded in mechanistic materialism.[11] Ironically, however, many of Lovecraft's followers 'wrote would-be "Lovecraftian" tales on the premise that in Lovecraft's fiction the religion of the Old Ones was meant to be true',[12] a practice which reaches its apotheosis in the works of Kenneth Grant and contemporary Chaos magicians, who insist that Lovecraft's work is a source of genuine magical insight.[13]

Moore's understanding of his own work – from that of a writer to that of a magician – is clearly one of continuity rather than an abrupt break. In fact, his reminder that 'there is a reason why Hermes and Thoth, the Gods of Magic, should be simultaneously the Gods of Writing' suggests that the categorisation of magic and writing as different types of practice is misconceived.[14] Moore's overwhelming preoccupation as both a writer and a magician is in exploring alternative experiences of reality and in altering the consciousness of his audience – or at the very least, of providing his readers with the tools to make these alterations themselves. However, while Moore's increasing investment in magical theory and practice does imbue works like *Promethea* with a twin sense of purpose and optimism, his magical calling did not in itself signal a turning-away from the darkness and violence characteristic of his seminal work on *Miracleman*, *V for Vendetta* and *Watchmen*.

Moore's first year as a magician saw the first of several Lovecraftian publications with Creation Books, resulting from editor David M. Mitchell's invitation to contribute to the short-story collection, *The Starry Wisdom*, a tribute to Lovecraft first published in 1994. Moore's contribution to this volume, 'The Courtyard', together with two additional stories, 'Recognition' and 'Zaiman's Hill' (published the following year in *Dust: A Creation Books Reader*), are the remains of a much larger project, *Yuggoth Cultures*, based around Lovecraft's sonnet cycle, *Fungi from Yuggoth*. Each story takes its title from one of the sonnets in the cycle and draws inspiration from the style and content of Lovecraft's corpus (including the prose as well as the poetry) to provide a pastiche that does not simply imitate but actively interprets and transposes its source material. In the context of the mid-1990s, these pieces share with *From Hell* and *Voice* a meditation on the interrelationship of the occult and the repressive violence of the law ('The Courtyard'), a concern over the psychic significance of landscape and geography ('Zaiman's Hill') and an anxiety over the ambivalent associations amongst magic, sexual violence and insanity ('Recognition'). These stories have been republished in various formats since 2003.[15] In 2006, Creation Oneiros also released a redesigned and expanded version of *The Haunter of the Dark and Other Grotesque Visions*, containing adaptations and artwork by John Coulthart, himself a collaborator in the Moon and Serpent Grand Egyptian Theatre of Marvels, a magical arts group coeval with Moore's earliest magical experiences. This expanded edition contains prose evocations to accompany Coulthart's 'The Great Old Ones', presenting a reinterpretation of the sefiroth in the context of Lovecraft's mythos. These prose poems bring together Moore's study of magic and his longstanding interest in Gothic horror, complementing the other Lovecraft pieces by exploring the chaos and violence associated with both creativity and desire. December 2009 saw Avatar's release of the 'Hornbook' preview of *Neonomicon*, a four-part comics sequel to 'The Courtyard', written by Moore with art by Jacen Burrows and published in 2010–11.

In addition to offering one of his few extant links to the comics medium, however, Moore's reinterpretations of Lovecraft also provide an important – one might even say dangerous – supplement to the presentations and representations concerning magic in his interviews, essays, performance pieces and the multi-volume *Promethea* series. They provide an opportunity to consider the intersection of his longstanding work in the Gothic tradition with his more recent explorations of magic and creativity. Specifically, they yield insight into the darker aspects of the area of collective consciousness Moore has termed 'Ideaspace',[16] simultaneously delineating the conjunction of creativity and magical practice, on the one hand, with reading and revision on the other. Moore's insistence on the overlap between the literary and the magical – 'to cast a spell, as far as I understand it, is simply to spell'[17] – suggests that the recitation of a spell is itself a process closely connected to acts of adaptation and rereading. Indeed, a convincing case can be made for suggesting that Moore's magic is self-consciously comparable to that of Lovecraft's three heroes in 'The Dunwich Horror'. He confronts the materialist philosophy and the conservative ideology embedded in Lovecraft's texts more directly than those who seek to elevate the Cthulhu mythos to a cult status, while at the same time remaining faithful to Lovecraft's own description of the weird tale as 'a narrow though essential branch of human expression'.[18]

'The Great Old Ones': magic and the satanic sefiroth

Lovecraft links the Gothic – which he variously identifies with cosmic fear, horror and supernatural terror – to a 'psychological pattern or tradition as real and as deeply grounded in mental experience as any other', one which is 'coeval with the religious feeling' and which he proceeds to relate to supernatural folklore and magic.[19] Moore expands on this linkage, for whereas Lovecraft limits this sort of psychological sensitivity to a certain strand of the Gothic, he extends it to include all imaginative works, situating a magical impulse that is closely akin to that of the Gothic at the core of all creative endeavour: 'you have invocations and evocations if you're a magician; you also have those things if you're a poet. And they mean pretty much the same thing in both cases.'[20] A further aspect of the connection between psychology and tradition is suggested by the fact that many of Lovecraft's tales are clearly indebted to predecessors such as Arthur Machen and Edgar Allan Poe, a cultural inheritance that is further related to the mutual borrowings between writers that Lovecraft himself encouraged in the development of his mythos. Moore's insistence on the fundamental kinship between magic and art suggests not only considerable cross-fertilisation between artistic and occult cultures, but also that the artist and the magus may share a similarly iconoclastic comportment in their relation to tradition.

That this sort of interpretative conflict has a longstanding history in the occult is suggested in Harold Bloom's discussion of the Kabbalistic antecedents for his theory of misreading or 'misprision'. Bloom emphasises the Kabbalah's 'work of *interpretation*, of revisionary replacements of Scriptural meaning by techniques of *opening*', and he notes that '*Zohar*, most influential of Kabbalistic books, is the true forerunner of Post-Enlightenment strong poetry, not in its grotesque content or its formless forms, but in its *stance towards the precursor text*, its revisionary genius and mastery of the perverse necessities of misprision.'[21] Lovecraft's own pastiching of anthropological, religious and occult texts – as well as works of fantasy and supernatural fiction – demonstrates a similarly revisionary stance, but one which seeks to open a way to scientific rather than mystical enlightenment. Lovecraft seeks an imaginative expansion of perception, a process that shares characteristics with many strands of mysticism; but, whereas the mystic seeks to gain greater knowledge of, or unification with, the divine, as Robert Price notes, Lovecraft 'sought to simulate the removal of the natural *limits on human perception* so as to provide a full view of the horribly empty (naturalistic) cosmos'.[22]

Moore likewise speaks of creativity in terms of an expansion of consciousness for his readers, 'providing something to people [. . .] that might, in some way, alleviate their situation, give them a different point of view'.[23] He also demarcates the powers of magic and imagination in Kabbalistic terms, noting the association of the ninth sefirah on the Tree of Life, Yesod, with the 'well from which both the magician and the artist draw', and remarking that 'though situated "higher" than the earthly and material sphere of Malkuth [. . .] Yesod at the same time represents the underworld of our subconscious and oneiric faculties, the eerie and chthonic realm of Hecate'.[24] However, while Moore himself relies on the Tree of Life as both a map and a metaphor, he rereads and revises it, continuing the practice of expansion and explication of occultists like Aleister Crowley, who inherit their practice from earlier Kabbalists.[25] The most extensive engagement comes in *Promethea*, in which the Tree, reimagined variously in the form of a circuit board, hopscotch game and London Underground map, provides the narrative structure for issues 13 to 23. But, whereas *Promethea* offers a visual and verbal path through the dark and light aspects of the sefiroth that culminates in a union with divine light, Moore also generates an entirely horrific account in 'The Great Old Ones'.[26]

These 'Evocations' consist of a series of prose poems that provide a monstrous reworking of the Tree in which the ten sefiroth are accorded ten personal names from Lovecraft's mythos such that Kether is linked to Yuggoth, Chokmah to Hastur, and so on. In some respects, this work resembles the Kabbalistic tradition of the 'left emanation', in which 'the ten "holy" Sefiroth have their counterparts in ten "unholy" or "impure" ones',[27] though Moore also includes two further divine aspects, Daath – the eleventh sefirah usually not included in the Tree and here identified with Lovecraft's Azathoth – and Ain –the nothingness that precedes creation, here associated with Kadath. Lovecraft's mythos thus enables Moore to engage in a contemporary rereading of the sefiroth which links the Gnostical school of medieval Kabbalism to the contemporary magic scene à la Kenneth Grant (who is quoted at the outset of the evocations). These work to further Moore's exploration of language by unfolding its potential for corruption rather than concentrating on its messianic potential – this latter was the emphasis throughout much of *Promethea* and tends to be the focus in interviews discussing magic. If, as Moore contends, fictional worlds provide access to different modes of consciousness, then Gothic works are capable of giving a local habitation and name to the more horrific impulses and aspects of experience. Lovecraft thus offers Moore a nomenclature and style for articulating an ontology of chaos, while the tradition of the satanic sefiroth offers the symbolic template with which to organise these dark visions.

Thus Chesed is inflected with the personal characteristics of Yog-Sothoth: 'HERE is the Father, and the child shall cry His name atop that fateful, watchful hill' (IV). There is more than a nod here towards 'The Dunwich Horror', in which the barely-human spawn of Lavinia Whateley conjures his father, Yog-Sothoth, on top of Sentinel Hill. Notably, during the final climax, when the three scholars confront the transdimensional gatekeeper, Lovecraft represents the uncanny aspect of language whose iterative capacity allows it to be co-opted by the other, issuing from an elsewhere space that has become too close to home. The text obsesses over the distortion of '*indisputably English* syllables' into a mephitic gibberish capable of dissolving worlds with words: 'from what black wells of Acherontic fear or feeling, from what unplumbed gulfs of extra-cosmic consciousness or obscure, long-latent heredity, were those half-articulate thunder-croakings drawn?'[28] This anxiety is itself reiterated in Moore's evocation: 'He is that power, howling and paretic, that adverse paternity with which no truce is possible. In Him, meaning collapses and is pulverised. In Him, apocalypse is swaddled' (IV). This is a very different apocalypse than that promised in *Promethea*, but it is nevertheless tied directly to Moore's own understanding of chaos as an elemental component of the communicative arts. Elsewhere, he notes the semantic distinction between noise and signal, which he links to 'Thoth the language god and his pet ape, the gibbering Cynocephalus, the monkey with the typewriter'; however, there remains a paradox at the heart of this dichotomy: 'the noise is capable of holding much more information than the signal [. . .] a page of Joyce's *Ulysses* is almost wholly noise and therefore holds a massive quantity of coded data'.[29]

'Recognition': fictional patrimonies

The disturbance inflicted upon the hearer by noise from beyond walls and windows is the subject of Moore's story 'Recognition', which explores the particular perturbation caused by the guttural sounds of copulation and the shouting of neighbours. The story opens with a scene reminiscent of Lavinia and Yog-Sothoth in 'The Dunwich Horror' – a graphic account of a woman being raped by a devil; however, in the fifth paragraph it is revealed that these are the 'paretic visions' and 'feverish tableaus' created in the mind of a travelling salesmen (identified as Lovecraft's father, Winfield), violent visions induced by the sounds of sex from the room below in the mind of a man who believes his wife is being punished for his own sexual misconduct.[30] This is Moore retelling Lovecraft retelling Machen, but with a particular linguistic turn, as brute mechanical noise is converted into a magical incantation capable of invading consciousness with alien meaning: 'downstairs the chanted protest of the bedsprings is commenced once more and viral imagery is seething in the dark behind the salesman's eyelids, overlays of spirochetal consciousness; alien signals flickering along the raddled spine' (p. 10). Here the reader familiar with Lovecraft's biography might decode an allusion to the spirochetes that caused the syphilis that led to the historical Winfield's institutionalisation in 1893. However, while it is tempting to read 'Recognition' as an imaginative account of the incident that precipitated Winfield's admission to Butler Hospital, the apparently historical facts in 'Recognition' are themselves fictions. Winfield was indeed forcibly restrained after an incident in a hotel room, but the actual occurrence is unknown, presenting a blank screen on which Moore can project his own text; moreover, if there were any doubt that this is fiction rather than history, Moore's story also subtly but significantly modifies its spatio-temporal coordinates – 'Recognition' is set in Boston, whereas the historical incident occurred in Chicago; moreover, it is set in 1898, the year of Winfield's death and five years after his institutionalisation.[31] Such spatio-temporal dislocations make it clear that Moore's concern is with the relationship between language and altered states of consciousness rather than deciding on the state of his protagonist's mental health or grounding his text in an appeal to historical veracity.

Whatever their source, the fictive Winfield's visions lead him to a verbal outburst that appears pathological and involuntary: 'nothing stems his pentecostal stream [...]. He is the monstrous father and his cheeks bulge with new syllables; a dreadful tertiary language that his son will one day echo in the loathsome coinages he picks to name his pantheon, his only children. From the open window of his hotel room, Yog Sothoth howls into the world's stink' (p. 11). Elsewhere Moore compares magic and psychoanalysis as two artistic attempts to delineate consciousness,[32] and the coda to 'Recognition' offers a quasi-Freudian reading of Lovecraft. Alluding to Lovecraft's lighthearted claim that he is 'descended from his Elder deities', the narrator of 'Recognition' asserts that here Lovecraft 'almost managed to decrypt the bas-reliefs raised in the R'lyeh of his sunken mind' and wonders 'would he have screamed his father's name, like Wilbur Whateley's brother, from a hilltop: College Hill, or Sentinel?'[33] Moore here exercises a twofold misprision – of text ('The Dunwich Horror') and history (the biographies of Winfield and his illustrious son) – the strength of which resides in an ability to open a meta-narrative level within the text itself.

Moreover, in his description of Winfield as Yog Sothoth shouting from a window, Moore provides yet another metaphor for readerly engagement with texts produced by authors who themselves know not what they do. Just as the tail-end of 'Recognition' substitutes the bellowing of son for father, so too the reader replaces the neighbour subjected to the unsolicited assault of verbal noise. In Moore's deeper soundings of

Lovecraft's worlds, in works like 'The Courtyard' and *Neonomicon*, this preoccupation with what language does to whoever is overhearing it comes to the fore. Indeed, in adapting the Lovecraftean heterocosm, Moore confronts the reverse side of the redemptive capacities of language and sexuality posited in works like *Promethea* and *Lost Girls*, emphasising the madness-inducing potential of a language capable of violating the self in an assault that is indissociable from sexual violence.[34]

Psychogeography in 'Zaiman's Hill'

Moore has expressed fears that the creation of works that are 'too immersive' will have 'a crippling effect on the mass imagination',[35] a concern which may well be reflected in the fact that his own fictional worlds are shot through with metanarrative fissures that confront the reader with a dialectic between imagination and perception operative within the mimetic process. Visual and verbal languages, in their ability to encode and communicate art and magic, share with sexuality and corporeality more generally a comportment towards alterity capable of transforming the phenomenal world of the self; however, this latent potential for sensory and sensual penetration also demonstrates a disturbing propensity for violence and violation.

This relational dimension of the self directly intersects with Moore's interests in psychogeography, which, as noted in different ways by both Round and Murray above, inform Moore's Gothic works formally and thematically. Moreover, a considerable proportion of art's alchemical effects derive from its capacity to inform the bearing of the self in its environment. 'Our reaction to various locations seemed to me to be dependent upon the richness of the web of association that we connected with these sites', Moore remarks, reflecting on the situational emphasis in his performance pieces, and noting that 'if you are a practising magician or poet and have a web of symbol systems with which to decode even chance appearances and events [...] then your experience will be richer and more meaningful'.[36] However, while psychogeography provides a means of divining such associations from the sociocultural history of a place, even art that is historically unconnected to a particular location can serve to structure and mediate present perceptions of it.

'Zaiman's Hill', a story 'compiled from notes and various jottings

[...] made during a very uncomfortable wilderness holiday',[37] represents the landscape of the Brecon Beacons within a web of association drawn from the alien worlds of Lovecraft: 'in shower-spattered streets below ground, dim, pellucid, our fingers trace wet shapes: the cold, pregnant messages of R'lyeh.'[38] In disanchoring the Lovecraftian world from its New England moorings and applying it to the Welsh countryside, Moore demonstrates the efficacy with which the fictional can colonise the real. Moreover, the deployment of imagery adapted from an American horror writer to describe the landscape encountered camping in Wales here serves to highlight the uncanny disjunctions brought about by sociopolitical interventions that have transformed both the built and natural environment:

> it was in the middle of [...] these huge, dead, silent pine forests that had been planted by the National Trust. And because the canopy cuts out any light there is absolutely no birdsong, there is nothing growing [...]. You've just got these huge dark dead woods.
> There are reservoirs where they actually flooded the whole valley, and there are still submerged villages – church spires that can be seen at low tide [...]. [F]ish don't live there because if you've got a huge body of water draining from a pine forest, the water is naturally highly acidic.
> There were also massive limestone caves at [...] [Dan-yr-Ogof] [...] with these natural formations which were about the most Lovecraftian things I've ever seen. They were like Lovecraft monsters rendered in stone, growing out of the walls of the caverns.[39]

The uncanny here results from a sense that humans have brought death to the environment, but the story itself effaces the distinction between human and inhuman, effecting a Lovecraftian dissolution of anthropocentrism: 'the stone threatens terrible life, dreams of meat [...] fashions a geo-organic menagerie, every conceivable quirk of biology prefigured here in these waxed carboniferous ruptures' ('Zaiman's Hill', p. 186). Subterranean spaces open the mind to the fact of humanity's precarious life, while at the same time the 'birdless dark', 'drowned hamlets' and 'acid lagoon' assert its destructive capacities (p. 185).

This reworking of Lovecraft suggests that adaptation is best conceptualised as a web of association containing manifold symbolic intersections. Within Moore's corpus alone, the subaqueous town is reminiscent of the vampire city depicted in issue 39 of *Swamp Thing*, whose Gothic environmentalism is discussed in detail by Gray and

Bradshaw above; however, in the context of Gothic adaptations more broadly, the application of Lovecraft to the Welsh countryside represents a homecoming of sorts. Indeed, anchored as Lovecraft's fiction is within specific locales, it bears the unmistakable traces of previous authors not indigenous to the landscapes being described. Thus, 'The Dunwich Horror' is itself informed by 'The Great God Pan', a tale set in part in Wales and authored by Arthur Machen, a Welshman. 'Zaiman's Hill' thus calls attention to the symbolic exchanges amongst texts and the ways in which these serve to mediate between the human self and the physical environment.

When Heterocosms Go Bad: 'The Courtyard' and *Neonomicon*

While 'Zaiman's Hill' suggests that the negotiation between self and the exterior world involves an effacement of the distinction between the real or exterior world and fictional or subjective worlds, the possibility that such self-reconfigurations can go badly wrong is explored directly in 'The Courtyard' and the follow-up mini-series, *Neonomicon*. In these works, the violence of language is presented in the context of rape and attendant forms of corporeal violation and dismemberment. Both works are set in a heterocosm that draws heavily on the Lovecraftian mythos with added elements of science fiction. Set in 2004, 'The Courtyard' details a fictional future a decade from its original publication date, while *Neonomicon* begins in late summer 2006, two years after the events in the earlier story. Both draw extensively on terms, ideas and images from Lovecraft, but – at least initially – the most obvious physical difference in this alternative world is the fact that the cities are enclosed within giant domes to protect their inhabitants, a nice metaphor for the human skull with its sensory inlets that are required for life but are also a potential source of contamination from without. Indeed, on a thematic level both works engage with two interrelated anxieties omnipresent across Lovecraft's work: the angst generated by uncertainties about one's identity and the often ambiguous line that separates sanity from a descent into madness.

'The Courtyard' is focalised through a first-person narrator whose opening description of his location – Red Hook, named after the squalid waterfront district in Lovecraft's 'Horror at Red Hook' – not only introduces the Lovecraft intertext but blurs the boundaries between the worlds of fact and fiction. Thus, the residents of Clinton Street (the road name is taken from Lovecraft) have 'been petitioning [...] for a name-change since our chief executive fucked up the Syria thing in 1995' (p. 137).[40] In addition to similarities in the setting, typical Lovecraftian fears — especially concerning race and sex — are embodied in the character of the narrator, whose smug intolerance is applied to various minorities in general and, in particular, to his schizophrenic neighbour, Germaine, whose existence he equates with the excrement he finds smeared on the sink and faucets of their shared bathroom: 'I'm afraid that my feelings concerning Germaine's Mom and Pop are exactly the same as the feelings I had for their daughter while shaving: I just wish these people would clean up their own shit' (*ibid.*). Whereas the protagonist of 'Red Hook' is a police officer, 'The Courtyard's' narrator is an FBI agent, and most of the story details the final hours of his investigation into a set of murders perpetuated by unrelated individuals but adhering to a clear pattern that suggests an underlying connection: 'All fifteen are without heads or hands, torsos sculpted like those garnish vegetables that you get at the fancier restaurants, carved into roses; the separate layers of skin, fat and muscle peeled back in triangular flaps into flowers of meat' (p. 138). Such gruesome descriptions are rare, and the story's horror develops specifically out of the contamination of one imaginary by another through the medium of Aklo, a language invented by Machen but referenced in three of Lovecraft's short stories.[41]

Initially, the narrator assumes Aklo is a drug that might connect the murders, and successfully convinces the dealer, Johnny Carcosa, to give him some. It is only after Carcosa has begun whispering the Aklo words in his ear that he realises the mistake:

> A pinwheel of nautillus fronds is dissolved into sparks by my vitreous humour as huge old grammatical structures collapse into place. Aklo isn't a drug. There's no drug with mind-altering properties halfway as powerful. Aklo's a language.
>
> Ur-syntax; the primal vocabulary giving form to those pre-conscious orderings wrung from a hot incoherence of stars, from our birthmuds pooled in the grandmother lagoon; a stark, limited palette of earliest notions, lost colours, forgotten intensities. ('Courtyard', p. 145)

The first-person focalisation, coupled with the fact that the narration is in the present tense, means that the text directly mimics the linguistic effects of Aklo in real time: 'the word bursts inside me like summer thunder, sends scarabs and swastikas rippling over the screen of my eyelids. "Wza-y'ei." A mental floor gives way beneath me' (ibid.). As the narrator's perspective supports the plot-structure, his mental transformation directly affects the narrative, disrupting its linearity and revealing a horrific anagnorisis that radically reconfigures the relationship between narrator and implied reader:

> I now grasp that this isn't Clinton Street, nor is it truly me walking across it. We're both merely part of a brief verbalized reconstruction I'm making to you, Germaine, as I kneel here in your room, bent above you.
> I want you to know that the tape on your mouth isn't there to prevent you from making a noise: it's to stop the Dho-Hna flowing in through the wrong aperture, which of course could spoil everything for you.
> I know you're still worrying over your hands, but please don't. They're quite safe, I assure you. The thing is to focus yourself on the Wza-y'ei; the concept of not-hands. No. No, don't black out. There. That's better. (p. 146)

This passage makes explicit the psychological violation involved in every act of narrative address by repositioning the reader in a clearly defined and uncomfortable position as the victim of violence.

This interpolation of the reader functions as a reminder of the risks attendant upon the transformative capacity of art – the blurring of fictional and factual worlds is not always a happy experience. Written several years after 'The Courtyard', *Promethea* utilises an analogous metanarrative device to situate the reader in a position of apocalyptic awakening, as when the prophetess directly addresses the reader: 'Know that I love you in this room, this womb of warm and gathering shadows . . . / [. . .] / Rejoice. Your world is ended. / [. . .] / Time's jail-yards are unlocked.'[42] The revelation in 'The Courtyard', however, is horrific, anticipating an awakening that is the diabolical inverse of mystical enlightenment. Indeed, just as the narrator has become infected by the very madness he was sent to investigate, so too the implied reader is forced to take the position of the schizophrenic Germaine and to recognise the proximity between imagination and delusion.

When Moore returns to the heterocosm of 'The Courtyard' in *Neonomicon*, this metanarrative impulse – and its subsequent association with sexual violence – is made more explicit. Billed as 'a sequel to *The Courtyard*',[43] *Neonomicon* not only recounts events that take place after the short story – the narrator, now named as Agent Sax, has been institutionalised and the case taken up by Agents Brears and Lamper – but it also follows up on the blurring of fact and fiction by making this a constituent feature of the plot. Thus, in Chapter 2, Brears advises her colleagues that 'every element in this case is connected to the writings of H.P. Lovecraft', calling attention to fact that all the details of incidents treated as historical fact in *Neonomicon* and earlier in 'The Courtyard' can be found in 'two stories, Horror at Red Hook and Shadow over Innsmouth'.[44] Subsequently, the work further effaces the distinction separating Brears's world from ours both verbally, when she discusses Kenneth Grant's belief that 'Lovecraft's whole mythology was genuine in some way', and visually, showing her in possession of occult works, like Grant's *The Magical Revival*, and scholarly texts, such as S.T. Joshi's *H.P. Lovecraft A Life* (II.12.ii, II.13.iv, IV.16.iii–IV.17.iv). Finally, Burrows's limited-edition covers of *Neonomicon*'s 'auxiliary' print run further emphasise the metanarrative dimension of the series by including author, artist and Lovecraft himself in vignettes in a manner that suggests they are themselves characters or stars in the piece (see Figure 14.1).

The sexual aspect of the violence in 'The Courtyard' is left implicit – a further homage to Lovecraft who, as Brears indicates in another intertextual reflection, only provides 'dark hints' about sex, 'unnameable couplings, stuff like that' (II.7.iii); in *Neonomicon*, however, it becomes explicit, with Brears and Lamper infiltrating a cult of swingers using sexual energies to summon a Lovecraftian monstrosity, which proceeds to repeatedly rape Brears. As in the evocations to 'The Great Old Ones', violent sexuality here becomes linked to the summoning of a dark power. Moreover, sexual violations become associated with textual ones by virtue of the fact that the cult leaders own a shop that sells not only Lovecraftian books, but also Lovecraft-inspired pornography and sex toys. While this combination of merchandise causes confusion for Lamper – 'What's with all the occult books? I thought we were running down the sex angle?' (II.12.i) – it makes perfect sense in view of occult traditions linking sexuality with mystical or magical knowledge. Likewise, the link between sexual violence and the interpenetration of the real world by one or more heterocosms is suggested in Chapter 3,

14.1 Alan Moore and Jacen Burrows, *Neonomicon*, I (2010), auxiliary cover

where as a result of her ordeal with the monster, Brears finds herself in an alternate dreamspace (see Figure 14.2). Here she encounters Johnny Carcosa, the Aklo dealer from 'The Courtyard', who explains, in his characteristic lisp, that 'Thith ith R'lyeh. R'lyeh ith in you' (III.7.iv). As at the end of 'Recognition', here too Lovecraft's submerged city becomes associated with the depths of the mind associated both with inspiration and (sexual) neurosis (III.7.ii), an intersection between imagination and abject impregnation reconfigured on the penultimate page, when R'lyeh is subsequently identified with Brears's womb (IV.24.iii).

Earlier in the narrative, the final frames of Chapter 1 present a compelling metaphor for art's capacity to alter or destroy the boundaries between worlds. Set in the text's 'real' world, Carcosa, who moments before was interacting with the agents as a fully-fledged character, melds into a wall-mural, evading capture and destabilising the world-views of those left behind. Brears is furious and alarmed – 'his picture, it wasn't even on the wall when we came in' – and Lamper attempts to calm her. Throughout this page (see Figure 14.3), the viewer's perspective of each frame rises steadily such that the last frame depicts the view from outside the city's glass dome, suggesting the viewpoint of an extraterrestrial waiting to get in and adding an ironic connotation to Lamper's assurance that 'Everything's Good' (I.25).

As vehicles for the doctrine of cosmic indifference, Lovecraft's stories harness a fear of alterity in order to undermine anthropocentric worldviews. While Moore's work does not endorse the social prejudices implicit and explicit in Lovecraft's texts (associating them with repressive violence and mental instability), it does harness this fear, transforming a key Lovecraftian motif, the invasion of the human universe by monstrosities from another world, into a metaphor for the darker implications of art's redemptive capacities. These stories – like Lovecraft's own – are works of bricolage, compiled from multiple sources in a spirit that is creative and critical rather than simply iterative. Moore's works suggest that the heterocosm is not only a concept that can be applied to fiction across a range of media, but also a metaphor for the sort of world-building that is at the heart of both magic and art. Moreover, in adapting Lovecraft's heterocosms within works that employ various metanarrative devices, these stories expose the horror at the heart of magical experience. While the world-building enterprises

14.2 Alan Moore and Jacen Burrows, *Neonomicon*, III.4–5

14.3 Alan Moore and Jacen Burrows, *Neonomicon*, I.25

promoted in *Promethea* may indeed offer help and solace to a beleaguered humanity, all worlds are not equal and everything is not good, as Lamper himself discovers when, in Chapter 2, he is shot with his own gun. Read collectively, Moore's Lovecraftian tales suggest that the fact that a particular world can be imagined, does not necessarily mean that it should be brought into being. Like predecessors such as William Blake, Moore not only understands that the imagination's potential to redeem is bound up with its capability for destruction, but also unflinchingly explores the darker dimensions of human experience:

> People who are profound of spirit are not going to see everything as a delightful spiritual Disneyland. Far from it. They are going to be people who see the world at its worst *and* can embrace that, who can understand that in some ways it is all part of the tapestry of existence, that the excremental parts of it are in some ways every bit as holy as the more exalted parts of the human experience.[45]

Notes

1. H.P. Lovecraft, 'The Dunwich Horror', in *Necronomicon: The Best Weird Tales of H.P. Lovecraft*, ed. Stephen Jones (London: Gollancz, 2008), pp. 264–97 (p. 292).
2. 'Beyond our Ken', Review of Kenneth Grant's *Against the Light*, *KAOS*, 14 (2002), 155–62.
3. The short story, 'Allan and the Sundered Veil', is appended to the account of the first outing of the League; see Moore and O'Neill, *The League of Extraordinary Gentlemen*, 2 vols (La Jolla, CA: America's Best Comics, 2003), I, n.p. Though this story represents a significant engagement with Lovecraft, it is clearly imbricated within the narrative history and fictional worlds represented in a larger series, *The League*, and therefore differs from the works discussed here, each of which are self-contained and all of which share a similar provenance, being first-published by Creation Books (with the exception of *Neonomicon*, which directly references 'The Courtyard' and carries on from the republication of the Creation Books stories by Avatar Press, as discussed below).
4. See *Of Grammatology*, trans. Gayatri Chakrovorty Spivak (London: Johns Hopkins University Press, 1997), pp. 138–9: 'the strop-catapult [*bricole*] seems originally to have been a machine of war or the hunt, constructed to destroy. And who can believe the image of the peaceful *bricoleur*?' (p. 139; original emphasis and interpolation).
5. *Ibid.*, p. 139 (original emphasis).

6 Linda Hutcheon, *A Theory of Adaptation* (New York and London: Routledge, 2006), p. 14.
7 For a detailed catalogue of Lovecraft adaptations across a wide range of media, see Don Smith, *H.P. Lovecraft in Popular Culture: The Works and their Adaptations in Film, Television, Comics, Music and Games* (Jefferson, NC: McFarland, 2006).
8 For a survey of the often contradictory political and aesthetic positions articulated in Lovecraft's fiction and letters, see especially Sunand T. Joshi, *A Subtler Magick: The Writings and Philosophy of H.P. Lovecraft* (Berkeley Heights, NJ: Wildside, 1999), pp. 13–50.
9 David Punter, *The Literature of Terror: A History of Gothic Fictions from 1765 to the Present Day*, 2nd edn, 2 vols (London: Longman, 1996), II, p. 39.
10 David Oakes, *Science and Destabilization in the Modern American Gothic: Lovecraft, Matheson, and King* (London: Greenwood, 2000), p. 29.
11 Joshi notes that 'the central tenet in what Lovecraft called his "cosmic indifferentism" is mechanistic materialism' (*Subtler Magick*, p. 29).
12 Robert M. Price, 'Lovecraft's "artificial mythology"', in *An Epicure in the Terrible*, ed. David E. Schultz and S.T. Joshi (London: Associated University Presses, 1991), pp. 247–56 (p. 250).
13 See, e.g., Kenneth Grant, *The Magical Revival* (London: Muller, 1972).
14 'Beyond our Ken', p. 159.
15 All three of the short stories have been recently republished in a newly expanded edition: 'Recognition', 'The Courtyard' and 'Zaiman's Hill', in *The Starry Wisdom*, ed. David M. Mitchell (London: Creation Oneiros, 2010), pp. 9–12, 137–46, 185–6; hereafter cited in the main body of the text. This edition was released under the Creation Oneiros imprint in 2010 as an accompaniment to Mitchell's follow-up collection, *Songs of the BlackWürm Gism: Hymns to H.P. Lovecraft*, published in 2009 with cover art by Moore. From 2003 to 2006, Avatar republished all three stories in various formats, adapted for comics by Antony Johnston with artwork by Jacen Burrows ('The Courtyard' and 'Recognition') and Juan Jose Ryp ('Zaiman's Hill'); these works, and more, are reprinted in *Alan Moore's Yuggoth Cultures and Other Growths*, ed. William Christensen (Urbana, IL: Avatar Press, 2007).
16 For further discussion of Ideaspace, see 'Alan Moore interviewed by Eddie Campbell', *Egomania*, 2 (2002), 1–32 (pp. 18–22); reprinted in Alan Moore and Eddie Campbell, *A Disease of Language* (London: Knockabout Comics, 2010), pp. 109–40.
17 *Alan Moore Spells It Out*, interview with Bill Baker (Milford, CT: Airwave, 2005), p. 11.
18 H.P. Lovecraft, *Supernatural Horror in Literature* (New York: Dover, 1973), p. 106.

19 *Ibid.*, p. 13.
20 *Alan Moore Spells It Out*, p. 10.
21 Harold Bloom, *A Map of Misreading*, 2nd edn (Oxford: Oxford University Press, 2003), p. 4 (original emphasis).
22 Price, 'Artificial Mythology', p. 248 (original emphasis).
23 *Alan Moore Spells It Out*, p. 30.
24 'Beyond our Ken', p. 160.
25 For a short summary of Crowley's use of the Tree of Life, see *The Book of Thoth* (San Francisco, CA: Weiser Books, 1974), pp. 30–8, 265–70; for a brief survey of the development of the Tree of Life within Jewish mysticism, see Gershom Scholem, *On the Kabbalah and its Symbolism*, trans. Ralph Manheim (New York: Schocken Books, 1969), pp. 68–9, 107–17.
26 Alan Moore, 'The Great Old Ones: Evocations', in John Coulthart, *The Haunter of the Dark and other Grotesque Visions* (London: Creation Oneiros, 2006). This work is unpaginated but each evocation is accorded a number from 0 to XI, which will be used for citations in the main body of the text.
27 Gershom Scholem, *Major Trends in Jewish Mysticism*, 3rd edn, revised (New York: Schocken Books, 1961), pp. 177–8.
28 'Dunwich Horror', p. 296 (original emphasis).
29 'Beyond our Ken', p. 161.
30 'Recognition', in *The Starry Wisdom*, ed. D.M. Mitchell, rev. edn (London: Creation Oneiros, 2010), pp. 9–11 (pp. 9–10); hereafter cited in the main body of the text.
31 For a brief biography of Winfield Lovecraft, see S.T. Joshi and David E. Schultz, *An H.P. Lovecraft Encyclopedia* (Westport, CT: Greenwood, 2001), p. 155.
32 Alan Moore, 'Fossil Angels', posted by Glycon, *Livejournal* (20 Oct. 2010): http://glycon.livejournal.com/13888.html.
33 'Recognition', p. 11.
34 For further discussion of redemptively subversive sexuality in Moore's work, see Matthew J.A. Green, '"The end of the world. That's a bad thing right?": Form and Function from William Blake to Alan Moore', in *Blake 2.0: William Blake in Twentieth-Century Art, Music and Culture*, ed. Steve Clark, Tristanne Connolly and Jason Whittaker (Basingstoke: Palgrave Macmillan, 2012), pp. 175–86; and Green, '"She Brings Apocalypse": Sex, Imagination and Redemptive Transgression in William Blake and the Graphic Novels of Alan Moore', *Literature Compass*, 8:10 (2011), 739–56.
35 'Legendary Comics Writer Alan Moore on Superheroes, *The League*, and Making Magic', interview by Adam Rogers, *Wired*, 17:3 (23 Feb. 2009): www.wired.com/wired/issue/17-03.
36 'Moore interviewed by Campbell', p. 7.

37 'The Story behind the stories', Alan Moore interviewed by William Christensen, in *Yuggoth Cultures*, pp. 105–15 (p. 107).
38 'Zaiman's Hill', in *The Starry Wisdom*, ed. D.M. Mitchell, rev. edn (London: Creation Oneiros, 2010), pp. 185–6 (p. 186); hereafter cited in the main body of the text.
39 'Story behind the stories', p. 107.
40 The event alluded to is fictional – and set in the year after 'The Courtyard' was first published – but President Clinton was in office when the story was written.
41 N.G. Christakos, 'Annotations', in *Alan Moore's 'The Courtyard': A Companion*, ed. William Christensen (Urbana, IL: Avatar, 2004), pp. 44–58 (p. 48).
42 Alan Moore, J.H. Williams III and Mick Gray, *Promethea*, 5 Books (La Jolla, CA: America's Best Comics, 2000–05), B5.VI.14.i–ii.
43 *Alan Moore's* Neonomicon *Hornbook* (Urbana, IL: Avatar, 2009), frontmatter.
44 Alan Moore and Jacen Burrows, *Neonomicon* (Urbana, IL: Avatar, 2011), II.2.i, II.1.iv; hereafter cited in the main body of the text.
45 Alan Moore, personal interview, 25 Jan. 2011.

Bibliography

Primary sources: Alan Moore

Comics and graphic novels

Moore, Alan (and various artists/writers), *AARGH! [Artists Against Rampant Government Homophobia]* (Northampton: Mad Love, 1988).

——, *Alan Moore's Yuggoth Cultures and Other Growths*, ed. William Christensen (Urbana, IL: Avatar, 2007).

——, Alfredo Alcala, Stephen Bissette, John Totleben, Rick Veitch et al., *Saga of the Swamp Thing*, 6 vols (New York: Vertigo, 2009–11); vol. 1 reprints *Saga of the Swamp Thing*, 20–27 (Jan. 1984–Aug. 1984); vol. 2 reprints *Saga of the Swamp Thing*, 28–33 (Sept. 1984–Feb. 1985) plus *Swamp Thing Annual*, 2 (1985); vol. 3 reprints *Saga of the Swamp Thing* 35–38 (Apr. 1985–July 1985) and *Swamp Thing* 39–42 (Aug. 1985–Nov. 1985); vol. 4 reprints *Swamp Thing* 43–50 (Dec. 1985–July 1986); vol. 5 reprints *Swamp Thing* 51–56 (Aug. 1986–Jan. 1987); vol. 6 reprints *Swamp Thing* 57–64 (Feb. 1987–Sept. 1987).

——, Joe Bennett, Rick Veitch and Alex Ross, *Supreme: The Story of the Year* (West Carrollton, OH: Checker Book Publishing Group, 2002).

——, Chuck Beckum, Rick Bryant, Alan Davis, Gary Leach, John Totleben, Rick Veitch et al, *Miracleman*, 1–16 (Aug 1985–Dec 1989); issues 1–6 reprint material from *Warrior* 1–21 (Mar 1982–Aug 1984).

——, Stephen Bissette and Rick Veitch, 'The Mirror of Love', in Alan Moore and various artists/writers, *AARGH! [Artists Against Rampant Government Homophobia]* (Northampton: Mad Love, 1988), pp. 2–9.

—— and Brian Bolland, *Batman: The Killing Joke,* deluxe edn (London: Titan, 2008).

—— and Jacen Burrows, *Neonomicon* (Urbana, IL: Avatar, 2011).
—— and Eddie Campbell, *The Birth Caul* (Paddington, QLD: Eddie Campbell Comics, 1999); reprinted in Alan Moore and Eddie Campbell, *A Disease of Language* (London: Knockabout Comics, 2010), pp. 5–56.
—— and Eddie Campbell, *From Hell: Being a Melodrama in Sixteen Parts* (London: Knockabout Comics, 2006).
—— and Eddie Campbell, *Snakes and Ladders* (Paddington, QLD: Eddie Campbell Comics, 2001); reprinted in Alan Moore and Eddie Campbell, *A Disease of Language* (London: Knockabout Comics, 2010), pp. 57–108.
—— and Eddie Campbell, *A Disease of Language* (London: Knockabout Comics, 2010).
—— and Alan Davis, *Captain Britain* (New York: Marvel Comics, 2001).
—— and Melinda Gebbie, *Lost Girls* (Marietta, GA: Top Shelf, 2009).
—— and Dave Gibbons, 'For The Man Who Has Everything', in *Superman: Whatever Happened to the Man of Tomorrow*, deluxe edn. (New York: DC Comics, 2009), pp. 85–124; reprints *Superman Annual*, 11 (June 1985).
—— and Dave Gibbons, *Watchmen* (New York: DC Comics, 2005).
—— and Dave Gibbons, *Watchmen*, Absolute edn (New York: DC Comics, 2005).
——, Michael T. Gilbert, William F. Loebs and Ken Bruzemak, 'The Riddle of the Recalcitrant Refuse', *Mr. Monster*, 3 (Oct. 1985); reprinted in *The Extraordinary Works of Alan Moore: Indispensable Edition*, ed. George Khoury (Raleigh, NC: TwoMorrows, 2008), pp. 129–44.
—— and David Lloyd, *V for Vendetta* (London: Titan, 2009).
—— and Kevin O'Neill, *The League of Extraordinary Gentlemen: Volume I* (La Jolla, CA: America's Best Comics, 2000).
—— and Kevin O'Neill, *The League of Extraordinary Gentlemen: Volume II* (La Jolla, CA: America's Best Comics, 2003).
—— and Kevin O'Neill, *The League of Extraordinary Gentlemen: The Black Dossier* (La Jolla, CA: America's Best Comics, 2007).
—— and Kevin O'Neill, *The League of Extraordinary Gentlemen: Century: 1910* (London: Knockabout Comics, 2009).
—— and Steve Parkhouse, *The Complete Bojeffries Saga* (Northampton, MA: Tundra Press, 1992).
—— and Bill Sienkiewicz, 'Shadowplay – The Secret Team', in *Brought*

to Light: A Graphic Docudrama (Forestville, CA: Eclipse Books, 1989), pp. 1–30 (all works included in this text are paginated separately).

———, Chris Sprouse, Alan Gordon et al., *Tom Strong*, Book 1 (La Jolla, CA: America's Best Comics, 2000).

——— and Curt Swan, 'Whatever Happened to the Man of Tomorrow?' in *Superman: Whatever Happened to the Man of Tomorrow*, deluxe edn. (New York: DC Comics, 2009), pp. 10–60; reprints *Action Comics*, 423 (Sept. 1986) and *Superman*, 583 (Sept. 1986).

——— and Rick Veitch, 'The Jungle Line' in *Superman: Whatever Happened to the Man of Tomorrow*, deluxe edn. (New York: DC Comics, 2009), pp. 61–84; reprints *DC Presents* 85 (Sept. 1985).

———, J.H. Williams III and Mick Gray, *Promethea*, 5 Books (La Jolla, CA: America's Best Comics, 2000–05).

——— and Oscar Zarate, 'I Keep Coming Back', in *It's Dark in London*, ed. Oscar Zarate (London: Serpent's Tail, 1996); reprinted in *Alan Moore's Yuggoth Cultures and Other Growths*, ed. William Christensen (Urbana, IL: Avatar, 2007), pp. 83–94.

———and Oscar Zarate, *A Small Killing* (Urbana, IL: Avatar, 2003).

Essays and other non-fiction

25,000 Years of Erotic Freedom (New York: Abrams, 2009).

Alan Moore's Writing for Comics (Urbana, IL: Avatar Press, 2003); reprints material from *Fantasy Advertiser*, 92–95 (Aug. 1985–Feb. 1986).

'Behind the Painted Smile', in Alan Moore and David Lloyd, *V for Vendetta* (London: Titan, 2009), pp. 267–76.

'Beyond our Ken', Review of Kenneth Grant's *Against the Light*, *KAOS*, 14 (2002), 155–62.

'Fear of a Black Flag', *Dodgem Logic*, 2 (Feb.–Mar. 2010), 2–5.

'Fossil Angels', posted in the online journal of Glycon [Pádraig Ó Méalóid], *Livejournal* (20 Oct. 2010): http://glycon.livejournal.com/13888.html.

'Frankenstein's Cadillac', *Dodgem Logic*, 4 (June–July 2010), 2–11.

'Going Underground', *Dodgem Logic*, 1 (2009), 2–7.

'Introduction', in Moore et al., *Saga of the Swamp Thing* (New York: DC Comics, 1987), pp. 7–12.

'Minutes', in Alan Moore and Dave Gibbons, *Watchmen*, Absolute edn. (New York: DC Comics, 2005), n.p.

Interviews and correspondence

'A chat with Alan Moore' (DC Comics/Lynn Vanucci Productions, 1985): www.youtube.com/watch?v=ze3rCvyiISA&feature=related.

'A For Alan', interview with Heidi Macdonald, *The Beat* (1 Nov. 2005): http://web.archive.org/web/20070305213808/http://www.comicon.com/thebeat/2006/03/a_for_alan_pt_1_the_alan_moore.html.

'The Alan Moore Interview', interview with Barry Kavanagh, blather.net (17 Oct. 2000): www.blather.net/articles/amoore/index.html.

'Alan Moore interviewed by Eddie Campbell', *Egomania*, 2 (2002), 1–32; reprinted in Moore and Campbell, *Disease of Language*, pp. 110–40.

Alan Moore: Portrait of an Extraordinary Gentleman, ed. Gary Spencer Millidge and Smoky Man (Leigh-on-Sea: Abiogenesis Press, 2003), pp. 307–16.

'Alan Moore Reflects on Marvelman: Part 1', interview by Kurt Amacker, *Mania* (3 Sept. 2009): www.mania.com/alan-moore-reflects-marvelman_article_117413.html.

'Alan Moore Reflects on Marvelman: Part 2', interview by Kurt Amacker, *Mania* (10 Sept. 2009): www.mania.com/alan-moore-reflects-marvelman-part-2_article_117529.html.

Alan Moore Spells It Out, interview with Bill Baker (Milford, CT: Airwave, 2005).

'Big Words', interview by Gary Groth, *Comics Journal*, 138–40 (Seattle: Fantagraphics Books, 1990).

'Correspondence: From Hell', correspondence between Alan Moore and Dave Sim, in *Alan Moore: Portrait of an Extraordinary Gentleman*, ed. Gary Spencer Millidge and Smoky Man (Leigh-on-Sea: Abiogenesis Press, 2003), pp. 303–45; reprints material from *Cerebus*, 217–20 (Apr.–Jul. 1997).

'The Craft', interview by Daniel Whiston, *Zarjaz*, 1.3–4 (24 May 2003); reprinted by *enginecomics.co.uk* (2005): www.enginecomics.co.uk.

'Dracula Reborn', interview by David Bogart, in *The Best of Vampirella: Lost Tales*, ed. David Bogard and Bon Alimagno (New York: Harris, 2008), n.p.

The Extraordinary Works of Alan Moore: Indispensable Edition, interview by and ed. George Khoury (Raleigh, NC: TwoMorrows, 2008).

'Hipster Priest: Unearthing the magical world of the comic book genius', interview by John Doran, *Stool Pigeon* (7 July 2010): www.thestoolpigeon.co.uk/features/alan-moore-interview.html.

'Legendary Comics Writer Alan Moore on Superheroes, *The League*, and Making Magic', interview by Adam Rogers, *Wired*, 17.3 (23 Feb. 2009): www.wired.com/wired/issue/17–03.

'Magic is afoot', interview by Jay Babcock, *Arthur*, 4 (May 2003): www.arthurmag.com/2007/05/10/1815/; reprinted in *Yuggoth Cultures*, ed. William Christensen, pp. 117–38.

'The Magic of Comics', interview by Jon Cook and George Khoury, *Comic Book Artist*, 25 (Raleigh, NC: TwoMorrows, 2003).

Magus: Transdisciplinary Approaches to the Work of Alan Moore, with Melinda Gebbie and Paul Gravett (Chair), Plenary discussion panel, University of Northampton (28–29 May 2010): www.youtube.com/watch?v=Y-wwwCmuDHI&feature=player_embedded.

'A Portal to Another Dimension', Alan Moore and Dave Gibbons interviewed by Neil Gaiman, *Comics Journal*, 116 (July 1987): 80–7 (p. 83); reprinted in *The New Comics: Interviews from the Pages of* The Comics Journal, ed. Gary Groth and Robert Fiore (New York: Berkley, 1988).

'The Rational Shaman', interview by Jay Babcock, *LA Weekly* (10 January 2002): www.laweekly.com/2002–01–10/news/the-rational-shaman.

'Round table discussion with Alan Moore and Dave Gibbons', first published in *Fantasy Advertiser*, 100 (Mar. 1988): www.johncoulthart.com/feuilleton/2006/06/24/watchmen/.

'The Story behind the stories', Alan Moore interviewed by William Christensen, in *Alan Moore's Yuggoth Cultures and Other Growths*, ed. William Christensen (Urbana, IL: Avatar, 2007), pp. 105–15.

'Tea and Sorcery', interview by Alex Musson and Andrew O'Neill, *Mustard*, 4.2 (2009), 14–29.

'Watchmen', round table discussion with Alan Moore, Dave Gibbons et al. {*feuilleton*} (24 June 2006): www.johncoulthart.com/feuilleton/2006/06/24/watchmen/; reprints *Fantasy Advertiser*, 100 (Mar. 1988).

Performances/happenings

The Moon and Serpent Grand Egyptian Theatre of Marvels, Bridewell Theatre, London, 16 July 1994; CD recording: David J, Alan Moore and Tim Perkins (Cleopatra Records, 1996)

The Highbury Working: A beat séance, The Garage, Highbury, London, 20 Nov. 1997; CD recording: Alan Moore and Tim Perkins (RE:play, 2000).

The Moon and Serpent Grand Egyptian Theatre of Marvels, Angel Passage, South Bank Centre, London, Feb. 2001; CD recording: Alan Moore and Tim Perkins RE:play, 2001).

Snakes and Ladders, Conway Hall, London, 10 Apr. 1999; CD recording: Alan Moore and Tim Perkins (RE:Play, 2002).

Poetry and prose fiction

'The Great Old Ones: Evocations', in John Coulthart, *The Haunter of the Dark and Other Grotesque Visions* (London: Creation Oneiros, 2006), n. p.

The Mirror of Love, with photographs by José Villarrubia and intro. by David Drake (Atlanta, GA: Top Shelf, 2004).

———, 'Recognition', 'The Courtyard', and 'Zaiman's Hill', in *The Starry Wisdom*, ed. David M. Mitchell (London: Creation Oneiros, 2010), pp. 9–12, 137–46, 185–6.

———, *Voice of the Fire* (Atlanta, GA: Top Shelf, 2009).

Television and film

'Husbands and Knives', in Matt Selman (writer) and Nancy Kruse (dir.), *The Simpsons*, 19.7 (20th Century Fox Television: 18 Nov. 2007).

'Metamorphosis', *Prisoners of Gravity*, Season Three (TVOntario: broadcast 3 Dec. 1992).

The Mindscape of Alan Moore, dir. DeZ Vylenz (London: Shadowsnake Productions, 2003).

'Monsters, maniacs, and Moore', dir. Norman Hull, ed. Kevin Lester and prod. David Naden, *England Their England* (Central Independent Television, 1987): www.youtube.com/watch?v=Ucba9NtF3cE.

Other primary sources

Ackroyd, Peter, *Hawksmoor* (London: Penguin, 1993).
'Another Whitechapel Murder', *The Times* (10 Nov. 1888).
Bissette, Steve, 'A monstrous talent: an interview with Steve Bissette', interview by Wellington Srbek: http://maisquadrinhos.blogspot.com/2008/05/when-i-think-about-which-comic-book.html.
——, 'Growing Up with Dinosaurs', interview by David Ehrlich, *International Journal of Comic Art*, 4:1 (Spring 2002), 97–133.
Brown, Isaac Baker, *On the curability of certain forms of insanity, epilepsy, catalepsy, and hysteria in females* (Hardwicke, 1866).
Burke, Edmund, *A Philosophical Enquiry into the Origin of Our Ideas of the Sublime and Beautiful*, new edn (London: J. Dodsley, 1787).
Byron, Glennis (ed.), Bram Stoker, *Dracula* (Peterborough, ON: Broadview, 1998).
Coleridge, Samuel Taylor, 'The Rime of the Ancient Mariner', in *Lyrical Ballads, with a few other poems* (London: J & A Arch, 1798).
Ellis, Warren and Marek Oleksicki, *Frankenstein's Womb* (Rantoul, IL: Avatar, 2009).
Forbes Winslow, L. (letter), *The Times* (12 Sept. 1888).
'The Fourth Whitechapel Murder', *Daily News* (10 Sept. 1888), p. 6.
Gibbons, Dave, 'Pebbles in a Landscape', interview by Bhob Stewart, *Comics Journal*, 116 (July 1987): 97–103 (p. 99).
Godwin, William, *Caleb Williams* (Oxford: Oxford University Press, 1998).
——, *An Enquiry Concerning Political Justice*, 2 vols (London: Robinson, 1793).
——, *Mandeville*, ed. Pamela Clemit (London: Pickering & Chatto, 1992).
——, *St Leon: A Tale of the Sixteenth Century*, ed. William Brewer (Peterborough, ON: Broadview, 2006).
Grant, Kenneth, *The Magical Revival* (London: Muller, 1972).
Gull, William, 'On a Cretinoid State Supervening in Adult Life in Women', *Transactions of the Clinical Society of London*, 7 (1873/74), pp. 180–5.
Henry, Lenny, 'Under the Settee with Len', from Alan Moore and Steve Parkhouse, *The Complete Bojeffries Saga* (Northampton, MA: Tundra Press), n.p.

Hoffmann, E.T.A., *Prinzessin Brambilla* (Stuttgart: Reclam, 1986).
'Horror Upon Horror. Whitechapel is Panic-Stricken at Another Fiendish Crime', *Star* (8 Sept. 1888).
Interview with Sir James Risdon Bennett (physician), *Evening News* (1 Oct. 1888).
Kames, Lord (Henry Home), *Elements of Criticism* (London: A. Millar, 1765).
Kaufman, Gerald, 'Michael Foot: Brilliant but wrong, wrong, wrong', *The Times* (4 Mar. 2010).
Keats, John, *The Letters of John Keats: A Selection*, ed. Robert Gittings (Oxford: Oxford University Press, 1970).
League of Extraordinary Gentlemen, dir. Stephen Norrington (20th Century Fox, 2003).
Le Fanu, Sheridan, 'Carmilla', in *In a Glass Darkly* (Oxford and New York: Oxford University Press, 2008), pp. 243–319.
Lovecraft, Howard Phillips, *Necronomicon: The Best Weird Tales of H.P. Lovecraft*, ed. Stephen Jones (London: Gollancz, 2008).
———, *Supernatural Horror in Literature* (Mineola, NY: Dover, 1973).
Maturin, Charles, *Melmoth the Wanderer*, ed. Douglas Grant (Oxford: Oxford University Press, 1998).
Melia, Don et al. (eds), *Strip Aids*, (London: Willyprods/Small Time Ink, 1987).
Mitchell, David M. (ed.), *Songs of the Black Würm Gism: Hymns to H.P. Lovecraft* (London: Creation Oneiros, 2009).
Morrison, Grant and Paul Grist, *St. Swithin's Day* (Leicester: Trident, 1990).
'The Murder in Whitechapel', *The Times* (10 Aug. 1888), p. 12.
O'Neill, Kevin, 'Kevin O'Neill reveals the secrets of the League of Extraordinary Gentlemen and Marshal Law', interview by Owen Vaughan, *TimesOnline*, 25 Feb. 2009: http://entertainment.timesonline.co.uk/tol/arts_and_entertainment/books/fiction/article5767132.ece.
Punch (15 Sept. 1888).
'The Reign of Terror in Whitechapel', *Evening News* (1 Oct. 1888).
Savage, G., 'Homicidal Mania', *Fortnightly Review*, 50 (1888), 448–63.
Shakespeare, William, *Macbeth*, ed. Kenneth Muir (London: Thomson Learning, 2003).
Shelley, Mary, *Frankenstein: The 1818 Text*, ed. Marilyn Butler (Oxford:

Oxford University Press, 1993).
Sinclair, Iain, *White Chappell, Scarlet Tracings* (London: Penguin, 2004 [1987]).
Sutherland, Henry (letter), *The Lancet* (22 Sept. 1888), 603.
Swamp Thing, dir. Wes Craven (USA: Swampfilms/Embassy Pictures, 1982).
Thatcher, Margaret, Speech to the Royal Society (27 Sept. 1988), *The Margaret Thatcher Foundation*: www.margaretthatcher.org/speeches/displaydocument.asp?docid=107346.
Totleben, John, 'John Totleben', interview with George Khoury, *Rough Stuff*, 1:4 (Spring 2007). 24–42.
Veitch, Rick and Alfredo Alcala, *Swamp Thing: Spontaneous Generation*, (New York: Vertigo, 2006); reprints issues 71–76 (Apr.–Sept. 1988).
Walpole, Horace, *The Castle of Otranto* (Oxford: Oxford University Press, 1996).
Wein, Len and Berni Wrightson, *Swamp Thing: Dark Genesis* (New York: DC Comics, 1991).
'What We Think', *Star* (10 Sept. 1888).
'The Whitechapel Horrors', *Evening News* (10 Sept. 1888).
'The Whitechapel Murder', *East London Advertiser* (8 Sept. 1888).
'The Whitechapel Murders', *The Lancet* (29 Sept. 1888), 637.
Winslow, L. Forbes (letter), *The Lancet* (22 Sept. 1888), 603.

Secondary sources

Adorno, Theodor, 'The Schema of Mass Culture', trans. Nicholas Walker, in *The Culture Industry*, ed. Jay M. Bernstein (London: Routledge, 2001), pp. 61–97.
Armitt, Lucie, 'The Magical Realism of the Contemporary Gothic', in *A Companion to the Gothic*, ed. David Punter (Oxford: Blackwell, 2000).
Auerbach, Nina, *Our Vampires, Ourselves* (Chicago, London: University of Chicago Press, 1995).
Bakhtin, Mikhail, *Rabelais and His World*, trans. Hélène Iswolsky (Bloomington: Indiana University Press, 1984).
Baldick, Chris, 'Introduction', in *The Oxford Book of Gothic Tales*, ed. Chris Baldick (Oxford: Oxford University Press, 1992), pp. xi–xxiii.
Bär, Gerald, *Das Motiv des Doppelgängers als Spaltungsphantasie in der Literatur und im deutschen Stummfilm* (Amsterdam: Rodopi, 2005).

Barker, Martin, *The Haunt of Fears: The Strange History of the British Horror Comics Campaign* (London: Pluto Press, 1984).

Barreda, Peter Patrick, 'Ouroboros: the Serpent in the Spirit', in *The Mandala Zone* (2004): www.mandalazone.com/essay-0407.html.

Bate, Jonathan, *The Song of the Earth* (London: Picador, 2000).

Baucom, Ian, *Out of Place: Englishness, Empire, and the Locations of Identity* (Princeton, NJ: Princeton University Press, 1999).

Beineke, Colin, '"Her Guardiner": Alan Moore's Swamp Thing as the Green Man', *ImageText: Interdisciplinary Comics Studies*, 5:4 (Spring 2011): www.english.ufl.edu/imagetext/archives/v5_4/beineke/.

Belsey, Catherine, 'Reading Cultural History', in *Reading the Past: Literature and History* ed. Tamsin Spargo (Basingstoke: Palgrave Macmillan, 2000), pp. 103–17.

Bennett, Tony and Janet Woollacott, *Bond and Beyond: The Political Career of a Popular Hero* (Basingstoke: Macmillan, 1987).

Bernard, Mark and James Bucky Carter, 'Alan Moore and the Graphic Novel: Confronting the Fourth Dimension', *ImageTexT: Interdisciplinary Comics Studies*, 1:2 (2004): www.english.ufl.edu/imagetext/archives/v1_2/carter.

Bloom, Harold, *Agon* (New York: Oxford University Press, 1982).

—, *A Map of Misreading*, 2nd edn (Oxford: Oxford University Press, 2003).

—, *The Anxiety of Influence* (Oxford: Oxford University Press, 1975).

Bookchin, Murray, 'The Concept of Social Ecology', in *The Ecology of Freedom: The Emergence and Dissolution of Hierarchy* (Oakland, CA: AK Press, 2005), pp. 80–108.

Botting, Fred, *Gothic* (London: Routledge, 1996).

—, 'In Gothic Darkly: Heterotopia, History, Culture', in *A Companion to the Gothic*, ed. David Punter (Oxford: Blackwell, 2000).

—, 'Preface: the Gothic', in *The Gothic*, ed. Botting (Cambridge: D.S. Brewer, 2001), pp. 1–7.

—, *Limits of Horror: Technology, Bodies, Gothic* (Manchester: Manchester University Press, 2008).

— and D. Townsend (eds), *The Gothic: Critical Concepts in Literary and Cultural Studies*, 4 vols (London: Routledge, 2004).

Brantlinger, Patrick, *Rule of Darkness: British Literature and Imperialism, 1830–1914* (Ithaca, NY: Cornell University Press, 1988).

Bresnick, Adam, 'Prosopoetic Compulsion: Reading the Uncanny in

Freud and Hoffmann', *Germanic Review*, 71:2 (1996), 117.
Brewster, Scott, 'Seeing Things: Gothic and the Madness of Interpretation', in *A Companion to the Gothic*, ed. David Punter (Oxford: Blackwell, 2000), pp. 281–92.
Brock, Marilyn, 'Introduction', in *Wollstonecraft to Stoker: Essays on Gothic and Victorian Sensation Fiction* (Jefferson, NC: McFarland, 2009).
Bruhm, Steven, *Gothic Bodies* (Philadelphia: University of Pennsylvania Press, 1994).
Buell, Lawrence, *The Environmental Imagination: Thoreau, Nature Writing and the Formation of American Culture* (Cambridge, MA: Harvard University Press, 1995).
——, *Writing for an Endangered World: Literature, Culture and the Environment in the United States and Beyond* (Cambridge, MA: Harvard University Press, 2001).
Butler, Judith, *Gender Trouble: Feminism and the Subversion of Identity* (London: Routledge, 1990).
——, *Bodies that Matter: On the Discursive Limits of 'Sex'* (London: Routledge, 1993).
——, *Frames of War* (London: Verso, 2009).
Campbell, Ramsey, 'Foreword', in Alan Moore, Stephen Bissette and John Totleben, *The Saga of Swamp Thing* (New York: DC Comics, 2009), pp. 9–11.
Canuel, Mark, *Religion, Toleration, and British Writing, 1790–1830* (Cambridge: Cambridge University Press, 2002).
Castricano, Jodey, *Cryptomimesis* (London: McGill-Queen's University Press, 2001).
Cavallaro, Dani, *The Gothic Vision: Three Centuries of Horror, Terror and Fear* (New York, London: Continuum, 2005).
Chard, Chloe, 'Introduction', in Ann Radcliffe, *The Romance of the Forest*, ed. Chloe Chard (Oxford: Oxford University Press, 1999).
Christakos, N.G., 'Annotations', in *Alan Moore's 'The Courtyard': A Companion*, ed. William Christensen (Urbana, IL: Avatar, 2004).
Christensen, William (ed.), *Alan Moore's 'The Courtyard': A Companion* (Urbana, IL: Avatar, 2004).
Clemit, Pamela, *The Godwinian Novel: The Rational Fictions of Godwin, Brockden Brown, Mary Shelley* (Oxford: Clarendon Press, 1993).
Collins, Jim, 'Batman: The Movie, Narrative: The Hyperconscious', in *The Many Lives of the Batman: Critical Approaches to a Superhero and his*

Media, ed. Roberta E. Pearson and William Uricchio (London: BFI Publishing, 1991), pp. 164–81 (p. 165).
Connor, Steven, *The English Novel in History – 1950–1995* (London: Routledge, 1996).
Coupe, Laurence (ed.), *The Green Studies Reader: from Romanticism to Ecocriticism* (London and New York: Routledge, 2000).
Coverley, Merlin, *Psychogeography* (Harpenden: Pocket Essentials, 2006).
Crowley, Aleister, *The Book of Thoth* (San Francisco, CA: Weiser Books, 1974).
Currie, Mark, *Postmodern Narrative Theory* (Basingstoke: Macmillan, 1998).
Davenport-Hines, Richard, *Gothic: Four Hundred Years of Excess, Horror, Evil and Ruin* (New York: North Point Press, 1998).
Day, William Patrick, *In the Circles of Fear and Desire: A Study of Gothic Fantasy* (Chicago: University of Chicago Press, 1985).
The DC Comics Encyclopaedia: The Definitive Guide to the Characters of the DC Universe, Scott Beatty and Robert Greenberger (New York: DK Publishing, 2004).
Deefholts, Susan L., 'Hazarding Chance: Reading Angela Carter's Wise Children', *Margin* (2003): www.angelfire.com/wa2/margin/nonficSLD3.html.
Deleuze, Gilles, *Cinema 2: The Time Image*, trans. Hugh Tomlinson and Robert Galeta (London: Athlone, 1989).
Deleuze, Gilles and Félix Guattari, *A Thousand Plateaus*, trans. Brian Massumi, *Capitalism and Schizophrenia* (London: Continuum, 2004).
Derrida, Jacques, 'Fors: The Anglish Words of Nicolas Abraham and Maria Torok', in N. Abraham and M. Torok, *The Wolf Man's Magic Word: A Cryptonymy* (Minneapolis: University of Minnesota Press, 1986), xi–xlviii.
——, *The Gift of Death*, trans. David Wills (London: University of Chicago Press, 1995).
——, *Of Grammatology*, trans. Gayatri Chakrovorty Spivak (London: Johns Hopkins University Press, 1997).
——, *Specters of Marx*, trans. Peggy Kamuf (London: Routledge, 1994).
Dijkstra, Bram, *Idols of Perversity: Fantasies of Feminine Evil in Fin-de-Siècle Culture* (New York and Oxford: Oxford University Press, 1986).
Di Liddo, Annalisa, *Alan Moore: Comics as Performance, Fiction as Scalpel* (Jackson: University Press of Mississippi, 2009).

Dryden, Lynda, *The Modern Gothic and Literary Doubles: Stevenson, Wilde and Wells* (Basingstoke: Palgrave Macmillan, 2003).

Dubord, Guy, *Society of the Spectacle* (New York: Zone Books, 1999).

Duncan, Randy and Matthew J. Smith, *The Power of Comics: History, Form and Culture* (New York: Continuum, 2009).

Durozoi, Gérard, *History of the Surrealist Movement* (Chicago: University of Chicago Press, 2002).

Eco, Umberto, 'The Myth of the Superman', in *The Role of the Reader: Explorations in the Semiotics of Texts* (London: Hutchinson, 1979) pp. 107–24.

Ellis, Markman, *The History of Gothic Fiction* (Edinburgh: Edinburgh University Press, 2000).

Fay, Elizabeth A., *A Feminist Introduction to Romanticism* (Malden, MA: Blackwell, 1998).

Foucault, Michel, *Madness and Civilisation*, trans. Richard Howard (London: Routledge, 2007 [1959]).

——, 'Of Other Spaces', trans. Jay Miskowiev, *Diacritics*, 16:1 (Spring 1986), 22–7.

Frank, Frederick S., 'Glossary', in Horace Walpole, *The Castle of Otranto and the Mysterious Mother* (Peterborough, ON: Broadview Press, 2003), pp. 341–50.

Freud, Sigmund, 'The Uncanny', in *The Uncanny*, trans. David McLintock (London: Penguin, 2003), pp. 121–62.

Gentile, Kathy Justice, 'Sublime Drag: Supernatural Masculinity in Gothic Fiction', *Gothic Studies*, 11 (May 2009), 16–31.

Gilbert, David and Rebecca Preston, '"Stop being so English": Suburban Modernity and National Identity in the Twentieth Century', in *Geographies of British Modernity*, ed. David Matless and Brian Short (Oxford: Blackwell, 2003), pp. 187–203.

Gilroy, Paul, *After Empire: Melancholia or Convivial Culture* (Abingdon: Routledge, 2004).

Goddu, Teresa A., 'American Gothic', in *The Routledge Companion to the Gothic*, ed. Catherine Spooner and Emma McEvoy (London: Routledge, 2007), pp. 63–72.

'Godwin, William (1756–1836)', Mark Philp, *Oxford Dictionary of National Biography*, ed. H. C. G. Matthew and Brian Harrison: http://0www.oxforddnb.com.catalogue.ulrls.lon.ac.uk/view/article/10898.

Goffman, Erving, *Asylums: Essays on the Social Situation of Mental Patients and Other Inmates* (Harmondsworth: Penguin, 1973).

Gravett, Paul, *Graphic Novels: Stories to Change Your Life* (London: Aurum, 2005).

—— and Peter Stanbury, *Great British Comics: Celebrating a Century of Ripping Yarns and Wizard Wheezes* (London: Aurum, 2006).

Green, Matthew J.A., '"She Brings Apocalypse": Sex, Imagination and Redemptive Transgression in William Blake and the Graphic Novels of Alan Moore', *Literature Compass*, 8:10 (2011): 739–56.

——, '"The end of the world. That's a bad thing right?": Form and Function from William Blake to Alan Moore', in *Blake 2.0: William Blake in Twentieth-Century Art, Music and Culture*, ed. Steve Clark, Tristanne Connolly and Jason Whittaker (Basingstoke: Palgrave Macmillan, 2012), pp. 175–86.

Groensteen, Thierry, *The System of Comics*, trans. Bart Beaty and Nick Nguyen (Jackson: University Press of Mississippi, 2007).

Gross, Louis, 'Redefining the American Gothic: From *Wieland* to *Day of the Dead* (1989)' (Ann Arbor: UMI Research Press, 1989).

Halberstam, Judith, *Skin Shows: Gothic Horror and the Technology of Monsters* (Durham, NC: Duke University Press, 1995).

Hall, Stuart, 'Culture, Community, Nation,' *Cultural Studies*, 7:3 (1993), 349–63 (p. 356).

——, 'The Great Moving Right Show', in *The Politics of Thatcherism*, ed. Stuart Hall and Martin Jacques (London: Lawrence & Wishart, 1983), pp. 19–39.

——and Martin Jacques, 'Introduction', in *New Times: The Changing Face of Politics in the 1990s*, ed. Stuart Hall and Martin Jacques (London: Lawrence & Wishart, 1989), pp. 11–22.

Hamilton, Paul, 'Coleridge and Godwin in the 1790s', in *The Coleridge Connection: Essays for Thomas MacFarland*, ed. Richard Gravil and Molly Lefebure (New York: St. Martin's Press, 1990), pp. 41–59.

Hatfield, Charles, *Alternative Comics: An Emerging Literature* (Jackson: University Press of Mississippi, 2005).

Hobsbawm, Eric, *The Age of Extremes: The Short Twentieth Century 1914–1989* (London: Abacus, 1994).

Hoeveler, Diane Long, *Gothic Feminism: The Professionalization of Gender from Charlotte Smith to the Brontës* (University Park: Pennsylvania State University Press, 1998).

Hogle, Jerrold E., 'Frankenstein as Neo-Gothic: From the Ghost of the Counterfeit to the Monster of Abjection', in *Romanticism, History and the Possibilities of Genre*, ed. Tilottama Rajan and Julia M. Wright (Cambridge: Cambridge University Press, 1998), pp. 176–210.

——, 'Introduction: The Gothic in Western Culture', in *The Cambridge Companion to Gothic Fiction*, ed. Jerrold E. Hogle (Cambridge: Cambridge University Press, 2002), pp. 1–20.

——, '"Christabel" as Gothic: The Abjection of Instability', *Gothic Studies*, 7:1 (May 2005): 18–28.

Holland, Norman and Leona Sherman, 'Gothic Possibilities', in *Gender and Reading: Essays on Readers, Texts, and Contexts*, ed. Elizabeth A. Flynn and Patrocinio P. Schweickart (Baltimore: Johns Hopkins University Press, 1986).

Horkheimer, Max, 'The Revolt of Nature', in *Green History: a Reader in Environmental Literature, Philosophy and Politics*, ed. Derek Wall (London: Routledge, 1994), pp. 235–7.

Horner, Avril and Sue Zlosnik, *Gothic and the Comic Turn* (Basingstoke: Palgrave Macmillan, 2005).

Howard, Jacqueline, *Reading Gothic Fiction: A Bakhtinian Approach* (Oxford: Clarendon Press, 1994).

Howells, Coral Ann, *Love, Mystery, and Misery: Feeling in Gothic Fiction* (London: Athlone, 1978).

Hurley, Kelly, *The Gothic Body: Sexuality, Materialism, and Denigration at the Fin de Siècle* (Cambridge: Cambridge University Press, 1996).

Hutcheon, Linda, *A Theory of Adaptation* (New York, London: Routledge, 2006).

Jackson, Rosemary, *Fantasy: The Literature of Subversion* (London: Routledge, 1981).

Jensen, Jeff, 'Watchmen: An Oral History', *Entertainment Weekly: EW.com* (21 Oct. 2005): www.ew.com/ew/article/0,,1120854_1,00.html (accessed 10 July 2010).

Johnson, Dan, 'Wein and Wrightson: The Roots of Swamp Thing', *Back Issue*, 1:6 (Oct. 2004), 3–14.

——, 'Bissette and Veitch: Old Monster, New Tricks', *Back Issue*, 1:6 (Oct. 2004), 48–66.

Johnston, Antony, 'Alan Moore: Voice of the Fire', *Spike Magazine* (2008): www.spikemagazine.com/0399voiceofthefire.php (accessed 27 Apr. 2010).

Joshi, Sunand T., *A Subtler Magick: The Writings and Philosophy of H.P. Lovecraft* (Berkeley Heights, NJ: Wildside, 1999).

——, and David E. Schulz, *An H.P. Lovecraft Encyclopedia* (Westport, CT: Greenwood, 2011).

Kannenberg, Gene, Jr, *500 Essential Graphic Novels* (New York: Collins Design, 2008).

Kastbjerg, Kristine, 'Dressed up in the body of an old woman': Gothic conventions in Ingemann, Andersen, Blixen and Hoeg', *Scandinavian–Canadian Studies*, 18 (2009), pp. 24–42.

Kawa, Abraham, 'What if the Apocalypse Never Happens?: Evolutionary Narratives in Contemporary Comics', in *Comics & Culture: Analytical and Theoretical Approaches to Comics*, ed. Anne Magnussen and Hans-Christian Christiansen (Copenhagen: Museum Tusculanum Press, 2000), pp. 209–24.

Keeping, J., 'Superheroes and Supermen: Finding Nietzsche's Übermensch in *Watchmen*', in *Watchmen and Philosophy: A Rorschach Test*, ed. Mark D. White (Hoboken, NJ: Wiley, 2009), pp. 47–60.

Keller, James R., *V for Vendetta: A Critical Study of the Graphic Novel and Film* (Jefferson, NC: McFarland, 2008).

Kelly, Gary, 'Politicizing the Personal: Mary Wollstonecraft, Mary Shelley and the Coterie Novel,' in *Mary Shelley In Her Times*, ed. Betty T. Bennett and Stuart Curran (London: Johns Hopkins University Press, 2000), pp. 147–69.

Kerridge, Richard, 'Ecothrillers: Environmental Cliffhangers', in *The Green Studies Reader: From Romanticism to Ecocriticism*, ed. Laurence Coupe (London: Routledge, 2000) pp. 242–9.

Kilgour, Maggie, *The Rise of the Gothic Novel* (London: Routledge, 1995).

Kline, Benjamin, *First Along the River, A Brief History of the US Environmental Movement* (USA: Rowman & Littlefield, 2007).

Klock, Geoff, *How to Read Superhero Comics and Why* (New York: Continuum, 2002).

Kortsch, Christine Bayles, *Dress Culture in Late Victorian Women's Fiction: Literacy, Textiles, and Activism* (Farnham: Ashgate, 2009).

Kristeva, Julia, *Powers of Horror: an Essay on Abjection*, trans. Leon S. Roudiez (Chichester and New York: Columbia University Press, 1982).

Kukkonen, Karin, *Neue Perspektiven auf die Superhelden: Polyphonie in Alan Moores 'Watchmen'* (Marburg: Tectum, 2008).

Kumar, Krishnan, *The Making of English National Identity* (Cambridge: Cambridge University Press, 2003).
Kupperberg, Paul, 'The Time Has Come!', in *Superman: Whatever Happened to the Man of Tomorrow*, deluxe edn (New York: DC Comics, 2009), pp. 6–9.
Laclau, Ernesto and Chantal Mouffe, *Hegemony and Socialist Strategy*, 2nd edn (London: Verso, 2001).
Ledger, Sally, *The New Woman: Fiction and Feminism at the Fin de Siècle* (Manchester: Manchester University Press, 1997).
Levy, Ellen, 'The Philosophical Gothic of St Leon,' *Caliban*, 33 (1996), 51–62.
Lewis, Jeffrey, 'The Dual Nature of Apocalypse in *Watchmen*', in *The Graphic Novel*, ed. Jan Baetens (Leuven: Leuven University Press, 2001), pp. 139–43.
Leys, Colin, *Politics in Britain: From Labourism to Thatcherism*, rev. edn (London: Verso, 1989).
Little, Ben, '*2000AD* – Understanding the "British Invasion" of American Comics', in *Comics as a Nexus of Cultures: Essays on the Interplay of Media, Disciplines and International Perspectives*, ed. Mark Berninger, Gideon Haberkorn and Jochen Ecke (Jefferson: McFarland, 2010), pp. 140–52.
Lovelock, James, *Gaia: A New Look at Life on Earth* (Oxford: Oxford University Press, 1979).
Luckhurst, Roger, *Science Fiction* (Cambridge: Polity Press, 2005).
Luke, Timothy W., *Ecocritique, Contesting the Politics of Nature, Economy and Culture* (Minneapolis: University of Minnesota Press, 1997).
Malpas, S. and P. Wake (eds), *The Routledge Companion to Critical Theory* (London and New York: Routledge, 2006).
Matthews, J.H., *Surrealism and Film* (Ann Arbor: University of Michigan Press, 1971).
Mattozzi, Alvise, 'Innovating Superheroes', *Reconstruction*, 3:2 (Spring 2003): http://reconstruction.eserver.org/032/mottazzi.htm.
McCall, Jessica, 'V for Vendetta: A Graphic Retelling of Macbeth', *Popular Culture Review*, 20:1 (Winter 2009), 45–60.
McCloud, Scott, *Understanding Comics: The Invisible Art* (New York: HarperPerennial, 1994).
McCormick, John, *British Politics and the Environment* (London: Earthscan, 1991).

McCue, Greg S. with Clive Bloom, *Dark Knights: The New Comics in Context* (London: Pluto Press, 1993).
McFarland, Thomas, *Coleridge and the Pantheist Tradition* (Oxford: Oxford University Press, 1969).
McGrath, Patrick and Bradford Morrow (eds), *The Picador Book of the New Gothic* (London: Picador, 1993).
McInnis, David, 'Mind-Travelling, Ideal Presence and the Imagination in Early Modern England', *Early Modern Literary Studies*, 19:7 (2009), 1–23.
Miall, Duncan S., 'Gothic Fiction', in *A Companion to Romanticism*, ed. Duncan Wu (Oxford: Blackwell, 1999), pp. 345–54.
Mighall, Robert, *A Geography of Victorian Fiction: Mapping History's Nightmares* (Oxford: Oxford University Press, 2003).
——, 'Gothic Cities', in *The Routledge Companion to the Gothic*, ed. Catherine Spooner and Emma McEvoy (London: Routledge, 2007), pp. 54–62.
Miles, Robert, 'Europhobia: The Catholic Other in Horace Walpole and Charles Maturin', in *European Gothic: A Spirited Exchange 1760–1960*, ed. Avril Horner (Manchester: Manchester University Press, 2002), pp. 84–103.
——, 'Gothic Romance as Visual Technology', *Gothic Technologies* (Dec. 2005): www.rc.umd.edu/praxis/gothic/intro/miles.html.
——, *Gothic Writing, 1750–1820: A Genealogy* (Manchester: Manchester University Press, 2002).
Millidge, Gary Spencer, *Alan Moore: Storyteller* (Lewes: ILEX, 2011).
Mills, Brett, *Television Sitcom* (London: BFI, 2005).
Mills, Jonathan, 'V for Verbal Violence' (7 May 2001): www.ninthart.org/display.php?article=5.
Minot, L.A. and W.S. Minot, '*Frankenstein* and *Christabel*: Intertextuality, Biography, and Gothic Ambiguity', *European Romantic Review*, 15:1 (2004), 23–49.
Mishra, Vijay, *The Gothic Sublime* (New York: State University of New York Press, 1994).
Monleón, José B., *A Specter is Haunting Europe: A Socio-Historical Approach to the Fantastic* (Princeton NJ: Princeton University Press, 1990).
Moretti, Franco, *Signs Taken for Wonders: On the Sociology of Literary Forms*, trans. Susan Fischer, David Forgacs and David Miller (London: Verso, 1988).

Morgan, Harry, 'Graphic Shorthand: From Caricature to Narratology in Twentieth-Century *Bande Dessinée* and Comics', *European Comic Art*, 2.1 (2009), 21–39.

Morgan, Jack, *The Biology of Horror: Gothic Literature and Film* (Carbondale: Southern Illinois University Press, 2002).

Morgan, Michele, *Simple Wicca* (Newburyport, MA: Conari, 2000).

Morrison, Grant, *Supergods* (London: Jonathan Cape, 2011).

Mota, Pedro, 'Alan on the Other Side of the Mirror', in *Alan Moore: Portrait of an Extraordinary Gentleman*, ed. Gary Spencer Millidge and Smoky Man (Leigh-on-Sea: Abiogenesis, 2003), p. 34.

Mouffe, Chantal, *The Democratic Paradox* (London: Verso, 2005).

Myers, Victoria, 'William Godwin and the Ars Rhetorica,' *Studies in Romanticism*, 44:3 (2002), 415–44.

Myrone, Martin, 'Superheroes', in *Gothic Nightmares: Fuseli, Blake and the Romantic Imagination* (London: Tate Publishing, 2006), pp. 73–99.

Naess, Arne, *Ecology, Community and Lifestyle: Outline of an Ecosophy*, ed. and trans. David Rothenberg, 8th edn (Cambridge: Cambridge University Press, 2001).

Nevins, Jess, *A Blazing World: The Unofficial Companion to* The League of Extraordinary Gentlemen Volume Two (Austin, TX: MonkeyBrain, 2004).

——, *Heroes & Monsters: The Unofficial Companion to* The League of Extraordinary Gentlemen (London: Titan, 2003).

——, *Impossible Territories: An Unofficial Companion to* The League of Extraordinary Gentlemen: The Black Dossier (Austin, TX: MonkeyBrain, 2008).

Nyberg, Amy Kiste, *Seal of Approval: The History of the Comics Code* (Jackson; University of Mississippi Press, 1998).

Oakes, David, *Science and Destabilization in the Modern American Gothic: Lovecraft, Matheson, and King* (London: Greenwood, 2000).

Oldridge, Darren, 'Casting the Spell of Terror: The Press and the Early Whitechapel Murders', in *Jack The Ripper: Media, Culture, History*, ed. Alexandra Warwick and Martin Willis (Manchester: Manchester University Press, 2007), pp. 46–55.

Paglia, Camille, *Sexual Personae: Art and Decadence from Nefertiti to Emily Dickinson* (New York: Vintage, 1991).

Paik, Peter Y., *From Utopia to Apocalypse: Science Fiction and the Politics of Catastrophe* (Minneapolis: University of Minnesota Press, 2010).

Parkin, Lance, *Alan Moore* (Harpenden: Pocket Essentials, 2001).
Paul, Jean, *Siebenkäs* (Berlin: Insel, 1987).
Paulson, Ronald, 'Gothic Fiction and the French Revolution', *English Literary History*, 48:3 (1981), 532–54.
Pirie, David, *A Heritage of Horror: The English Gothic Cinema 1946–1972* (London: Gordon Fraser, 1973).
Pite, Ralph, *The Circle of our Vision: Dante's Presence in English Romantic Poetry* (Oxford: Clarendon Press, 1994).
Poovey, Mary, 'Ideology and the *Mysteries of Udolpho*', in *Gothic: Critical Concepts in Literary and Cultural Studies*, ed. Fred Botting and Dale Townsend, 2 vols (London and New York: Routledge, 2004), II, pp. 116–36.
Porter, Roy, *Madmen: A Social History of Madhouses, Mad-Doctors and Lunatics* (Stroud: Tempus, 2004).
Price, Robert M., 'Lovecraft's "Artificial Mythology"', in *An Epicure in the Terrible*, ed. David E. Schultz and S. T. Joshi (London: Associated University Press, 1991), pp. 247–56.
Punter, David (ed.), *A Companion to the Gothic* (Oxford and Malden, MA: Blackwell, 2000).
——, 'The Ghost of a History', in *A Companion to the Gothic*, pp. viii–xiv.
——, *Gothic Pathologies: The Text, the Body and the Law* (Basingstoke: Macmillan, 1998).
——, 'Introduction: Of Apparitions', in *Spectral Readings: Towards a Gothic Geography*, ed. Glennis Byron and David Punter (Basingstoke: Macmillan, 1999), pp. 1–8.
——, *The Literature of Terror: A History of Gothic Fictions from 1765 to the Present Day*, 2nd edn, 2 vols (London: Longman, 1996).
—— and Glennis Byron, *The Gothic* (Oxford: Blackwell, 2004).
Pykett, Lynn, *The 'Improper' Feminine: The Women's Sensation Novel and the New Woman Writing* (London: Routledge, 1992).
Quiring, Björn, '"A fiction that we must inhabit" – Sense Production in Urban Spaces According to Alan Moore and Eddie Campbell's *From Hell*', in *Comics and the City: Urban Space in Print, Picture and Sequence*, ed. Jörn Ahrens and Arno Meteling (London: Continuum, 2010), pp. 199–213.
Richardson, Angelique and Chris Willis (eds), *The New Woman in Fiction and in Fact: Fin-de-Siècle Feminisms* (Basingstoke: Palgrave Macmillan, 2001).
Roberts, Marie, *Gothic Immortals: The Fiction of the Brotherhood of the Rosy Cross* (London: Routledge, 1990).

Rosen, Elizabeth K., *Apocalyptic Transformations: Apocalypse and the Post-Modern Imagination* (Lanham, MD: Lexington Books, 2008).

Round, Julia, '"Be vewy vewy quiet: we're hunting Wippers." A Barthesian analysis of the construction of fact and fiction in Alan Moore and Eddie Campbell's *From Hell*', in D. Hassler-Forest and J. Goggin, eds, *The Rise and Reason of Comics and Graphic Literature: Critical Essays on the Form* (Jefferson, CA: McFarland, 2010), 188–201.

———, 'Cryptomimetic Tropes in Yoshinori Natsume's Batman: Death Mask', *Foundation*, 37:106 (Summer 2009): 41–52.

———, 'Fragmented Identity: The Superhero Condition', *International Journal of Comic Art*, 7:2 (2005), 358–69.

———, 'Gothic and the Graphic Novel', in *A New Companion to the Gothic*, ed. David Punter (London: Blackwell, 2012), pp. 335–49.

———, 'London's Calling: Alternate Worlds and the City as Superhero in Contemporary British-American Comics', in J. Lent (ed.) *International Journal of Comic Art*, 10:1 (Spring 2008), 24–31.

Royle, Nicholas, *The Uncanny* (Manchester: Manchester University Press, 2003).

Sabin, Roger, *Adult Comics: An Introduction* (London: Routledge, 1993).

———, *Comic, Comix and Graphic Novels: A History of Comic Art* (London: Phaidon, 1996).

Sadleir, Michael, *The Northanger Novels* (Oxford: Oxford University Press, 1927).

Sale, Kirkpatrick, *The Green Revolution, The American Environmental Movement 1962–1992* (New York: Hill & Wang, 1993).

Sanders, Julie, *Adaptation and Appropriation* (London, New York: Routledge, 2006).

Santala, Ismo, 'Voice of the Fire', *The Modern Word* (2004): www.themodernword.com/reviews/moore_fire.html.

Savage, G., 'Homicidal Mania', *Fortnightly Review*, 50 (1888), 448–63.

Scholem, Gershom, *On the Kabbalah and its Symbolism*, trans. Ralph Manheim (New York: Schocken Books, 1969).

———, *Major Trends in Jewish Mysticism*, 3rd edn revised (New York: Schocken Books, 1995).

Schulz, Andrew, *Goya's Caprichos: Aesthetics, Perception and the Body* (Cambridge and New York: Cambridge University Press, 2005).

Schüwer, Martin, *Wie Comics erzählen: Grundriss einer intermedialen*

Erzähltheorie der grafischen Literatur (Trier: WVT, 2008).
Scott, Rebecca, 'Alan Moore, *Voice of the Fire* (Top Shelf, 2003)', *Green Man Review* (2003): www.greenmanreview.com/book/book_moore_voiceofthefire.html.
Shildrick, Margrit, *Embodying the Monster* (London: Sage, 2002).
Showalter, Elaine, *The Female Malady: Women, Madness and English Culture, 1830–1880* (London: Virago, 1991).
——— (ed.), *Daughters of Decadence: Women Writers of the Fin de Siècle* (London: Virago, 1993).
Simmel, Georg, 'The Metropolis and Mental Life', in *Simmell On Culture*, ed. David Frisby and Michael Featherstone (London: Sage, 1997), pp. 174–85.
Singer, Marc, "Unwrapping the Birth Caul", in *Alan Moore: Portrait of an Extraordinary Gentleman*, ed. Gary Spencer Millidge and Smokey Man (Leigh-on-Sea: Abiogenesis Press, 2003), pp. 41–6.
Smith, Andrew, *Gothic Literature* (Edinburgh: Edinburgh University Press, 2007).
———, *Gothic Radicalism* (Basingstoke: Palgrave Macmillan, 2000).
———, *Victorian Demons: Medicine, Masculinity and the Gothic at the Fin-de-Siècle* (Manchester: Manchester University Press, 2004).
———, William Hughes and Diane Mason (eds), *Fictions of Unease: The Gothic from Otranto to The X-Files* (Bath: Sulis Press, 2002).
Smith, Andy W., 'Gothic and the Graphic Novel', in *The Routledge Companion to Gothic*, ed. Catherine Spooner and Emma McEvoy (London: Routledge, 2007), pp. 251–9.
Smith, A.L., 'Postmodernism/Gothicism', in *Modern Gothic: A Reader*, ed. V. Sage and A.L. Smith (Manchester: Manchester University Press, 1996).
Smith, Don, *H.P. Lovecraft in Popular Culture: The Works and their Adaptations in Film, Television, Comics, Music and Games* (Jefferson, NC: McFarland, 2006).
Smith, Murray, 'Flatulent Conceptions: "The Young Ones," Inoculation, and Emesis', in *Television Studies: Textual Analysis*, ed. Gary Burns and Robert J. Thompson (London: Praeger, 1989), pp. 57–78.
Spicer, Andrew, 'Occasional Eccentricity: The Strange Course of Surrealism in British Cinema', in *The Unsilvered Screen: Surrealism on Film*, ed. Graeme Harper and Rob Stone (London: Wallflower Press, 2007), pp. 102–14.

Spooner, Catherine, *Contemporary Gothic* (London: Reaktion, 2006).
Spooner, Catherine and Emma McEvoy (eds), *The Routledge Companion to the Gothic* (London: Routledge, 2007).
Stein, Atara, *The Byronic Hero in Film, Fiction, and Television* (Carbondale: Southern Illinois University Press, 2004).
Stein, Daniel and Frank Kelleter, 'Great, Mad, New: Populärkultur, serielle Ästhetik und der frühe amerikanische Zeitungscomics', in *Comics: Zur Geschichte und Theorie eines populärkulturellen Mediums*, ed. Stephan Ditschke, Katerina Kroucheva and Daniel Stein (Bielefeld: Transcript, 2009), pp. 81–118.
Taylor, Stan, *The National Front in English Politics* (London: Macmillan, 1982).
Teiwes, Jack, 'A Man of Steel (by any other name): Adaptation and Continuity in Alan Moore's "Superman"', *ImageText* 4.55 (2011), 17: www.english.ufl.edu/imagetext/archives/v5_4/teiwes/.
Thompson, Richard Lowe, *The History of the Devil, the horned god of the West* (London: Kegan Paul, Trench, Trubner & Co., 1929).
Thomson, Iain, 'Deconstructing the Hero', in *Comics as Philosophy*, ed. Jeff McLaughlin (Jackson: University Press of Mississippi, 2005), pp. 100–29.
Todorov, Tzvetan, *The Fantastic: A Structural Approach to a Literary Genre*, trans. Richard Howard (Ithaca, NY: Cornell University Press, 1973).
Turner, Victor, *The Ritual Process: Structure and Anti-Structure* (New York: Aldine de Gruyter, 1997).
van Gennep, Arnold, *The Rites of Passage*, trans. Monika B. Vizedom and Gabrielle L. Caffee (Chicago: Chicago University Press, 1960).
Vardoulakis, Dimitris, 'The Return of Negation: the Doppelgänger in Freud's "The Uncanny"', *Substance*, *110* (2006), 100–16.
Veeder, William, 'The Nurture of the Gothic, or How Can a Text Be Both Popular and Subversive'?, in *American Gothic: New Interventions in a National Narrative*, ed. Robert K. Martin and Eric Savoy (Iowa City: University of Iowa Press, 1998).
Walkowitz, Judith R., 'Jack the Ripper and the Myth of Male Violence', *Feminist Studies*, 8:3 (Autumn 1982), pp. 543–74.
Walsh, Neil, 'Voice of the Fire', *SF Site* (2004): www.sfsite.com/12b/vf190.htm.
Warner, Marina, *Phantasmagoria* (Oxford: Oxford University Press, 2006).

Warwick, Alexandra, 'Blood and Ink: Narrating the Whitechapel Murders', in *Jack The Ripper: Media, Culture, History*, ed. Alexandra Warwick and Martin Willis (Manchester: Manchester University Press, 2007), pp. 71–87.

Warwick, Alexandra and Martin Willis (eds), *Jack The Ripper: Media, Culture, History* (Manchester: Manchester University Press, 2007).

Watt, James, *Contesting the Gothic: Fiction, Genre and Cultural Conflict 1764–1832* (Cambridge: Cambridge University Press, 1999).

Webber, Andrew J., *The Doppelgänger: Double Visions in German Literature* (Oxford: Clarendon Press, 1996).

Wertham, Frederick, *Seduction of the Innocent* (New York: Rhinehart, 1953).

Wheatley, Helen, *Gothic Television* (Manchester: Manchester University Press, 2006).

Whitson, Roger, 'Panelling Parallax: The Fearful Symmetry of Alan Moore and William Blake', *ImageTexT: Interdisciplinary Comics Studies*, 3:2 (2007): www.english.ufl.edu/imagetext/archives/v3_2/whitson/.

Whittaker, Jason, 'From Hell: Blake and Evil in Popular Culture', in *Blake, Modernity and Popular Culture*, ed. Jason Whitaker and Steve Clark (Basingstoke: Palgrave Macmillan, 2007), pp. 192–204.

Williams, Raymond, *Marxism and Literature* (Oxford: Oxford University Press, 1977).

Wilmut, Roger and Peter Rosengard, *Didn't You Kill My Mother-in-Law? The Story of Alternative Comedy in Britain from The Comedy Store to Saturday Live* (London: Methuen, 1989).

Wolk, Douglas, *Reading Comics: How Graphic Novels Work and What They Mean* (Cambridge, MA: Da Capo Press, 2007).

Wright, Angela, *Gothic Fiction: A Reader's Guide to Essential Criticism* (Basingstoke: Palgrave Macmillan, 2007).

Index

2000AD 34

AARGH! [Artists Against Rampant Government Homophobia] 99n
Abberline, Frederick 145, 150–1
abhuman, the 30, 37, 240
abject, the 4–5, 7–17, 27, 33, 59, 66, 73, 88, 104–5, 161, 167, 235, 239–41, 252n, 269
Ackroyd, Peter
  Hawksmoor 140, 152, 156n, 222
adaptation 14–17, 160–1, 165, 170, 174–5, 195–6, 199, 204–9, 210n, 211n, 247, 253–72
Adaptation Studies 195
Addams Family, The 22, 29–30
Aklo 265–6, 269
Alcala, Alfredo 60n, 136–9n
Alfgiva 237, 240, 244
alien 30, 87, 113, 126, 150, 163, 221, 261, 263
alienation 11, 34, 43, 73, 86, 123, 134, 136, 154, 180, 186, 192, 215, 220, 224, 231
alienation effects 43
Alighieri, Dante 124–5, 131, 137, 229
  Inferno, The 124–5
alter ego 10–11, 162, 171, 220
  see also doppelgänger
alterity 30, 218, 239, 262, 269
  see also otherness
Anarchism 3, 10, 37, 46, 111, 114, 150–1, 181, 184–5, 188–9
apocalypse 254
  environmental 42–3
  nuclear 89, 93–5
Apollonian, the 142, 167
Arcane, Gregori 71–2, 110, 124–7
Arkham Asylum 129, 217
arthrology 92, 93, 101n
authoritarianism 33, 55
autonomy 13, 27, 45, 88, 91, 156, 189–90, 197–200, 205–6, 208–9

Bakhtin, Mikhail 70, 111, 117n
Bangs, Sophie 65
Batman 7, 12–13, 51, 65, 99, 103, 116n, 162–8, 172, 177n
becoming 5, 12, 115, 181, 198
Bedlam 142, 147
Benjamin, Walter 80

Bissette, Stephen 18n, 43–51, 57–60, 61–2n, 72–3, 75, 83n, 123, 128, 133, 135, 136–9n
Bizarro 173–4
Black Mercy 162–3, 165–6, 170–5, 177n
Blake, Edward 182–3, 189
Blake, William 16, 18n, 85, 101n, 124, 137n, 233n, 272, 275n
Blazing World 160
blood 54, 67, 88, 110, 129, 136, 144, 173, 187, 198, 207–8, 224–5, 227, 239–40
Bloom, Harold 258, 274n
Body, the 8, 72, 74, 86–8, 129–30, 144, 148, 153, 164, 177n, 217, 220–1, 236–7
Bojeffries, Ginda 22–3, 30, 38
Bojeffries, Jobremus 22–3, 30
Bojeffries, Reth 22, 30, 38
Bolland, Brian 19n
Bond, Campion 200, 202
Bradbury, Ray 103, 115
Brears, Merril 267–9
Brecht, Bertolt 43, 59
Brecon Beacons, 263
bricolage 15–16, 199, 211n, 254, 269, 272n
Bronte, Emily
  Wuthering Heights 170–1
Brujería 126–8
Burke, Edmund 87, 100n, 244–5n, 251n
Burrows, Jacen 256, 267–71, 273n, 275n
Butler, Judith 8–9, 12, 18n, 19, 170–1, 177
Byron, Lord George Gordon 90

Cable, Abigail 6–7, 122–9, 133–4, 137–8n
Cable, Matt 134
Campbell, Eddie 76–80, 83, 100, 156–7n, 176n, 215, 222–4, 227–30, 233–4n, 273–4n
Campbell, Ramsey 123, 137n
cannibalism 126
canon 3, 49, 88, 122, 148, 159
  see also Gothic; literary
capitalism 55
Carcosa, Johnny 265, 269
carnivalesque, the 111
Carter, Angela 244–5
Carter, Randolph 5
Catholic Church 107, 113
Catholicism 27, 113
censorship 55, 196
Cernunnos 248

Index

Chapman, Annie 83, 141, 143, 150
Chick, Uncle 237
childbirth 11–12, 148, 167, 224, 227–8, 231, 235, 242, 265
Clare, John 131, 237, 244, 248, 251
climate change 42, 47, 130
Clinton, President William Jefferson 265
Cold War, the 89, 91, 97
Coleridge, Samuel Taylor 124–5, 131, 137n, 183, 187–8
  Rime of the Ancient Mariner, The 187–8
Comedian, the *see* Blake, Edward
comedy 27–8, 30, 125
  alternative comedy 36–8
  classical / literary 21, 113
  situation comedy 21, 29–30
Comics Code Authority 11–12, 29, 196
Conservative Party (UK), The 33–4, 39
Constantine, John 126–8, 130, 135
coterie 180–2, 185–93
Coulthart, John 256, 274
counter-Gothic 180
Craven, Wes 44, 60
crime 7, 54, 103–4, 108–9, 129, 130, 140–5, 150–1, 165, 186–7, 221, 255
Cromwell, Oliver 228–30
Crowley, Aleister 227, 258, 274
cryptomimesis 8, 236, 240, 245–6
Cthulhu mythos 255, 257

Dacre, Charlotte 196
Danielewski, Mark Z. 245
Dante *see* Alighieri, Dante
darkness 13, 54, 76, 79, 110, 151, 154, 165, 255
daughter 12, 22, 67, 137n, 162, 166, 184, 265
Deadman 124
death 13–15, 65, 89, 94–6, 106, 108, 110, 115, 134, 141, 148–9, 153–4, 162–3, 166, 182, 186–7, 191, 197, 203, 220, 227, 230, 236, 238–42, 264
deconstruction 8, 10
Dee, John 238
degeneracy 149, 197
demon 14, 15, 27, 119n, 124–5, 133–4, 142, 218, 222, 248
demonology 133–4
Dent, Harvey 129
Derleth, August 244
Derrida, Jacques 15–16, 19, 211, 246
desire 10–11, 13, 67, 70, 74, 113, 154, 161–3, 166–73, 182, 186, 197–8, 200, 203–4, 211n, 222, 232, 256
detective 128, 167, 182–3
Dionysian, the 142, 167
domestic, the 10, 23, 28, 33, 109–10, 161–2, 166–7, 173, 189–90, 218, 226–7, 259
doppelgänger 9–10, 13, 38, 65–81, 218, 220–1
double *see* doppelgänger
Dracula 14–16, 54, 199–200, 203–4, 208
Dracula see Stoker, Bram
dream 3, 12, 61, 67, 125, 132–3, 136, 145, 151, 163–75, 186, 221, 227–30, 238, 243–5, 263, 268–9
Dreiburg, Daniel 183–6, 189–92
drugs 89, 107, 265
Du Maurier, Daphne
  Rebecca 142
dystopia 34, 76, 81, 103–5

Eco, Umberto 55, 62
ecocriticism 42–3
ecology 42–62
  deep ecology 46, 48–9, 54
  ecofeminism 46
  social ecology 43, 54, 59
Eddowes, Catherine 141, 145–6
Elinor and Mary (*Voice of the Fire*) 245
Elliot, Jordan 11
embodiment 7–8, 27, 86, 95, 108, 123, 142–4, 146, 152–3, 156, 169, 187, 198, 204–5, 211n, 235, 239, 243, 248, 265
Englishness 21, 26–7, 33–8
enlightenment (mystical / spiritual) 230–1, 258
Enlightenment (historical / philosophical movement) 6, 15, 43, 46, 88, 132–3, 187, 217, 258
excess 28, 30, 50–1, 66, 70–3, 80, 86–7, 99, 154, 156, 173, 182, 216, 221, 239

family 14, 21–3, 26, 29–30, 33, 38, 65–6, 162, 165–71, 185, 220, 265
fantasy 14, 34, 122, 149, 160
  as a genre 26–8, 37–8, 68, 124, 143, 258
  personal fantasy 163, 166, 169–70, 173, 177n, 225
Fascism 34, 36, 105, 109–12
father 75, 77, 79–80, 104, 113–14, 117n, 127, 145, 162, 166, 169–70, 173, 259–61
Faust 112, 188
Fawkes, Guy 109, 247
film 16, 22–4, 26, 28, 44, 48, 76–7, 124, 126–7, 195, 204–9, 210n, 217, 225
Floronic Man 48, 74, 76, 123, 125, 129, 131
Fortress of Solitude 162
Foucault, Michel 146, 153, 157–8n
Frankenstein, Victor 182–5, 187, 190–2
Frankenstein's monster 85, 105, 127, 137–8, 216
Freemasonry 80, 152–3,
Freud, Sigmund 6–7, 18n, 19n, 73, 261
Friedrich, Caspar David 164

Fuseli, Henry 138n

Gaia hypothesis 46, 130–1, 138
Gaiman, Neil 98n, 217, 241, 246
Gebbie, Melinda 9, 159, 262
gender 6, 30, 54, 147, 171, 203–5
genre 12, 22, 28, 43–4, 67–9, 86, 103, 130–1, 134, 170, 175, 216, 231
 see also fantasy; Gothic genre; science fiction; superhero
Gibbons, Dave 84, 88–9, 91, 93, 98, 137n, 160, 169–70, 176, 177, 179, 182, 193–4n, 224
Gilman, Charlotte Perkins 244
Glycon 230
gods 3–4, 30, 228, 230, 255
Godwin, William 10, 54, 108, 116, 179–95
 Caleb Williams 104–5, 108–9, 180, 182–5
 Enquiry Concerning Political Justice 184, 189
 Mandeville 189
 St. Leon 180–90, 192
Goffmann, Erving 105–6, 116–17n
Gordon, Commissioner James 12–13
Gotham City 6–7, 51, 129, 133, 138n
Gothic genre 4–7, 10–15, 44, 67–8, 86–8, 103, 113, 115n, 121–2, 161, 164, 170–5, 215–17
Goya, Francisco de 131–4, 138n
 El sueño de la razón produce monstruos 132, 135
Grant, Kenneth 232, 255, 259
Gray, Dorian 204–8
Green Gothic 7, 122, 128–31
Green Man 47, 61n
Green Party, The 46, 130
Green World, the 48, 51, 122, 129, 130–1, 133, 136
grotesque 12, 23, 27–8, 30, 38, 44, 125, 218, 220, 256, 258
guilt 10–11, 35, 37, 108, 127, 218–21, 227
Gull, Dr. William (fictional) 70, 76–81, 142–56, 222–4
Gull, Dr. William (historical) 157n

Halloran, Jack 14–15
Hammer Film Productions 28–9
Hammond, Evey 10, 65, 109–14, 117n
Harker, Jonathan 14–15, 206
haunting 9–10, 14, 37, 65, 72, 87, 104–5, 122, 136, 142, 149, 164, 174, 215–17, 226, 235–43, 246
Hawksmoor, Nicholas 77–80, 150, 222, 225
Hawthorne, Nathaniel 54
hegemony 4–5, 9, 13–15, 34, 47, 55, 99n,
Henry, Lenny 37, 41n
heterocosm 85, 159–60, 254, 262, 264–72
heterogeneity 4, 15
heteronormativity 99

heterotopia 146, 150
Hinton, James 77, 79–80, 146–7
history 8, 15, 22, 27, 42, 54, 71, 81, 91, 109, 131, 142–3, 145–6, 151–2, 156, 215, 222, 226, 235–6, 239, 241, 245–6, 261, 267, 272n
Hitler, Adolph 80, 145
Hoffmann, Ernst Theodor Amadeus 69, 82n
Hogarth, William
 The Four Stages of Cruelty 147
Hole, Tim 218–21
Holland, Alec 44, 47, 61n, 71–3, 122–3, 126–7, 134
homosexuality 34, 69–70, 86, 115–6, 202
horror 12, 14, 26, 28–30, 43–4, 48–9, 54, 56, 59, 70–1, 84–91, 121–34, 172, 175, 196–7, 216–20, 228, 236, 256–69
Houma, Louisiana 50, 126, 133
Hyde, Mr. Edward *see* Jekyll, Dr. Henry/Hyde, Mr Edward

ideal 9, 12, 30, 65, 104–5, 110, 114, 184, 186
ideal presence 174–5
ideal reader 122, 131, 136
Ideaspace 222, 228, 231–2, 257, 273n
identity
 class 37, 54
 national / regional 35–37, 39n, 154, 236
 performance of 69–70, 167, 171–2
 personal / individual 9–10, 14–15, 66, 70–6, 81, 86, 95, 103, 106, 109, 156, 172, 184, 197, 227, 235, 240, 264
 secret 48, 129–31, 162, 172
ideology 54, 144, 255, 257
immortality *see* mortality / immortality
imperialism 8, 27, 91, 221–2
imprisonment 34, 51, 65, 96, 106–14, 163–9, 172, 206
incest 113–14, 154, 162
Inchmale, Trevor 23, 26, 30, 33
indeterminacy 37, 42, 49, 70, 76
indexicality 26, 33
insanity *see* madness
intertextuality 7–8, 10, 16, 28, 54, 59, 85, 99, 103, 110, 117, 121–39, 147, 159–61, 220, 253–4, 265
Invisible Man, the 202–3

Jack the Ripper 76–9, 140–2, 145, 147, 151, 154, 156, 221, 225–6
James, Henry 244
Jekyll, Dr. Henry / Hyde, Mr. Edward 143–4, 199–200, 202
Johnston, Antony 246, 251, 273
Joker, The 12–13, 65, 129, 167
Jor-El 167, 169

Joyce, James
  Ulysses 260
Juspeczyk, Laurie 90, 126, 183
justice 7, 59, 88, 93, 108–9, 165, 168–9, 217
Justice League, The 131

Kabbalah 107
Kafka, Franz 107–8, 220, 258
  'Metamorphosis' 220
  The Trial 220
Kames, Lord Henry Home 174, 178n
Kandor 164–6, 171–2
Keats, John 132, 136, 138n
Kelly, Marie Jeannette (Mary Kelly) 83n, 147–8, 153, 156
Kent, Clark 171–2
Kristeva, Julia 8–9, 15, 18n, 27, 39n, 121, 124, 239–40, 250
Krypto 173–4
Krypton 11
Kryptonite 161, 166, 169, 173

Labour Party (UK), The 38, 130
Lamper, Gordon 267, 269, 271–2
language, 4–5, 8, 30, 56, 114, 128, 143, 227, 238, 246–50, 254, 259–65
Larkhill 65, 105–11, 114, 117n
law 7, 12–13, 65, 80, 103–5, 108, 138n, 168, 237, 256
Le Fanu, Sheridan
  'Carmilla' 10, 66–9, 73, 81n
League of Extraordinary Gentlemen, The (film) 195, 204–9
Lees, Robert 145
Lewis, Matthew 28, 196, 236
  The Monk 27, 106
Lichtenstein, Roy 227
liminality 10, 28, 44, 73–4, 103–4, 111–15
literary, the 3–6, 10, 27, 43, 51, 76, 84, 103–10, 122, 124, 127, 142, 159, 163, 187, 195–6, 199, 215–20, 245, 249, 255, 257
  see also canon
Lloyd, David 18n, 34, 103, 115, 117n
Lombroso, Cesare 149
London 8, 80, 140–56, 197, 200, 204, 221–6, 230
Long, Malcolm 89, 95, 190, 192
Louisiana 7, 49–50, 56, 59–60, 126, 133, 138n
love 7, 9, 114, 125, 167–9, 175, 182, 185–6, 189, 230
Lovecraft, Howard Phillips 3, 5, 8, 17n, 21–2, 30, 232, 253–75
  'The Dunwich Horror' 253, 259–61
  Fungi from Yuggoth 256
  'Horror at Red Hook' 264–5
  'Through the Gates of the Silver Key' (with E. Hoffmann Price) 5, 17n
Lovecraft, Winfield 260–1, 274n
Lovelock, James 130–1
Lucian of Samosata 230

Machen, Arthur 228, 230, 257, 260, 265
  'Great God Pan, The' 264
madness 12–13, 49, 65, 70, 89, 112, 114–15, 127, 140–58, 167, 171, 173, 181, 215, 224, 228, 231–2, 236, 238–9, 247, 256, 262, 264, 266
magic 3–5, 7–8, 11–14, 49, 55, 122, 134, 152, 160, 170–1, 217–18, 222, 226–7, 230–2, 244, 246–50, 253–62, 267, 269
magical realism 38, 239, 244–5
Manhattan, Dr 90–1, 94, 96, 126
  see also Osterman, Jonathan
Marvelman *see* Miracleman
Mason, Hollis 181, 183–4
Masons, the *see* Freemasonry
Maturin, Charles 108, 116n
  Melmoth the Wanderer 106
memory 5, 12, 69, 112, 134, 145, 198, 218, 221–2, 226–8, 232, 235, 245
metamorphosis 33, 35, 49, 199
metanarrative / metafiction / metatextuality 17, 59, 66, 69, 73, 109–10, 188, 254, 261–2, 266–7
Metropolis 172
metropolitan 27, 152, 154, 156
Miracleman 11–12
misprision 258, 261
Mongul 162–5, 169–73
monologism 70, 73, 110
monstrosity 6–7, 14–15, 27, 33, 44, 48–9, 54, 71–2, 85, 105, 122–9, 133, 136, 137–8n, 141, 143, 149, 153, 191–2, 205–6, 218, 228, 232, 259, 261, 263, 267–9
Moon and Serpent Grand Egyptian Theatre of Marvels, The 227, 233n, 256
Moore, Alan (works by)
  Batman: The Killing Joke 12–13, 19n, 65, 116n, 167
  Big Numbers 236
  Birth Caul, The 8, 215–18, 226–32, 233n
  Bojeffries Saga, The 16, 21–38, 38n
  Captain Britain 215
  'Courtyard, The' 8, 256, 262, 264–9, 272–3n, 275n
  Disease of Language, A 226–32, 233–4n, 273n
  'For the Man who has Everything' 10–11, 159–75, 176n
  From Hell 4, 8–10, 16, 70, 73, 76–81, 82–3n, 84–5, 100n, 140–56, 167, 173, 215–18, 221–7, 231–2, 233n
  'Great Old Ones, The' 8, 256–59, 267, 274n

'I Keep Coming Back' 221–6, 233n
League of Extraordinary Gentlemen, The 16, 159–2, 175n, 195–209, 210–12n, 254
Lost Girls 9, 159, 262
Marvelman see *Miracleman*
Miracleman 5, 7, 11–12, 17–19n, 255–6
'Mirror of Love, The' 7, 18, 99n
Neonomicon 5, 8, 256, 262, 264–72, 275n
'New European, The' (*Vampirella*) 14, 19n
Promethea 7, 11, 18, 65, 255–62, 266, 271–2, 275
'Recognition' 256, 260–2, 269, 273n, 274n
'Riddle of the Recalcitrant Refuse, The' (*Mr. Monster*) 6, 17n
'Shadowplay – The Secret Team' 18n
Small Killing, A 8, 65, 215–21, 225, 227–32, 233n
Snakes and Ladders 8, 215, 217, 226, 232, 233–4n
Supreme 174
Swamp Thing 3–7, 10, 12–13, 16, 18n, 42–60, 61–2n, 70–7, 79, 83n, 84, 110, 121–36, 137–9n
Tom Strong 174
V for Vendetta 9, 18n, 34, 65, 103–15, 116n, 137n, 181, 236, 255
Voice of the Fire 3–4, 8, 17n, 235–50
Watchmen 10–12, 16, 84–98, 99n, 115, 125–6, 137n, 160, 179–93, 215, 217, 224, 255
'Whatever Happened to the Man of Tomorrow?' 11–12, 161, 173–4, 176n
'Zaiman's Hill' 256, 262–4, 273n, 275n
morality 9, 74, 86, 88, 90, 94, 99n, 104, 108, 115, 117n, 122–36, 148–9, 168, 173, 179–80, 187–92
Moriarty, Professor James 202
Morrison, Grant 167–8
  Arkham Asylum 217
  Dan Dare 34
  Invisibles, The 90, 217
  St. Swithin's Day 34
  Supergods 177
Morrison, Toni 54
mortality / immortality 15, 123, 180, 185–6, 190, 203
mother 67, 145, 163, 227, 237, 244
Munsters, The 16, 21–2, 29–30
murder 9–10, 67, 74–7, 80, 108, 112, 114–15, 122, 136, 140–56, 182–3, 186–7, 189, 191, 220, 222, 224–5, 238, 241, 244, 246–7, 265
Murray, Wilhelmina 16, 195–209, 211–12n
myth 3, 5, 9, 55, 77, 123–7, 154, 167, 216, 230, 236, 239, 246, 249–50, 255–9, 264, 267

Nemo, Captain 160, 199, 205–7
New Right, the 33, 45, 47, 56
New Woman 196–204, 208–9
New York City 96, 218
Nicholls, Judge Augustus 238
Nichols, Polly 83n, 141, 145, 152–3
Nietzsche, Friedrich 16
nihilism 88–91, 100n, 182
Nite Owl *see* Dreiburg, Daniel; Mason, Hollis
Norrington, Stephen 195
Northampton 8, 21, 26, 46, 230, 235–6, 239, 243, 248
nuclear waste *see* toxic waste
Nukeface 55–9

O'Neill, Kevin 175n, 195, 201, 205, 211, 212n, 254, 272n
Old Ones, the 8, 21, 255–9
Olun 238
ontology 9, 47, 73, 259
oppression 10, 54, 109, 115, 171, 173, 196, 220–1
optimism 96–8, 179–82, 187, 255
Orwell, George 115n
  1984 103
Osterman, Jonathan 186, 189, 192
  see also Dr. Manhattan
otherness 15, 37, 48, 69, 71, 105, 143–4, 146, 161, 167, 183–93, 216, 218, 220, 239–40, 243, 254, 259, 269
Otranto 87, 159
ouroboros 235, 242–3, 251n
Ozymandias 90–6
  see also Veidt, Adrian

pain 67, 71, 94, 96, 170, 172, 236, 240, 244
Pan 248, 264
paranormal, the 21–2, 128
Parkhouse, Steve 21, 24–5, 31–2, 38, 39n, 41n
Patchwork Man 44
performativity 70, 109, 111, 171–2, 175, 227, 246
Perkins, Tim, 230
perverse, the 4, 12, 114, 143, 218, 220, 258
Pig Boy, the 237, 241–2
pleasure 9, 143, 170, 185, 215
Podlasp, Grandpa 22–3, 30, 37
Poe, Edgar Allan 257
  'Man of the Crowd, The' 220
  'William Wilson' 220
politics 3–10, 16, 21, 33–8, 42–7, 54–6, 59–60, 73, 97, 99n, 109, 112–13, 115n, 121–4, 127–33, 136, 169, 179–82, 192, 202, 263, 273
polyphony 50, 70
popular culture 4, 16, 26, 28, 43, 46, 55, 124,

127, 159, 170, 217–18
possession (spirit) 240
postimperialism 34–5, 38
postmodernism 59, 217
post-traumatic stress 10
Price, E. Hoffmann 17n
Prothero, Lewis 110–11, 117n
psychoanalysis 12, 261
   see also Freud, Sigmund; Kristeva, Julia
psychogeography 221–2, 226–8, 232, 235–6, 242, 248, 262–4
pulp 3, 21, 123, 130, 255
Punch 140–1, 149, 156n
punishment 110, 124, 165, 237

Quatermain, Allan 199–209, 220n, 272n

R' lyeh 261, 263, 269–70
race / racism 35–7, 54, 127, 185–6, 255, 265
Radcliffe, Ann 10, 105, 108, 217, 236
   Italian, The 27, 104, 108, 196
   Mysteries of Udolpho 104
rape 9, 110, 151, 202, 260, 264, 267
reader, the 11, 23, 26, 33, 36, 43, 47, 49, 59, 66, 68–9, 73, 77, 79, 81, 87–8, 92–3, 96–7, 115, 121–36, 142, 145, 162–71, 174–5, 179, 181, 224–6, 231–2, 240–2, 247, 254–5, 258, 261–2, 266
Reagan, President Ronald 33, 45, 56, 122, 128, 130, 181
reason 28, 89, 123, 131–4, 140–7, 151–2, 154, 164, 167, 174, 207, 217
rebirth 97–8, 107, 114, 243
Red Hook 264–5
Red World, the 136
religion 4, 90, 113, 124, 129, 143, 151, 154, 240, 255, 257, 258
repression 6, 10, 12, 54, 66–7, 69–71, 73, 86, 154, 159, 161, 165, 185, 218, 227, 231, 232, 256
revenge 13, 104, 109–10, 112, 114, 122, 127, 130, 202, 208
revolution 84, 97, 111, 122, 249
   French Revolution 86, 180–1, 184–5
rite of passage 106, 109, 114
Robin 99, 162, 164–5, 168–9, 172–3
Rodin François-Auguste-René
   The Thinker 71
Romanticism 16, 43, 68, 86, 124, 127, 128, 131–3, 138n, 163, 183–4, 188, 190
Rorschach 70, 86, 88–92, 182–3, 189, 190–2
Rossetti, Dante Gabriel 228
Rouse, Alfie 238, 242
Rousseau, Jean-Jacques 132
   La Philosophie 132

Saussure, Ferdinand de 249
Sawyer, Tom 204–5
Sax, Aldo 264–7
Schwartz, Julius 162
science fiction 34, 91, 103, 216, 264
secret identity *see* alter ego; doppelgänger; identity
sefiroth 256–9
self 4–6, 9–10, 12, 16, 27, 50, 65, 68–73, 87, 106, 113, 123, 134, 167, 171–2, 197–8, 216–17, 220, 231, 239–43, 262, 264
Senlis, Simon de 237, 244
Sextus, Caius 239, 244
sexuality 6–11, 34, 66–70, 86, 99, 113–14, 116n, 142–3, 147, 150, 160–1, 164–71, 174, 196, 198, 202–5, 208–9, 211–12n, 224–5, 238–9, 241, 254, 256, 260, 262, 267, 269, 274n
shagfoal 238, 242, 248
Shakespeare, William 110, 117n
   Hamlet 47, 61n, 71, 110
   Macbeth 110, 117n
Shelley, Mary 10, 44, 127, 131, 136, 180–7, 217
   Frankenstein 44, 87, 104–5, 127, 137n, 163, 179–92
Shelley, Percy 95, 131, 183
Siddall, Elizabeth 228–30
Sienkiewicz, Bill 18n,
Silk Spectre *see* Juspeczyk, Laurie
Silver Age, the 55, 160–5, 168, 173–4
Simmel, Georg 154–6, 158n
Sinclair, Iain 222
   Lud Heat 143, 152
   White Chappel, Scarlet Tracings 143, 152–4, 157–8n
slavery 127, 150
son 22, 38, 65, 162, 165–8, 173, 261
space 16, 23, 27–8, 30, 34, 44, 49, 51, 69, 77, 82, 86–7, 91–2, 96, 104, 110–11, 115, 146, 152, 163, 216, 222, 231–2, 235, 254, 259, 263, 269
   see also heterotopia; psychogeography
spectral, the 4, 8–9, 18, 61n, 153, 170, 172
spectre 27, 42, 72
spelling (and spells) 143, 248–50, 253, 257
Stevenson, Robert Louis 3, 143, 149, 220
   The Strange Case of Dr. Jekyll and Mr. Hyde 142–3, 154, 199
Stoker, Bram 14, 195
   Dracula 14, 16, 54, 195–209, 210n, 212n
story / storytelling 3–5, 12, 14–15, 19n, 59, 126, 236, 238–9, 245–59
Stranger, the 124
Stride, Elizabeth 83n, 141, 145, 148, 157n
subjectivity 48–50, 55, 66, 69–70, 77, 107, 114, 154, 170–1, 220, 246, 264

sublime, the 5, 9, 42–3, 54, 87, 90, 100n, 137n, 152, 163, 170, 173, 180, 218, 228, 231
subversion 44, 51, 55, 68–9, 71, 84, 97, 111, 129, 131, 146, 152, 154, 195, 200, 209, 215, 247, 274n
Sunderland, General Avery Carlton 124
superhero 7–13, 48, 51, 85–6, 89–90, 103, 115, 131, 136, 138n, 161, 164, 166, 168, 171–2, 174–5, 217
superhero genre 8, 50, 55, 84–6, 89–90, 94, 97–8, 103, 139n, 160–8, 173–5, 196, 216–17, 220, 226
Superman 9–11, 131, 160–75, 177n
supernatural, the 4, 14–15, 54, 68, 126, 170, 176, 216, 245, 248, 257–8
surrealism 21, 23, 27–30, 33, 37–8, 41n, 220
Swamp Thing 42–60, 61n, 71–77, 110, 121–36, 137n
Swamp Thing (film) 44, 60n

technocracy 7, 46, 51, 60
technology 7, 123, 197
television 14, 21–2, 29, 36–7, 39n, 111, 195, 209, 224
terror 15, 54, 85, 90–1, 108, 126, 133–4, 141, 143, 165, 170, 175, 231, 236, 244, 257
terrorism 7, 13, 111–12, 129, 185
Thatcher, Margaret, Prime Minister 16, 33–4, 36, 45, 103, 115n, 122, 128, 130, 137–8n, 181
Thoreau, Henry David 131
Todorov, Tzvetan 26, 39, 68, 82n
Torso Garden, the 238, 244
torture 12, 34, 114, 147, 151
total institution 105
Totleben, John 43–53, 57–8, 60, 61–2n
toxic waste 47, 55–6, 130
transgression 11–13, 84, 90, 98–9, 161, 166–75, 196, 200, 204, 209, 212, 250
trauma 10, 12, 65–6, 68, 103, 114, 218, 232, 240
Tree of Life, the 258, 274n
Turner, Victor 104, 116n
Two-face *see* Dent, Harvey

uncanny, the 4, 7–10, 14, 16, 19, 21, 23, 26, 28, 54, 66, 68, 70–6, 91, 134, 142–3, 160, 165, 215–32, 236, 239, 245, 259, 263
underground comics 3, 43, 44
underworld 3, 125, 154, 250, 258
urban Gothic 7, 51, 80, 89, 133, 154, 221
utopia 70, 81

vampire 3, 6, 14, 21–2, 26, 30, 66, 68, 126–7, 136, 197–8, 205–9, 212n, 263
Veidt, Adrian 70, 82n, 88, 182–92
 see also Ozymandius
Veitch, Rick 18n, 60n, 125, 131, 136–9n
Verne, Jules 160, 199
 Twenty Thousand Leagues under the Sea 199
Victoria (Queen) *See* Wettin, Queen Alexandrina Victoria
Victorian period 21, 26, 28, 66, 69, 79, 81, 124, 142, 146–51, 196–200, 204, 208, 210
violence 8–10, 12–15, 29, 37, 42, 70, 74, 80, 88–9, 96–7, 109, 111, 114, 134, 136, 141, 144, 151, 161, 164, 202, 215, 217, 221–2, 224–6, 232, 236, 254–6, 260–9
vulnerability 9–10, 13–14, 16, 123, 138, 166, 203, 208, 217, 239

Warrior 17n, 21–3, 29–30, 34, 37, 110, 115n
weakness 11, 106, 148, 200
Wein, Len 3, 44, 60–1n, 71–2, 82–3n
Wells, Herbert George 3, 91
 Invisible Man, The 199
werewolf 3, 21–2, 26, 35, 127, 136
Wertham, Fredric
 Seduction of the Innocent, 29, 168, 177n, 196
Weston, Big John 237
Wettin, Queen Alexandrina Victoria 22, 37, 142
Whitechapel 141–54
wife 35, 125, 150, 162, 166, 169, 171, 184, 190, 197–8, 206, 230, 260
wilderness 6–7, 43, 48–9, 133, 263
wish fulfillment 167, 169, 170
witch 3, 23, 44, 49, 126, 240, 245, 249
Wollstonecraft, Mary 54
Wonder Woman 162–5, 168, 170, 172, 177n
Woodrue, Jason 48, 74, 76, 123, 125, 129, 131
 see also Floronic Man
Wordsworth, William 131
Wrightson, Berni 3, 44, 60–1n, 71–2, 82–3n
writing 3–5, 7–8, 12–14, 17, 59, 121, 124–6, 238, 248–50, 255, 267

Young Ones, The 36–8, 41n

Zarate, Oscar 218–20, 225, 227, 233n
Zlüdotny, Festus 22, 26, 30
Zlüdotny, Raoul 22, 26, 30, 35–7
zombie 3, 127

EU authorised representative for GPSR:
Easy Access System Europe, Mustamäe tee 50,
10621 Tallinn, Estonia
gpsr.requests@easproject.com

www.ingramcontent.com/pod-product-compliance
Ingram Content Group UK Ltd.
Pitfield, Milton Keynes, MK11 3LW, UK
UKHW041920140426